Whigs and Hunters

E. P. Thompson

Whigs and Hunters

THE ORIGIN OF THE BLACK ACT

PANTHEON BOOKS

A Division of Random House, New York

First American Edition

Copyright © 1975 by E. P. Thompson

All rights reserved under International and Pan-American Copyright Conventions. Published in the United States by Pantheon Books, a division of Random House, Inc., New York, and simultaneously in Canada by Random House of Canada Limited, Toronto. Originally published in Great Britain by Penguin Books, Limited, London.

Library of Congress Cataloging in Publication Data
Thompson, Edward Palmer, 1924-
    Whigs and Hunters: The Origin of the Black Act.
    Appendices (pp. 262–292) : 1.   The Black Act.—2. Alexander Pope and the Blacks.
    Bibliographical notes: pp. 295-300
    Includes index.
    1.   Great Britain.   Laws, statutes, etc. Black Act, 1723.   I.   Great Britain. Laws, statutes, etc. Black Act, 1723   1976.   II.   Title.
KD785.2B55T48   1976   345'.42'02   75-23168
ISBN 0-394-40011-9
ISBN 0-394-73086-0 pbk.

Manufactured in the United States of America

456789

TO
CHRISTOPHER HILL
MASTER OF MORE THAN AN OLD OXFORD COLLEGE

'Jesu!' said the Squire, 'would you commit two persons to bridewell for a twig?'

'Yes,' said the Lawyer, 'and with great lenity too; for if we had called it a young tree they would have been both hanged.'

Henry Fielding, The Adventures of Joseph Andrews

Contents

List of Illustrations

11. Breaking the wall of Richmond Park
    (From *Two Historical Accounts of the Making of the New Forest and of Richmond New Park*, 1751)

12. Walpole as Ranger of Richmond Park
    (Courtesy The Marquess of Cholmondeley; photograph Thomas Agnew & Sons)

13. Deer hunters, 1720
    (Taken from a painting by Byng, a friend of Kneller of *c.* 1720, and engraved for John Hutchins, *History and Antiquities of the County of Dorset*, 3rd edn, 1869, vol. iii. For this copy I am indebted to the kindness of the Curator of the Dorset County Museum and the Dorset Archaeological and Natural History Society)

14. Bobson, a famous running horse
    (Courtesy The British Library. From *A Collection of the Most Famous Running Horses*, 1739, in the print room, case 166, no. a 38)

15. Sir Francis and Lady Page at rest
    (Detail of monument by Henry Scheemakers in Steeple Aston church; photograph Edwin Smith)

16. Sir Jonathan Trelawny, Bishop of Winchester, by Sir Godfrey Kneller
    (Courtesy Christ Church, Oxford)

17. 'Royalty, Episcopacy, and Law' by Hogarth
    (Courtesy The British Library. See *Catalogue*, op. cit., no. 1734)

Abbreviations

Add. MSS	Additional Manuscripts
Brit. Mus.	British Museum (now British Library)
C(H) MSS	Cholmondeley (Houghton) Manuscripts, Cambridge University Library
DNB	*Dictionary of National Biography*
Hist. MSS Comm.	Historical Manuscripts Commission
History of Blacks	Anon., *The History of the Blacks of Waltham in Hampshire; and those under the like Denomination in Berkshire* (1723)
ON	*The Ordinary of Newgate, His Account of the Behaviour, Confession, and Dying Words, of the Malefactors who were Executed at Tyburn* (various dates)
PP	Parliamentary Papers
The Proceedings	*The Whole Proceedings upon the King's Commission of Oyer and Terminer and Gaol Delivery for the City of London* etc. (various dates)
Rec. Off.	Record Office
VCH	*Victoria County History*
Waterson	See Note on Sources

Public Record Office. To save unnecessary typesetting, I have not entered 'PRO' before each reference to papers located there. With the single exception of C(H) MSS, *all* references by letter to documents which appear in the footnotes without a location-reference refer to papers in the PRO. The following are the main classes:

Assi.	Clerks of Assize
C	Chancery

Crest.	Crown Estate Commissioners
DL	Duchy of Lancaster
E	Court of Exchequer
F	Forestry Commission
FEC	Commissioners of Forfeited Estates
KB	Court of King's Bench
LR	Exchequer, Auditors of Land Revenue
LRRO	Land Revenue Records and Enrolments
PC	Privy Council
SP	State Papers
T	Treasury
TS	Treasury Solicitor
WO	War Office
Works	Ministry of Works

Dates etc. All dates in this book (before the change in the calendar) are old style – as I found them – except that 1 January and not 25 March is taken as the beginning of the New Year. In a few cases of letters dated between 1 January and 25 March the ascription to the year must remain uncertain.

In transcribing eighteenth-century manuscripts I have not bound myself by any convention. In general I am careful to keep the original spelling and I have kept the original abbreviations and capitalization where it seemed to be intrinsic to the sense or feeling of the author.

The place of publication of books is given only when this was outside of London.

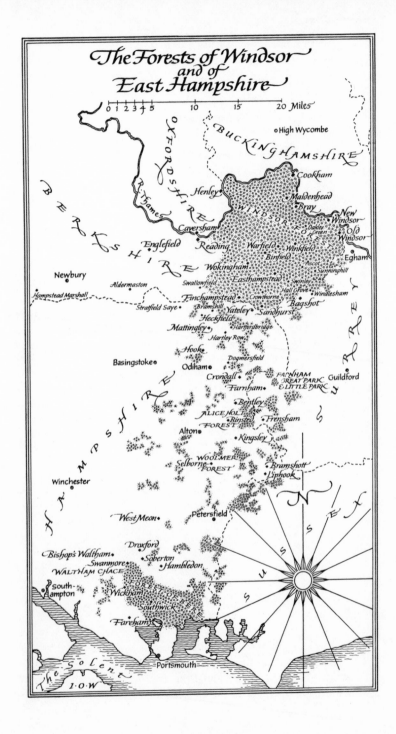

The Forests of Windsor
and of
East Hampshire

0 1 2 3 4 5   10   15   20 Miles

BUCKINGHAMSHIRE

o High Wycombe

OXFORDSHIRE

Cookham

Henley
Maidenhead
Bray
New
Windsor
Oakley
Green
Old
Windsor

BERKSHIRE

R. Thames

Caversham

WINDSOR FOREST

Englefield
Reading
Warfield
Winkfield
Ascot
Egham

Wokingham
Birfield
Sunninghill

Newbury

Aldermaston
Swallowfield
Easthampstead
Hall Grove
Winles
Windlesham

Hampstead Marshall
Stratfield Saye
Finchampstead
Crowthorne
Bagshot

Bramshill
Yateley
Sandhurst

Heckfield

Mattingley
Hartfordbridge

Hartley Row

Hook

Basingstoke
Odiham
Dogmersfield

Crondall
FARNHAM
GREAT PARK
& LITTLE PARK
Guildford

Farnham

Bentley

ALICE HOLT
FOREST
Binsted
Frensham

HAMPSHIRE
SURREY

Alton
Kingsley

WOOLMER
FOREST
Selborne
Bramshott
Liphook

Winchester

West Meon
Petersfield

SUSSEX

N

Droxford
Bishop's Waltham
Swanmore
Soberton
Hambledon
WALTHAM CHACE

South-
ampton
Wickham
FOREST OF BERE
Southwick

Fareham

Portsmouth

The Solent
I.O.W.

Preface

There is a sense in which this book is an experiment in historiography, although not of a kind which is likely to meet with approval. Five or six years ago, when I was at the University of Warwick, a group of us commenced to prepare work for a book on the social history of crime in the eighteenth century in England. I offered, rashly, to submit a contribution on the origins of the Black Act. I knew nothing about this, but the importance of the Act in eighteenth-century legal history made it seem essential (for all our work) that something be found out. I supposed that sufficient documentation would have survived to enable me to write a brief study, without too much difficulty.

The supposition was wrong and the difficulties proved to be serious. The central legal documentation as to trials of Blacks has been lost. Only one contemporary pamphlet offered any account of them. The press offered only scanty reports – and some of these soon turned out to be misleading. To prepare even a simple narrative of events proved very difficult. (I am not yet sure that I have succeeded.) To offer a considered analysis was even more difficult, because not only the events but their context had been lost to historical knowledge. Thus the press and scattered indications in state papers showed that some disturbances centred on Windsor Forest. It seemed to me that the incidents revealed a resentment by foresters at the operation of forest law. But the standard authorities all assured me that forest laws (the Swanimote courts and the like) all fell into disuse at the time of the Commonwealth and were never thereafter revived. I had therefore to begin at the beginning, and to reconstruct the government of the forest in 1723. Similarly, it became clear that the 'Waltham Blacks' nourished a peculiar ill will towards successive bishops of Winchester. But almost nothing was known about the reasons for this, and very little has been written about the administration and finances of the Church more generally in the early eighteenth century. Thus, once again, it was necessary to reconstruct the episcopal context before one could see the Blacks within it.

What made this exercise more hazardous was that I had neither read nor researched very much on any aspect of social history before 1750. Most historians do not put themselves at risk in this kind of situation, and they are wise not to do so. One normally reads very widely into a 'period', before or alongside one's researches, accepting the received context offered by previous historians, even if at the conclusion to one's work one is able to offer modifications to this context. I decided to work in a different way. I was like a parachutist coming down in unknown territory: at first knowing only a few yards of land around me, and gradually extending my explorations in each direction. Perhaps three quarters of this book (for my essay soon became too large for the co-operative book) is based upon manuscript sources. One source led me to the next; but, also, one problem led me to another. Deer-hunters in Windsor Forest led me to forest government, to the courtiers with their parks, and thence to Walpole, to the King (and to Alexander Pope). Deer-hunters in Hampshire led me to Bishop Trelawny and his stewards, to the eccentric Warden of Bere, Richard Norton, and, again, to Walpole and his courtiers. Deer-hunters in the environs of London led me, by routes far more direct than I had any reason to expect, once again to Walpole. As I pursued each line of investigation I left it to a fairly late stage before I attempted to familiarize myself with the available historical writing. In fact, there proved to be very little of this, except, of course, when I came to Walpole and the Court; and here my debt to other historians will be apparent.

This might appear to be less 'an experiment in historiography' than a way of muddling through. But I hope that it has turned out to be a little more. Since I started with the experience of humble foresters and followed up, through sketchy contemporary evidence, the lines that connected them to power, there is a sense in which the sources themselves have forced me to see English society in 1723 as they themselves saw it, from 'below'. I have avoided, until late in this book, any general description of that society which could have come to me from the constructions of other historians. I cannot of course pretend to have approached the theme without prejudices and preconceptions: certainly I did not expect to find a society which was uncorrupt or wholly just. But the method and the sources have placed my preconceptions under some controls. Hence when I come, in the last chapters of this book, to look a little sourly at Walpole, Baron Page or Lord Hardwicke, and at the legal system and Whig ideology more generally, I think it possible that I may see them much as they were to be seen at the time, by William Shorter, the Berkshire farmer, or John Huntridge, the Richmond innkeeper.

I have little doubt that experts in early-eighteenth-century society will call me to order, very properly, for my inadequate self-education, at some points, and for my treasonable views of Whiggery. Not all Englishmen, in 1723, were small forest farmers or customary tenants, and no doubt this way of writing history gives an intense but partial view. Someone must have benefited from Walpole's administration; although having read most of the state papers and most of the surviving newspapers for the years 1722–4, I am at a loss to know who this was, beyond the circle of Walpole's own creatures.

I write in this way to tease Professor Plumb and his followers, from whose work I have learned a good deal. At least this work of reconstruction has done one thing which always gives a historian some pleasure. It has not only recovered to view an episode which had become lost to historical knowledge. It has also recovered an episode which was not known to contemporaries at the time. Some part of it was known, of course: occasional bits of gossip survive in private papers which show that far more went the rounds than Walpole ever permitted to be published in the press. And a good deal of it was known to Walpole, Townshend and Paxton. But even they did not know what the Reverend Will Waterson was writing in his private memorandum book, nor how their successors would turn the Black Act to new occasions. So that one puts together at the end, as one always hopes to do, an account which at many points is inferior to contemporary knowledge, but which is, in certain other ways, superior.

I have tried to write the book in much the same way as I undertook the research. First, the context of Windsor Forest, the episodes, the analysis. Second, much the same procedure for the Hampshire forests and the 'Waltham Blacks'. Finally, we move towards London, getting ever closer to the measures and ideology of the Whigs, to the men who made the Black Act and to the law which they made.

This study was originally planned as part of the collection of studies which has been edited by myself, Douglas Hay and Peter Linebaugh, as *Albion's Fatal Tree* (Pantheon, 1975). Although it grew too large for that book, I benefited throughout from the co-operative discussions, and the exchange of references and of criticisms, which gave rise to that work. My coeditors were especially helpful in passing to me information and in reading my early drafts; help also came from all of the extended seminar which originated at the Centre for the Study of Social History at the University of Warwick. In particular I must thank Jeanette Neeson for references from the *Northampton Mercury* and elsewhere; Malcolm Thomas for bibliographical advice; and Pamela James for typing a final draft. An old friend, E. E. Dodd, has undertaken various research commissions for me, in the Public Record Office and at the Surrey Record Office. Howard Erskine-Hill, Trevor Griffiths and John Beattie have been kind enough to read and comment on my manuscript, and Pat Rogers (with whom I cross swords in the text) has kept me informed as to his own work.

In the course of my research dozens of people have patiently answered my inquiries, and I must apologize for being unable to acknowledge them all individually. Mrs Elfrida Manning, of the Farnham Museum Society, was especially helpful; and I must also thank the Reverend Frank Sergeant, formerly of Bishop's Waltham; Mrs Monica Martineau of the same town; Mr A. P. Whitaker, the Winchester City Archivist; Mr Charles Chenevix Trench; Mr George Clarke (for information about Viscount Cobham); Mr Gerald Howson; Mr G. Ferard and Mrs Pamela Fletcher Jones. John Walsh, Eric Jones and A. R. Michell all sent me useful references. Particular thanks are due to those who allowed me to consult and draw upon their archives: I must acknowledge the gracious permission of Her Majesty the Queen to consult the Royal Archives (Stuart Papers) as well as the Constable's Warrant Books in her library at Windsor Castle; the Master and Fellows of St John's College, Cambridge and of Christ Church College, Oxford; the Rt Hon. the Earl St Aldwyn (for the papers of Charles Withers, and also for permission to reproduce the portrait of Withers which hangs in Williamstrip Park); the Marquess of Cholmondeley (for the Cholmondeley (Houghton) papers of Sir Robert Walpole, now in the Cambridge University Library); the Marquess of Downshire, for permission to consult the Trumbull correspondence in the Berkshire Record Office; the Dean and Chapter of Winchester Cathedral; His Grace the Duke of Marlborough (for the papers of Sarah, Duchess of Marlborough and of the Earl of Sunderland, at Blenheim Palace); the Town Clerk of the Royal Borough of Windsor (Windsor borough records); and Mr Richard Allen, the Headmaster of Ranelagh School, Bracknell (for the Waterson memorandum books). I must also thank the Librarian of the Henry E. Huntington Library, San Marino, California, and Miss Anne Caiger, the Assistant Archivist, for sending me copies of materials on Enfield Chase in the Stowe Collection, Brydges Papers. I am also greatly indebted to the Librarians, Archivists and staff at the foregoing and at the following institutions: the British Library; the Bodleian Library; Cambridge University Library; Reading Reference Library; the Public Record Office; the County Record Offices in Berkshire, Hampshire, Surrey, and also Middlesex, Norfolk and Norwich, West Sussex and Oxford; the Portsmouth City Record Office; the Guildford Muniment Room; the Lambeth Palace Library; the National Register of Archives; the Royal Commission on Historical Manuscripts; and Nottingham

University Library (Portland Papers). The archivists and their assistants at the Berkshire and Hampshire offices have been especially helpful, both in correspondence and on my several visits, and Miss Hazel Aldred in Hampshire drew to my attention several documents which I would otherwise have missed. Transcripts of Crown-Copyright records in the Public Record Office appear by permission of the Controller of H.M. Stationery Office, and my thanks are due to the Public Record Office for permission to reproduce the map of Windsor Forest (Plate 4). The map on p. 26 was drawn by Leo Vernon.

Worcester, April 1975

Introduction: The Black Act

The British state, all eighteenth-century legislators agreed, existed to preserve the property and, incidentally, the lives and liberties, of the propertied. But there are more ways than one of defending property; and property was not, in 1700, trenched around on every side by capital statutes. It was still not a matter of course that the legislature should, in every session, attach the penalty of death to new descriptions of offence.

Premonitions of this development can be noted in the late seventeenth century. But perhaps no event did more to habituate men's minds to this recipe of state than the passage into law of 9 George I c.22, which came to be known as 'The Waltham Black Act' or simply as 'The Black Act'. This was enacted in the four weeks of May 1723. It was drawn by the Attorney and Solicitors-General upon the order, *nem. con.*, of the House of Commons. At no stage in its passage does there appear to have been debate or serious division; a House prepared to debate for hours a disputed election could find unanimity in creating at a blow some fifty new capital offences.[1]

The first category of offenders within the Act is of persons 'armed with swords, fire-arms, or other offensive weapons, and having his or their faces blacked', who shall appear in any forest, chase, park or enclosed ground 'wherein any deer have been or shall be usually kept', or in any warren, or on any high road, heath, common or down . . . By a layman's

---

1. Read for the first time, 30 April; second time, 1 May; committee of the whole House, 4 and 9 May; amendments engrossed, 13 May; read third time, 18 May; passed in Lords, 21 May; royal assent, 27 May. The only evidence of any division is the rejection, on 13 May, of an amendment offering to ensure that no person prosecuted under the Act could be punished a second time for the same offence under a different statute. No such lenity was allowed. *Commons Journals*, XX, *passim*; *Lords Journals*, XXII, p. 208.

reading, it would appear that such persons must also be engaged in one of the various offences listed below. But the Act had scarcely been passed before it was enlarged by successive judgements, so that arming and/or Blacking might constitute in themselves capital offences.[1]

The main group of offences was that of hunting, wounding or stealing red or fallow deer, and the poaching of hares, conies or fish. These were made capital if the persons offending were armed and disguised, and, in the case of deer, if the offences were committed in any of the King's forests, whether the offenders were armed and disguised or not. Further offences included breaking down the head or mound of any fish-pond; maliciously killing or maiming cattle; cutting down trees 'planted in any avenue, or growing in any garden, orchard or plantation'; setting fire to any house, barn, haystack, etc.; maliciously shooting at any person; sending anonymous letters demanding 'money, venison, or other valuable thing'; and forcibly rescuing anyone from custody who was accused of any of these offences. In addition, there was a provision by which if a person was accused of any of these offences on informations sworn by credible witnesses and returned to the Privy Council – and if such person was then proclaimed by the Privy Council and ordered to surrender himself (and if he failed to so surrender) – he could, if apprehended, be deemed guilty and be sentenced to death without further trial.

There were certain other provisions intended to expedite the operation of legal process, which overrode customary procedure and the defences of the subject. The accused might be tried in any county in England, and not only in the county where the offence was committed. In addition, the hundred in which the offence was committed was made collectively liable to pay the damages caused by any of the offences, through the medium of a special levy on all inhabitants.

Several of these offences were of course already felonies. But even where this was so, as in the case of arson, the definition in the Black Act was more comprehensive. Sir Leon Radzinowicz has written:

> There is hardly a criminal act which did not come within the provisions of the Black Act; offences against public order, against the administration of criminal justice, against property, against the person, malicious injuries to property of varying degree – all came under this statute and all were punishable by death. Thus the Act constituted in itself a complete and extremely severe criminal code . . .[2]

In his thorough and lucid examination of the Act he has shown more than

1. For the Act in full see Appendix 1, pp. 270–77.
2. Leon Radzinowicz, *A History of English Criminal Law and its Administration from 1750*, 1948, I, p. 77.

fifty distinct offences for which capital punishment was provided. An even stricter but more legalistic multiplication, which takes into account the different categories of person committing each offence (whether armed, or disguised, whether principals in the first or second degree, accessories, etc.) gives a total of between 200 and 250.[1] Moreover, the Act was so loosely drafted that it became a spawning-ground for ever-extending legal judgements. Despite the eighteenth-century's reputation for legal precision, it seems unlikely that any early-seventeenth-century lawyer trained in the school of Sir Edward Coke, and with his nice respect for the liberties of the subject, would have tolerated the passage into law of such an ill-drawn statute.

It is a remarkable statute, and it has drawn an expression of surprise from our most eminent historian of the criminal law: 'It is very doubtful whether any other country possessed a criminal code with anything like so many capital provisions as there were in this single statute.'[2] Although a tendency to attach the death penalty to new descriptions of offence can be noted in previous decades, the Black Act of 1723, which coincided with the year of Walpole's final political ascendancy, signalled the onset of the flood-tide of eighteenth-century retributive justice. Its passage suggests not only some shift in legislative attitudes, but also perhaps some complicity between the ascendancy of the Hanoverian Whigs and the ascendancy of the gallows.

It has been generally assumed that the Act must have been passed under the pressure of some overwhelming emergency. It was, in the first place, to remain operative for three years only, although in fact it was successively re-enacted with further accretions.[3] For Lecky the Blacks were 'a gang of deer-stealers . . . so numerous and so audacious that a special and most sanguinary law . . . was found necessary for their suppression'.[4] Successive historians have scarcely advanced upon this: since the Act was passed, it may be assumed that it was 'necessary' to pass it.[5] Even Radzinowicz, the historian who has examined its provisions with the greatest precision, assumes that it was an 'exceptional measure' which

1. See the detailed examination of all the provisions of the Act in Radzinowicz, op. cit., I, pp. 49–79 and also the same author's earlier article on the Black Act in the *Cambridge Law Journal*, IX (1945) which includes a few reflections not repeated in the book.

2. Radzinowicz, *Cambridge Law Journal*, p. 72.

3. See below, p. 206.

4. W. E. H. Lecky, *A History of England in the Eighteenth Century*, 1913 edn, II, p. 113.

5. As this goes to press a more seriously informed account (and apology) for the genesis of the Act has appeared from the pen of Professor Pat Rogers: 'The Waltham Blacks and the Black Act', *Historical Journal*, XVII, 3 (1974), pp. 465–86. For some discussion of this, see below, pp. 192–5.

was 'brought into existence by a sudden emergency, which gave rise to intense feelings of fear'.[1]

Perhaps it was. But a 'sudden emergency' whose date is mis-remembered[2] and which has left so little trace in the public print of the time[3] is an unprovable, if comforting, hypothesis. At any rate, it is a matter which should be explored further. And this is the occasion for the present study. I have set myself the task of approaching (through sources which are often inadequate) the following questions. What occasioned the passage of the Act? Who were the 'Waltham Blacks'? Was the passage of the Act furthered by any identifiable lobby of special interests, or may it be considered as an act of Government *tout court*? To what functions was the Act (when passed) applied, and how did it take its place as part of the eighteenth-century code? Why was it so easy for the legislators of 1723 to write out this statute in blood?

1. *Cambridge Law Journal*, pp. 73, 75.
2. J. H. Plumb, *Sir Robert Walpole*, 1960, I, p. 237 offers 1726 as the date; Sir Leon Radzinowicz offers the regnal year (1722).
3. Attention to the Blacks in contemporary newspapers was so scant that not a single paper published an account of the two major trials. There appears to have been only one popular pamphlet about the Blacks, as contrasted with the mass of ephemera surrounding such folk heroes and villains as Jack Sheppard and Jonathan Wild. I have found no broadsheets, ballads or chapbooks about them. No 'emergency' can have left less impression in print nor imprinted itself more feebly on the popular memory.

PART I

Windsor

1: Windsor Forest

There was certainly no national 'emergency' relating to any Blacks in 1723. But there were some local disorders. The two areas where these took place were Windsor Forest and some forest districts of east and south-east Hampshire. The Waltham Blacks were named, not after Waltham Forest in Essex, but after Waltham Chase, near Bishop's Waltham, in Hampshire. The first official notice of any Blacking appears in a proclamation of March 1720 against night-hunting in disguise in Windsor Forest. Fourteen men on horseback, armed with guns, together with two men on foot with a greyhound, had coursed red deer in the late afternoon in Bigshot Walk, with their faces blacked, and some 'with straw hats and other deformed habits'. Four deer were killed and a keeper was threatened.[1] Three years later, in February 1723, there was another, and more sensational, proclamation. This claimed that 'great numbers of disorderly and ill-designing persons' had associated themselves under the name of Blacks in the counties of Berkshire and Hampshire. They were armed, broke into forests and parks, killed and carried off deer, rescued offenders from the constables, sent menacing letters to gentlemen demanding venison and money, and threatening murder or the burning of houses, barns and haystacks. They had assaulted persons, 'shot at them in their houses, maimed their horses and cattle, broke down their gates and fences, and cut down avenues, plantations, and heads of fish-ponds, and robbed them of the fish . . .'[2]

The disturbances were confined to forest areas, or to private estates with deer-parks or fisheries. There were significant differences in the government of the Berkshire and Hampshire forests, and also in the

---

1. *London Gazette*, no. 5836, 22–6 March 1720.
2. PC 2, 88, pp. 188–91. Brit. Mus., press-mark 21 h 4 (171).

nature of the disorders in the two counties, and it will be convenient to examine these separately.

Windsor Castle in the early eighteenth century was only some two and a half hours from the centre of London by fast coach. Queen Anne frequently moved her court to Windsor in the summer and the Privy Council came posting down for business. George I, when not in Hanover, preferred Hampton Court or Richmond (both well stocked with deer) for summer resort, but he also on occasion was at Windsor.[1] The forest presented, during his reign, an extreme contrast in scenery and in life-styles. Windsor itself and its immediate environs offered, as the summer residence of courtiers, the refinements of civilization. Apricots and peaches grew in the gardens of fashionable Thames-side 'villas',[2] and great courtiers like the Earl of Ranelagh and the Duke of St Albans had established palatial seats within easy riding distance of the Castle. A few miles away lay Bagshot Heath, a notorious resort of highwaymen:

> Prepar'd for war, now *Bagshot-Heath* we cross
> Where broken gamesters oft repair their loss –

So wrote John Gay in 1715, and matters remained the same in 1723.[3] Defoe described Bagshot Heath in that year as '. . . not only poor, but even quite steril, given up to barrenness, horrid and frightful to look on, not only good for little, but good for nothing; much of it is a sandy desert, and one may be frequently put in mind here of Arabia Deserta. . .'[4]

Windsor Forest itself was over thirty miles in circumference and took in about 100,000 acres, with, in addition, some purlieus on its margins which remained subject in part to forest law.[5] Some part of this forest was made up of parkland and of widely spaced mature oaks, intersected by straight rides; other parts were enclosed arable and meadow land; on other parts were thick coppices, bushes and man-high bracken in which deer could hide or shake off a dog; and yet other parts were moorland, on the edges of which squatters had settled. The forest, in fact, was so by

1. See J. P. Hare, *The History of the Royal Buckhounds*, Newmarket, 1895, pp. 258–61.

2. One of the earliest uses of the word 'villa' is in Pope's 'Windsor Forest' (1713). For the apricots and peaches, and the round of dining out on venison and riding out in the parks, see Swift's *Journal to Stella*.

3. 'Epistle to Burlington' (1715?), *Poetical Works of John Gay*, ed. G. C. Faber, New York, 1926 and 1969, p. 153. Gay also drew the character of 'Robin of Bagshot' (a near relative of Walpole's) in the *Beggar's Opera*. The exploits of such heroes in 1723 included the robbing, at 5 a.m., of the Exeter stage: *Gloucester Journal*, 25 March 1723. Such episodes were sometimes attributed, without any basis, to the Blacks.

4. D. Defoe, *A Tour through the Whole Island of Great Britain*, 1962 edn, I, p. 143.

5. South in his 'Account of Windsor Forest' (1759) gave the figure of 92,200 acres: Crest. 2. 1628. By the end of the century the area had shrunk to 59,600 acres: Second Report of the Commissioners on the State of Windsor Forest, *PP*, 1809, IV.

virtue of legal and administrative designation, rather than by any unitary economic organization. The Crown owned Windsor Little Park, more than three miles around, and Windsor Great Park which was reported to Defoe to be fourteen miles around.[1] But of the forest's fifteen or more major manors, the Crown owned only Bray and Cookham, and shared in the manors of New and Old Windsor. The other manors, and much of their lands, remained in private hands.

To the uncultivated eye a forest appears simply as uncultivated land – an expanse of woodland and heath which has been left 'wild', and in which wild animals, including deer, may run at will. But a forest has its own complex economy; and where forest settlements had become numerous the competing claims of red and fallow deer, lesser game, hogs, cattle, sheep, and human demands for timber, firing and transport, were subject to intricate regulation.

In theory not only were deer 'the principal beauty and ornament of the forest',[2] but the needs of their economy overrode every other need, since the especial function of this royal forest was to provide the King with relaxation from the cares of state. This function was established in law, invoked by the King's officers,[3] and celebrated in literary tradition:

> Here have I seen the King, when great affairs
> Give leave to slacken, and unbend his cares,
> Attended to the Chase by all the flower
> Of youth . . .[4]

The tradition was upheld in practice, although not in so stately a manner, by Queen Anne who (Swift reported in 1711) 'hunts in a chaise with one horse, which she drives herself, and drives furiously, like Jehu, and is a mighty hunter, like Nimrod'.[5]

The royal prey, however, did not reproduce itself abundantly and

1. Defoe, op. cit., I, p. 311. Defoe was told that the Little Park was 'particular to the Court', while the Great Park was 'open for riding, hunting, and taking the air for any gentlemen that please'. So far as hunting goes this was certainly untrue.

2. Nathaniel Boothe, Esq., Steward of the Court, *The Rights of His Majesty's Forest Asserted, in a Charge given at a Swanimote-Court held in the Castle-Court belonging to the Honor and Castle of Windsor, before the Verderers of the Forest of Windsor, the 27th of September 1717,* 1719, p. 6.

3. When Earl Tankerville, Chief Justice in Eyre, was accused of being too free in his grants of game warrants in 1717, he was urged by Lord Cobham, the Constable, to 'reflect how much the Beauty of the Pallace of Windsor and the Diversion of the Royal Family depends upon the preserving of the Forrest': Constable's Warrant Books (Royal Library, Windsor Castle, Room I, IB6b), I, fo. 22. See also *Hist. MSS Comm. 15th Report, App. VI (Carlisle)*, Carlisle to Halifax, 29 December 1723.

4. 'Cooper's Hill', *The Poetical Works of Sir John Denham*, New Haven, 1969, p. 81.

5. Swift, *Journal to Stella*, 31 July 1711.

unbidden. Deer require extensive feeding-grounds, both for grass and for the leaves of bushes and lower branches of trees ('horn-high'). Their tastes are delicate but various: they favour, in particular, young corn or vegetable crops, the bark of young trees (in winter), and occasional luxuries, such as apples. The princely red deer and the common fallow deer (with both of which Windsor was stocked) consort together no more happily than the red and grey squirrel. The species tended to keep their distance, and to need the distance for their keep. Tolerant of cows, both species competed directly with sheep and horses which, like deer, bite the grass close. Serious competition with sheep could drive the deer from the forest into neighbouring cultivated land, and few wooden fences or 'railes' could hold them in for long. In the winter their feed was supplemented by hay or by 'browse wood' ('lops and tops, or tender twigs from the trees', branches of holly, etc.) which was cut by the keepers and left lying for the deer to strip of leaves and bark. In mid-summer the deer required to be left free of all disturbance while they fawned, and during 'fence month'[1] extensive tracts of forest, whether fenced or not, were to be left utterly untroubled. In addition, certain favourite haunts of the deer were to be left as 'preserved grounds' throughout the year; and since the deer themselves could be almost as damaging as goats to that other great forest product – the timber – from time to time copses and new plantations had to be fenced against deer and cattle alike, until the trees were large enough to survive their browsing.

This was by no means the end to the royal claims over the forest. In an attempt to enforce these claims, Nathaniel Boothe, Steward of the Windsor Swanimote Court, gave a detailed Charge to the court in September 1717, which he later published in order to counter 'the railing and ignorance of those people who condemn the Laws of the Forest'. His Charge, which lamented the 'manifest destruction' of vert and venison, attended in particular to the position of those who dwelt in forest purlieus. Although deer, when they come out of the forest 'lose something of their former freedom, yet they are expected back again'. 'Most men reckon the deer his own that he can find out of the forest, but this is a great mistake', for, if in the purlieus, they could be taken only on stringent conditions: no man might hunt (a) on the Sabbath, (b) nor before sunrise nor after sunset, (c) nor during 'fence-time', (d) nor oftener than thrice a week, (e) nor taking with him more than his own household servants, (f) nor further than his own lands extended, (g) nor unless his lands were worth 40s. a year, (h) nor (if within seven miles of the forest) within forty days before

1. 21 June to 21 July. For shrewd observations on the competing claims of deer, cattle, hogs, etc., see Anon. ('A Commoner'), *A Letter to the Commoners in Rockingham Forest*, Stamford, 1744.

or after the King's hunting, (i) nor might he let his dog follow the deer back into the forest, 'but standing there, must call back his dog and blow his horn, and if his dog has kill'd the deer, yet he may not have him, unless his dog seized him in the purlewe, and the beast by his force drew him into the forest'. This feat, however, it was most unlikely that a truly law-abiding and loyal dog could accomplish, since the inhabitants of forest purlieus might only keep hunting dogs if these had been 'lawed' – that is, three fore-claws chopped off, thus laming the dog so badly that it could not chase deer. The inhabitants of purlieus (as well, of course, as of the forest proper) were prohibited from keeping bows, engines, toils, guns, nets, snares . . .[1]

Boothe's Charge gives the complete claim of the Crown. It was of course in some respects quaint and archaic; thus, dogs were probably no longer being 'lawed' in 1717 (although dogs caught hunting by the keepers were certainly destroyed), and the common interpretation of the law as it affected purlieu lands was less nice.[2] But within the forest proper there was nothing archaic about the claims of the Crown. All was subordinated to the economy of the deer. Those arable oases which Pope so admired, when –

> . . . 'midst the Desart fruitful Fields arise,
> That crown'd with tufted Trees and springing Corn,
> Like verdant Isles the sable Waste adorn . . .[3]

might not be fenced so high that the deer could not pass through them to their customary feeding-grounds. Whether the land was privately owned or not, no timber could be felled without licence from the forest officers. Peat and turfs might not be cut in preserved grounds (whoever owned those grounds). Deer might not be killed on any pretence whatsoever.

At least, this was so in theory. The practice was more intricate. Claim and counter-claim had been the condition of forest life for centuries. On the one hand, the nobility and the local gentry had been nibbling and continued to nibble; here a small private deer-park, there a pond with private fishing-rights, here an exclusive claim to rights to manorial soil. Sometimes these claims were supported by grants or the evidence of favours from previous monarchs.[4] On the other hand, the customary

1. Boothe, loc. cit.

2. In a case arising in Sherwood Forest in 1708 and sent to the Attorney and Solicitors-General for their opinion, they held that the law might be interpreted more simply: killing deer in purlieus might be done on one's own purlieu land and by 'fair chase': Portland MSS, Nottingham University Library, PW2 619–26.

3. Alexander Pope, *Windsor Forest*, lines 26–8.

4. The Trumbull family of Easthampstead, for example, held a deer-park and lands

tenants of the several manors had pressed forward, on every occasion, their own claims to unrestricted grazing, timber and peat-cutting on their commons.[1] And finally there was the problem of squatters and in-comers, who pretended to no legal right but who asserted the same claims as their neighbours. Very probably the population of the forest was increasing in the first decades of the eighteenth century, and had been increasing for nearly a century. No worthwhile figures exist, and one must be content with indications. In 1640 a petition of the grand jury of Berkshire protested that 'free men' had been forced through fear of the press-gang to forsake their homes and hide in the woods.[2] Some may have stayed. Others (old Cromwellian soldiers in the main) may have stayed when, in the Commonwealth, Windsor Great Park was parcelled out into some thirty farms; their tenancy did not, of course, survive the Restoration.[3] Population certainly thickened in the north-east of the forest, around Maidenhead, Bray, Cookham and Windsor (the area of greatest gentry settlement) with attendant servants and services.[4] But it is clear from the Court Books of the Verderers that squatting and 'purprestures' (or illegal petty enclosures) went on continuously in the forest interior as well: in one forest walk, Bearwood, some 'three or four score' cottagers were presented for unlicensed settlement in 1687 alone.[5] Other forest parishes,

---

on a grant from Charles I, on the condition of keeping 200 deer for the King's use: E. P. Shirley, *Some Account of English Deer Parks*, 1867, p. 132. In the early years of the eighteenth century Sir William Trumbull, Pope's patron, and for many years a Verderer, observed forest law meticulously and took no venison except by warrant of the Chief Huntsman, Will Lorwen: see Berks Rec. Off. Trumbull Add. MSS 135.

1. The claims of the tenants, and often of all 'inhabitants', were unusually large. For the important cases of Winkfield and Sandhurst, see below, pp. 48–53. Customs claimed by three forest or purlieu manors in 1735 show: Wargrave, common of pasture for all manner of cattle without stint; Warfield, all 'tenants and inhabitants' common of pasture without stint and 'without restraint of any season', the right to cut turf, heath, fern and furzes and to dig loam and sand 'without any leave, lycence or molestation', and (for copyholders) the right to fell timber without licence; Waltham St Lawrence, un-restrained right of common for 'all and every tenant and occupyer of lands and tene-ments': Berks Rec. Off. D/EN M 71/1, M 73/1, M 82/A/1. The people of Cookham, Bray and Binstead claimed similarly extensive grazing and timber rights, and the tenants of Wokingham claimed the right to take wood as necessary and without licence, as well as the right to take turf in the waste except in fence month: South, op. cit., 1759, Crest. 2. 1628, pp. 29–30, 41–2, 76. When similar claims were made at the last Justice Seat in Eyre in 1632 they were universally disallowed (see below, p. 36 n. 5), so that one can assume that they date back to their forcible assertion during the Commonwealth.

2. Brit. Mus. Harl. MSS 1219, fo. 31.

3. South, op. cit., p. 25; T. E. Harwood, *Windsor Old and New*, 1929, p. 175; W. Menzies, *The History of Windsor Great Park and Windsor Forest*, 1864, p. 15.

4. South, op. cit., p. 15.

5. These squatters were treated with humanity, no further action being taken, 'it

with rising poor-rates, were anxiously attempting to prevent new settlers.[1]
The population of the forest (somewhat reduced in area) was estimated at
17,409 in 1801.[2] No comparable figures exist for the 1720s, but for what
it is worth one may contrast the figures for selected forest parishes of the
'Compton' religious census of 1676 with those of 1801 to indicate the
trajectory of growth:[3]

THE POPULATION OF WINDSOR FOREST: SELECTED PARISHES

	1676	1801
Binfield	345	1,045
Bray	1,098	2,403
Cookham (with Maidenhead)	687	2,239
Easthampstead	168	566
Finchampstead	250	463
Sunninghill	262	700
Warfield	650	823
New Windsor	1,025	3,361
Winkfield	250	1,465

A substantial bureaucracy existed to enforce forest law upon this
growing population, although in the approved eighteenth-century manner
the senior officers were in the main sinecurists and absentees. The chief
officer beneath the King was the Constable and Governor of the Castle,[4]
most of whose duties were performed by a Deputy Lieutenant. From
June 1717 this last post was held by Colonel Francis Negus, a very
influential courtier, who served in this capacity throughout the episode of
the Blacks.[5] Beneath him came a Chief Woodward and a Rider of the

appearing to us that many of them were poor and aged people and such as doe receive
bread & almes of their respective parishes': Verderers' Court Books, LR3.2.

1. e.g. Sunninghill Vestry Book (Berks Rec. Off. D/P/126/8/1), entry for 26 January
1718; and Winkfield Churchwardens' Accounts (Berks Rec. Off. D/P/151/5/2) for
general tendency for poor-rates to rise.

2. *PP*, 1809, IV, p. 323.

3. W. Money, 'A Religious Census of the County of Berkshire in 1676', *Berks, Bucks
and Oxon Archaeological Journal*, II, Reading, 1899, pp. 22–6. The 'Compton' census
may afford some approximate evidence as to *adult* population, but the degree of this is
disputed: the figures in the table therefore indicate only comparative growth-rate of
parishes.

4. Sir Richard Temple, Viscount Cobham, 1716–June 1723; the Earl of Carlisle,
June 1723–8. Thereafter the Duke of St Albans. The full title was Constable of Windsor
Castle, Keeper of the Parks, Forests and Warrens, Governor and Captain of the Castle
and Forts.

5. Negus had long experience of the forest, serving as Woodward, and as Ranger of

Forest, and then a further hierarchy of titular and actual officialdom. Each Walk in the forest (Old Windsor, New Lodge, Easthampstead, Swinley, Bigshot Rails, Billingbear, Bearwood, etc.) had a nobleman or gentleman as titular Master, Warden, Ranger or Bailiff, with salary, perquisites of wood and game, and the use of the relevant lodge.[1] Sarah, Duchess of Marlborough, had gained (through her earlier favour with Queen Anne) the rangership of Windsor Great and Little Parks. Unlike most of the others, she was a busy and vociferous Ranger; deprived of her element of royal or political favour, she remained too big for even Walpole to cut down to size, and she survived for decades, like a huge amphibious creature, thrashing her tail among the courtiers at Windsor and making what annoyances she could. The Blacks no doubt enjoyed the spectacle, and they seem to have left her alone.

The effective duties of the forest were performed by thirteen or fourteen under-keepers, four gamekeepers, a vermin-killer and their servants. (There was also a parallel organization, staffed by some of the same personnel, of royal huntsmen – a Master of Buckhounds, a Chief Huntsman, yeomen prickers and servants.) These posts carried small salaries – for under-keepers £20 per annum – and if not supplemented from other sources would scarcely have constituted a livelihood.[2] But the best posts were in fact lavishly supplemented by perquisites. Some of these were expressed, such as the use of their own sub-lodges, a hay allowance for the deer, a scale of payment for each stag, buck or hind officially killed, the use of old fence-posts for firing, etc.; others were unexpressed but perfectly well understood and sanctioned by usage, such as the culling for their own use of the occasional ('wounded') deer, a fairly free hand with timber, small game and herbage; still others were the wages of a customary corruption (the covert sale of venison on their own account, or the accept-

Bigshot Rails and Sandhurst Walk and Chief Forester of the Bailiwick of Finchampstead, as early as 1704: Hare, op. cit., p. 242. He still held all these offices, except that of Woodward, in 1716, and continued to hold them when he became Deputy Lieutenant.

1. 'The lodges in those parks, are no more lodges, but palaces': Defoe, op. cit., p. 311. Such offices as these keeperships (the Duke of Chandos said) would sell in some forests at £1,200 or £1,500: C. H. C. and M. I. Baker, *Life and Circumstances of James Brydges First Duke of Chandos*, Oxford, 1949, p. 388.

2. And perhaps did not in exceptional and ill-favoured cases. The 'poor distressed keepers of the Bailiwick of Surrey' claimed in 1726 that they were at the expense of keeping horses and hounds to drive deer back into the forest, had been paid no wages for five years, that the Out-Ranger (Brigadier Munden) had appropriated the money (£600 p.a.) out of which their wages should have been met to his own use, and that they were in debt and likely to perish in gaol: T1.255 (30). In 1716, when several years' salary was due to the under-keepers in Windsor, the Duke of Kent was persuaded that 'some of those poor men who subsist chiefly by that salary do at this time want bread': T1.198 (67). He may have been persuaded too easily.

THE GOVERNMENT OF WINDSOR FOREST, CIRCA 1723

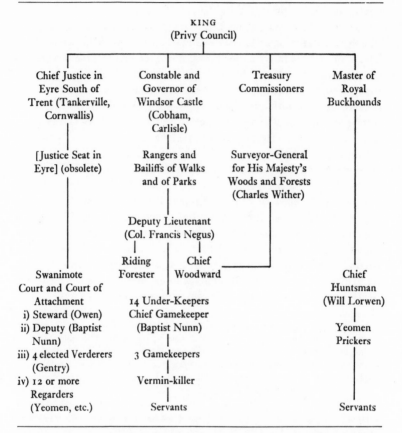

This is the forest bureaucracy proper. But foresters might also be subject to the local authority of their own lord of the manor and his manorial court; and, of course, of J.P.s, who had an existence independent of any of these lines of authority.

The Surveyor-General for Woods was responsible only for matters of timber, repairs, etc. But the Lords Commissioners of the Treasury had a finger in all pies, finding all salaries, court expenses, enlargement of lodges, etc. And the Treasury Solicitor was concerned in all major prosecutions.

The lines of authority could be crossed (or united) by pluralities: thus Will Lorwen the Chief Huntsman was also under-keeper of New Lodge Walk, while Baptist Nunn was Deputy Steward of the forest courts and chief gamekeeper, to which he added the under-keepership of Linchford Walk and the post of Janitor and Keeper of the Outward Gate of Windsor Castle (yet another bureaucracy there).

ance of bribes from poachers as a payment for silence).[1] Not satisfied with this, the senior officials were pluralists who accumulated several posts in their own hands, and who were continually using their influence in the forest courts to secure additional favours.

This was the executive force. But the position of these officials was complex, since they operated half within forest law, and half within statute law. Two Justices in Eyre (one north, the other south of the Trent) had the authority to enforce forest law. The niceties of this law varied from forest to forest, but it is at least clear that it was not quite as ineffectual as some authorities have supposed.[2] In Windsor offenders could first be complained of at the Court of Attachment, or 'Forty Days Court', and then (if the complaint was found good) be presented at the Swanimote (or Swainmote) Court, which was held infrequently, at either Windsor or Wokingham. The Swanimote Court was constituted of the King's Steward, four judicial Verderers (elected, like county members, by the freemen) and twelve or more Regarders appointed from the different districts of the forest.[3] It had power to convict and to assess a fine, but it remained a 'court of attachment' only; its sentences were not enforceable, until they had been certified under the seal of Verderers and jury and then tried at the court (or Justice Seat) of the Chief Justice in Eyre. However, no Justice in Eyre had actually *sat* in the forest since the reign of Charles I; hence no offenders had been formally sentenced for nearly 100 years.[4]

1. The total budget for the salaries of twenty-three forest officials in 1717 was only £537 9s. 11½d. (Constable's Warrant Books, I, fo. 13 *verso*). It is impossible to set an exact value on the perquisites of keepers; the best attempt was made later in the century in the New Forest (*Commons Journals*, XLIV, 1789, p. 558). A keeper who started off with a salary of £20 p.a. would be unlucky, when he had added to this fees for driving the walks, fuel wood (or allowance in lieu), allowance for repair of lodges, use of lodge, fees for killing deer, profit from the sale of browse wood, sale of rabbits, use of his own grazing in forest, etc., to emerge with less than £100 p.a., and this on his own confession, before undeclared advantages are considered. Many gained very much more. The scale of fees for authorized killing of deer in 1721 was £2 a stag, £1 a hind, and 10s. a buck: T1.235 (46); in some cases they also had the valuable perquisites of the skin, shoulders and antlers of the deer (Brit. Mus. Add. MSS 35,996, fo. 69).

2. See e.g. Sir William Holdsworth, *A History of English Law*, 1956 edn, I, pp. 105–7. The best general accounts of the law are in William Nelson, *Manwood's Treatise of the Forest Laws*, 1717; and G. J. Turner, *Select Pleas of the Forest*, Selden Society, 1901, introduction.

3. South, op. cit., *passim*, says there should be twelve Regarders, appointed (a) by the patent of the King, (b) by the Chief Justice in Eyre, or (c) temporarily sworn in for a particular Swanimote. But in 1725 seventeen Regarders served at the Swanimote, and in 1728 the Duke of Newcastle appointed (or reappointed) twenty-four Regarders (Verderers' Court Books, LR3.3).

4. Memorial of Cracherode, the Treasury Solicitor, 25 November 1719 in T1.223 (6); memorial of Negus in Constable's Warrant Books, I, fo. 18 *verso*. See also P. Lewis,

In these circumstances it is easy to ridicule the forest courts as obsolete monuments to antiquity, kept alive solely to provide a rationale for certain sinecurists.[1] In 1809 parliamentary commissioners found the Swanimote Court's judgements to be 'easily evaded, like a lawed dog, too mutilated to catch their game'.[2] This is to misread the evidence, as it relates to the early eighteenth century. The courts did have certain powers which, if insufficient to deter the wealthy offender, were certainly sufficient to give pain to the poor. First, they could 'attach' offenders, either in their persons (if caught red-handed) – and there was a dungeon or 'coal hole' in the Castle where they could be held – or in their goods, pending either bail or trial at the Swanimote.[3] Second, the forest officers had summary powers of confiscation, of guns and snares, dogs, and of unlicensed loads of timber or peat. Third, offenders found guilty at the Swanimote could be bound over to attend the next Justice Seat in Eyre upon recognisances far too high for a poor man to find.[4] Finally – and perhaps arising from the

---

Historical Inquiries Concerning Forests and Forest Laws, 1811, p. 36. Sir William Jones left clear notes on the cases and arguments at the last Justice Seat in Eyre for Windsor Forest in September 1632. This notorious set of judgements was part of Charles I's attempt to enhance his forest revenues; almost every case was decided against the foresters; offenders were heavily fined; lords of the manor and parishes had their claims to ancient rights refused; and even loyal officers were fined for inscribing accounts on paper (instead of parchment) or neglecting the proper forms. The memory of this Seat must have turned the foresters into republicans, and done something to prevent the revival of the Seat after the Restoration: see Jones 266–94, *English Reports*, vol. 82, pp. 139–55.

1. In fact, at Windsor's last Swanimote in 1728 it appeared that the Verderers and Regarders were not being paid their ancient fees: for the Verderer two horses, a saddle, a sword, five lances, a spear, a buckler and 200 silver shillings; for a Regarder a horse, lance and buckler and fifty shillings; for a keeper a lance, a cross-bow, and fifteen shillings: LR3.3.

2. *PP*, 1809, IV, p. 9.

3. Boothe, op. cit. pp. 13–14; keepers were urged to attach offenders 'by their goods or cattle' at the Court of Attachment, 26 July 1687 (LR3.2), but there is no evidence that this was being done after 1716. But offenders certainly were on occasion held in gaol: thus two were committed for contempt in September 1717 for not attending the Swanimote; another offender was in custody at the 1725 Swanimote: LR3.3.

4. Unfortunately the Verderers' Court Books, which survive, enter presentments but very rarely give any clue as to the outcome – at the best a cryptic 'ignoramus' or 'compuit'. Some Minutes of the Court survive, however, for 1688, which give an indication: thus W. Platt, yeoman of Old Windsor, was presented for keeping a gun and toil (trap or net) in his house; a true bill found, and he was ordered to enter into recognisances of £40 for himself and £20 each for two sureties on condition that he (in the usual form) 'shall personally appear at the next Justice in Eyre seat to be holden in the said forest'. The same sum was used to bind over a husbandman for an encroachment; but only £10 and £5 for an offender grubbing bushes: Berks Rec. Off. DE/N O 11. A prosperous offender was bound over, at £20, for 'staffherding sheep' in 1717: LR3.3.

last power – it had clearly become a custom for the courts to accept a fine in 'composition', thus waiving both the never-never-land of the Justice Seat and the recognisances which must otherwise be found.[1] Very probably this composition, in small offences, stood at about £5.[2]

The matter has become obscured in legal history because the big offender – the gentleman or large yeoman who was enclosing his lands against the deer and felling timber wholesale without licence – could afford without difficulty to find his recognisances, and could then continue his offence with impunity. Against such offenders the Crown attempted to proceed by exposing them to the far more costly process of an Information in the Court of Exchequer. The small offenders, under the watchful eyes of the forest officers, and dependent upon them for licences and other favours, could scarcely attempt such defiance; and even if the Justice in Eyre never sat, he had the power to send for offenders by his messengers, 'which will put them to so much charge & trouble that the people will not venture to transgress the order'.[3]

This was the last vestige of his judicial function. But in true eighteenth-century fashion, the office of Justice in Eyre remained as a source of privileges and perquisites even where its functions had lapsed. These included the right to grant (but in fact to sell)[4] warrants to chase all game except deer in the royal forests.[5] He could also take each year a number of deer for his own use, and he had the power to grant (or sell) warrants and

---

1. R. H. Hilton, discussing 'The Swanimote Rolls of Feckenhem Forest' (*Worcestershire Historical Society, Miscellany I*, Worcester, 1960, pp. 39–40), distinguishes between 'the more serious offences against venison', which were referred to the justice in eyre, and other offences, where the court could (as in a manorial court) make its own by-laws and exact its own fines and penalties. This may also explain Windsor procedures.

2. The evidence is presumptive. (1) The frequent entry of 'compuit' beside presentments in the Court Books; (2) Edward Young, Surveyor-General of Woods, recommended to the Treasury the revival of the Swanimote Court in 1717 since 'the fines and punishments the Verderers have a power of levying' have good effects (T1.208 (1)); (3) earlier Swanimote records (e.g. *temp.* Charles I) show the use of summary fines for small offences, and a fine of £5 for coursing deer (Berks Rec. Off. D/ED L 36); (4) memoranda on the New Forest in 1717 indicate the practice of 'composition' for fines, and a standard £5 fine for wood theft: T1.209 (24); and for the forest of Essex, *temp.* Charles I, see W. J. Fisher, *The Forest of Essex*, 1887, pp. 99–100.

3. Constable's Warrant Books, II, fo. 43 *verso*.

4. Fisher, op. cit., pp. 95 and 202, suggests the price of a licence might be twenty guineas to the Justice in Eyre, and (1723 in Essex) 3 dozen of wine to the Court's officers.

5. When King George (through his Constable, Lord Cobham) instructed that because of the waste of game no more warrants should be granted, the Earl of Tankerville was indignant: 'since the memory of man tis the first time that a Lord Chief Justice in Eyre's Warrant has bin refused to be served, who by a grant under the Great Seal of England has and is Master of all His Majesties forests': Tankerville to Cobham, 1 January 1718, Constable's Warrant Books, I, fo. 22.

licences to fell timber and to enclose or build in the forest.[1] For the rest, his duties appear to have been met by issuing occasional proclamations from London, and drawing his salary of £1,500. The post usually went not to a lawyer but to a courtier, the Chief Justice in Eyre (a surveyor noted) 'commonly being an officer of greater dignity than knowledge in the laws of the forest'.[2]

The Swanimote Court therefore functioned as a local forest court, with its own judges (the Verderers), grand jury (of Regarders), and petty jury (of freeholders). Nor should it be assumed that it was a wholly pliant instrument of royal authority. Utilitarian bureaucrats might later see it as a toothless old relic, but in fact it was the shadowy survival of a concept both more functional and more democratic than any of their own creations. It sought to bring equilibrium to the forest economy by reconciling the interests of the King, of the large landholders and gentry, and of the substantial freeholders, tenant farmers and yeomen foresters. The Regarders were chosen from among the most substantial farmers.[3] At every election of Knights of the Shire and of Verderers (Colonel Negus complained in 1719) 'the country people take an extra-ordinary liberty'.[4] Hence even at the zenith of Walpole's power, Tory Verderers could be returned, and Tories with vociferous constituents. Whig ministers and officials showed little liking for forest courts, except for the brief episode in Windsor between 1716 and 1725 when they attempted to turn the courts towards their own uses. Charles Withers, the Surveyor-General for Woods, complained that in those forests where courts were kept 'divisions among the Verderers generally screen offenders'.[5] To its credit, the ancient Swanimote Court of Windsor was allowed to fall into desuetude at the end of the 1720s after turning with an audible snarl upon its

1. Such licences were entered regularly in the Verderers' Court Books (e.g. LR3.3) and examples are also in Berks Rec. Off. E/ED E 42 (signed by Baptist Nunn, in 1722, as Deputy or Clerk of the Court) and in W. Lyon, *Chronicles of Finchampstead*, 1895, pp. 270–71. The Clerk of the Court formally received 1s. for entering each licence (LR3.3, October 1728, scale of court fees) but presumably the Chief Justice required a payment, and the Clerk could exact a *douceur* to secure his favour.

2. South, op. cit., Crest. 2. 1628. The Earl of Tankerville was Chief Justice in Eyre from 1716 to 1722. On his death he was succeeded by Lord Cornwallis: SP44.361, fo. 131; *St James's Journal*, 21 June 1722.

3. Two Regarders were appointed from each of the main Walks or Bailiwicks of the forest. The names which I can identify, from 1725 and 1728, are of substantial farmers. Their duties included viewing and presenting encroachments, etc., in their own areas, and viewing timber to be felled.

4. Constable's Warrant Books, I, fo. 19 *verso*.

5. Copy of Memorandum to Treasury Lords, n.d. (1722?) in Earl St Aldwyn's MSS PPD/7.

Hanoverian masters.[1] Research into other forests might well reveal that the old forest courts died out, not because they were impotent but because they continued to express, however feebly, the interests of the foresters.

The forest's equilibrium was certainly imperilled in 1717, when the Swanimote Court was revived as a direct consequence of the 'ill state and condition of the forest'.[2] Old people could still remember the outrageous freedoms taken in the Commonwealth days, when the deer had been slaughtered wholesale, the Great Park turned over to farms, and the foresters had enlarged their 'rights' beyond previous imagining. A Berkshire correspondent wrote, in 1722, to the Bursar of St John's College, Cambridge, lamenting the consequences of 'the godly days of Oliver Cromwell, when Church and College lands were laid waste'.[3] The Duchess of Marlborough was still, in 1728, trying to prevent carriages, timber-teams and carts from forcing the gates of the Great Park and claiming right of way: 'There never was any road in that part of the park, unless it were in Oliver Cromwell's time, when the King was not in possession of his crown: and then it is probable there might be roads . . .'[4] For forest areas the Restoration brought counter-revolution in a score of practical and painful ways. Charles II expelled the new farmers, restocked and extended the parks and revived forest law.[5] The courts appear to have acted vigorously in the reign of James II. In the last year of his reign exceptional measures were taken against deer-stealers, sixteen offenders being committed to the care of the janitor of Windsor Castle. The Glorious Revolution of 1688 seems to have been a signal for a general insurrection against the deer; no doubt the foresters hoped that the 'godly days' of Oliver Cromwell were about to return.

They were soon disillusioned. At a Court of Attachment on 27 December 1688 about 150 'deer hunters and killers' were presented. The parishes most strongly represented were Winkfield (thirty-two) and Bray (thirty-four). This was followed, in May 1689, by a proclamation of the Chief Justice in Eyre, forbidding all peat and turf cutting in the forest without licence or leave from the keepers. (This proclamation clearly overrode established parochial rights.) For a further year the 'Forty Days Court' was held regularly and it was made abundantly clear that King William intended to maintain his predecessor's prerogatives. But after 1690 the

1. See below, p. 97.

2. Constable's Warrant Books, I, fo. 14 and *verso*.

3. J. Morris to Bursar, Sunninghill, 3 April 1722, calendar of estate papers, St John's College, Cambridge, drawer 109 (184).

4. Sarah Churchill to Townshend, copy, 25 July 1728, Blenheim MSS F1.40.

5. South, op. cit., Crest. 2. 1628, pp. 25–6; Menzies, op. cit., p. 15.

regimen appears to have relaxed (although disputes continued about peat and turf cutting in Winkfield and in Sandhurst). With the accession of Queen Anne the courts began to doze and to drift down the stream. In September 1704 it was announced that it was the Queen's pleasure that the warren at Swinley Rails should be destroyed: destructive rabbits should give way to hares.[1]

There can be little doubt that Queen Anne's reign saw a genial laxity in forest government; perhaps her frequent presence in the forest was more effectual in curbing offences than frequent court-keeping. Pope spent his childhood in the forest, and celebrated this mild regimen in his first major poem, 'Windsor Forest'.

> Rich Industry sits smiling on the Plains,
> And Peace and Plenty tell, a STUART reigns.

When George I came to the throne it suddenly appeared that rich industry (for the graziers and forest farmers) could be seen in an altogether different guise. The railing of the Great Park was so rotten that the deer 'daily get out, and are killed by the country people'.[2] As regards the Little Park, funds for railing had been misappropriated, the keepers had not been paid for four or five years,[3] so many people in Windsor town had got keys to the gates that 'the park is almost become common', the palings round the new plantations of trees were so broken that the colts broke in and barked and spoiled them, the deer-pens, deer-racks and vermin-traps were in ruins, and the surviving deer were at daily risk:

> The deer gets out of the park [wrote one keeper] so that we can't tell what to do with them and goes into the gardens at Windsor town and are killed and the gardeners says that they have a world of mischief done with them that they can't bare with them nor will not and likewise they goes down to Old Windsor to the farmers hay ricks and they kill them . . .[4]

The sums required – and occasionally appropriated – for maintaining the fences etc. were very large, although they often found some way of disappearing into private purses somewhere between the Treasury and the actual officers of the forest.[5]

1. Verderers' Court Books, LR3.2. See table below, p. 46.

2. Petition of the keepers of Windsor Great Park, T1.181 (53).

3. Non-payment of keepers' wages was 'of great disservice to the Crown, it being impossible for these people to subsist so long without money, had they not indirect means of getting, which tis feared falls heavy on His Majesty's Woods and venison': E. Young to Treasury Commissioners, 7 February 1716, T1.198 (22).

4. Papers accompanying memorial of Sarah, Duchess of Marlborough, in T1.198 (22), (27) and (34).

5. In 1670 no less than £7,574 was allocated by the Treasury for the palings of the

If this was the condition of the two royal parks, it may be expected that the outer forest was, from the standpoint of those with the care of His Majesty's vert and venison, in an even more deplorable state. A memorandum was drawn up by Colonel Negus (in about 1717) to show 'how it comes that there are so few deer'. The digging of heath, turfs and peat in forest areas had been so extensive 'that it has been impossible for the deer to find any shelter or quiet'. Turf and firing were being taken by the inhabitants not only for their own use but also for sale outside the forest. The deer were 'continually disturbed and the keepers insulted by the drivers of those carts'. The old ridings were out of repair, being used as common roads by the country people whose carts had reduced them to 'great holes' and 'boggs'. Common rights for sheep were being abused, stints disregarded, and 'everybody feeds as many as they please'. The excessive number of warrants to hunt granted by the Chief Justice in Eyre, although in theory for small game only, and the number of sine-curists claiming deer as their perquisite of office led to depredations on the fallow deer. In Swinley Walk the fences around the new coppices were down, and the deer were eating their own future cover. Under all these pressures the deer were 'forced to seek shelter in the woods and coverts on the skirts of the forest, where they have been commonly shot by the common people'. Four out of every five deer culled by the keepers were found to have some mark of shot on them. No doubt the advancing technology and increasing availability of firearms would, in itself, have provoked this crisis.[1]

Memorials of the keepers in November 1719 add new complaints to those of Colonel Negus. So many woods, coppices and hedgerows were being felled, grubbed and assarted (cleared for cultivation) that the people 'threaten a total destruction of the covert'. 'The heath and turf is yearly carryed off . . . so that as the covert of wood is destroyed in the enclosures, the covert in the open country is destroyed by selling the heath.' 'People within the forest make their hedges so very high, and spike their gates in such a manner, that it is impossible for the deer safely to pass and repass.' In the parish of Winkfield in the heart of the forest offenders were encouraged by a local gentleman, Robert Edwards, who had bought some old sheltering-grounds of the deer, and enclosed

---

Great Park. In 1715 Sarah Churchill was demanding more than £3,000 to repair the rails of the Little Park; she maintained that a few years previously the Surveyor-General of Woods (Wilcox) had misappropriated 'great sumes' allocated to this purpose from wood sales: papers in T1.198.

1. Copy of memorandum in Constable's Warrant Books, I, fos. 18–19; estimate of Surveyor-General for repairing old ridings, 3 April 1717, ibid., I, fos. 15–16 *verso*; papers in T1.206 (51).

these with a fence nine feet high over a length of a mile and two furlongs, thereby beating the deer from their usual feed and forcing them out of the forest. He had fenced off another plot of contiguous land, leaving a passage for the deer between the two of less than 100 yards in width; hence the deer, in moving between the wood and the heathland, were an easy prey for the toils of deer-stealers. Other Winkfield farmers were following his example. Under these circumstances, Negus wrote in a covering letter, the keepers 'are quite disheartened from executing their offices, and if some way can't be found out to cheque Mr Edwards it would be better for the King to give up his forest'.[1]

The King did not, as it happens, do this. His first forest hunt, and perhaps his first visit to Windsor, took place in September 1717. There was a regular fanfare for Hanover. Tables were set out for the respectable denizens; the King gave '*confitures aux femmes de la compagne*'.[2] Nathaniel Boothe delivered himself of his archaic Charge.[3] And the first full Swanimote Court was held since 1708. But it is unlikely that the King gave '*confitures*' to Colonel Negus and the forest officers; he was sportsman enough to read the signs and to see that this celebrated royal forest of the English did not, in the matter of game, come up to Hanoverian standards. Thereafter, he maintained a close interest in the forest.[4] And the forest bureaucracy bore down on the foresters accordingly.

1. Papers accompanying memorial of A. Cracherode, Treasury Solicitor, 25 November 1719, in T1.223 (6). To deal with offenders of the substance of Mr Edwards, Cracherode recommended proceeding by an English Information in the Court of Exchequer. The proposal was warmly supported by the new Surveyor-General for Woods, Charles Withers: 'some few examples' of such prosecutions would be 'sufficient to terrify them in each forest' (Memorial to Treasury Commissioners, 2 March 1721, in T1.233); 'the expenses of such a suit, and the terror of the consequences of such a new way of prosecution, would soon put a stop to this evil' (further memorandum, n.d. (1722?), copy in Earl St Aldwyn's MSS, PPD/7). Such prosecutions were initiated in several forests in 1721 (T27.23, p. 153), some of which were stayed when the defendants submitted and offered to compound (ibid., p. 281, June 1722). No doubt this exacerbated the climate in which Blacking took place; but only one such Windsor prosecution (for carrying off the tops of trees) was still in hand in 1723 (T1.243 (1)).

2. Brit. Mus. Add. MSS 17,677 KKK 2, 28 September 1717.

3. See above, p. 30.

4. Evidence for the King's close interest in Windsor Forest is sparse but conclusive. After his visit to the forest in September 1717 he instructed Negus that all further warrants from the Chief Justice in Eyre should be refused (see above, p. 38 n. 5.) and that no game or venison should be killed 'upon any pretence whatsoever' (Constable's Warrant Books, I, fo. 22). Memoranda on forest matters were on occasion sent on to him in French (e.g. T1.206 (51b)). In July 1723 he ordered a restraint of all hunting in Swinley Walk, 'wherein his Majesty chooses to take diversion himself': LR3.3. Walpole's attempt to nominate a sinecurist to a rangership occasioned one of King George's moments of stubbornness: the King (Townshend reported to Walpole) had 'some

They had, in fact, anticipated the King's displeasure. The first evidence of tougher forest rule is seen in the previous year. A new Whiggish forest officialdom was appointed, headed by the very rich military adventurer, Viscount Cobham. When his Deputy Lieutenant died in June 1717, Colonel Negus (who already held several forest posts) was appointed in his stead.[1] It is reasonable to assume that Negus, who was Member of Parliament for Ipswich and also acting Master of the King's Horse, was the ally of Townshend and Walpole and of the hard Hanoverian Whigs.[2] The immediate effect of the changes may be seen in the level of presentments of offenders at the Court of Attachment or 'Forty Days Court'. After the last (and only) Swanimote of Anne's reign, this court continued to meet from time to time, with occasional presentments of offenders for encroachments, unlicensed timber cutting, etc. Thereafter the court almost ceased its functions, until April 1716, from which point the presentments rose steeply. Whereas at the 1708 Swanimote no true bills were found against forest offenders, at the next Swanimote (1717) when King George first visited the forest ninety-one true bills were found. Most of these were presented at a Court of Attachment hurriedly called three weeks before the King's visit: twenty-two were for heath and peat cutting, thirteen for encroachments, ten for unlicensed cottages or buildings, five for fences too high for the deer to pass (including Robert Edwards, the King's antagonist in Winkfield), four for offences in grazing sheep and one for keeping greyhounds. From 1717 until 1725 presentments were maintained at a high level. Thereafter they slackened off.[3] (See table, p. 46.)

These presentments covered a dozen forest offences. There were

---

doubts whether it would not interfere with his hunting': 4 November 1725, Brit. Mus. Add. MSS 32,687: see also J. M. Beattie, *The English Court in the Reign of George I*, Cambridge, 1967, pp. 101, 140. See also p. 235 below. I have not consulted the King's papers at Hanover, where no doubt more evidence could be found.

1. For Negus's previous posts, see above, p. 33 n. 5. He replaced, as Deputy Lieutenant, Richard Nevile, who died in June 1717: Constable's Warrant Books, 1, fo. 12.

2. Control of posts close to the King's person was one of the prizes for which the political factions fought most ruthlessly. Walpole entered the government in October 1715, and in July 1716 alterations were made in the Cabinet intended to strengthen his position and Townshend's: Negus to be Master of Horse, Cobham to be Constable of Windsor Castle: *Hist. MSS Comm. 11th Report, App. IV* (Townshend), p. 102. When Negus was promoted to Deputy Lieutenant in June 1717, Walpole and Townshend were in temporary opposition. But Negus was too good a courtier to be caught wholly in the toils of faction: he gave his name to the drink (warm wine and sugar) which he had once dispensed to soothe a dispute between Whigs and Tories: see *DNB*. See also below, p. 203 and Plumb, *Sir Robert Walpole*, 1960, 1, ch. 6.

3. Verderers' Court Books. LR3.2, 3.3.

offences against game: a gentleman presented in July 1717 with his servants and five spaniels for 'killing a heath poult which I catcht him drawing of'; a yeoman, in May 1718, for being abroad at night with a greyhound and a dog; and, in February 1719: 'I present that I heard the burst of a gun and made toward it & I found Thomas Marlow setting by a coppice called Long Grove in . . . Wingfield in Swinley Walk with a gun by him . . . being on a Sunday, he was the servant to Edward Boyer of Old Bracknell, baker.' There were presentments for building cottages or cart-houses; for felling timber or for grubbing coppices; for taking in land from the waste. But the most frequent presentments were against turf, peat and heath-cutters. These centred upon waste areas in the centre and south-west of the forest, at Winkfield, Sandhurst, Sunninghill and near Wokingham, where the Crown and the manors (and their customary tenants) contested each others' claims.

Let us look at this 'forest' once again, with the aid of the surveyor's map of 1734. It contained only two substantial nucleated settlements: Windsor to the north and Wokingham (or Ockingham, Oakingham) to the south-west. Windsor was a thriving and expanding corporate borough; admissions to its freedom in the late seventeenth and early eighteenth centuries show luxury trades (goldsmiths, clock-makers, confectioners, vintners, glovers, armourers, etc.), building trades, food marketing and distribution, leather and wood industries.[1] Wokingham was governed by a very small, very tight group of self-nominating burgesses – mainly merchants and shopkeepers – and since apprentices were not admitted to the freedom, it is more difficult to identify the trades. It had the expected occupations of a small market-town – bakers, butchers, apothecary, pharmacist, ironmonger, barber, tallow chandler, hosier – as well as trades in leather, wood and building.[2] But the control of the burgesses was so tight that it was self-defeating; and much new settlement was evidently taking place outside the borough boundaries.

Apart from these two towns, there were few nucleated settlements: hamlets, farmsteads and cottages straggled over the forest. In the centre and west there were good arable clays, and huge areas, assarted from the forest centuries before, were farmed in open fields. To the south, around Bagshot and Sandhurst, were the Bagshot sands, which supported little but fern, furze and heath. Wokingham shared some of both kinds of soil, two thirds of the parish's lands being arable and pasture, privately owned,

1. Guildhall archives, Royal Borough of New Windsor, Freedom Book RO/f: Hall Book, 1653–1725, WI/AC a 1.
2. Wokingham Common Council Book, Berks Rec. Off. WO/AC a 1.

TRUE BILLS FOUND AT WINDSOR SWANIMOTE COURTS

Date	Reigning monarch	Encroach-ments[1]	Timber offences[2]	Turf cutting	Game offences[3]	High fences[4]	Other[5]	Total true bills
1687	James II	14	14	3	6	—	8	54[6]
1688	James II	46	1	—	3	—	2	52
1690	William and Mary	2	2	5	2	—	1	12[7]
1692	William and Mary	6	2	3	3	—	1	15[8]
1697	William III	1	—	—	—	—	—	1
1701	William III	—	—	—	—	—	—	—[9]
1708	Anne	—	—	—	—	—	—	—[10]
1717	George I	32	8	34	6	6	5	91
1725	George I	19	2	31	4	—	—	56
1728	George II	18	2	—	—	—	2	22[11]

Notes: The accuracy of this table cannot be assured. Swanimote courts were held from time to time (in September) when the forest officers wanted them. The Courts of Attachment (or Forty Days Courts) were held regularly, and the Verderers' Books keep what appears to be an accurate record of offenders brought before these. When a true bill was found at these, the cases were held over for judgement by the Verderers and jury at the next Swanimote. But the books contain only rough notes of proceedings at the latter; presumably the formal records were enrolled (on parchment) and forwarded to the Chief Justice in Eyre. I have used both sets of records to draw up this table; only those found *billa vera* at the Court of Attachment proceeded to the Swanimote. But not all of these did so; apart from those who might die or leave the area in the interval between attachment and judgement, the forest officers might decide not to present the case against them. Such problems make any exercise in counting hazardous, but the table certainly indicates the falling and rising levels of presentments.

1. Offences of two kinds: encroaching on forest land (the average amount taken in being about ½ acre), and unlicensed building of cottages, out-houses, barns, etc.

2. Again of two kinds: felling timber or branches without licence and without the 'view' of the Regarders, and felling coppices (for hurdles, posts, basket-making) or grubbing and 'assarting' hedgerows.

3. Killing or hunting deer; keeping 'toyles' (nets and snares), guns, hunting dogs; and (two cases, 1688) taking coneys.

4. Fences too high for the deer to pass and repass to their feeding-grounds.

5. The most important being offences concerning sheep: (i) overstocking the forest; (ii) keeping sheep on 'preserved grounds' during 'fence month' – in 1688 200 offenders were presented for this, but they do not appear to have been referred to the Swanimote (possibly the forest officials failed to establish their precedents in the case); (iii) 'staff-herding' – i.e. sending out sheep with a follower. This frightened off the deer, and enabled the sheep to pick the best grazing. Other offences included burning the heath, digging the greensward, building unlicensed brick-kilns or sand-pits and taking hogs to hire.

6. There were nine other presentments at this court for unidentified offences.

7. Some 150 men were presented, including some from almost every forest parish, on

27 December 1688, for pursuing or shooting at deer (presumably in celebration of James II's dismissal from the throne), but none of these cases went forward to the 1690 Swanimote.

8. At this court two other men were presented for turf-cutting, found *ignoramus* (i.e. not guilty), and then committed into custody for misbehaviour.

9. Five presentments – all found *ignoramus*.

10. There appear to be no presentments, and only one order made.

11. This court shows the highest acquittal rate of the series (apart from 1701): 45 per cent, or 18 found *ignoramus* as against 22 *billa vera*. Seventeen out of 19 timber cases were found *ignoramus* but only 1 out of 19 cases of encroachment. This suggests that the Regarders and jurors were willing to defend common grazing-land against private appropriation, but were determined to assert the farmers' right to fell the timber on their own land. It is also significant that the forest officers did not even try to present any turf-cutters. From their point of view a non-compliant Swanimote Court might as well be wound up; and it was.

---

and one third – sandy and barren waste – over which the farmers maintained common rights, being owned by the Crown.[1] Although the enclosure and fencing of one's own land was permissible, the forest officers held that this might not be done to an extent which would hinder the free movement of the deer. This claim of the Crown had in effect been expelled by force from Surrey in the seventeenth century, when the people of Egham had again and again sallied out to attack the deer.[2] In Berkshire the forest officers stuck rigidly to their claim: in true forest areas the villagers must suffer the deer to stray into their corn and crops – indeed, they had a duty to support the King's deer, in return for their own grazing rights on the wastes; they could on no account kill them, and at the most they might drive them back from the fields into the woods and waste.[3]

Hence the deer had freedom of movement over the whole Berkshire forest area. But in fact they were expected to gather in a number of walks, within each of which were parks or 'rails' which marked out their fawning and preserved grounds for quiet feeding. The most important of these were Old Windsor, Cranborne and New Lodge in the north; Swinley and Easthampstead in the centre; Bigshot Rails further south; and Billingbear in the west. The overwhelming majority of deer, both red and fallow, were in the first four walks; and of these, Swinley Rails was the farthest from Windsor and the most exposed to attack.

1. South, op. cit., Crest. 2.1628, p. 75.

2. See below, p. 55.

3. Boothe, op. cit., pp. 2–6. So dependent had the deer become upon arable crops that in 1718 when additional red deer were sent into Swinley Walk Viscount Cobham suggested that an area of the waste should be enclosed for the cultivation of turnips and grain for the use of the deer: Constable's Warrant Books, 1, fo. 23 *verso*: and below, p. 236.

To a layman's eye the true forest of woodland and 'wild' country would have ended abruptly, less than five miles from Windsor at Winkfield Plain. Here there were three large arable open fields, comprising some 500 acres.[1] The parish of Winkfield was very large: twenty miles in circumference and taking in about 8,500 acres, it extended from north to south, almost across the forest. To the north it took in Cranbourne Park and edged New Lodge; in the centre it took in Ascot, and to the south it took in Swinley Rails and extended to the borders of Bagshot and of Sandhurst. It had no nucleated centre, and few gentry; it was, and had long been, yeoman's country, with large and small freeholds, customary tenures, and with privately owned coppices cut down regularly for fencing-posts, hurdle-making and basket-making.[2]

The trades in the parish included tailors, carpenters, weavers, coopers, butchers, bakers, innkeepers, etc. But the greatest number of people were farmers and farm servants. The manor of Winkfield took in more than half of the parish, and some one hundred customary tenants. Until the time of Henry VIII it had belonged to the monastery of Abingdon, and when the latter was dissolved most of its lands were granted away from the Crown, with the exception of Swinley, which was the property of the subsidiary abbey of Stratford-le-Bow. In the reign of James I, the tenants had been granted unusually extensive rights by the then lords of the manor, including rights to their own timber and the right to 'digg, take, and carry away turf, gravel, sand and loam, heath, ferne and furzes, wherever they shall be found on the Lord's waste'.[3] Perhaps in consequence of these rights, Winkfield had several sandpits and hungry lime-kilns and brick-kilns, fuelled with heath. Like the neighbouring manor of Sandhurst, it also had a thriving trade in peats, sold outside the parish.[4]

Around the rights to cut turf and heath in Winkfield was centred a conflict which had gone on for at least a century and was to continue for

1. This is not an exact contemporary survey, but rests on a 1613 survey (Winkfield Commonfield 220 acres, Millfield 174 acres, Wellfield 103 acres, Townfield 35 acres) which Waterson claimed as being still, in general, accurate: Waterson (Ranelagh) 1 and Waterson (Reading), pp. 288, 303. The fields were still shown at the 1817 enclosure; Berks Rec. Off. D/P 252/26 B.

2. Various perambulations in Waterson; Crest. 2.1628, p. 51 (which gives a larger acreage than Waterson).

3. John Pulteney, the Surveyor-General of Lands, in a private report to the Treasury, 30 April 1725, cited an 'indenture' of 3 James I between the lord and lady of the manor (Sir Richard and Dame Mary Ward) and the tenants, ceding these rights to the latter; and, in addition, the rights to sell or convert their copyhold estates, cut and carry away their timber, hedge their holdings, etc. T1.255 (8).

4. Presentments of various dates in LR3.3; Constable's Warrant Books, 1, fo. 18 verso.

decades. It was one of those tripartite conflicts between the King and his officers, the lords of the manor, and the customary tenants (and inhabitants) in which each party held documents and could cite precedents, but which in practice was decided by force and by stealth. Between 1717 and 1723 force rose to the point of armed conflict. A few years before the conflict had risen to a high point of law in a trial between the Crown and the lords of the manor in the Court of Exchequer.

We have an opportunity to glimpse what was going on, from surviving memoranda left by the vicar of Winkfield, the Reverend Will Waterson.[1] Waterson seems to have been an exceptional parish priest. He came into the parish in 1709, as the first master of Ranelagh School, a charity school founded by the Earl of Ranelagh explicitly for the poor children of the parish. While he fulfilled the charity's purposes for fifty years, he added to the poor children the children of freeholders and yeomen (whom he took as his own paying pupils). In 1717 he added to this the duties of vicar of the parish, a post which he held independent of any local patronage. As parish priest, he thought it 'a necessary part of his duty . . . to enquire into the civil and political state of the whole parish, as well as to minister to people in an ecclesiastical and spiritual way'. Thus he maintained the school (often in the face of great difficulties); inquired into the use and abuse of parish charities; and also concerned himself with the parishioners' common rights. When he had first come to Winkfield, he found 'the people did not know by what title they held their estates, or in what respects they were *free from*, or subject to, the *forest laws*'. He proceeded first to enlighten himself (using records in the Surveyor-General's office and in the Bodleian Library), and then to enlighten his parishioners. His influence, both as the parish 'memory' and as its schoolmaster, may even – deplorable as he would himself have regarded such an outcome – have had some bearing upon the emergence of the Blacks.[2]

Waterson's own view was unequivocal: '*Liberty* and *Forest Laws* are incompatible.' His views as to the local lords of manors and park owners have largely been destroyed, although enough fragments survive to make it clear that he doubted the pretensions and even the titles to property of several of the great gentry and nobility of the forest, while he certainly thought little of their virtue:[3] 'I shall say no more of their civil rights'

1. For a fuller account of these records, see Note on Sources, below, p. 299. Unless otherwise stated, information on Winkfield in the next five pages is from these books.

2. 'A malicious and groundless complaint,' Waterson noted at the end of his life, 'was made some years ago . . . that the Charity Schools are nurseries of Rebellion': Waterson (Reading), p. 113.

3. Most of the relevant pages in the Waterson (Reading) Book have been torn out (below, p. 299). At p. 156 he comments on John Baber, son-in-law to the Earl of Ranelagh and owner of Sunninghill Park (who had refused to pay tithes), that 'men who

(one fragment concludes) 'it being no . . . part of modesty and prudence to ask them for a favour which perhaps is not safe to trust out of their own hands.'[1] His views as to 'the impertinency' of the forest officers were explicit.[2] His account of the conflict around the rights of Winkfield was this. Although many precedents could be cited from the time of Elizabeth and James I to show that the tenants had been granted extensive rights and that the parish had been freed, at least in part, from forest law,[3] from the time of James II there had been attempts by the forest officers to encroach on these rights. Swinley Rails, an enclosure two miles around and including 191 acres, lay in the midst of the manorial waste at the southern end of the parish. The enclosure belonged to the Crown, but forest officers had sought to extend their claim to the surrounding area, denominating it 'preserved' or 'reserved ground', forbidding all heath and turf cutting, setting up posts to mark their claim, until 'it came at last to be call'd the property of the Crown'. Upon this 'the parishioners came to a resolution to assert their right, and accordingly cut turf there'. This drew on, in 1709, the Exchequer case, in which the Crown laid claim to the entire waste with its herbage and fish-ponds. But this costly process led to no decision, 'the managers for the Crown thinking fit to drop it before it came to an hearing'. In the view of Waterson and his parishioners, this showed 'that the cause was bad' on the Crown's side.[4]

But the matter had not been decided. No doubt fearing the consequences of an adverse decision, the Attorney-General in 1712 simply failed to attend the court, and the Winkfield defendants were left to 'go without day'. If all had depended on the civil law this would have been a favourable decision, and would have left them unmolested in the possession of their waste. But the Crown simply returned to a campaign of harassment in the forest courts, assuming therein as fact what it feared to test in the civil courts. It was from 1716 that presentments for turf and heath cutting in Swinley, Sandhurst and Sunninghill began to become numerous. And the greatest attention focused on Swinley. When King George paid his

will neither imitate the subtility of the serpent nor the innocency of the dove, deserve no pity'. In his parish register (Berks Rec. Off. D/P/51/1/4) he occasionally made such entries as this: 'N.B. Anne Cook registered as baptiz'd in the year 1726 was the reputed child of Capt. Hawley and his maid'. (An attempt was made by someone to delete this entry.) His comments on the trustees of parochial charities (Waterson (Ranelagh) 1, *passim*) are sometimes savage.

1. Waterson (Reading), top p. 37: the previous thirty-six pages have been torn out.
2. See esp. below, pp. 99–100.
3. Waterson assembles formidable evidence, including a patent of 2 Elizabeth (Waterson (Ranelagh) 11, pp. 457–75), customs decreed in Chancery 1605 (ibid., pp. 358–9), early perambulations (ibid., p. 352), the survey of 1613, etc.
4. See Exchequer Commission, depositions, 8/9 Anne Hilary, 9 Berks, E134, and decree 11 Anne Hilary E126.20.

brief visit to Windsor in 1717, it was to Swinley Walk that he was taken for his shooting;[1] he was scarcely likely to have found himself so many miles from Windsor if Colonel Negus had not conducted him in that direction.

Meanwhile another threat developed in the north of Winkfield parish. The forest officers decided to restock New Lodge Walk with the large and athletic red deer. This Walk lay between the parishes of Winkfield and Bray, and marched down to the edge of the arable fields of both. The deer, Will Waterson recalled, 'became an intolerable oppression and nuisance to the neighbourhood', and 'a bone of contention' between the Crown and the parish of Bray. That it did not become such a bone to Winkfield was due to the providential intervention of Mr Robert Edwards. An asthmatic London ironmonger in search of health and a gentry seat, he had bought Winkfield Place in 1709. When New Lodge Walk was stocked with red deer, Edwards purchased for £600 the grounds in-between the Walk and Winkfield Plain, 'to make all easie that had lands on Winkfield side', and also for a hunting-seat for himself. After purchase he 'thought it adviseable to make such a strong impregnable fence next the common as to be proof against all attempts of the red deer'. For this (as we have seen) he was presented at the Forty Days Court, although the grand jury of Regarders, at the Swanimote of 1717, found the bill '*ignoramus*'. 'If a man has paid for making his land free,' asked Waterson, 'what should hinder him from making what fence he pleases?' No doubt this was the consensus of the parish, and found weight also with the Regarders.

Whereas in the case of Swinley the forest officers when disappointed in the civil courts fell back on the forest courts, in this case they attempted the reverse. It was two years later, in 1719, that Colonel Negus and the keepers took their case to the Treasury Solicitor, who recommended proceeding by informations in Exchequer.[2] Meanwhile they resorted to their summary powers, relying upon the authority of the Chief Justice in Eyre. Nearly forty years later Will Waterson recalled his memories of that time, when

The people durst not cut a copice, nor fell a timber tree without a special licence from the Justice-in-Eyre, which was necessarily attended both with trouble and expense. It happened that a farmer being minded to grub a certain hedge-row, and setting labourers to work upon it, their tools were seiz'd, and they themselves drag'd up to London to answer for the reputed trespass . . .[3]

1. Carlisle to Cornwallis, 10 July 1723, Constable's Warrant Books, II, fo. 45.
2. See above, p. 43 n. 1.
3. This is no doubt an example of the summary powers of the Chief Justice in Eyre referred to above, p. 38.

'Such arbitrary proceedings', he added, enabled ministers to 'make a property of the King' and alienated the affections of his subjects.

No doubt the turf-cutting was a nuisance. Colonel Negus complained that it frightened the deer, the soil was deeply rutted by carts, and the carters and cutters had opportunities to poach the game.[1] But from the point of view of the agrarian economy it was the deer which were a nuisance, and the King could keep all and more than he needed in his own parks. In any case, the Crown was certainly attempting to exceed its rights[2] and the forest officers may have been acting from motives of personal self-interest.[3]

But the issue was not quite as clear-cut as this; other interests than those of 'foresters' on one hand and 'the Crown' on the other were involved. Thus, while Winkfield sought unrestricted common right not only for its own freeholders and customary tenants but also for all its inhabitants, it was at equal pains to exclude from these rights the inhabitants of the neighbouring parish of Warfield.[4] Moreover, the interests of Winkfield's farmers and of its manorial lords were not identical. Both parties, of course, wished to throw back the claims of the Crown. But it was scarcely in the interests of the lords of the manor to defend the very large claims of the inhabitants upon the wastes – claims grounded upon the customs decreed in the time of James I.

By 1717 Winkfield Manor had become a petty, weak and divided lordship. One ninth was owned by Grey Neville of Billingbear, near Twyford, about whom we know nothing – or next to nothing.[5] Eight ninths belonged to Anthony Meeke, who also lived outside the parish, in Bray, and who appears only to have owned two or three farms in Winkfield.[6]

---

1. Cited by Pulteney, T1.255 (8).

2. And knew this. Thus the Attorney-General avoided any Exchequer Decree in 1712 (above, p. 50), the Surveyor-General of Lands knew very well of the existence of the indenture of 3 James I (p. 50 n. 3 above), and an attempted action by the Crown against Anthony Meeke for waste of timber was dropped in 1724 when the Law Officers reported that Winkfield waste, although still subject to 'vert and venison', was outside the property of the Crown (Constable's Warrant Books, II, fo. 51 *verso* to 55 *verso*; Hardwicke MSS, Brit. Mus. Add. MSS 36,140, fos. 110–14).

3. See below, pp. 96–8.

4. Against whom they secured an Exchequer decree, 11 Anne Hilary, E126.20.

5. When Neville died in May 1723, Thomas Hearne noted that he was 'a gentleman good for nothing, being debauch'd, & of no principles of virtue or religion, but a downright Republican'. But a 'republican', in Hearne's eyes, was much the same as a Hanoverian Whig: *Remarks and Collections of Thomas Hearne*, Oxford Historical Society, 1907, VIII, p. 72. Grey Neville was also lord of the manor of Wargrave, an extensive manor which took in Warfield to the west of Winkfield.

6. Papers in T1.255 (8). In deeds in Berks Rec. Off. (D/E2 45). Meeke is described as being of the parish of St Margaret's, Middlesex.

It was scarcely a lucrative property for either of them. Their annual income from quit rents amounted to £16 9s. 6d.; to this an additional £4 or £5 p.a. might be added by fines, court fees, sale of turfs, etc.[1] Their most valuable assets appear to have been some seven or eight fish-ponds (for carp and trout), one of them large enough to serve as a decoy for waterfowl. The manorial lords, once extricated, in 1712, from the Exchequer case, set about enlarging their ponds, no doubt inundating the pits where the inhabitants had taken gravel and peat.[2] The water would have extinguished rights both of herbage and of turbary (turf-cutting) for the commoners, and this may go some way to explain why fish-ponds were among the targets of the Blacks. In any case, this exercise in initiative did little to extricate Meeke from his financial difficulties. In 1724, after the episode of the Blacks, he was weary of his charge and seeking to sell his eight-ninths lordship to the Crown. Since it transpired that he had already (in 1721) mortgaged the lordship to a Mr Rogers (against a debt of £360) for 500 years, we are unable as yet to record the outcome.[3]

Hence the yeomanry of Winkfield – freeholders and customary tenants – were in conflict about common rights both with the forest officers and with their own manorial lords; and since these rights were extensive and extended to all inhabitants, the labourers were likely to have taken the side of the yeomen. In the manor of Sandhurst to the south it is probable that a comparable set of relations and a comparable situation of conflict existed, although the parish had no schoolmaster–vicar to record its history. Here also – and at Wokingham, Finchampstead and Easthampstead – we have conflicts over rights of turbary which derived from orders in restraint of pre-existent usage, dating from the time of James II.[4] Here also we appear to have a weak and financially encumbered lord of the manor. Thomas Solmes, the lord, claimed the right to take one acre of peat annually from one of three pleasant sites: Vilemere Bottom, Kitholes

1. Accounts of the lords of the manor survive for 1716 and 1717 in Berks Rec. Off. D/EN M 19.

2. It is clear from Exchequer records (p. 50 n. 4 above) that fishing rights in the ponds were fiercely contested. In both 1716 and 1717 the lords of the manor paid out more for work on two new pond-heads than their total manorial receipts: Berks Rec. Off. D/EN M 19.

3. Papers in T1.255 (8); Berks Rec. Off. D/E2 45; Constable's Warrant Books, II, fos. 51–5. At least some part of the manor was in fact sold to the Crown in about 1726: Crest. 2.1628, p. 51. But some court rolls remained in private hands until about 1959 when they were inadvertently burned by the owner's solicitors (private information kindly supplied by Mr C. Ferard). *VCH Berks*, III (1923) gives the date of final purchase by the Crown as 1782 (p. 87).

4. These orders in restraint of heath- and turf-cutting in all these manors are derived from precedents *temp.* James II cited in Colonel Negus's memorandum of 1717, Constable's Warrant Books, I, fos. 18–19.

Bottom or The Merk. He was watched not only by Colonel Negus but also by his own freeholders and tenants who, if he took out too much, threw it back again into the pit.[1]

In September 1717 at the Swanimote Robert Shorter, his son, and two others were presented for cutting turf in Sandhurst on the order of Thomas Solmes. Six years later Shorter was to die in prison as a convicted Black, his son was to be a fugitive, and his brother William, also a fugitive, was to be spoken of as the 'King' of the Windsor Blacks. Presented before the same court was John Perryman of Bray, for making unlawful fences ten feet high around his own land to the hindrance of hunting and of the deer getting to their feed; he also was to be accused as a notorious Black. Thomas Hatch, junior, presented at the same court for cutting heath at Winkfield in 'quiet breeding and feeding grounds', was to end, as a Black, on the gallows. James Barlow of Winkfield, victualler, presented at the same court for building a cart-house and enclosing four pole of land, was to be indicted not only as a Black but as a suspected Jacobite. Thomas Stanaway, senior, and his son, together with William Dee, parish clerk, were also presented (at an earlier court) for cutting and carrying away a load of heath out of the preserved ground next to Swinley Rails – those very grounds which the Crown had failed to establish rights over in the Court of Exchequer. Thomas Stanaway, junior, was to become a fugitive and an outlaw, accused of taking part, with Hatch, in the murder of a keeper's son. Undoubtedly the Swanimote Court in September 1717 brought men together, in roles to which they had long been allocated. It was, on that happy Hanoverian day when the King gave out '*confitures*', the beginning of another kind of association.[2]

The Blacks left no manifesto, no articulate apologia; not even a sub-stantial deposition survives from which we can recover their case. Hence it proves all the more necessary that we place them in the most complete context, so that from this context and their actions we can deduce some-thing of their motives. Their motives must always remain, in some part, obscure. But from 1717 onwards their actions are very clear. They hustled the forest officers and they attacked the forest deer.

1. There was an attempt in 1717 to get Thomas Solmes 'turned out of the manor', but he seems to have survived it: LR3.3 and Constable's Warrant Books, I, fo. 19. The Sandhurst dispute dragged on into the second half of the eighteenth century and made a nine-course meal for the lawyers: see TS11.425.1349. Some of the evidence comes from witnesses (e.g. Robert Shorter, William Gale and Joseph Payce) who refer back to the 1720s: esp. Lib. B317. For disputes about turf-cutting and common rights in other forest manors in these years, see Sunninghill Vestry Book, November 1712, September 1742, Berks Rec. Off. D/P/126/8/1; C. Kerry, *History and Antiquities of the Hundred of Bray*, 1861, p. 186; Easthampstead, 1705 and 1729, Berks Rec. Off. D/ED C 34 and Trumbull Add. MSS 135.   2. Verderers' Court Books, LR3.2 and 3.3.

2: The Windsor Blacks

There are better population statistics for the deer in Windsor Forest than for the human denizens. The keepers made annual counts, and warrants survive for authorized slayings and cullings. From these and other sources it is possible to propose some quantities.

According to Norden's survey of 1607 there were in Windsor Forest (excluding Windsor Great and Little Parks and those parts in Surrey which were later disafforested) 377 red deer and 2,689 fallow.[1] The strict enforcement of forest law during the reign of Charles I[2] built up a head of steam, until, in 1640, the grand jury of Berkshire presented a petition against 'the innumerable increase of deer, which if allowed to go on a few years more will neither leave foode nor roome for any other creature in the forest'.[3] Republican zeal during the Civil Wars and Commonwealth succeeded in greatly reducing the numbers of these royal favourites, and in expelling the forest almost altogether from Surrey. In 1641 the inhabitants of Egham sallied out in daytime, eighty and a hundred strong, and destroyed the deer; when the Restoration threatened to restore the forest to Surrey, they sallied out once again.[4] By 1649 there were no deer remaining in Windsor Great Park.[5]

1. Brit. Mus. Harl. MSS 3749: copy in Berks Rec. Off.
2. See C. and E. Kirby, 'The Stuart Game Prerogative', *English Historical Review*, XLVI (1931), pp. 239–54.
3. Brit. Mus. Harl. MSS 1219, fo. 31 (s.5).
4. The Surrey battleground appears to have been Inglefield Heath, between Egham and Old Windsor. The Crown did not cede this gracefully after the Restoration. In 1679 the Privy Council was attempting to deal with 'dangerous riots' in and about Egham, which involved deer-stealing and the rescue of offenders; when the J.P.s attempted to seize six or seven of the latter, they came with about forty others 'who cried out that they would all suffer alike', and who refused to deliver their guns: PC2.68, pp. 127, 138–9. Judge Jeffreys was sent down with a Special Commission to punish those who had 'risen upon some of the King's deer, which had lain upon their corn, and killed them':

55

There was an ancient enmity between democracy and these gentle creatures. Royalty returning, in 1660, the forests were restocked; but the fallow deer never recovered (outside of the Parks) the strength of 1607:

DEER IN WINDSOR FOREST (BERKSHIRE ONLY)[1]

Date	Red deer	Fallow deer
1607	377	2,689
1697	258	203
1698	379	274
1699	500	300
1700	559	466
1717	379	536
1720	388	587
1721	419	589
1722	289	577
1723	376	707
1724	357	880
1725	415	976
1726	456	839

What appears from this table is a substantial fall in the number of red deer (royalty's particular prey) between 1700 and 1717, and a further steep fall between 1721 and 1722. The fallow deer were not affected in the first period, but their rate of natural increase was halted in the second. The figures for the red deer conceal a much more serious fall, since the forest was restocked from outside sources several times.[2] But while this

---

but he was outwitted by his own grand jury: see Onslow MSS, *Hist. MSS Comm. 14th Report IX*, pp. 485–6, and below, pp. 140–41. In the eighteenth century the Crown still appointed Surrey Out-Rangers, and clung to a little forest jurisdiction on the Surrey side of the county border, from Bagshot down to Linchford Walk (adjoining Farnham Chase), which harboured fewer than a dozen red deer.

5. G. M. Hughes, *A History of Windsor Forest, Sunninghill and the Great Park*, 1890, pp. 50–57.

1. Sources: (i) 1607, Norden's Survey (p. 55 n. 1 above); (ii) 1697–1700, Berks Rec. Off. D/EN o 13; (iii) 1717, 1720–26, Constable's Warrant Books and Verderers' Books. But Norden (1607) shows 2,108 fallow deer in the two parks, whereas Sarah, Duchess of Marlborough (below, p. 95 n. 1) claimed 4,000 to 5,000. If we accept a figure of 4,500, then the corrected totals for fallow deer would be: 1607, 4,797; 1726, 5,339.

2. T1.147 (27) are the accounts of W. Lowen for fetching 100 red deer from Haughton

fall may be attributed to poaching, neither Negus's report of 1717 nor the report of the Treasury Solicitor in November 1719 make any reference to organized poachers or Blacks: they refer simply to the 'country people' or to deer-stealers. It is the second period only (1721) in which the fall can be attributed to Blacks.[1]

Over the forest as a whole, red deer declined from 379 in 1717 to 289 in 1722. It is possible to identify more precisely the Walks in which the decline took place:

TOTALS OF RED DEER IN EACH FOREST WALK[2] (*At November*)

	1717	1720	1721	1722
Bigshot	25	47	37	24
Easthampstead	21	17	20	14
Swinley	133	133	142	54
New Lodge	131	116	136	128
Cranborne	17	21	30	27
Billingbear	14	17	17	12
Old Windsor	35	29	28	34
Totals	379	388	419	289

Thus in these years most Walks showed either no rate of increase, or a very slight decline, but the significant fall (1721–2) was in Swinley, lying within the parish of Winkfield. Without doubt this was poachers' work.

Poaching has always been endemic in any forest area, and has no doubt been coeval with the forest's existence. 'Blacking' or disguise had long been used by poachers. Deer could rarely be taken by stealth (as could pheasant, hare or salmon), and disguise was the poacher's first protection.

Park to Windsor, by wagon, barge and ship, in 1711 (total £312 2s. 3d., including 10s. 'for handsaws to cut off their horns'). The deer appear to have been shipped, after some preliminary journeying, at Hull. See also Hughes, op. cit., p. 74; J. P. Hare, *The History of the Royal Buckhounds*, Newbury, 1895, p. 239. In 1717 the Duke of Marlborough gave to the King a further forty head of stags and some hinds: Constable's Warrant Books, I, fo. 23 *verso*; and in 1722 more deer came from Woodstock to Windsor: LR3.3.

1. There are full records of deer officially killed by warrant, etc. and these show that the fall in numbers cannot be occasioned by this: see Constable's Warrant Books, *passim*. Epidemics among the deer cannot be discounted, but whereas these are sometimes mentioned in the sources, there is no mention of them during the years of steep decline.

2. Constable's Warrant Books and Verderers' Books, *passim*. The deer could, of course, move or be driven by poaching and huntsmen from one Walk to another.

'Blacking' is found in medieval Kent,[1] and 1 Henry VII c.7 refers to the hunting of deer in vizors with 'painted faces' or in disguise. Severe laws, supplemented by rewards offered to informers, inevitably engendered a conspiratorial secrecy among the poachers. There might, indeed, have been something in the nature of a direct tradition, stretching across centuries, of secret poaching fraternities or associations in forest areas.[2] Blacking certainly continued in certain parts into the nineteenth century.[3]

By 1 Henry VII c.8 (1485) deer-hunting with disguises or at night was made a felony. But this Act was reduced to nullity by humane legal judgements in the reign of Elizabeth. Coke in his *Institutes* could not conceal his contempt for what remained (after some 150 years) 'this new and ill penned law'. 'It is the first law that was made for the making of any hunting felony, against that excellent and equall branch of *carta de foresta*' (by which no man might lose either life or limb for killing a wild beast): 'The old statutes concerning the forests are called the good old laws, and customes . . . and therefore this new act of H.7. is too severe for beasts that be *ferae natura*, whereof there can be no felony by the common law . . . and therefore the judges have made a favourable construction . . .'[4] The Act was not enforced in the seventeenth century, and the attempt to disinter it in the Proclamations of 1720 and 1723[5] indicates the reversal of a long-sustained trend towards clemency.[6]

Action against deer-poachers in the seventeenth century appears to have taken place at two levels. Genteel poachers, especially if in royal forests, were offending against the royal prerogative, and could be proceeded against in the Court of Star Chamber[7] and, after the Restoration, before the Privy Council.[8] Plebeian poachers could be dealt with in other ways:

1. *Kent Records: Documents Illustrative of Medieval Kentish Society*, ed. F. R. H. du Bouley, Kent Archaeological Society, 1964, pp. 217, 254–5. These Kent Blacks were servants of the Queen of the Fairies.

2. See Charles Chevenix Trench, *The Poacher and the Squire*, 1967, *passim*; H. Zouch, *An Account of the Present Daring Practices of Night-Hunters and Poachers*, 1783.

3. See C. Kirby, 'English Game Law Reform', *American Historical Review*, XXXVIII (1932), p. 364, for the great battle of 'Blacked' poachers and gamekeepers near Berkeley Castle in 1816.

4. See Coke, 3 Inst. 74–7.

5. See above, p. 27.

6. The Act was not in fact successfully brought back into use. No doubt the difficulties were such that the Black Act was enacted to replace it.

7. C. and E. Kirby (op. cit., p. 245) suggest that evidence that the Star Chamber actually acted against deer-poachers is wanting. But see on this point *Notes and Queries*, 3rd Series, XII, pp. 181–3.

8. See C. and E. Kirby, op. cit. But Windsor offenders brought before the Privy Council in 1673 and 1677 do not appear to be genteel: they included a farmer, a yeoman and a husbandman. The Council let them off lightly, discharging them on a promise of

in the forest courts, by the gamekeepers' summary powers, or under several statutes in the ordinary courts of law. After the Restoration, the law was successively tightened and penalties raised.[1] 13 Charles II c.20 (1661) imposed a fine of £20 or up to one year's imprisonment, while offenders could also be prosecuted under more comprehensive game legislation, such as the clauses against unqualified persons keeping hunting dogs or snares, in 22 and 23 Charles II c.25 (1671). In 1691 a further Act was passed (3 and 4 William and Mary c.10) 'for the more effectual discovery and punishment of deer stealers'. Its preamble referred to 'divers lewd, sturdy and disorderly' persons 'making amongst themselves as it were a brotherhood and fraternity'. The penalty for coursing deer, whether in royal or private parks, remained at £20; but the penalty for killing or wounding one was increased to £30. One third of the fine was to go to the informer (generally the gamekeeper or his servant), one third to the poor of the parish and one third to the owner of the deer. Goods could be distrained to the value of the fine, and if the offender had no goods of sufficient value he was to be imprisoned for a year and pilloried for a day.

Two further Acts were passed in 1719. One was a private bill; but since it was introduced by Major-General John Pepper, a loyal Hanoverian and Warden of His Majesty's Chase at Enfield, it can scarcely be regarded as private in character. This Act plugged loopholes in the legal process, extended penalties (£50 this time) to keepers 'in confederacy with deer-stealers', and stiffened penalties for breaking down the fences of deer-parks. The other, prepared by the Law Officers, increased the penalty for killing or wounding deer from a fine to seven years' transportation.[2]

The Act of 1691 was certainly put to use, but not without difficulties. The preamble to 5 George I c.15 makes it evident that deer-stealers often had good lawyers, and succeeded in evading their fines by removing their cases, by writs of *Certiorari*, into superior courts at Westminster. Where the offender did not do this, he could sometimes wriggle out in other ways. Witnesses could be intimidated, or have second thoughts, like informers against offenders in Sherwood Forest who suddenly discovered scruples about taking oath on the Bible.[3] For the rich, a fine of £30 was not sufficient to deter the eager poacher, who kept this sum (or, more

---

good behaviour; the punishment appears to have been in the incidental expense, and the anxious solemnity of appearing before the highest Council in the land: see PC2.63, fos. 166, 170; PC2.64, fos. 114, 118, 154, 161; PC2.65, fo. 450.

1. The best contemporary survey of the laws operative in the 1720s is in *The Game Law: or, the Laws Relating to the Game*, 1727, Two Parts.

2. 5 George I c.15 and c.28; *Commons Journals*, XIX, 24 February and 10 March 1719. General Pepper is discussed below, pp. 170–79

3. Sir Francis Molyneux to Newcastle, Brit. Mus. Add. MSS 32,686, fos. 243–4.

probably, a smaller *douceur* for the keeper) on hand in case he was caught.[1]

For the poor it was a different matter. Conviction could certainly lead to a year's imprisonment.[2] Even so, prosecution under the Act of 1691 does not seem to have been common in Windsor Forest before the 1720s. A complex unwritten code appears to have governed the forest officers and the magistrates. If a gentleman offended against the game laws, the officers were likely to prosecute him indirectly, through his servants or even his gamekeeper. Correspondingly, if no great alternative 'interest' was at risk, the gentleman or yeoman was expected to do what he could to get his own servants out of trouble. To submit tamely in the face of a prosecution of one's own servant was to lose face in the forest community. When an Easthampstead man named Humphrys was convicted and imprisoned in 1705, Sir William Trumbull, the lord of his manor, exerted himself through his vicar to raise collections to meet the cost of the fine. Negotiations were opened with the keepers and with the overseers of the poor of Old Windsor in an effort to reduce their portions of the fine. The officers of the neighbouring parish of Sunninghill seconded the negotiations, fearing – as it transpired – that one of their own parishioners who had been an accomplice of Humphrys might also be compromised.[3] Yet Sir William Trumbull, in his alternative role as a conscientious Verderer, was also one of the judges of the forest court. From time to time similar complexities of rivalry and interest can be glimpsed: in 1728, when Lord Sidney Beauclerk had been poaching pheasant in Windsor Great Park, the keepers convicted his 'man', but the New Windsor overseers 'forgave him' their share of the fine 'in compliment to my Lord Sidney, tho' they took it from the poor'.[4]

Recourse to statute law was unpopular in the forest districts. If a parishioner was imprisoned, then his family was only thrown upon the poor rates. The keepers were more likely to get co-operation from the foresters if they affected an easy-going toleration of small offences. And such recourse was also unpopular with the magistrates in the forest areas. Colonel Negus lamented in 1717 that 'the Statute has provided severe penalties in case any one kills a deer, but the keepers have found so little protection from the Justices of Peace that they are tyred by the insults of the country people & almost afraid to act'.

1. See W. Chafin, *Anecdotes and History of Cranbourn Chase*, 2nd edn, 1818, p. 40 *et passim*.

2. For examples, see below, pp. 142, 172.

3. Letters from the Reverend John Power (who in effect acted as Steward during Sir William's absence) to Sir William Trumbull, December and January 1705-6, Berks Rec. Off. Trumbull Add. MSS 135.

4. Blenheim MSS, F1.40.

'When any offences are committed,' the Treasury Solicitor reported two years later, 'the keepers can scarce prevail with the Justices to take their affidavits, and when they do they will not levy the penalties.'[1] The reluctance of the Justices of the Peace to act is explained further by Negus in the same year: '. . . as to the Justices of the Peace I think there can be no effectual remedy but making some new ones, for these at present ask why we don't punish the offenders by the forest laws, and are unwilling to execute the statute laws upon forest offences.' In January two keepers had come upon two men in Winkfield Lane between 11 and 12 at night with 'great staves or poles in their hands' and a 'large tall greyhound'. They seized the men (two servants) and shot the dog. John Baber, J.P., 'would not levy the penalty for having a greyhound nor commit the offenders, so that they laugh at the keepers: Justice Baber alledges that the keeper having shott the dog he could not levy the penalty for a dead dog.' In March one William Herring of Bray was seen by keepers coursing red deer with a greyhound and a lurcher: James Hayes, J.P., would not levy the penalty 'but bids the keeper make up the matter. Herring tells the keepers tho' they stand and look at him he will course the deer.'[2]

One wishes to know more of what lay behind the phrase 'make up the matter'. Clearly, forest custom expected some passage of money between offenders and their captors. When Michael Rackett and a party were seen hunting deer in July 1722 they were followed to his house by a keeper 'who saw them dressing a hind's calf they had killed and Rackett gave him a guinea to hold his tongue . . .'[3] Doubtless this was the common form.

But the Justices of the Peace may have had other motives for inaction. One or two staunch Tories may have been hostile to any measure of Hanoverian Whigs. In any case, the stricter enforcement of forest law after 1716 was leading to collisions between the forest officers and local gentry. Edward Baber, presumably a relative of Justice Baber of Sunninghill Park, was presented at the Swanimote Court in 1717 for encroaching forty poles. (It occurs to one also that if Justice Baber was lenient towards deer-poachers he might purchase, by this means, some immunity from their attacks on his own park.) Lords of forest manors presented at the Court of Attachment between 1716 and 1720 included the lords of Sandhurst, Barkham, Finchampstead, Winkfield and Swallowfield; their offences turned upon disputes as to rights of soil, turbary, timber, encroachments and the right to depute their own gamekeepers

1. Constable's Warrant Books, I, fo. 19.

2. Memorial of Treasury Solicitor (Cracherode) to Treasury Commissioners, 25 November 1719, with accompanying depositions from keepers and with Negus to Cobham, n.d.: all in T1.223 (6).

3. Notes in SP35.47, fo. 72.

(for all game except deer) on their own lands. Such presentments were little more than pinpricks; but a gamekeeper (even a royal gamekeeper) cannot stick pins into a gentleman with impunity. In the same years perhaps a dozen gentlemen were presented for coursing or hunting small game within the forest. To local gentry, accustomed to the licence of Anne's reign, this must have encouraged apoplexy.[1]

Hence the authorities were in some disarray. It was not in the interests of local gentry to strengthen the powers of a forest bureaucracy which might inhibit their own pursuit of game and inquire too closely into their perquisites and manorial rights. But the existence of forest law provided an alibi for the infrequent use of statute law. And yet, at this point, the surviving sources present us with a puzzle. If we read one series of sources, large-scale Blacking – attacks on deer by groups of men, mounted, armed and in disguise – commenced in earnest early in 1719 or early in 1720 and reached a climax in 1721–3 (in the first of these years the red deer in Swinley Walk fell from 142 to 54).[2] But our other main series of sources – the Verderers' Books and Constable's Warrant Books – give little evidence of this crisis. The vigorous revival of the forest courts after 1716, as reflected in presentments at the Courts of Attachment, appears to be most intense in the years 1716–20; and the greatest number of presentments are for turf-cutting, encroachments, etc.; fewer are for offences against game or deer, and after 1720 all types of presentment fall away.[3]

The explanation for the discrepancy in the evidence is most probably this. Since both magistrates' and forest courts were proving ineffective, the conflict degenerated into extra-legal forms and was fought out as a direct confrontation of force. By May 1719 deer-poachers incurred the

1. Verderers' Books, LR3.3 *passim*. The dispute between the keepers and local lords of the manor as to the deputation of gamekeepers was especially fierce: in February 1718 the guns and nets were seized from the pretended gamekeepers of the lords of the manor of Barkham (Ellis St John, for whom see below, pp. 107–8) and of Finchampstead. These replied with an action at law: LR3.3 (February and March 1718); T27.22, p. 308; Constable's Warrant Books, I, fos. 25, 27. The complaint as to the ineffectiveness of forest J.P.s frequently recurs in other forests. In 1743 the Duke of Chandos offered a plausible account of their behaviour in Enfield Chase to the Lord Chancellor, Lord Hardwicke: 'when my officers bring any of the offenders before them, they [the justices] declare publickly they'll not meddle nor make with them, nor will they grant any warrant . . . some pretending that they shall have their houses burnt about their ears if they should, and others, I am apt to think, from being concern'd underhand with them, in buying wood from them at cheap rates . . .': C. H. C. and M. I. Baker, *The Life and Circumstances of James Brydges, First Duke of Chandos*, Oxford, 1949, p. 391.

2. See Proclamations, above, p. 27; table of deer, above p. 57; and Baptist Nunn's Accounts, below, pp. 65–6

3. See table of presentments, above, p. 46.

threat of transportation (under 5 George I c.28) and in 1720 the forest officers secured a royal proclamation against disguised hunters, supplemented by the bait of the large sum of £100 rewards. In 1721 they attempted a new and unusual legal process by prosecuting deer-stealers in the Court of Exchequer.[1] But these successive measures, coming on the heels of the assault on forest usages in the forest courts, were calculated to band the discontented foresters more closely together, to foster secrecy and 'fraternities', to force freelance deer-stealing to give way to attacks by substantial mounted parties in disguise; in short, the fear of transportation and the fear of informers gave rise directly to Blacking. In the result, the authority of the forest officers crumbled away around them.

Some of the keepers fell back upon the maximum exertion of their summary powers: a gamekeeper might confiscate turfs, timber and even tools and carts; seize offenders and fetch them before the Justice in Eyre in London; throw down fences and encroachments; confiscate game, nets, snares and guns; and search houses in the forest.[2] And keepers had the further power to seize and kill hunting dogs. No power provoked fiercer resentment than this. A good greyhound or lurcher was a substantial investment; the dog may have been obtained with difficulty and from a distance, and its training – no less than that of an expert sheep-dog – may have occupied months. Again and again the killing of dogs sparked off some act of protest or revenge.[3]

Thus the confrontation in Windsor Forest between 1720 and 1723 was, in the most immediate way, a conflict of force between Blacks and keepers. Moreover, for two or three years the Blacks achieved a hegemony in the

1. The Treasury Solicitor's particulars of causes under prosecution, 9 June 1721, T1.234 (27), shows two cases proceeding against deer-stealers and their rescuers in Windsor Forest. I have been unable to trace the outcome of these cases, although other cases in Exchequer at this time (e.g. against timber offenders in the New Forest) suggest that the process was slow, cumbersome and inconclusive.

2. It is my impression that within the forest proper search of suspected houses could be undertaken without warrant. Outside the forest, or in its purlieus, a Justice's warrant was required. A specimen warrant ordering constables and tithingmen to assist William Lorwen to search markets, transport going to and from markets, buildings, alehouses etc., and to seize game, guns, toils etc. (1726) is in the memorandum book of a Berkshire J.P., Ralph Howland, Brit. Mus. Add. MSS 38,824, fos. 32–3.

3. See below, pp. 65, 104 and Douglas Hay in D. Hay, P. Linebaugh and E. P. Thompson, eds., *Albion's Fatal Tree*, 1975, pp. 215–16. When a greyhound bitch belonging to William Cooke, labourer, of Wing, Buckinghamshire, was seized in 1727, he threatened that if the dog was not returned within a fortnight he would come, with twenty or thirty companions, cut down the pales of a gentleman's park and drive out the deer. And come they did. Proclamation of Cooke under the Black Act, PC1/4/22 and *London Gazette*, no. 6574, 18–22 April 1727. The park belonged to William Gore of Tring.

forest. If fines were levied, if guns or dogs were seized, they descended by night on the keepers' outlying lodges and took these back by force. Some keepers gave in before the pressure, and seem to have supplied venison or money to the Blacks in self-protection.[1] There were fewer presentments at the Forty Days Courts after 1720, both because these were proving ineffectual and because some keepers had been intimidated; as Negus noted in June 1723, the keepers had failed in their duties owing to the 'insolence & force of the Blacks'. He also made clear the intimate connection between the deer-hunters and the aggrieved turf-cutters of Winkfield, Sandhurst and Wokingham: 'Since the Blacks took the liberty to bid defyance to all the Laws and Orders relating to the forest, the preserved grounds have been likewise spoiled by the heath & peat cutters.'[2]

Blacking arose in response to the attempted reactivation of a relaxed forest authority. This provoked resentment among foresters generally, whether small gentry (outside the charmed circle of Court favours), yeomen, artisans or labourers. The resort of deer-poachers to more highly organized force may be seen as retributive in character and concerned less with venison as such than with the deer as symbols (and as agents) of an authority which threatened their economy, their crops and their customary agrarian rights. These Blacks are not quite (in E. J. Hobsbawm's sense) social bandits, and they are not quite agrarian rebels, but they share something of both characters. They are armed foresters, enforcing the definition of rights to which the 'country people' had become habituated, and also (as we shall see) resisting the private emparkments which encroached upon their tillage, their firing and their grazing. Their armed encounters with keepers arose because these keepers were defending their antlered charges with greater vigilance and greater force of arms. For 1716 also sees the rise to prominence of an enforcement officer who was not an absentee or a sinecurist, but whose (at times literally) sleepless activity brought him into weekly conflict with the Blacks: Baptist Nunn.

Baptist Nunn was the son of a keeper, and also farmed land in the forest area.[3] Whereas the old chief huntsman and senior gamekeeper, William

---

1. The under-keeper of Linchford Walk was dismissed in January 1722 for 'killing the game which your office was to preserve': Constable's Warrant Books, I, fo. 32. This outlying Walk in Surrey had seven red deer in 1717, four in 1722.

2. Constable's Warrant Books, II, fo. 43.

3. He was admitted to a copyhold in Wargrave in 1716 (which may of course have been only one of several land holdings); Robert Nunn 'of Windsor Great Park', who may have been his father, was admitted to a tenure on 9 April 1717. Baptist Nunn also appears in a list of inhabitants of Warfield (within the manor of Wargrave) in 1717: court book of Wargrave, 1708–29, Berks Rec. Off. D/EN M 54; D/P/144/5/2.

Lorwen, was illiterate, Nunn had attended school at Bray, where the famous antiquary, Thomas Hearne, had been his school-fellow and later remembered him as 'a boy of good parts, & very forward to learn'.[1] In 1716 Nunn was appointed chief gamekeeper for all within three miles of the Castle.[2] In November 1718 he was also made Deputy Steward or registrar of the Swanimote Court, thus bridging in his two offices the royal authority and that of the Justice in Eyre.[3] These posts were not, taken singly, lucrative,[4] but by aggregating them and exploiting the perquisites they contributed not only to status but to substance.

But Baptist Nunn expected to be reimbursed in full for his expenses, and the detailed expenses claim which he later presented to the Treasury Solicitor[5] is our major source of information for the extraordinary war which was waged in 1722 and 1723 between the Windsor Blacks and forest officials. The accounts (which must surely have a pre-history) commence on 20 May 1722, and, characteristically, start with the seizure by Nunn of a greyhound which 'Shorter & gang' had used in killing deer. On 24 May:

		£	s.	d.
	Persons in the night to demand the dog & threatened to burn the house down & kill the s^{d} Nunn by wch he was oblig'd in out^{wd} show to send 3 messengers to the neighbouring town to cry the dog & make in wth some persons to inform himself from wch quarter they came & to meet y^{m} a^{bt} it	2	10	0
27	Message again wth fresh threats & forct to goe to Lond^{n} to Col. Negus & made an affid^{t} before Mr Blackerby	1	18	0
	Insuring my house & barns from burning	1	13	4
31	A fresh surprise. One appeard disguised wth a message of destruction, lay out y^{t} night			

On 5 June he was 'beset in Heath' and forced to fly back to Hartford Bridge. On 10 June:

1. *Remarks and Collections of Thomas Hearne*, Oxford Historical Society, 1907, VIII, p. 215. (Hearne was born in 1678, and his school-fellow Nunn must have been much the same age: this would make him forty-five in 1723.)

2. Constable's Warrant Books, I, fo. 6. Nunn also had responsibility for Cranbourne Walk, Old Windsor and Egham Walk.

3. LR3.3. In the latter office he signed (and received a fee for) the Justice in Eyre's licences to fell timber etc. in the forest: examples in Berks Rec. Off. D/ED E 42.

4. The salary for the gamekeeper of Old Windsor was £30 p.a. and that for registrar (or Deputy Steward) of the forest courts was £20.

5. In T1.244 (63). Extracts are reproduced, with some inaccuracies, in G. A. Kempthorne, ' "Blacking" in Berkshire', *Berks, Bucks and Oxon Archaeological Journal*, XVII (1911), pp. 113–20.

		£ s. d.

A message here from Blacks to demand 5 gunias & a buck
to be sent to Crowthorne or damage.

11   To London to Col. Negus who gave me 5 gs to give them   1   0   0

13   To Oakingham manageing a person to discover ye persons
who were to have the money & at last agreed ab^t a discovery, if performed to pay 5 gs. mere to discoverer and
gave him then and expenses   1   18   0

On 24 June he met this 'Oakingham correspondent' at Colnbrook 'who
told me they were determined to kill me if they had not the money . . .'
'We agreed about the management of the discovery.' On 27 June:

                       £ s. d

Blacks came in the night shot at me 3 times 2 bullets into
my chamb^r window & agreed to pay y^m 5 gs. at Crowthorne ye 30th inst

29   Sent 2 fawns one to Oakingham one to Hartford Bridge
wth a guinea each & a spye to each place thinking they
might drop in   2   2   0

Throughout the next few months the same intricate game of blackmail
and espionage was pursued. Nunn laid out his guineas among spies,
'correspondents' and informers as patiently as a poacher lays snares,
while at the same time he appeared to comply with the blackmail of the
Blacks, who were no doubt using time-honoured means to recoup fines
and to keep over-eager forest officers in their place. Nunn's superior
officials, Colonel Negus and Viscount Cobham, encouraged him and
received his reports in London; in Windsor he could rely only on the
support of fellow keepers.

On 30 June he succeeded in planting three witnesses outside the house
of a farmer, William Shorter; here they saw three men enter, and come
out again afterwards (in the company of Shorter), all disguised. The four
men then went to Crowthorne[1] to collect their five guineas. This was the
first firm evidence as to the identity of any Blacks, but Mr Owen, who
had replaced Boothe as Steward of the forest courts, was unimpressed
and refused to act. On 21 July Nunn was 'beset in the Heath' again, and
forced to 'fly back' to Finchampstead; on the 26th, 'Blacks at my house
again, shot & swore my death for endeavouring to detect them, forsook

---

1. A point on the Roman road at the junction of Sandhurst, and Bigshot and Easthampstead Walks, later known as Brooker's Corner (ibid., p. 114) – a bare and isolated
point in 1722.

my house for a fortnight' (£2 10s.). He attended several times in London with affidavits as to the disguising, but when he was advised to take informations upon oath against Shorter and his fellows he found that 'country Justices shufled. No oaths taken' (£1.10s.). To London again early in August for consultations with lawyers, and he was 'ordered to take care of myself for some time':

		£	s.	d.
Aug. 6	Gave correspond^t 2 gs, to make peace & got some venison & sent to y^m met some of them & expenses wth y^m	2	18	6

This suggests that Nunn pretended to 'make up' his differences with the Blacks, and to submit to their hegemony in the forest, since there were no further entries for ten weeks. But 'about Michaelmas fresh ravages nightly committed & fresh threatenings from all parts, deer killed everywhere in day time & keepers insulted'. At last Nunn succeeded in getting informations sworn on oath by the witnesses who had seen Shorter and his fellows disguising, but it was necessary to take evidences to London to do so. It is doubtful whether the matter was kept secret in the forest, since a fortnight later Nunn was 'assaulted by two persons in disguise'. Once again the local Justices of the Peace gave him no help. Thereafter his journeys to London became more frequent, and his company more exalted. In October, November, December, and in January 1723 he attended upon Lord Cobham and Colonel Negus. On 14 February he attended upon Lord Chief Justice Pratt with the informations concerning disguising. On 22 February he attended on the Attorney-General. At this stage prosecution was still being considered 'by common law'. The Lord Chief Justice was willing to issue warrants against Shorter and his three accomplices, but there was 'some difficulty about military forces to assist the civil magistracy'. Through February, March and into April 1723, against a background of 'fresh mischiefs and dayly threatenings', legal consultations continued, while Nunn continued to build up his network of spies. Finally, on 25 April, Nunn received at last instructions to act, upon no less authority than that of Robert Walpole.

Baptist Nunn (although he may possibly have been unaware of this) had not been, throughout the previous months, the only source of Government information. From the national standpoint the sensations of 1722 had not been about the Blacks at all (these scarcely broke the surface of the press) but about the Jacobite conspiracies associated with the names of Christopher Layer, Captain Kelly and Francis Atterbury (the Bishop of Rochester). The several plots included correspondence with the Pretender, serious but ineffectually supported preparations for another

Jacobite insurrection, and Layer's proposal to seize or assassinate the King at Kensington. These plots broke surface in May and June 1722 and the next twelve months saw an unrelenting pressure upon Papists and Nonjurors; the harassment of any oppositional press; the suspension of *habeas corpus*; new fines and new oaths of loyalty, aimed primarily at Catholics; the search for arms in Catholic households; and a realignment of political forces, greatly to the benefit of Walpole and Townshend.[1]

It was in August 1722 that one of the informants of the young Duke of Newcastle wrote to him of a man 'who had made discovery of a great number of ruffians lurking about Guildford, Farnham and other places in Hampshire & Berkshire compleatly horsed and armed, and associated under a pretence of deer stealing, but in reality intending to begin an insurrection when ordered . . .' He feared that this man 'is since made away with, no mortal having heard of him since his coming up to London and giving the intelligence'.[2] There can be little doubt that this man had not been made away with at all, except by Townshend and Walpole. He was certainly the Reverend Thomas Power, the curate of Easthampstead, who served the living in the place of his absentee father, the Reverend John Power. For there remains among the state papers the draft of a royal warrant, of 21 July 1722, authorizing Power to act as an agent among the Blacks, and to 'contract a farther intimacy with them in order to penetrate into the bottom of their treasonable intentions'; once again the 'pretence of deer stealing' was alleged to be in reality 'treasonable designs against our person and government'. A royal promise of indemnity for any consequences was given to Power.[3]

Whatever Townshend and Walpole may have really thought about the matter, and whatever tall stories Power had told them, this story did not altogether strain belief. England, in the aftermath of the South Sea Bubble, was a profoundly disaffected country and there were many elements of discontent which could have given substance to a serious Jacobite conspiracy. The Thames valley near Windsor was an area of dispersed Catholic settlement, some of it perhaps brought there by an earlier order for Papists to withdraw ten miles from London (1695).[4] The sensation of the Jacobite conspiracies in May 1722 was accompanied by

1. See J. H. Plumb, *Sir Robert Walpole*, 1960, II, pp. 44–9; C. B. Realey, *The Early Opposition to Sir Robert Walpole, 1720–27*, Kansas City, 1931, *passim*; Romney Sedgwick, *History of Parliament: The House of Commons 1715–1754*, 1970, esp. I, introduction; G. V. Bennet, 'Jacobitism and the Rise of Walpole', *Historical Perspectives*, ed. N. McKendrick, 1974.

2. J. Poyntz to Newcastle, 3 August 1722, Brit. Mus. Add. MSS 32,686, fos. 232–3.

3. SP 35.32, fo. 24.

4. L. Fitzgerald, 'Alexander Pope's Catholic Neighbours', *Month*, CXLV (1925), pp. 328–33.

searches for arms among Catholic inhabitants of the forest,[1] and when Layer's conspiracy indicated the assassination of the King as a possible strategy, no doubt Power's story of armed Jacobites, disguised as deer-stealers, lurking near Windsor, deserved at least momentary attention. If not effective Jacobites now, they could become so in a favourable turn of events.[2]

But this view can scarcely have been held seriously, or for long, by Townshend and Walpole, who were in a position to receive, through Lord Cobham and their own Law Officers, the well-informed and detailed evidence of Baptist Nunn. Nor can the Jacobite *'peur'* be used to explain the introduction of the Black Act to the House of Commons on 26 April, since the way had been prepared for this by long consultations with Nunn in previous months; and it was occasioned directly by an episode of bloodshed in Windsor Forest on 9 April 1723.

It will have been noticed that in the extraordinary year-long passage-of-arms between Nunn and the Blacks, while the gamekeeper had been 'beset on the heath', threatened, 'assaulted' and had his windows fired into, he had (it seems) suffered no actual bodily injury, and he had even mingled with Black emissaries and drunk with them. Nor is there any other record of injury or death attendant upon the actions of Windsor Blacks in 1722. But in April Andrew Hughes (or Hews), a poacher, had two guns seized from him by a keeper, and was fined £10. At midnight on 9 April six or seven Blacks rode into the forest on a mission of revenge. They forced a carpenter to guide them to the house of William Miles, a keeper. Here they demanded the return to Hughes of his guns and his fine, or they would come back within three days and burn the house. Miles's son, aged about twenty-two, put his head out of a window and shouted back at the Blacks. One of the Blacks fired his gun at the window, wounding the young man in the head. At the subsequent trial, it was pleaded that the gun was fired only *in terrorem*, from behind a wall; but whatever the plea, it did Miles no good since he died several days later from his wounds. The Blacks later descended on the house of Robert Friend, the Churchwarden of Old Windsor, who was holding the fine, and, by threatening to burn his house, forced him to give the money back. By one account they also carried off several deer, and boasted that 'they

1. See warrant of Ralph Howland, J.P., 20 May 1722, authorizing the constable of Cookham to search for Papists, reputed Papists, non-jurors and 'other disaffected persons', and seize ammunition, weapons and horses: Brit. Mus. Add. MSS 38,824. In September 1722 the discovery of a barge filled with gunpowder and arms at Reading caused a sensation, until it was found to be legitimate merchandise on its way to Bristol: SP35.33 (4); SP44.81, fos. 102–3. The 1717 'return' of popish recusants in Berkshire includes the names of no one subsequently to be accused of being a Black: FEC1, pp. 32–3.

2. This is discussed more fully below, pp. 164–6.

did not value the Proclamation that was out against them, for they could raise two thousand men in a night's time'.[1]

The death of young Miles was the first precipitant. On 24 April Nunn was in London and found Mr Cracherode, the Treasury Solicitor, 'resolv'd to take Blacks up & sent two down with assurances of forces & money that night'.[2] But meanwhile on 23–4 April at the Berkshire sessions at Newbury, an extraordinary drama had been acted out, which served as a further precipitant. Thomas Power of Wokingham, 'Clerke', was presented by the grand jury for riot and other misdemeanours and also for treasonable practices 'in aiding and abetting the raising of forces for the bringing of the person called King James the Third' into the kingdom; and he was committed to Reading gaol.[3] We are fortunate in having the voluble correspondence of Dr William Stratford, the rector of Little Shefford (Berkshire), which throws light on what would otherwise be an exceptionally murky episode. An 'odd thing' had happened at the last Sessions (he informed Edward Harley): a clergyman had had high treason sworn against him. One man had sworn that Power had offered to settle an estate of £14 p.a. on him if he engaged himself to enlist for the Pretender. 'Some say he [Power] had been endeavouring to deal with the "Blacks" for that purpose.' It was rumoured, among Stratford's neighbours, that Power's real design was to inveigle others and to discover the enemies of the Government; 'but there must have been treachery or treason, and he deserves to be hanged'.

Three days later, after Stratford had inquired around, he was able to present a more circumstantial account. Young Power was a man with a 'scandalous' reputation, whom Lady Trumbull had been trying to get removed from the curacy. No doubt learning that Nunn and the Government were about to act against the Blacks, he decided to gain some kudos for himself by jumping the gun. He collected three dragoons and went –

without any warrant, to search a house, as he pretended for some of the 'Blacks'. He found only a country fellow or two taking a pot of ale, but committed such disorders there that the people of the house got a warrant, and carried him before Mr. Barker . . . a justice near Reading. Barker committed him for a riot, but kept him for a week in the constable's hands, to see if anyone would bail him. He was so scandalous no one would. Barker asked him if he thought his

1. Warrant for committal of A. Hughes, 16 May 1723, SP44.81, fo. 242; deposition of Robert Friend, SP35.43, fo. 31; A. Boyer, *The Political State of Great Britain*, XXV, 1723, p. 666; *History of Blacks*, 1723, p. 14; *London Journal*, May–June 1723, *passim*; *Weekly Journal, or British Gazetteer*, 15 June 1723; SP35.65, fo. 152; *St James Evening Post*, 8–11 June 1723.

2. Nunn Accounts, T1.244(63).

3. Berks Quarter-Sessions Order Book, Berks Rec. Off. Q /SO 1, p. 156.

own father [the Rev. John Power, whose living at Easthampstead he served], if he were there, would bail him. He frankly owned he believed he would not. To gaol he went, but he told Mr. Barker he would send him a paper, if he would promise to return it, that would justify him in what he had done. . . A paper was sent, signed at the top, and counter-signed at the bottom, being as pretended an authority to converse with the Blacks in order to discover them, and leave also to talk treason and make any reflections he pleased on any of the Royal Family . . .

Power was eventually bailed by another Justice of the Peace named Fellow, who was clearly in Government's confidence. But by now the startled Berkshire magistracy (whom Walpole and Townshend had not kept informed) had become thoroughly restive. A substantial debate developed in the grand jury as to whether Power should not be committed for treason. While this was in progress,

Three men from Ockingham [Wokingham] came and swore high treason against him for speaking treason, and endeavouring to list them for the Pretender. This was not to be withstood. The fellow muttered somewhat of a paper, which he intimated would indemnify him. He said Colonel Negus had procured him the paper, and how should the King's enemies be discovered but by such men as he was? That the three men swore against him to save their own lives, he having already informed against them to my Lord Chancellor. But to gaol he is gone for high treason.[1]

We know a little more about the Reverend Thomas Power. A former commoner of Christ Church, he presumably did not receive very much of his absentee father's stipend of £300 p.a. for attending to his living. He seems to have married a local Wokingham woman for her money; and she was so truculent as to neglect to settle all her worldly goods upon him. A year or two before, Power had been assiduous in attempting to persuade her to make over the residue of her estate to him, which 'she being unwilling to consent to he lately threatened to hang her out of the window by one Leg', and, if she continued to be obstinate, to cut the string 'and so make an end of her'. Her neighbours, who heard of the affair, thought this exercise in persuasion excessive, and four of them, 'famed for chivalry', came to the aid of 'the distressed Dame'. One of them disguised himself as a woman, and knocked at Power's gate. When he came to inquire, the 'woman' seized him and shrieked for help. The others then leaped from the bushes, secured Power's arms (a blunderbuss and two guns), dragged him through a pond, took him a mile into the forest and tied him to a tree. The 'woman' there pretended to be the spirit of his wife's grandmother, and upon her plea a mock trial was held and Power

1. *Hist. MSS Comm. Portland, VII*, pp. 357–8.

was condemned to die. 'He, half dead with fear, not knowing whether they were in jest or earnest, desired time for his praying.' The 'knight errants' then fired over his head, and left him tied up in the forest, threatening worse treatment if he did not reform his behaviour to his wife.[1]

These 'knight errants' were possibly also Blacks,[2] and in view of the character of this Hanoverian public servant, we can better understand why 'three men from Ockingham' did their best to 'shop' him at the Newbury Sessions. These three were, almost certainly, William Shorter, a substantial yeoman farmer,[3] the same Shorter on whom Nunn had planted spies to 'observe disguising'; Edward Collier, a Wokingham felt-maker; and George Winn (or Wynne), a Wokingham clock-maker.[4] Their action proved to be a great folly.

For, even if the death of Miles's son had not forced Government's hand, the situation of Power (and the interest, indeed vexation, shown by the Berkshire grand jury) made action imperative. Such action was facilitated by the current suspension of *habeas corpus*. On 29 April Townshend issued his warrant to bring Power from Reading to London; on the same day a warrant was issued to bring Shorter, Winn and Collier to London for examination. Shorter had long been known to Government, from the information of Nunn (and also, presumably, of Power) as a leading Black. He had now given to Government an opportunity to seize him without the armed confrontation that might have been involved if he had been taken up in the forest. Two King's Messengers travelled to Wokingham, tracked down the three men, drank cheerfully with them to the health of the King, thanked them for their loyalty and for their detection of Power, summoned them to London to present their information against him more fully, offered them rewards and furnished them with immediate funds for horse-hire and expenses, and by these stratagems

1. Berks Rec. Off. Trumbull Add. MSS 137: F. Allen (tutor to young William Trumbull) to Mr Bridges of Brentwood, referring to 'a diverting tho' terrible disaster that has lately befallen our friend Power'. Dated 8 January 1722 and unclear whether old-style or new: I think 1723 more likely. Mrs Power was possibly Ann Ticknor, who owned (jointly with her sister) some hundred acres of arable and pasture in Wokingham and Binfield, as well as cottages, barns and orchards: see abstract of Aaron Maynard's title to four closes in Wokingham (*c.* 1760), which shows that Ann Ticknor married 'Mr Powers & died many years ago without issue & without doing any act to affect the said Closes': Berks Rec. Off. D/ER E 12.

2. Among other affidavits listed in state papers but now seemingly lost is one by Thomas Power in February 1723 'concerning an assault made upon him by five Blacks'. This might well refer to this episode, since Power would have wished to present this private matter as an injury which he received in the public service: SP44.81, fos. 235 *et seq.*

3 See below, p. 88.

4 *British Journal*, 11 May 1723; SP44.81, fo. 225.

decoyed them to the city where they were, of course, instantly placed under arrest.[1]

The operation was now being conducted directly by Walpole and Townshend, through the agency of Baptist Nunn. Owen, the Steward of the forest courts, continued to hesitate until, and beyond, the last moment.[2] On 2 May no fewer than twenty-three arrest warrants were made out for suspected Windsor Blacks. Walpole arranged with the Secretary of War for a detachment of Horse Grenadiers to accompany Nunn back to the forest, and Nunn himself bought 8 lbs of gunpowder and 12 lbs of ball (£2 7s.). On the night of 3 May some twenty-one suspects were captured,[3] and brought in heavily guarded wagons to London on the next two days. Further arrests were made over the next three weeks. On 16 May three more wagon-loads of prisoners from the area of Maidenhead and Bray were brought to town; the citizens of Maidenhead were no doubt astonished to see a muscular butcher seized and dragged off the local cricket field. On 20 May more arrests were made at Bagshot, Egham and Virginia Water. By this time at least forty Blacks had been arrested. Smooth as the operation was, there were certain failures. William Shorter, while being held under arrest by a Messenger, cut through the wainscot of his room with a penknife and escaped. (His brother, Robert, however, remained in custody.) Some others accused of being leading Blacks evaded arrest. On 4 June a well-prepared operation at Wokingham, supported by troops, ended without result: 'Search blow'd in Oakingham,' Nunn noted, 'some went away wth part cloaths on. Spent upon ye keepers for their expences, all wet to ye skinn . . . £1.18.10d.'[4]

1. *History of Blacks*, pp. 15–18.

2. The stewardship was in the gift of the Justice in Eyre, and Owen presumably was appointed in Boothe's place when Lord Cornwallis succeeded the Earl of Tankerville in June 1722; see above, p. 39 n. 2. John Owen was also under-steward and magistrate for Windsor Corporation from 1717 (Windsor Guildhall Archives, Hall Book 1653–1725, W1/AC a 1, p. 416 etc.): Windsor was within the Patronage of the Beauclerks (Dukes of St Albans) and Owen was presumably their nominee. Owen's resistance to the measures of his Deputy Steward (and Nunn had of course been appointed by his predecessor) might have stemmed from Cornwallis's jealousy of Cobham and Negus, from Beauclerk's jealousy of the Crown's increasing influence in Windsor, or even (but the suggestion seems absurd) Owen's own humanity. In any case, Baptist Nunn found it hard going; on 29 and 30 April he was dining with Owen at the Rose Tavern; on 1 May he waited on Owen once more at the Temple and found him 'cold'; on 2 May 'attended Mr Owen who still raised scruples notwithstanding all Mr Walpole's kind promises and my treats, spent 12s. 4d.': Nunn Accounts, T1.244 (63).

3. The prisoners were at first held in Warfield Church, and then taken to the general rendezvous at The Squirrel in Winkfield Plain. The Squirrel was later known as The Green Man: Waterson (Reading), p. 253.

4. Nunn Accounts, *passim*; *History of Blacks*, *passim*; SP44.81, *passim*; various

All this (it may be noted) took place before the passage of the Black Act, which only received the royal assent on 27 May. Hence the Crown prepared to proceed by a Special Commission of Oyer and Terminer, which opened at Reading on 6 June 1723.

The Special Commission was held before Baron Page, Baron Gilbert and Justice Denton. An Assize sermon was duly preached by the Reverend William Shaw upon the text: 'Whoso keepeth the law is a wise son, but he that is a companion of riotous men shameth his father' (Proverbs 38:7).[1] The business was dispatched in three days. It had been excellently prepared by Baptist Nunn. For a month he had moved ceaselessly between the forest and the Cockpit (where the Privy Council met), drumming up evidence, suborning witnesses, alternately bribing and threatening the prisoners. The arrested men were pitifully easy to break down. Every three or four days Nunn took down more confessions. On 6 May a guinea purchased one man's evidence against his fellows; two days later he was able to select the 'offenders making the most useful evidences'. Each confession led back to the forest to further arrests. On 22 May Burchett, a crucial 'evidence', was broken down in Newgate gatehouse over two shillings' worth of beer; he was to be the star witness who sent four men to the gallows.

In the week before the trials the wives and families of those prisoners who had turned King's evidence were supplied with money for subsistence; and four of the same men were thoughtfully given a guinea each 'to provide necessarys against the Assizes to appear like men'.[2] Nunn (who arranged this) also spent much time with Paxton, the Assistant Treasury Solicitor, drawing up the Crown briefs; he attended on the Attorney-General and on the Privy Council; and he gave particular attention to the selection of the jury:

25th May. At night with Undersheriffs abt Jury for Spec. Com. Had a copy of the pannell. Treated them	£1	4	2
Gave their Clerke altering pannell	£1	0	0
1st June. To Windsor with some of the jury. Spent	£1	9	4
Gave the person who warnd pt of jury	£1	1	0

---

reports in the London press. For the butcher seized on Maidenhead cricket field, see *Northampton Mercury*, 13 May 1723; and for William Shorter's escape, see *Evening Post*, 11–14 May 1723.

1. The publication of this was advertised in the press (e.g. *Gloucester Journal*, 7 October 1723) but I have been unable to trace a copy.

2. William Cox received 3s. a day, William Terry and James Stedman 10s. a week: T27.23, p. 404.

It was owing to his energy alone that more than fifty evidences were assembled for the trials.[1]

No show trial could have been more carefully prepared. For all that, it was an anti-climax. Nothing sensational came out. The Reverend Thomas Power was kept out of sight as carefully as Oliver the Spy was to be kept, nearly a hundred years later, away from the trial of Brandreth.[2] The London press dismissed the affair in a line or two. Dr William Stratford was dismayed at such a tame affair: 'The trials of our "Blacks" are over, and, to our comfort though to our disappointment too, nothing of treason or even of sedition appeared upon any of the trial. The extraordinary commission had no other business than to give due correction to the old sin of deer stealing.'[3] On 12 June Baptist Nunn rode to London to give directly to Walpole an account of the trials.[4]

'Due correction' in these cases amounted to four death sentences, for complicity in the killing of Miles's son. Six men were sentenced to seven years' transportation each (under 5 George I c.28), five of them for killing deer in the royal forest or parks, one for stealing Sir Robert Rich's tame deer.[5] Robert Shorter, who was probably William's brother, was sentenced to three months' imprisonment for cutting the head of a private fish-pond; and another man was imprisoned and fined for an assault on a keeper.[6] Perhaps two score accused were held over for trial at subsequent Assizes for Berkshire and Oxfordshire. A number of indictments were drawn against accused who had evaded arrest. In the midst of this expeditious judicial terror, formal rituals of justice reinserted themselves. It was found that there was a flaw in the indictments drawn against three of the men sentenced to transportation. Judgement in their cases was respited, but two of the three had the error corrected, and were transported from the next Assizes. The third, Joseph Mognar, lost his chance of a similar favour since he had already died in prison.[7]

King George left for Hanover early in June. Townshend and Walpole were intriguing against Carteret, and both Secretaries of State felt it

1. Nunn Accounts, *passim*.

2. Power eventually received his promised pardon on 15 June 1723: see SP35.43, fo. 106; SP 44.286, fo. 13; SP44.361, fo. 242.

3. Stratford to Harley, 18 June 1723, *Hist. MSS Comm. Portland, VII*, 362.

4. Nunn Accounts, 12 June 1723 (£1 10s.).

5. Stealing deer 'reduced to tameness, knowing them to be tame' was adjudged to be felony: *The Game Law*, 1727, I, p. 22, II, p. 51.

6. Minutes of Lords Justices, 13 June 1723, SP43.66; SP35.40, fo. 6; T1.243(63); Brit. Mus. Add. MSS 27,980, fo. 67.

7. Assi. 2.8 and T1.249 (1) for the further trial and transportation of Charles Grout and Joseph Mercer. The third man, whose name was variously given as Joseph Mognar, Mogny or Moyner, died shortly after trial: Foster to Paxton, 17 June 1723, SP35.43, fo. 130.

advisable to accompany the King to Hanover in order to keep their rival under observation.[1] This left Walpole for the first time in unchallenged pre-eminence in Britain. Affairs of state were presided over by a Regency Council of Lords Justices, headed by the Archbishop of Canterbury. Apart from the Archbishop (who, as we shall see, had the interests of the Bishop of Winchester to consider) one of the Council's more regular attenders was Earl Cadogan, acting Commander-in-Chief, whose own park at Caversham had been raided by the Blacks.[2] Although Cadogan and Walpole eyed each other with suspicion, they were not likely to have differed on the matter of deer-stealing; nor was another frequent attender, the Duke of Newcastle (as Lord Chamberlain), since he was plagued with similar problems in his capacity as Lord Warden of Sherwood Chase.

This august committee of park-keepers was much concerned with matters of detail. In particular, they wished to ensure that the offenders were hanged in chains in Windsor Forest. After the trials Delafaye, the Secretary to the Lords Justices, had informed Townshend: 'The proceedings against the Blacks will, it is to be hoped, cure that Distemper which possibly might have proved an Epidemical one, the Infection having begun to spread into more Countys. Some of the Malefactors condemned at Reading for the Murder will be hanged in Chains.'[3] To be hung in chains, with one's body left to rot within sight of relatives and neighbours, was a penalty worse feared than death.[4] The aggravated penalty was also, in these circumstances, a provocation to riot. On 20 June Delafaye was writing urgently to Baron Gilbert – he had not heard whether the condemned at Reading were dead yet or not:

I suppose that upon the Directions which were given you by the Lords Justices when you attended them you do of course give the proper directions for their being hanged in Chains. That matter was again debated at their Exc'ys meeting on Tuesday last upon a suggestion that the doing it might prove the occasion of more disorders—but their Exc'ys did not think fit to make any alteracion in their order but to let it stand . . .[5]

But in this exercise of justice their Excellencies had already been baulked. Two of the prisoners – one of those sentenced to transportation, and the other Robert Shorter – had already died in prison. This was perhaps not surprising: petitions of the poor prisoners in the gaol complained

1. See Plumb, op. cit., II, pp. 51–4; William Coxe, *Memoir of the Life and Administration of Sir Robert Walpole*, 1798, I, pp. 181–4.

2. See below, pp. 100–102. For Walpole's relations with Cadogan, see Coxe. op. cit., I, p. 189; Plumb, op. cit., I, pp. 253, 256, 282, II, p. 23.

3. Delafaye to Townshend, 14 June 1723, SP43.66.

4. See Hay, Linebaugh and Thompson, op. cit., p. 50.

5. SP44.289, fo. 18.

that they were 'almost poysoned by reason of the privy house' which 'is very full and noisome and overruns with excrements'.[1] Local feeling, it seems, had had enough, and the under-sheriff of Berkshire ordered the execution of the four condemned in the 'common Way', and not in chains.[2]

The men did not act the part either of heroes or of satisfactory villains. Three of the men were fathers of families, with ten children between them; of the other, we are only told that he was a stay-maker.[3] They were supposed to have confessed in prison to the murder of Miles's son, but said 'they were prompted to it by the instigation of Richard Burchett, the evidence against them, who offer'd them a bowl of punch, of a guinea price' if they would go to Miles's house and demand the return of the fine and guns – 'and that they had no intent to kill, but only to affright. They seemed to be very ignorant, but died penitent.'[4] Even so, the executioner had some difficulty in performing his duty. The condemned were all stricken with gaol fever, and so weak with lying in prison that one of them was 'borne between two to the Town-Hall and carry'd upon the hangman's back into the cart'. 'Partly with sickness and partly through the fear of death, none of them was able to speak or stand at the place of execution. Nay, it was actually believed by many who were present that some of them were dead before they were thrown off.'[5]

Throughout that summer the Lords Justices of the Regency Council evidently enjoyed their godlike exercise of the prerogative of mercy, normally reserved to the King. They confirmed that several army deserters were to be shot, or flogged to the brink of death. One interesting case arose which throws light upon the operation of justice. John East had been sentenced at Buckingham Assizes to transportation for deer-stealing. The King received, in his case, a formal recommendation from Lord Chief Justice Pratt (who had judged East) that the sentence be remitted. He enclosed a letter from Judge Denton (who had been one of three judges of the Reading Special Commission) earnestly supporting the recommendation. East (it transpired) had been convicted before Pratt for

1. Berks Rec. Off., Q/SO 1, 89 *verso*, 155 *verso*. See also Nunn Accounts 31 July 1723: 'Captain Cooper lay at my house a week because prison unwholesome.'

2. SP35.43, fos. 119, 130.

3. See below, p. 89.

4. *Northampton Mercury*, 17 June 1723. There was an odd silence as to the executions in the London press. The men were hanged on 11 June (Foster to Paxton, 17 June 1723, SP35.43, fo. 130), but as we have seen (above, p. 76) Delafaye, the Secretary to the Lords Justices, had still not heard of the executions on the 20th, and several days after they were dead and buried in Winkfield churchyard 'their Excellencies' were still debating the matter of hanging them in chains.

5. Capt. Charles Johnson, *A General History of the Lives and Adventures of the Most Famous Highwaymen, etc.*, 1734, pp. 456–9; C. Chevenix Trench, op. cit., p. 117; *Gloucester Journal*, 24 June 1723.

killing a deer in Denton's own park. Denton was satisfied that it was East's first offence: 'he has no confederates, but being in drink & living in the neighbourhood stept in to the park for this purpose.' Denton had been warmly pressed by his neighbours to secure a pardon: 'I am afraid that my sincerity or my interest will be very much questioned in the county if I should fail in this attempt. If I had thought any difficulty would be made in this affair I had convicted him on the other stat. [statute] for the penalty, but I thought the sentence of transportation would deter others . . .' John East had, in any case, been convicted on his own confession.[1] Their Lordships were not moved by these judicial pleas: they made no Order – leaving the law to take its course.[2]

One hopes that Judge Denton's credit in the county did indeed suffer. There is a little evidence that the gentry of Berkshire, Oxfordshire and Buckinghamshire had had their stomachs turned by the Power affair (which never broke the surface of the press, but which certainly became known by gossip among the gentry[3]) and by the Reading Special Commission. A number of accused Blacks were held over from Reading to the Berkshire Assizes at Wallingford and to the Assizes at Oxford. Once again, Baptist Nunn put out his best efforts; he scrutinized and altered the jury,[4] found money for the families of evidences,[5] and

---

1. Judge Alex Denton of Hillesdon, Buckinghamshire, to Delafaye, 8 September 1723, SP35.45, fo. 18. By 'the other stat.' Denton presumably meant the statute of 1691 imposing a £30 fine or one year's imprisonment. Denton did not of course judge and convict East himself; by 'I had convicted' he means that, in a private prosecution, he had the choice of indicting the offender under more or less severe statutes.

2. Minutes of Lords Justices, 5 and 12 September 1723, SP44.291. Those present on 5 September: Archbishop of Canterbury, Walpole, Cadogan, Argyll, Godolphin, Roxburghe. See also SP43.67, for Lord Chief Justice's memorandum recommending pardon to the King.

3. Even young William Trumbull, a schoolboy, was excited by the buzz of gossip: 'The whole talk of the County is about a late adventure of Mr Power: who fram'd a Project for ye Discovery of a set of People we call Blacks: & in order for the executing his deep designs had got a pardon sign'd by some great man to ensnare any whom he thought or suspected to be of their Gang, by vile means & some say by proposing treasonable healths. But before matters were ripe, this profound Plotter being overpower'd by Liquor unravelled all his Mysteries, & upon ye unlucky Discovery has been forced to fly, so that we are left destitute of our Pastor. He has since been seen at Redding in a Red Coat, & Sword': W. Trumbull to Rev. Ralph Bridges, 11 August 1723, Berks. Rec. Off. Trumbull Add. MSS 137.

4. Nunn Accounts:

<table>
<tr><td></td><td>£</td><td>s</td><td>d</td></tr>
<tr><td>July 25. Attended again in London desired pannells of Jury to be altered, with Under Sherriffs</td><td>1</td><td>16</td><td>8</td></tr>
<tr><td>26 & 27. Waited upon Mr Walpole to obteyn Perryman's Tryal respited. Promised amendment of Jury Spent with Under-Sherriffs</td><td>0</td><td>11</td><td>9</td></tr>
</table>

5. ibid.: 'Sent Stedman's poor family & Terry's by Mr Delafaye's consent for

brought twenty-seven witnesses to Wallingford. But, for all this, most of the accused were discharged, and two only were left for transportation.[1] Two more were sentenced to transportation for deer-stealing at Buckinghamshire Assizes, at least one of whom (John East) was certainly not a Black, and two more at Oxford.[2] These results fell far short of the expectations of the prosecution: on 15 and 16 August (Nunn notes) 'waited upon Mr. Walpole with Account of the bad proceedings at Wallingford & about reducing the Expences of State prisoners': (£1 10s. od.). It appears from notes of the Treasury Solicitor that the Law Officers had postponed the prosecution of several prisoners at the Berkshire Assizes at Wallingford for fear that the jury would refuse to convict.[3]

The two men sentenced to transportation at Oxford Assizes were found guilty of taking part in a raid on Earl Cadogan's park at Caversham. One of these men, Thomas Willets, condemned in the first week of August, was still lying in Oxford gaol at the end of November, and the Lords Justices received a petition in his favour endorsed by medical evidence from John Lahser, the Regius Professor of Physick; Willets was so reduced by fever, which had 'taken away his stomach', that his life was despaired of and he could not survive the voyage. This petition, like all others in favour of deer-stealers, was refused.[4]

Meanwhile the administration was chiding the Berkshire authorities for their inactivity. Walpole thought it necessary to write directly to one magistrate demanding more active prosecution of 'Blacks & other Deer Stealers': 'it is found by experience that they do but grow the more daring & insolent for a faint prosecution.'[5] In December the Lords Justices were informed of the 'backwardness' of the Berkshire bench to sign the necessary order for the transportation of several Blacks still living amidst the excrement of Reading gaol. 'Mr Forward who transports the fellons from Newgate hath agreed to take the said prisoners', but Fellow

---

subsistence 2 gs – £4.4.0.' Stedman was a carpenter from the Hampshire side of the border, at Yately: recognisances in Assi. 5.44 (2).

1. *Reading Mercury*, 5 August 1723. These two were Grout and Mercer, who had been held over from the Special Commission because of a flaw in the indictment.

2. *Northampton Mercury*, 12 August 1723; *British Journal*, 10 August 1723.

3. Memorial of A. Cracherode on causes under prosecution, Hilary Term, 1724. T1.243 (63). Of James Barlow, indicted for breaking the head of a fish-pond and speaking seditious words, it is noted 'the King's Councel thought it proper to deferr the Tryal, the Jury having in some Tryals given Verdicts contrary to Evidence'. There is a similar note beside the name of John Plumbridge in a further memorial in T1.249 (1).

4. SP35.46, fo. 46; SP44.291 (Minutes for 28 November).

5. Walpole to James Hayes (of Holly Port, Berkshire), 17 October 1723, SP44.81, fo. 316. This is the same Hayes whose inactivity had been complained of in 1719: above, p. 61.

(who was Sheriff of Berkshire and who now appears as the only truly subservient Hanoverian Justice of the Peace in Berkshire)[1] could not get *any* of his fellow magistrates to join him in signing the Order. The recalcitrant magistrates (seven in number) included Sir John Stanhope, Charles Viscount Fane and the two Members of Parliament for Reading.[2] It was not until July 1724 that four of the convicted Blacks – Charles Grout, John Chapman, Andrew Hughes and Joseph Mercer – set sail on the *Robert* for Maryland.[3] There is no mention of Willets; it is probable that he had already died.

1. See above p. 71 for his role in the Power affair.
2. Paxton to Delafaye, 5 December 1723, SP43.68; SP44.291 (5 December); SP35.47 fo. 7.
3. T53.31, p. 256.

3: Offenders and Antagonists

After so many words and so many episodes, the matter of Berkshire Blacking should now be clear. It is not. If this was a local, county emergency, why did the authorities encounter passive or active resistance from the Steward of the forest courts, jurors and Justices of the Peace in their attempt to deal with it? If it was a national emergency, with connections with Jacobitism, why did Townshend and Walpole employ a clerical *agent provocateur* to further it, and then delay any action for some nine months?

How far, in any case, were the Blacks organized? The press, which was well-tuned by government, carried accounts of secret oath-taking, confederacy, and of a quasi-monarchical, quasi-military organization headed by a 'King'. (For a few days William Shorter, the farmer, was thought to be this King.) One paper, describing the Blacks both of Berkshire and Hampshire, said they were at first made up of 'owlers' (smugglers), poachers and deer-stealers, but now 'a very considerable set of Jacobites . . . mix with 'em, in hopes of engaging a little army of Blacks in their cause'.[1] In a more lurid example, which again refers to both Berkshire and Hampshire, we have –

'Tis said this lawless band are firmly subjected by the most solemn oaths to a blind obedience of their Mock Monarch, King John, who may perhaps be a fit ally for another Idol and King, whose wicked agents have lately bid so fair for involving this nation in blood and confusion. An army of Blacks would be proper instruments for establishing the Kingdom of Darkness . . .[2]

Another, later, account, which is worthless as evidence but of interest as folklore, described the Waltham Blacks as 'a set of whimsical merry

1. *Post-Man*, 30 April–2 May 1723.
2. *Whitehall Evening Post*, 30 April–2 May 1723.

fellows', who dined at a forest inn upon venison prepared in eighteen different ways, washed down with claret. Members were only admitted to the 'society' after being tested for their security and discretion when in drink. They were then to equip themselves with a good mare or gelding, a brace of pistols and a gun. They were then 'sworn upon the horns over the chimney', and had a new name conferred for use within the society. 'The first article in their creed [is] that there's no sin in deer-stealing.'[1]

Such folklore might have applied differently to Berkshire and Hampshire realities, and the Hampshire evidence will be examined later. In the Berkshire case no method is open to us but painstaking examination of fragmentary and imperfect evidence. We will start with the offences charged against men in the Windsor Forest area.[2] Since the offences were committed before the Black Act became law, the only felony which could be laid against any of the accused was the murder of Miles's son, whether as principals or accessories.[3] For this, six men were indicted. Beyond this the Law Officers were in difficulties. Disguising was not felony, and blackmail could only with difficulty be construed as robbery. The strongest statute to hand, for most offenders, was 5 George I c.28 against unlawful hunting, which provided the penalty of seven years' transportation.[4]

Murder and unlawful hunting are clear offences. But the accused collected other charges along the way, for riot, assault on keepers, and threatening letters and behaviour. William Shorter (who was not re-captured) was indicted *in absentia* for robbing Baptist Nunn of five guineas, for stealing a tame hind from Thomas Hollier, for cutting the heads of fish-ponds belonging to two private gentlemen, and for killing deer in the park of the Earl of Arran (but not, it seems, in any part of the

---

1. This account, which has been transmitted by several subsequent historians, appears to have first gained currency in *Lives of the Most Remarkable Criminals*, ed. A. L. Hayward, 1927, pp. 171–4. First published in 1735, the account comes purportedly from a letter from a gentleman in Essex. This suggests that only ten years after the events, popular memory was confusing Bishop's Waltham in Hampshire with Waltham Forest in Essex. The account is highly improbable in several particulars, and of value only as folklore: as such, it is of interest.

2. Some offences are included in this discussion which were committed on the margins of the forest: at Caversham, and along the Berkshire–Hampshire border.

3. Stealing tame deer, knowing them to be tame, could also be felony: see *The Game Law* (1727), I, p. 22.

4. As late as 12 May 1723, only three weeks before the Special Commission opened at Reading, Government remained uncertain as to the best means of prosecution, and Townshend asked the Attorney-General whether he could prosecute Blacks 'upon the late Statute against unlawful hunting': SP44.81, fo. 235. Some were, of course, so prosecuted.

royal forest). A count, which is without doubt imperfect, gives us the following list of offences:

Murder (or accessory to)	6
Assault on keepers and their servants	12
Unlawful hunting of deer (royal forest)	20
Unlawful hunting of deer (private parks)	47
Fish-ponds (robbing and cutting banks) (all private)	17
Robbery (i.e. blackmail)	4
Sedition	2
Threatening letters	2
Attempted arson	1
Theft or illegal taking of wood	2
Poaching fish (private)	1
Total	114

This table requires some comment. First, it does not include offenders dealt with at quarter-sessions (whose records are lost) nor presented (mainly for turf-cutting) in the forest courts. Second, riot is not separately entered since offenders were charged with assault. The cases of murder all relate to the killing of Miles's son, for which four were condemned at the Reading Special Commission, one evaded arrest, and one accessory (Burchett) turned King's evidence. The robbery cases all concern the extortion with menaces of five guineas from Baptist Nunn.[2] The last two items (wood theft and poaching) may or may not relate to the Blacks, but are entered since they rose to Assize or comparable level in the same years. Finally, this is a table of offences, not of offenders; a number of men were, like William Shorter, indicted for several offences.

One point is noticeable: the very large number of offences (over 60 per cent) committed not against royal prerogative in the forest but against private gentry and noblemen. We will explore this problem shortly. But first we must examine an even more difficult question: who were these offenders? And this cannot be answered without some attention to the technical problems of recovering the evidence.

1. This table is drawn in the main from: (i) Particulars of the Causes now under Prosecution, prepared by A. Cracherode, the Treasury Solicitor, in 1723 and 1724, in T1.243 and T1.249; (ii) Assize records, esp. Assi. 2.8 and 4.18; (iii) warrants for arrest and committal in SP44.81. It is not possible to compile a useful table of convictions because (a) a number of persons indicted *in absentia* were never taken up; (b) the Crown dropped some cases without bringing them to trial; (c) the legal records are at points deficient.

2. This is the case already described in Nunn's Accounts, above, p. 66.

We may start with a provisional table, compiled from unexamined attributions. Of 120 persons indicted, or informed upon, for Black offences and deer-hunting in these years, no attribution of occupation can be found in fifty-six cases. There are sixty-four persons for whom such attributions can be found:

WINDSOR FOREST OFFENDERS (1722–4): ATTRIBUTED OCCUPATIONS[1]

Baronet	1		
Gentlemen	2	3	gentry
Farmers and yeomen		10	farmers
Innkeepers	2		
Butchers	2	5	tradesmen
Miller	1		
Carpenters	4		
Blacksmiths	3		
Clock-maker, farrier, fisherman, felt-maker, millwright, stay-maker, wheelwright – one of each	7	14	craftsmen
Labourers	24		
Servants	6	32	labourers
Inn servants, ostlers	2		
	Total	64	

If this was a fair sample it would suggest a make-up of approximately 50 per cent labourers; 21·5 per cent urban and rural craftsmen; 15·5 per cent farmers; under 8 per cent tradesmen; and 4·5 per cent gentry.

But it is not a fair sample, and may be greatly misleading. Sixteen of the twenty-four labourers are worthless attributions by a Clerk of Assize, relating to episodes at Caversham.[2] Thirteen other attributions (including six labourers and five craftsmen) are recovered from an uncharacteristic case, involving the baronet, Sir Charles Englefield, on the fringes of the forest,[3] and none of these thirteen men were informed against for other Black offences. It seems therefore more helpful to make a distinction

1. Compiled from various sources in state papers, Assize records, press, etc. The Wokingham clock-maker was acquitted.

2. In Assi. 4.18 the sixteen men are listed as 'of Caversham, labourer', under prosecution for taking part in two attacks on Earl Cadogan's park at Caversham. Attribution of place is clearly (from other evidence) the place where the offence was committed, not the residence of the accused; and in this kind of entry from Clerks of Assize no reliance whatsoever can be placed upon the attribution of occupation as 'labourer'.

3. See below, pp. 102–3.

between 'hard-core Blacks' and common poachers, etc. caught up in the same disturbances. About seventy of this 120 were regarded by the authorities as presumptive Blacks. Their names were collected by Baptist Nunn and his informants, or by Parson Power, and forwarded to the Secretary of State: these appear (but unfortunately without attribution of occupation) in his Warrant Book, or in the particulars of causes under prosecution drawn up from time to time by the Treasury Solicitor. Very few of them can be identified by occupation: all formal depositions, informations and even indictments for this central group of Blacks appear to be lost.[1] Of this seventy, the occupations of forty-seven remain unknown. Of the remainder:

HARD-CORE WINDSOR BLACKS: OCCUPATIONS

Farmers and yeomen	8
Servants	3
Labourers	2
Gentleman	1
Innkeeper	1
Butcher, clock-maker, farrier, felt-maker, fisherman, stay-maker, blacksmith, carpenter – one of each	8
Total	23

The composition of this 'sample' looks very different. But the figures, very probably, remain misleading, since, if we turn to other sources, a good deal may be inferred as to the status even of many of the forty-seven of unknown occupation. Such an exploration is difficult and open to error; the spelling of names is haphazard, the Crown sometimes issued warrants in the wrong name or the wrong Christian name, and the same names recur in the forest. Sons were named after fathers; the chief huntsman, William Lorwen (or Lowen), had not only a son but a brother named William.[2] In Winkfield there were several families named Hatch: 'the eldest branch of that family', Will Waterson recalled, 'time out of mind has had an handsome estate and a good interest' in the parish.[3] The head of this branch, in 1723, was Thomas Hatch, a Regarder, and a man evidently favoured by the forest officers.[4] But a Thomas Hatch of Winkfield was also hanged as accessory to the murder of young Miles.

1. See Note on Sources, below, p. 296.
2. J. P. Hare, *The History of the Royal Buckhounds*, Newmarket, 1895, pp. 222–4, 255.
3. Waterson (Ranelagh), 1. Two eighteenth-century Hatch gravestones still stand prominently in Winkfield churchyard, beside the path to the church door.
4. Verderers' Books, LR3.3 *passim*.

We do not know the relationship of the two Thomases[1] and can only with difficulty distinguish them from each other (and perhaps from other Thomases) in other parochial records. In the examination which follows I have wherever possible established an identification by two or more intersecting inferences. Where the evidence is slender I insert a cautionary qualification.

We will start at Bray, on the north-east edge of the forest. William Herring is one of the listed yeomen. He had been in trouble in 1718 for coursing red deer with a greyhound, had been reported to the Treasury Solicitor in 1719, was presented for an encroachment of two acres in 1720; and a William Herring paid quit-rent of 8d. for a tenement in neighbouring New Windsor.[2] The fisherman in the list is William Terry: he was early taken up, broken in Newgate, and was enlisted by Nunn as an evidence. 'Fisherman' suggests a labouring status, but Terry was at least as good as a yeoman. Between Maidenhead and Windsor there were several good private fisheries; in 1712 Terry had inherited from his father (in much the same way as a copyhold) the lease of a fishery belonging to Windsor Corporation, for a quit-rent of £6 5s. p.a. and an entry fine of £20.[3] It was probably Terry who informed on John Perryman, also of Bray, in notes which survive in the state papers:

> Perryman, some years since in the hard frost, killed a brace of deer. About a year and a half ago desired Stedman and Terry to bring their acquaintance to meet his people near the New Lodge to kill deer and advised them that if Lowen and his people should resist they should shoot them from behind trees, & burn the house.

– This and some more deer-hunting episodes.[4]

John Perryman is one of those listed as a farmer, of Oakley Green, between Bray and New Windsor. He was presented in the forest court in 1717 for making fences ten feet high against the red deer imported into New Lodge Walk.[5] He was indicted at the Special Commission at Reading for his part (with three others) in a riot and assault upon two keepers' servants, but his trial was repeatedly held over and probably

---

1. Since Thomas Hatch, the Black, is once referred to as 'Thomas Hatch, Junior' it is not impossible that he was the Regarder's son.

2. T1.223 (above, p. 61); LR3.3. LR13 (5).

3. SP35.43 (i) and (ii); SP44.81; SP35.47; Nunn Accounts; Windsor Corporation Archives, Windsor Hall Book 1653–1725, W1/AC a 1, p. 365. Terry may also have been one of the 'four fishermen of the King's water' at Bray, who shared a quit-rent of 33s. 4d. p.a. which had not changed since 1632; Berks Rec. Off. D/Est M1–3 (Bray rental, 1702); Charles Kerry, *History and Antiquities of the Hundred of Bray*, 1861, p. 81. See also below, p. 235 n. 4.

4. SP35.47, fo. 72.   5. See above, p. 54.

never took place. Undoubtedly he was able to bring influence (and probably money) to bear. He was a substantial farmer – a note by his name says he was worth £200 p.a. – and he was bound upon the very high recognisances of £1,000 (with two sureties at £500).[1] The office of Reeve for the manor of Bray went in rotation around the more substantial properties, and a John Perryman (presumably his father or himself) served in 1700 and 1715.[2]

One of those indicted with Perryman for assault on the keepers was Robert Hawthorne, one of the 'unknowns'. He was presumably a farming neighbour of Perryman's, who had the same reasons to resent the New Lodge deer. Also a farmer of substance, a Robert Hawthorne was Reeve for the manor of Bray in 1699 and 1714.[3] He evaded arrest and became for a time an outlaw.[4] Of the other two in this indictment, John Plumbridge remains unknown,[5] and John Chapman, who had been in trouble for poaching before, was a 'servant', very probably a farm servant. He was less lucky than his companions, and was transported.[6] If we assume that the last two came from Bray (as seems possible), we have six men in this group: two substantial farmers, a yeoman, a master of a fishery, a servant and one unknown.

South from Bray, New Windsor supplied the two labourers in the list of hard-core Blacks. William Alloway and John Churchman were charged with coursing deer in Windsor Great Park. The attribution of occupation, and even of parish, is suspect; these men could equally have

1. T1.243 (63); SP35.43, fo. 23; SP44.81, fo. 253. Perryman's trial was postponed in July 1723 after Baptist Nunn had waited upon Walpole (Nunn Accounts, 26 July) and was still being postponed in 1724: SP44.81, fos. 298, 316, 335; T1.249 (1). A London newspaper noted that among those seized as Blacks some were 'of considerable substance', and 'one now in Newgate is . . . of a very reputable family in Berkshire, and heir at law to a valuable fortune; and great application is making to men in power in his favour': *Applebee's Original Weekly Journal*, 25 May 1723. This passage might refer to Perryman, or possibly to Simmonds or Rackett (discussed below).

2. Berks Rec. Off. D/Est M1–5. Bray quit rentals show Perryman holding several properties ('Haverings', 'Wests', 'part of Punters', 'part of Marches' and 'Archlands' in Braywick). The office of Reeve was not unimportant and appears to have circulated every fifteen years between the most substantial property holders: Perryman served in his capacity as the occupier of 'Wests'.

3. ibid. Hawthorne served in his capacity as occupier of the property known as 'Wise's'.

4. SP44.81; T1.249 (1); SP35.43; SP35.47.

5. He could perhaps have been related to E. Plumridge, a brick-maker of Winkfield, who owned barns, outhouses and orchards in Cranborne Woods, and who left a token legacy in his will to his brother John: Bodleian Library, MS Wills Berks, 20, p. 33 (*probat.* 2 June 1728).

6. T1.223 (above, p. 61); T1.243 (63); T1.249 (1); SP44.81; SP35.40; SP35.47. Chapman may, however, have been a servant in Winkfield.

been yeomen, servants or craftsmen from the town.[1] New Windsor also supplied a substantial yeoman or farmer,[2] and Old Windsor an innkeeper, William Hart, who while not accused of being a Black got himself into deep trouble for allowing Blacks to drink at his house. Brought up to London for examination, he deposed that four named men, headed by William Shorter, together with six or seven others in disguise on horseback, were drinking at his inn on 9 April, 'when an attempt was made on Baptist Nun's house by some of them on horseback'. A reluctant witness, he was bound over on recognisances of £40 to appear in evidence; and to encourage him further he was presented at the Forty Days Court for keeping a disorderly house at the sign of The Fox 'and harbouring poaching, loose and disorderly company'.[3] This threat to his livelihood was sufficient to bring him as a witness to the Special Commission.

Undoubtedly the heart of hard-core Blacking would have been in the central and southern areas of the forest: Winkfield, Warfield, Easthampstead, Wokingham, Sandhurst and across the border (by Bagshot) into Surrey. Wokingham provided many suspects, but (in the absence of relevant manorial records and rentals) imperfect information. Four Shorters were deeply involved: two Williams and two Roberts, both fathers and sons. William Shorter, senior, was often referred to as the 'head' of the Berkshire Blacks. He was described as a farmer of Wokingham, owning freehold lands worth £80 p.a. and renting a further £200 p.a. – a very substantial man.[4] Of his son nothing is known, except that he evaded arrest and became (like his father after his escape) an outlaw.[5] From Wokingham also came the felt-maker, Edward Collier, sentenced to transportation for stealing a 'tame' deer,[6] and George Winn (or Wynne), the clock-maker, who had attended with Shorter and Collier at the Berkshire quarter-sessions to inform on Parson Power, but who was the only accused to be acquitted at the Reading Commission. Thomas Hamilton (or Hambleton), a Warfield farmer, was accused of killing a deer in the forest with some Winkfield men, and taking it to the house of

1. Assi. 2.8, 4.18; the attribution of occupation from Assize sources is, once again, suspect. Churchman's trial was still being postponed in 1725: SP35.57, fo. 9.

2. The records confuse a Charles, John and Thomas Simmonds or Symonds; a John Symonds was released on the high recognisances of £500 on 25 May 1723 and was subsequently discharged (*British Journal*, 15 June 1723); but there was also a Charles who was not taken; SP44.81, fo. 253; Assi. 4.18.

3. SP44.81; SP35.43, fo. 45; LR3.3.

4. *History of Blacks*, p. 13; *British Journal*, 4 May 1723. For Shorter's offences, see above, p. 82.

5. Three separate warrants were issued unsuccessfully for his arrest by the Secretary of State in May and June 1723: SP44.81.

6. SP35.40; Assi. 4.18. For Collier's subsequent history, see below, p. 238.

Thomas Hatch where it was dressed; he saved his own skin by becoming an evidence. He and William Hambleton (one assumes they were related) were presented (as 'of Wokingham') at the Forty Days Court in July 1722 for cutting and carrying off a load of turfs from 'preserved grounds' at Bigshot Rails.[1] The Robert Shorters, father and son, probably brother and nephew to William, were perhaps Wokingham men, in the service of Thomas Solmes, lord of Sandhurst manor; they were presented for cutting turf for him in 1717.[2]

Wokingham men often acted together with men from the contiguous parish, Winkfield. For this parish the evidence is a little fuller. Three of the four men hanged for the murder of young Miles came from Winkfield, and were buried together in the churchyard.[3] All must have been youngish men, and all had young families: John Gilbert was married in 1718, Thomas Hatch and Leonard Thorne in 1716. Both Hatch and Thorne appear to have held parish offices, as tithingmen, in 1721 and 1720 respectively.[4] Hatch had been presented for heath-cutting in 1717; we already know that he came from an established Winkfield family, and that deer-stealers went to his 'house' to dress the venison. The fourth man to be hanged, John Hawthorne, was described as a stay-maker and may have come from somewhere near Winkfield.[5] A John Hawthorn appears in Winkfield rentals; so also do the names of three other men identical with those of hard-core Blacks – John Cooper, who was charged with attacking fish-ponds in the company of Shorter, and who evaded arrest; Peter Lawrence, whose history is much the same; and Joseph

1. SP44.81; SP35.43; Nunn Accounts, *passim*; LR3.3; recognisances of Thomas Hambleton in Assi. 5.44 (2).

2. Some forty years later, during a dispute about rights of turbary in Sandhurst, a Robert Shorter (now a yeoman pricker) gave evidence that he had been born sixty-six years before, within a mile of Sandhurst manor, and had been a servant to Mr Solmes at the age of thirteen: TS11.425.1349. When Robert Shorter, senior and junior, were presented at the forest court (September 1717 – see above, p. 54) for turf-cutting in Sandhurst, they were presented as cutters for Mr Solmes, the lord of the manor: LR3.3.

3. *Northampton Mercury*, 17 June 1723. All came from the hamlet of Wingfield Row. Their burial ('*infurcati*') on 16 June 1723 is noted by the Reverend Will Waterson in the parish register; Berks Rec. Off. DP 151/1/3.

4. Churchwardens' Accounts, Winkfield, Berks Rec. Off. DP 151/5/2.

5. The *Northampton Mercury* gave the place as 'Waryhill': this might perhaps have been a misprint for Merryhill or Maryhill, to the west of Winkfield. This seems to agree with a list of householders drawn up in 1727 in the parish of Binfield, which shows a Katherine Grave renting 'Jno Hawthorn's': Berks Rec. Off., D/P/18/41. In 1734 Susannah Hathorne, 'late of Binfield', a widow, made a will in which it appeared that she had security for £100 in the form of a mortgage upon land of John Perryman, the Black, in Bray. This was probably John Hawthorne's widow, and Perryman may have extended some help to her: Bodleian Library, MS Wills Berks 21, p. 75.

Mognar, convicted of stealing deer in the forest, who died in prison.[1] Thomas Stanaway or Stanworth, indicted for the murder of Miles, was probably petty constable of Winkfield in 1720; he evaded arrest.[2] Richard Attlee turned evidence upon his companions, and rehabilitated himself to become Overseer for Ascot (within the parish of Winkfield) in 1731.[3] Thomas Clarke was a juror (and therefore presumably a customary tenant) on the manorial court of Sunninghill (close to Swinley Walk) in 1722.[4]

Two other men of Winkfield parish can be identified more precisely. John Punter (or Poynter) was certainly a substantial farmer. He had been reported to the Treasury Solicitor in 1719 for employing men in grubbing up more than two acres of coppices and hedgerows.[5] He was on the Winkfield vestry in 1718, and petty constable in 1722; turning King's evidence, he survived to become Overseer in 1730. He appears prominently in a 'List of Blacks' of May 1723.[6] So also does James Barlow, but he is a more complex offender. He first appears, during the reign of Anne, on the side of officialdom. In 1708 he was sworn gamekeeper of Cranborne, Old Windsor and Egham Walks; in 1713 (still gamekeeper) he was given a special licence to enclose two acres for his own use on Ascot Heath.[7] He was wise to have made hay while a Stuart sun was shining, since, with the Hanoverian accession, he was one of the first victims of the spoils system. His post as gamekeeper was taken off him in April 1715 and awarded to none other than Baptist Nunn. The former gamekeeper, now a victualler of Winkfield, was himself presented in 1717 for building a carthouse on four poles of waste land. These experiences disturbed his loyalty; he was described in Crown notes as 'a Jacobite', and his inn near Cranborne as 'a great meeting house', where the Blacks drank. He was indicted (with William Shorter and others) for cutting the heads of two private fish-ponds; and also, alone of the Winkfield men, for sedition, in saying, 'God damn the King and his Posterity. I hope to have a new master in a little time.'[8] His trial was repeatedly postponed, and the Crown

1. Manorial quit-rents, Winkfield, 1714, 1717: Berks Rec. Off. D/EN M 19; SP35.40; SP35.43; Assi. 4.18; SP44.81. But (see below) these three men may also have held land in Warfield.

2. Churchwardens' Accounts, Winkfield, Berks Rec. Off. DP 151/5/2; T1.243 (63).

3. ibid.; SP35.65, fo. 152; SP35.43.

4. Sunninghill Parish Book, Berks Rec. Off. D/P 126/8/1.

5. T1.223 (6): see above, p. 42.

6. SP35.43; SP44.81 (20 May, recognisances of £100); Churchwardens' Accounts, Winkfield, Berks Rec. Off. DP 151/5/2.

7. LR3.2. Ascot Heath commenced its life as a fashionable race-meeting during the reign of Anne; among prizes contested in the 1720s was the 'Stag Hunter's Plate', worth forty guineas: *Weekly Worcester Journal*, 23 July 1725.

8. Assi. 2.8; SP35.43; T1.243 (63); SP44.81 (23 May, recognisances £500); LR3.3.

evidently had no confidence in its own case.[1] But Nunn and the Law Officers pursued him vindictively, and clearly saw this gamekeeper-turned-poacher as one of the chief Blacks. In 1729 the indictment was still being held above his head.[2]

The parish of Winkfield neighboured Warfield to the south-west and Binfield to the west. Some men probably farmed land in several parishes. Binfield, a comparatively prosperous forest parish (Alexander Pope's old home), appears to have contributed little to Blacking.[3] Warfield, however, seems to have been as disturbed as Winkfield. It was a sparsely populated parish of desolate blacklands. There were 109 householders in Warfield in 1717 (nine of these widows) and ten poor ('certificate') families; of the householders at least four could have been Blacks.[4] Jonathan Cooke, who evaded arrest on a charge of killing deer in the Great Park, was perhaps the same man as one of that name presented in the forest court in 1718 for felling oaks on his own land without licence.[5] Joseph Mognar, Peter Lawrence and John Cooper are names which appear in both Winkfield and Warfield records. Thomas Hambleton may also have been a Warfield farmer. And other names suggest possible relationship to other accused men (Alloway, Grout, Simmons). It would be hazardous to carry inference too far. But we seem, again and again, to be finding men with small freehold or copyhold farms, sometimes scattered in several parcels in more than one parish, adjoining the heath and forest with their valued grazing and common rights. Such a man is John Cooper, perhaps the Black of that name, who was admitted in 1721 on the death of his father to two small tenures, Evelins and Hangers Corner; in a year's time he had surrendered them to another tenant. If we have the right Peter Lawrence, he was a Warfield weaver, with two acres of freehold and two even smaller customary tenures, together with barns, stables and an orchard. And so on. There can be little doubt that Baptist Nunn, a fellow Warfield parishioner, gathered into The Squirrel on 3 May a wagon-load of yeomen and of rural artisans with petty landholdings very much of this kind.[6]

Thus Warfield. We might extend this examination to other parishes,

1. It is possible that the case against Barlow depended upon the provocations of Parson Power, whom the Crown kept well away from the witness-box.

2. Assi. 9.2; and see above, p. 79 n. 3.

3. A list of Binfield householders (135 men and 4 women) compiled between 1721 and 1727 includes the names of no indicted Blacks: Berks Rec. Off. D/P/18/41. The exception (discussed above) may be John Hawthorne.

4. Warfield Churchwardens' Accounts, Berks Rec. Off. D/P/144/5/2. See also Eileen Shorland, *The Pish (Parish) of Warfield*, 1967.

5. LR3.3; SP44.81 (25 May, recognisances of £200); Berks Rec. Off. D/P/144/5/2.

6. Warfield Churchwardens' Accounts; court books of the Manor of Wargrave, Berks Rec. Off. D/EN M54; Bodleian Library, MS Wills Berks, 21, p. 159.

but it would prove tedious. But two other men on the hard-core list must be mentioned. There is nothing among surviving Crown papers relating to any of the men so far mentioned to support the more lurid stories in the press as to a highly organized conspiratorial fraternity, oath-taking, secret signs, 'monarchical government' and the rest. Only Barlow was accused of Jacobitism. The evidence suggests more informal organization, based on neighbourhood, kinship, common grievances and drinking companionship.[1] But with Richard Fellows we have a different case. He lived at Dawney, near Maidenhead, and was probably the butcher 'of a huge stature' seized on 10 May while playing cricket. He can also be identified as a tithingman for Maidenhead in 1721.[2] A butcher, of course, would be a man with excellent contacts for the sale of venison; but Fellows appears to have been involved for different reasons. He was committed on 18 May, charged with being 'confederated' with the Blacks and of soliciting others to join the confederacy. Against his name, and that of Edward Stevens, a farrier of Easthampstead, are jotted the words 'suspicion of High Treason'; but it is also noted that in Fellows's enlistment of men for the Blacks the Pretender was 'not mentioned'. Perhaps this is the reason why his trial, like Barlow's, was repeatedly postponed, being passed over in the end towards the Buckinghamshire Assizes.[3]

A more surprising man to be suspected as a hard-core Black was Charles Rackett, 'Esq.' of Hall Grove, Wingham, near Bagshot. The Secretary of State's warrant was issued for the arrest of him, his son Michael, and two of his servants on 18 May.[4] Crown notes allege: 'Mr. Rackett, his son, his servants, horses & dogs frequently were seen hunting and maliciously destroying the deer in Windsor Forest, particularly Anno

1. There were several pairs of fathers and sons among indicted Blacks: two pairs of Shorters, and pairs of Thorbers, Racketts and Coopers. There were also two Clarkes, two Hambletons, two Hawthornes, two Colliers and two Mercers – all of unidentified relationship.

2. Court rolls, Cookham 1721, Berks Rec. Off. D/Esk M 153; *Northampton Mercury*, 13 May 1723; *Weekly Journal, or British Gazetteer*, 18 May 1723; *Whitehall Evening Post*, 12 November 1723.

3. SP44.81, fo. 247; SP35.43, fo. 23. The Secretary of State's Warrant Book (SP44.81, fos. 236–7) shows that eight informations proving Fellows to have enlisted men for the Blacks were forwarded to the Attorney-General: these are now lost. Fellows's name appears among the causes under prosecution prepared by the Treasury Solicitor in 1723 and 1724, but with no specific charge beside it (in T1.243 and T1.249). He was bailed in 1724 (Assi. 2.8) in the sum of £100, and ordered to appear at the next summer Assizes for Buckinghamshire 'to answer for such matters' as would be presented against him: he is described here as a yeoman. I have not been able to trace the case further, but assume that this case, like Barlow's, may have been too far involved with the provocations of Parson Power to have convinced a jury.   4. SP44.81, fo. 261.

1722 . . .'[1] On one occasion they were seen by Thomas Sawyer, the keeper of Swinley Walk, to kill a hind calf. He followed them back to Hall Grove, where he found Rackett's son, Michael, with their two servants, dressing the calf. When the keeper asked to speak to Rackett, the latter 'begged of deponent not to take notice of it, offering him a guinea'.[2] Among Crown notes there is jotted beside Rackett's name, 'Jacobite . . . worth £20,000'.[3] Only one of the Racketts seems to have been taken up, probably the father who was bound over in £500 on 25 May.[4] Perhaps Michael, his son, fled. A press report supposed that the fugitive was the father; noting that some of the accused Blacks had evaded arrest, it added: 'among them one Mr. R—, a gentleman of a good estate; they tell us he is brother-in-law to the famous Mr. P—.'[5] He was indeed; Rackett was the husband of the half-sister of Alexander Pope, and he was also a fellow Catholic. Hall Grove was not far from Pope's own childhood home in Windsor Forest, and the poet kept up a close association with the Rackett family. Perhaps it was owing to Pope's good offices that the Treasury Solicitor dropped the case against Charles Rackett.[6] But things were not dropped as easily as that in the 1720s. No doubt much money was needed (indeed, at double rate to buy out a Catholic) and the finances of the family never recovered from some blow which fell at about this time. Pope's nephew, Michael Rackett, disappeared overseas; perhaps the price of the father's liberty was the son's outlawry.[7]

Two of the three servants in the hard-core list were Rackett's men, James Goddard and Daniel Legg. They were dealt with summarily, and spared more exalted trial.[8] And we can now see that this closer examination has very much qualified the earlier notion of social composition of the Blacks suggested by the unexamined statistics. In the hard-core list the two labourers are doubtful identifications, and the servants appear as part of a package where gentry or farmers hunt with their servants. While forty-seven of the seventy remain of 'unknown' occupation, something of their social status can be inferred. Thus they include the kin of men of

---

1. SP35.47, fo. 72.

2. 'Account of Michael Rackett's killing and dressing deer', in SP35.33.

3. SP35.43, fo. 23.

4. There is some confusion in the Secretary of State's Warrant Book, and although a 'Ragget' was taken on 19 May (SP35.43, fo. 57) it is not clear whether it was father or son. But it was Charles (the father) who was released on recognisances; SP44.81, fos. 258–9.

5. *London Journal*, 25 May 1723.

6. Neither Rackett appears in the Treasury Solicitor's list of causes under prosecution for 1723 and 1724 in T1.243 and T1.249.

7. For Pope and the Racketts see Appendix 2.

8. Nunn Accounts show (11 June) 'before Mr Hayes with Mr Rackett's man [men?] for conviction about killing deer in forest'.

substance (Michael Rackett, William Shorter junior); men whose presence in rentals suggests them as farmers, yeomen or craftsmen; men whose recognisances were far too high for a labourer to meet; a fisherman who turns out to be master of a fishery; and men who served as tithingmen, reeves, on the homage of court leets, or as petty constables – all offices which did not normally pass to labourers or servants. Undoubtedly the latter took part as auxiliaries or in freelance actions of their own. But theirs were not the actions which most rattled the authorities. In any case, to segregate the social categories in this way is perhaps to put the wrong question to the forest community. Rentals, wills and surveys show an unusual fragmentation of landholding – old assarts, encroachments, purprestures, a few score poles 'won' here and there from the forest. A labourer might well hold, on a nominal quit-rent, a tenement; might graze a few beasts in the forest; and rent a portion of land in another parish. A servant might be the son of a yeoman or craftsman who would soon follow a similar occupation in his turn.

This was yeoman's country, of a kind which Thomas Hardy would have understood. The heart of Blacking lay in the middling orders of the forest: a few gentry sympathizers, more substantial farmers, more again of yeomen and tradesmen or craftsmen, and a few of the poorer foresters. And from their offences we can identify their antagonists. First of all, there were the forest bureaucracy and their allies. Blacks were indicted for threatening and extorting money ('robbery') from Baptist Nunn, and for assaulting the keepers' servants and the keepers. And other offences which appear to have been committed against private persons may have been aimed at the same bureaucracy; thus Edward Collier was to be transported for stealing a 'tame' deer from Sir Robert Rich; but Rich was also titular Keeper (by inheritance) of Bearwood Walk. Barlow, Shorter and five others were indicted for cutting the head of a fish-pond in Winkfield of Edmund Halsey; Halsey was Ranger of Battles Bailiwick. Shorter and six others were indicted for stealing a tame hind from Thomas Hollier. Hollier, until he was sacked in 1722, had been under-keeper of Linchford Walk.[1] Robert Shorter was charged with attacking fish-ponds of Viscount Cobham, the Constable of the Castle.

This accounts for seventeen of the private cases in the table of offences (above, p. 83). The case of Hollier, and that of James Barlow (the ex-gamekeeper turned Black) should occasion reflection. It was not just an abstract forest authority which was in conflict with the farming community, but particular men who lived in the midst of their opponents. Although Hollier was dismissed for negligence or for collusion with deer-stealers, this does not mean that he was a friend of the Blacks. He might

1. Constable's Warrant Books, *passim.*

have submitted to intimidation, but at the same time have exploited his perquisites in ways which left resentment long after his dismissal. Barlow, on the other hand, may have nourished a hostility towards the man who replaced him (Baptist Nunn) fierce enough to have made him an advocate of Blacking.

In a situation of perquisites and blackmail there was obviously intense in-fighting going on, the details of which can never be recovered. But clues have been left here and there. A part of the forest bureaucracy formed almost a caste within the forest, self-recruiting and of long standing. Nunn was a gamekeeper's son; in the same way the sons of Hanningtons, Mileses, Sawyers, Lorwens, and Ironmongers succeeded upon their fathers. These families had no doubt won the confidence of Colonel Negus, the only executive, non-sinecurist member of the genteel officialdom. Other officers appear to have been displaced, with each change in senior administration or in the titular Ranger or Keeper of each Walk. The hard core of officials had more than ideology or a sense of duty to fight for; they stood to gain substantial spoils.

Sarah, Duchess of Marlborough, is not a reliable historical source. Deprived of royal favour in the last years of Anne, she never regained it during her long-continued life under two Hanovers; she nourished a healthy hatred of Walpole, and when declaring one of her many grievances she gave free rein to fantasy. But there is a passage in one of her budgets of grievance which deserves attention. She was furious at being rated for land tax on Windsor Little Park, of which she was Ranger (by a gift during Queen Anne's favour) and she did her best to represent this pleasant and rewarding sinecure as a costly obligation incurred in the royal service. She received for this duty only a hay allowance, out of which she could not even meet the keepers' wages. She was cross with Walpole, who had threatened her hay allowance, and who, after ignoring her for several years, had waited upon her in ingratiating mood: he had need (it turned out) to borrow £200,000. 'Whatever advantages so knowing a man as Sir Robert may make of his own park,' she commented, 'I find mine at Blenheim very chargeable':

And at Windsor 'tis much more so, because all the under servants look upon it to be the King's, and that they have a right to get all they can. . . And for the deer, they are the King's, and he may do what Sir Robert pleases with them. I make no advantage of the Park, but to eat sometimes a few little Welsh runts, and I have no more cows than I allow the under-keepers, which are to each six. . . I have laid out a great deal of money which is called being a good tenant, and I never was so mean as to bring any bills like other great men upon such occasions, for what I did for my own satisfaction.[1]

1. Sarah, Duchess of Marlborough to Dr Hare (copy), n.d. (September 1726?), Brit.

The first comment on this is no more than negative evidence. The Blacks, who attacked deer in the Great Park, Cranborne, New Lodge, Bigshot and Swinley Walks, did not attack the Little Park. This suggests that it is conceivable (scandalous as the imputation may be) that Sarah was a good Ranger, and did not, like the Rangers and titular Keepers of other Walks, turn her office into private property and milk it of every possible source of profit. Second, Sarah, if unreliable, was refreshingly devoid of noble cant. 'The under servants look upon it to be the King's, and that they have a right to get all they can . . .'

One must regard the forest officialdom as a distinct interest-group, and not as the loyal servants of a royal presence which, in the reign of George I, was mostly a royal absence. King George did not go shooting in Swinley Walk in 1717 because he had studied maps of the forest and put his finger on the spot; he was conducted there. The officials who conducted him were pursuing their own interests. Several of the old gamekeeper families were rising to the status of gentry and landholders in their own right. Illiterate fathers were handing over to literate and well-endowed sons. Will Lorwen, the chief huntsman and keeper of New Lodge Walk, commanded the disposal of some £600 to £1,000 p.a. in the first office, out of which an establishment of hounds and grooms had to be maintained; his son, William, was yeoman pricker at £80 p.a.; his brother was also on the establishment; a George Lorwen was, for a time, keeper of Sandhurst Walk. Lorwen was also under-keeper of New Lodge Walk, at a salary of only £20 p.a., with an addition of £6 1s. as 'housekeeper' of the handsome lodge.[1] Robert Hannington was under-keeper of Bigshot Rails (£20 p.a.), Augustine Hannington, senior, of Sandhurst Walk, and Augustine Hannington, junior, of Easthampstead Walk (£20 p.a.) and also Vermin Killer (£9 2s. 6d.); but other documents show them to be landholders and one at least of them was styled 'gent'.[2] William Miles was under-keeper of Old Windsor and Egham Walks (£20), and his son, who was killed, was in the service of Brigadier Honeywood, the titular Keeper of

Mus. Add. MSS 9,120. The reference to the 'bills' of 'other great men' could possibly refer to Walpole's improvements at Richmond Park; see below, p. 184. The rows between Sarah and Walpole about Windsor Little Park are also the subject of correspondence in Blenheim MSS, F1.40; and see W. Menzies, *The History of Windsor Great Park and Windsor Forest*, 1864, pp. 21–2; and Sarah's own *An Account of the Conduct etc.*, 1742, pp. 291–2, where she alleges that she had to keep up 'four or five thousand head of deer in the Park'. I think this may be fantasy: but, if anything like true, it means that there were as many deer in Windsor Forest in the 1720s as at the time of Norden Survey in 1607: see table, p. 56.

1. Constable's Warrant Books, *passim*; Hare, op. cit., pp. 222–4, 255.
2. Constable's Warrant Books; William Lyon, *Chronicles of Finchampstead*, 1895, pp. 209–10, 310; T1.235 (46).

Old Windsor Walk.[1] Thomas Sawyer was under-keeper of Swinley Walk and John Sawyer of part of Cranborne Walk (at £20 each); but John Sawyer was probably also the attorney of that name who appeared regularly at Windsor Borough Court.[2] The spoils system of these years may have been awarding not only the titular posts of rangers and keepers to noblemen and generals, but also the posts of under-keeper (several of which were becoming almost hereditary) to gentlemen, professional men, and the sons of forest officers who had climbed to that status. The actual work was performed by servants.

In a system of perquisites and spoils one can never hope to identify any individual's income. (We might be put on our guard by the case of Colonel Negus, who as Lieutenant or Deputy to the Lord Warden (Constable) received the derisory salary of £10 p.a.; but to this we must add several allowances as Ranger of three different Walks; £800 p.a. for executing the duties of Master of Horse; £260 p.a. as Avener and Clerk Marshal; and this is only the beginning of his accumulated roles.[3]) In the case of the under-keepers, known perquisites included the use of lodges, often with orchards, gardens, grazing; fees for the warranted killing of deer; important timber perquisites;[4] the sale of browse-wood; and the exploitation of the influence that went with office. In the aftermath of the tragedy of the Blacks, the normally compliant Regarders of the forest court showed, at the last two Swanimotes to be held for Windsor Forest, a flurry of guarded independence. They presented the under-keepers as a group for taking down dead trees without view (i.e. without licence or notice to a Regarder), and lopping too many branches from the trees under pretence of browse-wood. In addition the taking for their own use of deer found wounded or accidentally killed 'is grown to be a pernitious custome'. The old huntsman, Will Lorwen, had died, and they rounded belatedly upon his son, who had inherited his offices; he was presented for continuing an enclosure, unauthorized by the forest court, made by his father in New Lodge Walk of no fewer than 150 acres, 'to the prejudice of the neighbours to the places who have right of commoning there'.[5]

1. Constable's Warrant Books; LR3.3 (August 1720).

2. Windsor Corporation Archives, Court Books JBs 3 and 4.

3. Constable's Warrant Books; *The Present State of the British Court*, 1720, pp. 55–6; and below, p. 203.

4. Thus South in his 'Account' of 1759 said the keepers of Cranborne Chase (in Windsor Forest) had 'all profits arising by the herbage and browzewood windfall tree and dead branches mastage and chiminage', as well as fuel and wood for repairs: Crest. 2.1628. For other allowances, see pp. 34, 36 n. 1. The Hannington family received £93 for killing deer by warrant, 1715–21, T1.235.

5. Regarders' presentments, Swanimote Courts of September 1725, October 1728: Verderers' Court Books, LR3.3.

With these presentments we are probably only lifting the corner of a veil. Where there was no crusty and (perhaps) honest Ranger like Sarah looking on and limiting perquisites, the lesser forest officialdom were (in her words) getting 'all they can' from the 'King's' properties. Their lordly masters were, as we shall see, showing them the way. And Baptist Nunn, zealous as he was, may have been impelled by motives not only ideological and theoretic but also of self-interest. By 1723 he had accumulated the posts of gamekeeper of Old Windsor Walk (£30 p.a.) and Deputy Steward or clerk of the forest courts (£20 p.a.). In the second post he received acknowledged fees for all business, including the provision of licences from the Justice in Eyre for felling timber, cutting coppices, etc. It had been an ancient grievance of the foresters that the officers under the Justice in Eyre charged 'inordinate fees',[1] and there is no reason to suppose that the eighteenth century opened a new dispensation; certainly Will Waterson recalled that the obtaining of licences was attended 'both with trouble and expense'.[2]

Most offensive to the foresters were licences granted, or sold, under the warrant of the Justice in Eyre to hunt all game except deer within the forest. With such warrants London sportsmen – merchants, lawyers, army officers – could bring down to the country fashionable sporting parties at weekends, when the local farmers and gentry were being presented in the forest courts for taking game on their own lands. Even Negus protested in 1717 at the number of warrants so granted;[3] and after Nunn became Deputy Steward warrants for both hunting and for the felling of timber appear to have increased. In 1725 the rebellious Regarders presented that the scarcity of game in the forest was 'chiefly owing to the number of persons that too often hunt & shoot . . . under pretences of lycences'. And whatever advantage Nunn may have gained from these transactions, we can document more definitely one additional perquisite: from 1720 onwards he received annually a special licence to take for his 'own proper use' tens of thousands of peats and turfs from Sunninghill, next to Swinley Walk. Hence this very influential official was being licensed to carry off the very turfs over which there had been conflict for decades, an expensive and inconclusive Exchequer case, and for cutting which Winkfield and Wokingham men were being presented in the courts – and this not for the King's benefit but for his own.[4]

1. Brit. Mus. Harl. MSS 1,219 (Berks Grand Jury Presentment, 1641).

2. Above, p. 51. Nunn may have been the son of Robert Nunn, under-keeper of Windsor Great Park: T1.235 (46). See p. 64 n. 3 above. His brother, John Nunn, was also a keeper; see below, p. 237.

3. Constable's Warrant Books, I, fos. 14, 19 *verso*, 22.

4. Verderers' Court Books, LR3.3. Presumably Nunn's licence, although limited to an allowance of 14,000, or 10,000, of peats and turfs, would have given him authority

The forest farmers and the forest bureaucracy faced each other as fiercely antagonistic interests. It would have been easy to have explained Berkshire Blacking by some gesture towards an (unprovable) demographic crisis, precipitating increasing demands upon the forest's resources. But there is no convincing evidence as to any such crisis, demographic, ecological or agrarian. Farmers and forest officers had rubbed along together, in a state of running conflict, for many decades and they were to continue to do so for many more. What appears as crisis was a conflict in the broadest sense political. The Hanoverian accession had withdrawn the actual presence of the monarch from the forest, thus enhancing the influence of those noblemen and officials who derived their authority from 'the Crown'. The equilibrium thus disturbed would no doubt have righted itself, after one or two stormy episodes, if Nunn and his colleagues had not succeeded in bringing to their side the very powerful aid of Townshend, Walpole and the Law Officers and army. In this sense, the 'crisis', while arising from forest conditions, was accentuated by political intrusions from outside. What was at issue was not land use but *who* used the available land: that is, power and property-right. There was room enough for all the deer and game the King and Court could use in Windsor Little and Great Parks; the Crown was not, in any serious way, interested in exploiting as a source of revenue the timber of the royal forests;[1] in the rest of the forest area there was room enough for the farmers, brick-makers, lime-burners, quarrymen and hurdle-makers and craftsmen who inhabited it. The forest officialdom, by enlarging and reviving feudal claims to forest land use – essentially claims for the priority of the deer's economy over that of the inhabitants – were using the deer as a screen behind which to advance their own interests.

The sense of grievance of one Winkfield farmer, who had lived through the episode of the Blacks, still stirs within a passage he wrote down more than thirty years afterwards. After denouncing the injustice of the forest laws he continued:

None suffer more than those that feed,[2] and, if it was in their power, would preserve the game. But if one that does neither has a licence to kill and destroy [a licence from the Justice in Eyre], and I that do both, am scarce suffer'd to

---

to have carried off very much what he liked. Nunn also handled in 1722 and 1723 substantial Treasury grants for the repair of lodges, rails etc.: LR4.3 (7) and (34). For the Winkfield turf-cutting dispute, see above, pp. 49–51.

1. This was sufficiently shown in subsequent inquiries: see below, pp. 241–5.

2. Waterson refers here to the position in forest law under which it was assumed that the inhabitants of forest villages were granted extensive rights of commoning in the forest as a compensation for the fact that the deer would feed (and had a right to feed) on their own crops.

keep a gun in my house: if a keeper or game-keeper, that wears his master's livery, may come into my grounds, break down my hedges, trample over my corn with impunity, while I that am the sufferer dare not be known to have a bird in my house, I know both how to resent and how to revenge it, which every farmer knows too, as well as I; and this is the true reason why game in all forests is so very scarce, and why, probably, some resolute people take an insufferable liberty to kill the deer, which are the King's property, and therefore on no account to be molested.[1]

The voice is that of Winkfield's schoolmaster–vicar, Will Waterson, writing in his seventies, and carried away so far that he nearly forgot the clergyman in the farmer. It is probably as near as we shall ever get to hearing the voice of a Black in his own defence.

Why did Walpole and Townshend interest themselves so much in the forest? Why did Government intrude so forcibly into this local disturbance? One part of the answer lies in the high politics (and fear of Jacobitism) of the time, and it is more convenient to discuss it later.[2] Another part may become clearer if we look at some of the offences against private proprietors committed by the Blacks.

Some of these offences, as we have noted, were committed against individuals who were also, as titular keepers or Rangers, part of the forest hierarchy. Sixteen of those indicted for hunting deer in private parks were accused of taking part in two mass attacks on Earl Cadogan's new deer-park at Cawsham (or Caversham) near Reading, just across the Thames from the forest. The park was raided by armed and mounted men on 1 January, and again in July 1722, and sixteen fallow deer were slaughtered. William Cadogan was, like Viscount Cobham (the Governor of the Castle), an outstanding military adventurer, courtier and politician; one of the true victors of Marlborough's wars, at whose conclusion he was second in command to the Duke. Honour had succeeded upon honour. His command of German and his knowledge of Hanover's politics made him a favourite of the King. In 1716 he was created Baron Cadogan of Reading, in 1718 Earl Cadogan, in 1722 (on Marlborough's death) he became in effect (but not quite in fact) Commander-in-Chief of the armed forces and he was (when the King was absent in Hanover in 1723) an influential member of the Regency Council (the Lords Justices).

Cadogan purchased an estate at Caversham, where he pulled down the old manor house and constructed his own variant of Blenheim Palace. Of an estate of just over 1,000 acres, about one half was given over to gardens, lawns, woods and the great deer-park of 240 acres. The terrace before the house extended for a quarter of a mile; avenues and vistas were planted; canals and basins stocked with fish; statuary, obelisks, urns and

1. Waterson (Ranelagh), 1.   2. Below, Chapter 9.

'vazas' valued at £3,987 were placed in the gardens; there was a pheasantry, menagerie, and quail yard. The work was completed in 1723, but must have been at its height in the previous two years. Evidence does not survive, but it is improbable that such extensive landscaping could have been carried through without evicting cottagers and without displacing farmers from customary grazing rights.

In any case, Earl Cadogan's deer-park and fishing-canals and obelisks cannot have been loved by the local inhabitants, upon whom he had suddenly descended somewhat like Gulliver's flying island of Laputa. Nor had Cadogan succeeded in endearing himself to the citizens of Reading, just across the Thames. The borough was an open constituency, with some 600 electors, which he tried but failed to bring into his pocket. The citizens clearly identified him with the Hanoverian interest: in the election of 1714–15 he failed to secure the seat, in the face of crowds demonstrating under slogans of 'No Hanover, no Cadogan', and 'No Foreign Government!' His brother Colonel Charles Cadogan won the seat in 1716 but lost it again, after a bitter conflict, in 1722. The Tory Dr Stratford wrote to Harley:

Reading has dealt the most honourably of any borough I have yet heard of. They shut their doors against Cadogan's brother and another who came with him, and declared that, though they starved, they would not be bribed this election. They sent to two neighbouring gentlemen to come, and much ado they had to prevail with them to appear, though they were to be chosen *gratis*.

In the aftermath of his family's defeat, the town teemed with Cadogan's soldiers. The navigations in his park had done nothing to improve the condition of Watry Lane, the only road between Caversham and Reading, an important market route flooded and impassable for many weeks in the year. Cadogan had promised that if the borough chose his brother, he would drain and mend the road. The electors were left to do the work by public subscription (to which the Earl contributed not one penny) and by donations of their own gravel, labour and carts. High politics had a way of being felt in the pockets of the people.[1]

Somewhere within this record of the ostentatious refashioning by an alien and unpopular adventurer – a coarse, bull-necked Irishman[2] – of the

1. Assi. 2.8 and 4.18; *Particulars of the Manor of Caversham* and *A List of the Subscribers for mending the road from Reading to Caversham*, Reading, 1724, both in Bodleian, Quarto Rawl. 526; Colin Campbell, *Vitruvius Britannicus*, III (1725), pp. 11–12; W. Wing, *Caversham Park and Manor* (cuttings in Reading Ref. Lib., RH NW 4,490); *An Account of the Riots, Tumults and other Treasonable Practices since His Majesty's Accession to the Throne*, 1715, p. 8; *Hist. MSS Comm. Portland*, *VII*, pp. 316–23; Romney Sedgwick, *History of Parliament: The House of Commons 1715–54*, 1970, entries for Reading, Cadogan; *DNB*. And plate 5.

2. Cadogan had first served as a cornet on the victorious side in the Battle of the Boyne.

customary agrarian environment we may detect reasons why Blacks descended in force, in January and July 1722, upon his park. Robert Shorter was alleged to have taken part in the attack, and it is evident that the offenders came from several forest parishes. Another attack on a private park was much more of a local affair; it is probably highly uncharacteristic of Blacking in general (indeed, it involved no one accused of being a Black) but since – alone of all these episodes – depositions and examinations survive, we must squeeze out of it what information we can. It provides, at least, evidence as to the mechanics of one deer-stealing expedition.

On 17 December 1722, when Blacking was at its height in other parts of the forest, eleven men (with the support of two 'confederates') killed a fallow deer in the park of Mrs Anne Wright of Englefield, and carried it off (breaking down the park gates to get it out). Englefield was on the western edge of the forest, well outside its boundaries. Anne Wright was a daughter (and, subsequently, heiress) of Lord Francis Powlett, the eldest son of the fifth Marquess of Winchester; she had married the Reverend Nathan Wright, second son of Sir Nathan Wright, Lord Keeper of the Great Seal, and she brought the property, with its ancient deer-park, with her. But she had a neighbour who felt that he had an ancestral claim upon the deer rather more ancient than hers.

Sir Francis Englefield was one of Queen Mary's chief courtly supporters, a Catholic and a man of vast possessions. On Elizabeth's accession he had fled abroad, been outlawed, attainted of high treason, and (in 1585) his manors and lands forfeited to the Crown and granted to Sir Francis Walsingham. But the central jewel around which his many other properties were set was the manor of Englefield, which had been in his family's possession for upwards of 780 years. Forseeing his attainder, he had taken the precaution of settling this estate upon his nephew, with a saving clause which would revoke the grant if he should tender to his nephew a gold ring. After protracted dispute in the courts, the Queen passed a special statute confirming the attainder, tendered her own gold ring to the nephew, and seized the property. But in the next reign, an Englefield (his nephew's son) remained on the edge of the manor, holding a smaller property, and the ancient fishing rights; and there this stubbornly Catholic family remained for the next two centuries, over-watching their ancestral lands.

By the time of Sir Charles Englefield, in 1723, there had been 150 years of grievance and over 900 years of ancestral right. Sir Charles appears as a backwoods baronet, loyal to the old faith, faithful (if not to his wife) to his mistress, a 'person of no reputation' called Margaret Bye, who 'hath had several bastards 4 of which were born in [his] house at

Englefield'. He amused himself by feuding at law with the usurpers of the family estate. In September 1722 Anne Wright forbade Sir Charles to set with dogs and nets within Englefield Park. At about that time John Cannon, a local blacksmith, called on Sir Charles and found him in an ill humour about Mrs Wright: he said 'he would get some good honest fellows to destroy her deer'. Cannon said he knew a few fellows of that sort, and Sir Charles said there was half a guinea waiting for such men. Cannon assembled a good party, mainly from the neighbourhood: Tilehurst, Sulhampstead, Theale and (another blacksmith) from as far away as Newbury. They had three guns (one borrowed from a carpenter), two dogs, quarter-staffs, two hangars, powder and shot. They got their deer, carried their spoil through the broken park gates, and took it to Burghfield Mill (where it was probably sold to an unknown venison dealer). Seven of them met later at an alehouse, got two shillings apiece as a share in the sale of the deer; they then went on to John Cannon's house where they drank Sir Charles's health with Sir Charles's money.

But someone was indiscreet, and John Cannon later found himself prosecuted at the Assizes. Sir Charles provided five guineas for his defence, and promised to get him a reprieve if convicted, on condition that he kept mum. Cannon, who could expect transportation and who could probably also assess the improbability of any small Catholic squire getting a reprieve out of Walpole, turned evidence. The case ends with Sir Charles under threat of prosecution at the Assizes himself, and standing forlornly amidst the ruins of his ancestral pride: 'Sir Charles,' his solicitor assured Mrs Wright, 'cannot consistent with his honour submit to write anything that may seem to . . . excuse the fact that he is so perfectly innocent of'; 'Sir Charles . . . has no ill will or spleen towards her or hers . . .' He hoped that she would accept this assurance, which was as much as she could expect from any gentleman.[1]

Those involved in the attack on Englefield Park included two black-smiths, two carpenters, a miller, a mill-wright, four labourers and two servants from a local inn. It is the sort of affair which could just as well have happened fifty years before or fifty years later; it was Sir Charles's misfortune that it should have coincided with the zenith of the Blacks. But there were a number of other offences against private proprietors, several of which it has been impossible (since there is no record of prosecutions arising from them) to include in the table of offences. First,

1. The main papers in this case (presumably originating in the Wright family papers) are in Brit. Mus. Add. MSS 28,672, esp. fos. 97, 99–110; and 28,670, fos. 73, 76. See also information of John Digger, wheelwright, 16 July 1724 in Assi. 5.45; *DNB*; A. Harrison, *Englefield* (Typescript, Reading Reference Library, BLM/D); and *VCH Berks*, III (1923), pp. 408–9.

there were several cases of attacking the heads of fish-ponds and robbing the fish (an offence which the Black Act made capital). This was clearly, like the attacks on deer, retributive in character – a way of punishing the owners. In Winkfield it would appear that the lords of the manor were making new fish-ponds, perhaps in old quarries and peat-cuttings; and perhaps these – or the ostentatious landscaped parks which were becoming the rage among the gentry – were inundating common land and obliterating valuable common-right assets.[1]

There are further fragments of evidence from Berkshire and from other counties which suggest that these raids on fish-ponds were something more than the usual poaching affairs, and involved a serious contest over customary fishing rights. In 1725 Jonas Law, a Newbury barber and weaver, was indicted at Assizes for burning the fish-house and destroying the pots of a local fisherman, who had taken the rights to 'Old Steward's Water'. Law clearly felt that right was on his side, and he threatened that if he were forced to leave the country he would see that those who were the means of it 'should not live to be 100 years old'. Over the Hampshire border the heads of Sir Anthony Sturt's fish-ponds were broken, and, in another case involving fishing rights, a Crondall offender resisted arrest, declaring, 'They have no power to grant such warrants, neither will I obey their warrant nor King George's warrant.'[2]

Second, there were a number of attacks upon properties which lay (like Englefield Park) on the fringes of the forest. In the case of the Earl of Arran's park near Bagshot we have a direct poaching confrontation. After raiding Bagshot Park, the Blacks sent a letter to the Earl declaring – 'That since his Keepers, or Servants, had shot two or three of their most valuable dogs, they would at a convenient season balance accounts with him, and leave not a stick standing in his park or house.'[3] Lord Stawell's park at Aldermaston was robbed, an 'insolent' letter left on the pales, and a man was indicted for attempting to burn his house.[4] And there were also incidents of Blacking reported in the extreme north-east corner of

1. See above, p. 53. Halsey's fish-pond, for the attack on which seven men were indicted, was in Winkfield: Assi. 2.8, James Barlow, Lent Assize, Berkshire, 1724.

2. For Jonas Law, Assi. 5.45: also Assi. 5.44 (2) for Philip Harvey of Cholsley, shoemaker, indicted for drawing and robbing the fish-pond of George Bayley. A more puzzling reference was made by a 'Mr P—d' in his London letter to provincial papers, 17 October 1723: 'This day one of the Blacks was tryed at the Old Bailey for robbing a fishpond in Middlesex of 60 brace of carp in the night, and convicted on the new Act of Parliament.' If this was true it will have been the first conviction under the Black Act, but I have found no further mention of the case: *Newcastle Weekly Courant*, 26 October 1723; *Northampton Mercury*, 21 October 1723.

3. *London Journal*, 25 May 1723; *History of Blacks*, p. 15.

4. Assi. 2.8; recognisances of Thomas Restall of Padworth, blacksmith, in Assi. 5.44; *Northampton Mercury*, 30 December 1723.

Hampshire, just south of the Berkshire border (at Bramshill, Heckfield, Mattingley, Hartley Row and Stratfield Saye) and at Dogmersfield and Crondall, close to Farnham.

So stubborn and long-continued was Blacking in this area that it may (with Farnham in Surrey) have been the place of origin of the Blacks, and the Windsor Forest men may have followed this example.[1] It was certainly the place of communication between Hampshire and Windsor men, and when the latter were broken some of the outlaws fell back towards Hampshire through this district. Thus it belongs equally to the history of both counties, although it is most convenient to discuss it here.

Our first information of this area comes from two letters from Hampshire magistrates to Sir John Cope, of Bramshill on the Hampshire–Berkshire border, who was Member of Parliament for Tavistock (and subsequently for the county of Hampshire) and was (by now) a Walpole man. One letter of October 1722 described the death in Winchester gaol of John Nellier, a carpenter of Hartley Row, held as a Black. A note referring to 'your Deer Stealing Bill' suggests that Cope was already pressing for sterner legislation in Westminster. The other, in December, from H. Foxcroft of Calcot Park near Reading, runs: 'Last week Sir Anthony Sturt got Eads the butcher of Hartley-Row arrested in an action for trespass for cutting down the heads of his fishpond & robbing of it.' Two bailiffs were sent to execute the warrant, but Eads was at once rescued by two well-known deer-stealers from Mattingley and Hartley Row, who beat one bailiff 'inhumanly' in the process. Warrants had been issued to arrest the rescuers, 'but to no purpose; if we had taken them, they would have been rescued: our commissions are of little use without the assistance of the Government. We shall soon find the deer stealers very insolent if we can't obtain a Proclamation from the King with a reward & pardon . . .'[2]

Foxcroft added that 'Mr. Pitt' was coming to town. This was presumably 'Governor' Thomas Pitt, whose many properties included

1. While Crondall may have been an epicentre of Blacking I have been unable to find out much about it. F. J. Baigent's valuable *Collection of Records and Documents relating to the Hundred and Manor of Crondall* (1891) takes the story up only into the seventeenth century; it shows a vigorous 'yeoman' community, jealous of its customary rights held under 'a perfect state of inheritance in fee symple' (customary of 1565), and asserting rights to all timber except oak and ash. Crondall was the manorial possession of the Dean and Chapter of Winchester, whose records are still held in the Cathedral; a brief inspection of these suggests that fines for renewals of tenure may have been raised in the early eighteenth century contrary to the customs claimed by the tenants; but I was unable to undertake a systematic search.

2. E. Hooker to Sir John Cope, 8 October 1722, and H. Foxcroft to do., 9 December 1722, SP35.34 (ii), fos. 94, 95a.

Swallowfield Park just over the Berkshire side of the border and just within the forest. This park was raided, and the locks of Pitt's fisheries on the River Lodden were broken. The park of his kinsman, George Pitt, at Stratfield Saye or Stratfordsea, was also 'pillaged'.[1] These raids took place in 1723, several of them after the passage of the Black Act. Meanwhile Sir John Cope's zeal against the Blacks had won their attention; they showed their resentment by committing 'waste' on his lands at Bramshill, cutting down a plantation of young oaks valued at £500. (The 'waste' may in fact have been a delayed revenge for Cope's part in imprisoning the carpenter, John Nellier, who had died in Winchester gaol.) None of the measures of repression of 1723 quietened this area, and incidents continued for several years. In March 1724 Cope received a further (and remarkable) letter, this time from Ellis St John, a magistrate at Dogmersfield. The occasion was the reprieve of one Edward Turner, a reputed Black and one of the 'Crondall gang', who had been convicted for horse-stealing at Reading Assizes:

> I hear of nothing but Turner's reprieve. . . This has much alarmed my neighbours, & the more because Richard Terry, the father of vice, declares he will not suffer death but soon return home and what can we then expect but murder or burning houses? – the former I am well assured he has been guilty of . . .

> You know Richard Terry has the name of keeping greyhounds & toyles for his men Turner and Kemp and bids defiance to our orders & contemns our authority when we summoned him to appear before us to show cause why the penalty of five pounds should not be levyed on him for killing a hare on a Sunday, not that I am against mercy when due, but this fellow is the worst of mankind . . .

> You will oblige your country if you hint this affair to Mr Walpole for if such villains shall escape with impunity what must we poor Justices do? Why, either screen them and give them venison when they please, or else lay down our arms and follow them. The report of this reprieve has had already an ill effect, for Monday night your tenant South had his stable broken and lost his horse and Tuesday night the stable at the Post House at Hartley Row had the same fate and lost five very good horses. So, Sir John, your turn is to come . . .[2]

If anything the transition from deer-poaching to horse-stealing suggests an escalation of disorder.

On the face of it, the incidents fall easily into categories which call for

---

1. *History of Blacks*, p. 20.

2. SP44.81, fos. 240–42, 396; SP35.55, fo. 60b. Turner, 'late of Crondall', was condemned for stealing a mare at Lawrence Waltham and a gelding at White Waltham, both in July 1723. A decision was postponed in his case, and there is a note by his name: 'certified for by the Judge Dormer for the Secretary's Letter [i.e. reprieve] but not granted at the Secretary's office'. But Townshend eventually ordered Turner's transportation, 2 February 1725: Assi. 2.8; 5.44 (2).

little more explanation: poaching, crime. A carpenter, a farmer, a wheel-wright, and 'Mourne who keeps The Raven at Hook' were denounced as Blacks.[1] But one cannot read the character of a historical event from a glimpse of the face. Let us attempt a closer acquaintance. Who, for example, was Richard Terry, 'the father of vice'?

It comes with a sense of shock to discover that he was none other than the outgoing lord of the manor of Dogmersfield. His family had been settled there, with the lordship, since at least 1630;[2] several members had prospered in London and brought money back to the estate;[3] from other documents it would appear that the Terrys owned extensive lands in north Hampshire and south Berkshire in the early eighteenth century, but Richard Terry had certainly become by 1722 deeply embarrassed in his finances.[4] Embarrassed or not, he can scarcely have relished being summoned to pay a £5 fine for coursing hare on a Sunday over his ancestral lands, and this by a magistrate who was an upstart and a financial bully who was buying the Terrys out of their lordship. Ellis St John was born Ellis Mews, and he had grown with the speed of a gargantuan mushroom; by his first marriage, to Frances St John, he had acquired some property and a new name; by his second, to Martha Goodyer, he acquired a great deal more of the first; and in 1723 he still had yet one more wife and more properties to make. By his second marriage he had got the lordship of two manors in Windsor Forest (Barkham and Finchampstead, West Court) as well as lands in half a dozen other parishes. So confident was he of his status that he even played law against the forest officialdom,[5] until Blacking brought him vociferously to the side of authority. In Dogmersfield his wife Martha

1. Negus's notes (16 May 1723) on Hampshire Blacks: SP35.75, fo. 30a.

2. Hants Rec. Off. 15M50/709.

3. Hants Rec. Off. 15M50/729: this document of 1693 shows a William Terry of London 'Gent.', and John Terry, citizen and goldsmith of London, sharing the lordship of the manor.

4. Court book of Dogmersfield, ibid., 15M50/712 and documents in 15M50/725 and 1,055–6 show that Richard Terry owned lands in Crookham, lands and a petty manor in Crondall, and lands in Binstead; he may also have owned lands in Hurst, Berkshire (Brit. Mus. Add. MSS 28,672, fo. 136) and elsewhere. A conveyance of 1722 shows that his lands in Crondall were mortgaged for £1,000, and that these (with lands in Binstead, Berkshire) were being conveyed, in mortgage, to one Henry Field of Odiham for £2,000.

5. Presentments at the Court of Attachment show that Baptist Nunn and Robert Hannington seized guns and nets from two men who 'pretend to be gamekeepers' under Ellis St John and another lord of the manor (13 February 1718): St John was also presented for eight acres of encroachment in Finchampstead (LR3.3). On the first matter St John commenced an action against Nunn, who was supported by the Treasury Solicitor: Cobham to Treasury, T27.22, p. 308.

Goodyer brought him much land, and some share in the lordship. He bought up additional land ruthlessly, granting and foreclosing mortgages in order to bring copyholds into his hands, and initiating an aggressive policy of emparkment and eviction of customary tenants from the commons which, continued with equal vigour by his son, was to end by turning Dogmersfield into a 'lost village'.[1] He also seems to have turned one family of customary tenants into very active Blacks in the process.[2] Somewhere between 1721 and December 1723 the Terrys disappeared as lords of the manor, and Ellis St John (at first through his wife Martha) entered into possession.[3]

With Richard Terry and Sir Charles Englefield in mind, a further hypothesis begins to take shape as to the character of the Windsor Blacks. We appear to glimpse a declining gentry and yeoman class confronted by incomers with greater command of money and of influence, and with a ruthlessness in the use of both. The source of Ellis St John's wealth was the roulette-board of death and inheritance. The Wrights of Englefield had connections with the nobility and Court; they were pursuing similar vigorous measures to those at Dogmersfield, using the means of 'enfranchising' their copyholders and thereby extinguishing their rights in the waste and commons.[4] These new seigneurial lords had discovered that ancient manorial rights, of little value in themselves, could, with the help of dexterous lawyers, be cashed in for lands, parks, money. But to do this presumed two prerequisites: first, a callous disregard of customary usages and neighbourhood opinion, and second, sources of wealth external to the local agrarian economy, sufficient to fee lawyers, to buy influence (when needed) at Court, to collect in lands and tenures, to offer mortgages, to take advantage of their neighbours' financial troubles.

Such men as Terry and Englefield may possibly have felt scruples as to

1. See G. I. Meirion-Jones, 'Dogmersfield and Hartley Mauditt: Two Deserted Villages', *Proceedings of Hants Field Club and Archaeological Society*, XXVI, Southampton, 1970, pp. 111–27. This shows that Dogmersfield had about sixty-eight dwellings in 1674, and thirty-one in 1837.

2. The Over family: see below, p. 224.

3. This summary of Ellis Mews/St John is based on W. Lyon, *Chronicles of Finchampstead*, esp. pp. 165–72 and Hants Rec. Off. 15M50, esp. items 712, 720 (Dogmersfield steward's papers), 723, 725, 1,121 and 1,141.

4. The evidence for this comes not from Englefield but from another manor of the Wrights, Stratfield Mortimer (1713). Quit-rents of copyholders of course provided no revenue, and the only means of enlarging this was through increasing periodic fines (on surrender and renewal, etc.) and if by custom these were 'fines certain' this presented legal difficulties. The Wrights were advised that all privileges belonging to the copyhold estates (including rights of common) 'will be all destroyed and determined by the infranchisement of the copyhold', thus giving the lord possession of the commons and wastes – a convenient means of enclosure: Brit. Mus. Add. MSS 28,672, fos. 213–15.

the first. As to the second, the agrarian economy of the forest and of the north-east Hampshire fringe gives the impression of being a customary rather than a market-orientated capitalist economy. Customary rentals were derisory and leasehold rentals moderate;[1] even the new interlopers do not appear, at this stage in the century, in the guise of landlord–improvers – they were intent to establish status, a substantial country seat, fish-ponds, deer-parks, vazas and obelisks. To do this they had, in the first place, to bring in money from outside. And this, perhaps, provides a common link between all those whom the Blacks selected as their antagonists.

Some brought in their wealth from finance and trade, some from place and preferment in the Court and the army. Adjoining Dogmersfield was the manor of Heckfield, whose lord of the manor, Sir Anthony Sturt, was visited in his fish-ponds by the Blacks; Sturt was the son of a London mealman and commissioner of the excise, and was himself a Court sinecurist (a Gentleman of the Privy Chamber).[2] Their neighbour at Bramshill, Sir John Cope, M.P., was the son of a director of the Bank of England, and himself a director for many years: his son, Monoux Cope, was also a Member of Parliament.[3] In the forest itself, the higher officials and titular keepers were of course, by definition, men of the Establishment. Negus, Cobham and Cadogan were very close to the Court and the Government.[4] Brigadier Philip Honeywood had distinguished himself in Whig eyes in 1710 by being deprived of his regiment for drinking 'damnation and confusion' to the Harley administration; he was rewarded with the keepership of Old Windsor Walk and £500 p.a. as a Groom of the Bedchamber.[5] Sir Robert Rich, Keeper of Bearwood Walk, for the stealing of whose 'tame' deer Edward Collier was sentenced to be transported, was another of Marlborough's officers who had incurred similar

---

1. I have made no systematic examination of the movement of rents in the first three decades of the century in Berkshire; at Finchampstead (East Court Manor) quit rents were by some means doubled between 1712 and 1722, and ordinary leaseholds substantially increased (in some cases from about 10s. to about 12s. or 15s. an acre): Lyon, op. cit., pp. 307–10.

2. J. M. Beattie, *The English Court in the Reign of George I*, Cambridge, 1967, p. 33. The aggressive Ellis St John had also had a joust at law with Sir Anthony Sturt in 1721: St John was attempting to buy out a copyholder in Sturt's manor of Heckfield and claim it as freehold: Hants Rec. Off. 15M50/1,121.

3. Sedgwick, op. cit., I, p. 151 and entries for Sir John and Monoux Cope; *DNB*. See also below, p. 205.

4. And are discussed more fully below, pp. 202–3.

5. Sedgwick, op. cit., II, p. 147; *Commons Journals*, XX, p. 534 (18 May 1725). In 1722 Honeywood was appointed to command the Royal Regiment of Horse Guards in Lord Cobham's absence: WO 26/16.

military disgrace under Anne; in the 1720s he was a sound Whig Member of Parliament and held a sinecure at the Court of the Prince of Wales.[1]

Not all the properties attacked by the Blacks were those of Whig courtiers and moneyed men. One or two were courtiers of the previous reign, deeply entrenched in properties contiguous to the forest: Lord Stawell of Aldermaston[2] and the Earl of Arran, of Bagshot Park. Arran in fact was brother to the Duke of Ormonde, now serving with the Pretender; and Arran himself (it now turns out) was the 'shadow' Jacobite Commander-in-Chief in England – a fact which throws doubt on the allegations that the Blacks were Jacobite conspirators.[3] It is much more likely that the forest farmers bitterly resented the increasing number of parks created by royal or ministerial favour, which trespassed upon their rights, and the titles to which – as Will Waterson implied – were often dubious. As they farmed their fields and carried their disputed turfs, huge areas around them changed hands as stakes in the games of politics and finance, and the palatial seats of the successful – the Earl of Ranelagh, the Dukes of St Albans – over-watched their sparse economy. Bagshot Park was a recent creation, a gift by James II to his courtier, Colonel James Graham. Graham assigned the grant to Sir Edward Seymour for £2,500 in 1699, who in turn conveyed it in 1704, for the same sum, to the Paymaster-General, the Earl of Ranelagh, whose influence at Court was adequate to secure an additional reversionary term (of three lives) after which he was able to sell the grant at a profit to the Earl of Arran.[4] Such dizzy transactions can have provoked nothing but ill will from the foresters, whether the grant originated in Whig or Tory favour.

The best illustration of the incursion of money and favour into the forest is that of 'Governor' Thomas Pitt of Swallowfield. The grandfather of William Pitt, Thomas Pitt was the case-book 'nabob'. Having made a vast fortune as an East India 'buccaneer' (that is, an 'interloper' trading outside the East India Company's monopoly), he returned to England, bought up Old Sarum, did a deal with the Company, made more money in India, became Governor of Madras, and acquired, for some £20,000, a monstrous diamond weighing 410 carats, which had been smuggled from the mines hidden in the wound in a slave's leg. Returning to England he bought extensive estates in several counties, fussed around cutting and

1. Sedgwick, op. cit.; *DNB*.

2. Lord Stawell's name appears as a supporter of the Pretender in the 'State of England, August 1721' in the Stuart Papers, Royal Archives, Windsor, SP65.16.

3. A. S. Foord, *His Majesty's Opposition*, Oxford, 1964, p. 83; Sedgwick, op. cit., I, p. 64.

4. South's 'Account', p. 143, Crest. 2.1,628.

trying to sell his diamond, quarrelled vehemently with his wife and his sons (while settling some £90,000 on the latter), found himself in financial difficulties, accepted (in 1716) the post (and salary) of Governor of Jamaica (which he never visited), and finally succeeded in selling his diamond to the Regent of France, at a clear profit of £100,000. This enabled him to retire from his onerous duties in Jamaica, to buy more estates in England, and resume his seat in Parliament for Old Sarum, where he sat as one of a group of related Whig Pitts. His surviving correspondence – mainly insults against his wife and children and anxious complaints about the cutting of his diamond – show him to be a man of formidable avarice and malice.

He bought Swallowfield in 1719, and sat more there than in most of his other seats. The experience cannot have been pleasant for those who were sat upon. Between 1720 and 1725 he was planting, ornamenting and extending the old park. A man who had beaten the 'John Company' at its own game was not likely to be bothered by the restraints of forest custom. Even the tame Regarders were forced to take notice, presenting him in 1720 for felling ten acres of coppice without licence and in 1726 (but they waited until after his death for this) presenting his successor for having enclosed without licence a park three miles around, in Bigshot Rails, which included twenty-three acres of covert and wood belonging to the forest. In making no concession to forest law the Pitts had, however, run into one difficulty. 'There must be a Grant obtained from the King for the Parks at Swallowfield,' his son Robert was informed early in 1726, 'else any body may robb the Parke of all the deer, and cannot be prosecuted.'[1] Perhaps this was why no Blacks were hanged or transported for offences at Swallowfield; but then 'Diamond' Pitt, whose offences against the forest were greater, was not hanged or transported either – not even to Jamaica.

With such predators as these prowling the forest, the Blacks appear not as aggressors but as victims. Court favour and money were transforming the great properties, which enlarged with each generation. As Fuller had remarked, and as Lysons repeated, 'the lands in Berks are very skittish, and apt to cast their owners', and both expressed a wish that these might be better settled in their seats, 'so that the sweet places in this country may not be subject to so many mutations'. 'There are but few large estates in

1. Pitt's remarkably ugly correspondence is in *Hist. MSS Comm. Fortescue (Dropmore)*, I, *13th Report, App.* Part 3 and Brit. Mus. Dropmore MSS I, 4. See also *The Diary of William Hedges*, ed. H. Yule, 1889, vol. III, and Lady Russell, 'Swallowfield and its Owners', *Berks Archaeological Society*, III (1893). Also Verderers' Court Books, LR3.3; *DNB*; Sedgwick, op. cit.; and Geoffrey Holmes, *British Politics in the Age of Anne*, 1967, pp. 280, 283, who shows Pitt's earlier evolution as a Hanoverian Tory.

Berks', a local historian added, 'which have continued for many generations in the same family.'[1] This was true, at the top. But if we look a little
lower down the social scale, we gain an impression of permanence. Few
could boast, like Sir Charles Englefield, of 900 years of family presence.
Perhaps more, like Richard Terry of Dogmersfield, were of old gentry
families in decline. But Will Waterson commented on the absence of old
gentry families in Winkfield. Those few gentlemen who lived there were
recent settlers who had come, like Robert Edwards the London ironmonger, for the hunting and the country air, and 'for the more convenient
education of their children' at Eton and at Windsor:

> Such as were gentlemen's houses . . . are since dwindled into cottages & such
> as were then cottages are now advanced to gentlemen's houses, some of whom
> (though they are not many) would pass for palaces in former days; and yet
> neither they nor their owners were known to the parish . . . sixty years ago.

On the other hand, he noticed in the parish several families of long
standing, by *names* not *estates*; such farming and yeoman families as the
Hatches (who 'time out of mind' had had 'a good interest' in the parish),
the Punters and the Clarkes.[2] All these families provided Blacks, just as
in Bray there had been Perrymans and Hawthornes occupying the same
farms as their Black descendants from at least the 1650s.[3]

We are able to bring one such man clearly out of the records. This is
Thomas Bannister, a yeoman of Finchampstead. He was not perhaps a
leading Black, but in the aftermath of the Special Commission he was
caught dropping a threatening letter from 'John King of the Blacks' at the
stable door of Thomas Taylor, a Sandhurst husbandman. It seems that
Bannister held Taylor to be an informer who had contributed to the
execution of the Winkfield men. Taylor's windows had been broken, his
hedges cut, his cattle wounded and his cart-harness slashed. Possibly
others than Bannister were involved in these acts of retribution. But
eventually Taylor's son, who was keeping watch, saw Bannister come up
before dawn and push three notes through a hole in the stable door. The
notes are barely literate, some words perhaps in dialect or cant, and they
may have suffered in the course of transcription into legal documents.
One is addressed to three men, Taylor, Courtness and Watson, and seems
to run: 'thee kild the men. John King of the Blacks. James Courtness I
cutt you Sort. Richard Taylor, Richard Watson, thee Cut im and hamm
and Quartorum. 1724.' (The end of this might perhaps mean: 'you cut

---

1. Thomas Fuller, *The History of the Worthies of England* (1662), 1811 edn, I, p. 113;
Daniel Lysons, *Magna Britannia*, 1806, I, p. 179.

2. Waterson (Ranelagh and Reading), *passim*. All these names appear in late-sixteenth-
and early-seventeenth-century surveys, etc.

3. Kerry, op. cit., p. 13.

them and hanged and quartered them'.) Another note referred to 'John King of the Blacks and King of the Devill of Hell the best of Kings of Hell', and ended with threats of 'brimm and Stonne'. When Thomas Bannister was arrested he was allowed bail, and John Bannister, of the status of 'gent.' and a Regarder, was one of his securities. The rental of the customary tenants in the manor of Finchampstead shows:

Mr. Thos Banister	for Justices	6s. od.
Do	for late Stevens	4d.
Do	for Stony Piddle	6d.
Do	for Hawks Hill & the Mead	5s. od.
Do	for the late Richard Riders	4d.

'Mr.', in this rental, indicates a gentleman or perhaps-gentleman, rather than a yeoman farmer. Bannister belonged to a most ancient local family. A Robert Banastre came to Windsor Forest with the Conqueror, an Alard Banastre was lord of the manor of Finchampstead in 1120, and the family, although losing the lordship, maintained a continuous presence in the parish. In 1723 the eldest branch of the family was probably represented by John Banister, gent., his security, whose own servant, however, was taken up as a Black. 'The junior members of each generation,' a local historian remarks, 'appear to have become small farmers, and in some instances to have declined in prosperity . . .'[1]

Much the same was true of the Hatches of Winkfield, and perhaps of the Perrymans and Hawthornes of Bray. Such families must have had a rich and tenacious tradition of memories as to rights and customs (who could fish this pond and who could cut those turfs), an age-old antagonism to forest officers and courtiers, and a sense that they, and not the rich interlopers, owned the forest. In 1723 the last years of the Commonwealth were only sixty or seventy years away; undoubtedly the republican freedom from deer and from forest law was still remembered. And scanning the presentments in the Verderers' Books in that sixty-year interval, again and again one encounters the family names of men who were accused as Blacks. The most striking case of all is in the great presentment of deer-killers which followed on the heels of the Glorious Revolution. From Winkfield there came two Punters, two Gosdens, a Clark and a John Plumridge; from other parishes came a Richard and Thomas Perryman, a William Cook, a Fellows, a Maynard and two Shorters, father and son.[2] Men with these surnames, and sometimes with

1. Lyon, op. cit., pp. 190–95, 309; Assi. 2.8; SP44.81 (12 May 1723); Verderers' Court Books, LR3.3; *VCH Berks*, III (1923), pp. 242–3; recognisance and examinations in Assi. 5.44 (2).
2. Court of Attachment, 27 December 1688, LR3.2. See above, p. 40.

these Christian names, were high on the list of accused Blacks thirty-five years later. Some must have been children, nephews or grandchildren.

These forest farmers had no money from sinecures or killings on the stocks with which to manure their lands, and they remained stationary or declining, with a traditional economy, while the new rich moved in all around. And it is possible that, immediately before Blacking broke out, there was some final turn of the economic screw. The anonymous contemporary historian of the Blacks had no doubt as to what this agency was; Blacking (he wrote) commenced 'about the times of general confusion, when the late pernicious schemes of the South Sea Company bore all things down before them, and laid waste what the industry and good husbandry of families had gather'd together'.[1] Only the most careful recovery of many local histories could establish a relationship between these two events. But the blowing and breaking of the South Sea Bubble (1720–21) might possibly explain why Richard Terry was mortgaging and selling his lands after 1721; why Anthony Meeke of Winkfield was mortgaged up to the eyes in the same year; why Ellis St John found it so easy to collect Dogmersfield tenures into his hands; why John Baber, of Sunninghill Park, was shortly to become mortgaged in his turn, and was to excuse to his landlord (St John's College, Cambridge) his own arrears of rent on the grounds that his tenants were paying badly;[2] why farmers and yeomen were so angry, and why Blacking commenced at this particular time and extended to regions whose grievances were not identical. Someone (it is always supposed) must have lost out when the bubble burst; the rich and influential who were speculating were often able to get out in time – they had agents or relatives in London in weekly communication as to the state of the exchange, like Lady Trumbull of Easthampstead Park. It was the small speculator, the petty country gentleman or substantial farmer, jealous of the gains of his wealthy neighbours, who came late into the game, without experience and without London advisers, who was most likely to lose his all. In the county election of 1727, after 'the greatest struggle', and the greatest extent of bribery, 'that ever was known in this county', Berkshire was held by the Tories; in the view of Dr Stratford the decision was influenced by hostility to the Whig 'stock jobbers [who] swarm in this part of the world', offering 'incredible sums' for votes: 'the vilest surely of men, and much more pernicious to their country than any officers civil or military.'[3]

We will leave the Windsor Blacks. Several, like William Shorter, will

---

1. *History of Blacks*, p. 2.

2. John Baber, 14 February 1725, 8 March 1725, 30 June 1726, St John's College, Cambridge, typescript calendar, drawer 109, items 186–203.

3. *Hist. MSS Comm. Portland VII*, pp. 449–50.

appear briefly again, since some of the many outlaws who were never taken moved down into Hampshire. One or two final comments are required. First, it may be noticed that we have not yet examined the high politics of the affair, and the accusations of Jacobitism levelled against Barlow, Fellows, Rackett and others. This will be discussed, together with similar accusations in Hampshire, below (pp. 164–6). It is sufficient to say here that Blacking in Berkshire can be understood without any such ulterior theme; if there was some Jacobitism about it was an additive, coming from the intensity of confrontation between foresters and Whig courtiers, but not intrinsic to the social formula. Second, an observation on method may be in place. In the analysis above, much has depended upon a complex tissue of inference, often derived from fragmentary evidence. The structure of historical explanation which I have offered depends in part upon logic, and only in part upon fact. A few identifications may be wrong, although I doubt very much whether the general identification of social composition and conflict is wrong. More identifications might be made, and much could be discovered as to the fortunes of the farming foresters, by the patient work of local historians. It seems to me possible, and even probable, that now attention has been given to the Blacks, somewhere – among some unsearched gentry or public papers – important new information may come to light. This will undoubtedly upset some of my conclusions, although the work of upsetting should be made easier by what I have done. It is the paucity of central sources – lost gentry and official forest correspondence, the loss of the hefty package of informations and examinations (including the reports of Parson Power) which the Secretary of State sent to the Attorney-General – which has made necessary the difficult, and perhaps tedious, business of constructing a collective portrait from the small brushwork of inference.

But (finally) I do not regard such inference, from sources which the quantifiers describe as 'literary', as an inferior historical occupation. If Assize records had given us a neat series of occupations these would have looked well in a table; but the partial table which they did provide (above, p. 84) turns out to have been misleading. Only the careful provision of context can test the meaning of the figures. And perhaps too good a series of figures is an inducement to laziness in the historian. In any case, the absence of ready sources has forced me to look farther afield for contiguous evidence, and this chapter of inferences and conjectures has cost me more weeks of research, and more weeks of composing into some order, than any other part of this study.

PART 2

Hampshire

4: The Hampshire Forests

There were three small royal forests in south-eastern and north-eastern Hampshire. If one crossed the coast at Portsmouth it was possible to ride through forest territory, through Bere, Woolmer and Alice Holt, to Farnham in Surrey; and from thence to Bagshot Heath and to the Forest of Windsor. On both the Sussex and the Hampshire side of the border these were ancient smuggling routes, and the Portsmouth road had become during Marlborough's wars busy with travellers, supplies, discharged seamen and men in search of work.[1]

The royal presence was weak in Hampshire: it was represented neither by a Colonel Negus nor a Baptist Nunn. Alice Holt lay south-east of Farnham, contiguous to lands of the Bishop of Winchester. It was heavily wooded, with much good oak timber, and stocked with fallow deer. To the south of Alice Holt was a belt of private property, and then the forest of Woolmer, an unwooded expanse of peatbog, fern and sandy heathland, on which some red deer ran. Together, Alice Holt and Woolmer constituted a single forest, extending to 15,493 acres, of which 6,799 acres were in private hands and 8,694 belonged to the Crown.

But the Crown obtained no profit from this acreage. The timber of Alice Holt had been extensively felled during the Commonwealth, and, although replanted again at the Restoration, little of the timber was mature enough (in the 1720s) for felling. The government of the forest had been granted by King William to General Emanuel Scroop Howe, a staunch Whig and one of the Grooms of the Bedchamber. On his death, in 1709, the office of Lieutenant of the Forest devolved upon his widow, Ruperta. She was perhaps the nearest thing to a royal presence the forest

1. There was more than one route from Portsmouth to London. One could go by West Meon, Alton, Farnham, Bagshot, Egham and Hounslow; or by Petersfield, Liphook, Guildford, Ripley, Cobham and Kingston: see T1.246 (99).

was to see in the next three decades, being the natural daughter of Prince Rupert by the actress Margaret Hughes. She was also the friend of Sarah, Duchess of Marlborough, and a woman of similar spirit and capacity for command.

Some sort of forest government, with forest courts, elected Verderers, officers of the forest and the rest, persisted in Alice Holt. It also persisted, perhaps more effectively, in the Forest of Bere, which lay farther south, in the hinterland of Portsmouth. (One consequence of this was that – as in Windsor – the magistrates were reluctant to act in matters which, they said, should be subject to forest law.) Bere Forest was well-timbered, and was some twenty-five square miles or 16,000 acres in extent; but although the whole of this was subject to the range of the King's deer, the land itself was divided into eighteen 'purlieus' or 'royalties', of which two were owned by the King, two by the Bishop of Winchester, two by the Warden of the Forest, and the remainder by several private proprietors. Thus the Crown itself owned less than 1,000 acres of the forest, and timber rights elsewhere belonged to the owners of the purlieus. The Crown also had an indefinite right to such 'vert' or herbage as was necessary to maintain the King's deer throughout the forest; but these competed with the cattle of the commoners of surrounding villages, who asserted, both here and in Alice Holt and Woolmer, unstinted grazing rights.[1]

The Warden of the Forest of Bere at this time was Richard Norton, a rich and eccentric gentleman, resident in his own mansion and park at Southwick within the forest.[2] The grandson of a Cromwellian officer, he was a staunch Whig and fervent supporter of the Revolution Settlement. At one time a keen performer in amateur theatricals, he had been alarmed to find, one night, the Devil in person on his stage. Thereafter he became morose, separated painfully from his wife (who pre-deceased him),

1. Much valuable information on the history of the forests of Alice Holt, Woolmer and Bere is to be found in the Reports of the Commissioners appointed to inquire into the State and Condition of the Woods, Forests and Land Revenues of the Crown: for Alice Holt and Woolmer, *Commons Journals*, XLV, 1790, pp. 120 *et seq.*; for Bere, ibid., XLVII, 1792, pp. 1031 *et seq.* In 1706 Norton estimated that the Crown lands in Bere amounted to only 520 acres: T1.101 (79).

2. Norton, whose seat at Southwick was on the site of the old priory, bought the Wardenship in perpetuity from the Earl of Carlisle for 2,000 guineas: he was also Constable of Porchester Castle. In 1705–7 he proposed that some part of the forest be disafforested and improved, a proposal which was overruled by the Surveyor-General for Woods on the grounds that the forest, at that time, was still providing some valuable naval timber: see papers in T1.101 (30) and (79); at the same time Norton was engaged in furious controversy with the Earl of Scarborough, whose hunting in Bere (under a previous grant of three brace of bucks a year) 'destroys our little forest, & drives all our deer to the Devil, whence they scarce ever return to us again, but are waylaid & killed...': T1.114 (61), T1.115 (2).

quarrelled with his neighbours and became a recluse, living with his steward and a few servants (whom he treated as intimates) and devising codicils to a will which is sufficiently remarkable to claim our later attention.[1] For all this, 'Crazy Norton' was regarded with affection in the countryside, and appears to have exercised his authority as Warden effectively.[2]

Agricultural improvers and local historians found little to say in favour of the forests of Woolmer and of Bere. 'Partially on royal demesnes', Mudie writes of Bere:

but much more on the private purlieus, the worthless from all parts of the country came and established themselves, constructing miserable huts in concealed places, and living in a state of the utmost misery and depravity. There was scarcely a vice of which demi-savages can be guilty which these free-booters of the forest did not perpetrate; and not a hen-roost, or even a house, within a night's journey . . . was secure against their depradations . . .[3]

Vancouver in his survey of 1813 had Bere, Woolmer and the New Forest in mind when he spoke of the 'incalculable mischief' done by the deer, and his desire to see annihilated 'that nest and conservatory of sloth, idleness and misery, which is uniformly to be witnessed in the vicinity of all commons, waste lands, and forests'. Old as he then was, the Surveyor expressed his 'earnest wish' that 'he yet may live to see the day when every species of intercommonable and forest right may . . . be abolished'.[4]

This, however, was the voice of improving market agriculture. In the early eighteenth century the twenty-five square miles of the Forest of Bere was only sparsely populated. There was no church within the forest, and only scattered hamlets and squatters' dwellings. The benefits of the forest economy, here and at Woolmer, belonged to the 'borderers', the inhabitants of the substantial and relatively prosperous villages which ringed the forest on all sides. It is difficult to recognize the voices of Mudie and Vancouver in Gilbert White's delightful and scrupulously observant account of his own border village, Selborne – a village abounding 'with poor', many of whom (however) 'are sober and industrious, and live comfortably in good stone or brick cottages, which are glazed, and have chambers above stairs: mud buildings we have none'. They enjoyed an economy of corn, hops and pasture, supplemented by

1. See below, p. 222, and Hants Rec. Off. Daly MSS, 5M50/397.

2. Norton valued the wardenship highly as a symbol of status: it was 'attended with pleasures & sports', and 'is what every body would esteem as an honour to themselves and a credit to their fortune': Norton to Godolphin, 6 March 1707(?), T1.101 (30).

3. R. Mudie, *Hampshire*, Winchester, 1838, II, pp. 157–62.

4. C. Vancouver, *General View of the Agriculture of Hants*, 1813, p. 496.

spinning, by the felling and barking of timber, the quarrying of sandstone and, of course, poaching. The forests (White noted) are 'of considerable service to neighbourhoods that verge upon them, by furnishing them with peat and turf for their firing, with fuel for the burning their lime; and with ashes for their grasses; and by maintaining their geese and their stock of young cattle at little or no expense'. And other benefits could be listed: rushes for thatching and for lighting, maidenhair fern for besoms, wood for fences, hurdles and hop-poles, fruit and vegetable gardens for the fortunate, honey, wines and remedies for the good housekeeper.[1]

Selborne bordered upon Woolmer; similar villages – Soberton, the Meons, Clanfield, Fareham – bordered upon Bere. Nor was the district devoid of industry. Petersfield and Alton, only a few miles from the forests, were thriving towns, and the latter, a woollen centre, already in the 1720s had trade union traditions. The variety of trades may be illustrated by the case of Hambledon, a large village on the northern border of Bere. Documents, which by no means constitute any kind of complete census, show the existence of the following trades: cordwainers (five), bricklayers (four), carpenters (four), blacksmiths, coopers, grocers, mercers and drapers, tailors (two of each), and a butcher, collar-maker, glazier, painter, periwig-maker, saddler, sawyer, surgeon, tallow chandler and tanner, as well as many yeomen.[2] This scarcely suggests (in the 1720s) a situation of 'sloth, idleness and misery'.

Hambledon was a Church manor, within the see of Winchester. To the west of Bere (and contiguous to it) lay another episcopal manor, Bishop's Waltham; and to the north-east of Alice Holt lay one more, Farnham. Hampshire Blacking was centred upon these two episcopal nodal points, separated from each other by some twenty-five miles of forest and downland, and it was after the former that the Waltham Hunters or Blacks were given their name. Alongside the royal forests, a belt of Church property stretched across south-east Hampshire, all within the see of Winchester. This bishopric was one of the plums of the Church; in 1713 the rent-roll amounted to some £2,500 p.a.,[3] and this was before other sources of revenue (such as timber sales, tithes, ecclesiastical fees) were considered.

1. Gilbert White, *The Natural History of Selborne* in *Works*, 1802, I, pp. 23–4, 34, 334, 338, 375 *et passim*.

2. This is no kind of census, but a list of the trades of witnesses involved in a series of disputes before Winchester Consistory Court; Hants Rec. Off. Typescript List, C/10/A, cases 50, 52 and 53 (1723–5): supplemented by a few other trades cited in returns of Catholic estates (E174, Hants) and in the Hambledon timber case of 1717 (below, p. 136), 5 Geo. I. Michaelmas, E134.

3. Thomas Cranley to Bishop Trelawny, 11 February 1713, Hants Rec. Off. B/xivb/3/2 (11).

If the royal presence was weak, the episcopal presence was contentious and ambiguous. Bishops would come and go, but the families of customary tenants might succeed each other to the same fields and perquisites for generations. If a bishop was avaricious, he had to milk his properties of all possible revenue during his lifetime, and salt the money away in some other investment; he had no personal motive for dunging the land for his successor's harvest. To defend themselves, the tenants had to assert their customs in the manorial courts, and seek to ally themselves with the bureaucracy of the see's stewardship; since several of the bishop's officers held their places by patent for life, they were not necessarily subservient to the bishop's will. At the heart of the episcopal agriculture there were opposing interests; the situation was always complex and often tense.

Whatever precipitated Blacking, the antagonism between bishop and customary tenants went back for decades. Bishop Peter Mews died late in 1706, at the age of eighty-nine; in his last years he had perhaps not been a vigorous landlord.[1] During the vacancy of the see, which lasted for some six months, the tenants, especially at Farnham, appear to have made a vigorous assault on the timber and deer, and the Archbishop of Canterbury found it necessary to intercede with Government on behalf of the latter:

> Tho' during the Vacancy of the See of Winchester the Jurisdiction is in me, yet your Lordship knows the Deer in the Park at Farnham (which they say are nigh 500 head) are none of my Flock. The late Bishop (tho' free enough of his Venison) complained frequently to me of Deer Stealers, and I was informed last night that they are beginning their Trade again . . .[2]

Mews's successor was Sir Jonathan Trelawny, who ruled the diocese with vigour from 1707 until his death in 1721. A Trelawny of Trelawne, it is difficult to know how he became a priest. Subservient to James II until the eleventh hour, he distinguished himself in the Monmouth rebellion as 'a spiritual dragoon' –

> He bravely Monmouth and his force withstood
> And made the Western land a sea of blood;
> There Joshua did his reeking heat assuage,
> On every sign-post gibbet up his rage;
> Glutted with blood, a really Christian Turk
> Scarcely outdone by Jeffreys or by Kirke . . .[3]

1. It was complained after his death, that Bishop Mews 'was entirely careless of discharging the duty of his function' and had shown 'a total neglect of discipline in the diocese': see W. W. Capes, *Scenes of Rural Life in Hampshire*, 1901, p. 271.

2. Archbishop to Lord Wharton, 3 December 1706, Lambeth Palace Gibson MS 941.13.

3. Cited in Agnes Strickland, *The Lives of the Seven Bishops*, 1866, p. 384.

He was one of the Seven Bishops whose remonstrance preceded the Glorious Revolution; but his part in this remained passive, until the issue was clearly decided, when he swiftly transferred allegiance to William. He was rewarded first with Exeter and then with Winchester, although his elevation to the latter (according to Burnet) 'gave great disgust to many, he being considerable for nothing but his birth and his (election) interest in Cornwall'.[1]

Trelawny is generally seen as a High Church Tory, surviving into a Whig dispensation. But in truth he was an ardent Hanoverian; hiding his essential timidity within a cloud of bellicose rhetoric, any hint of the Pretender's return filled him with extreme alarm. Recalling his own part in the Glorious Revolution, he feared for his own head if a Stuart returned to the throne. When Marlborough's wars ended, he wrote to Archbishop Wake: 'I have hardly had a quiet night or a cheerful day since the advance of the peace to a certain people's liking. I can't but fear the Pretender is next oars; if so, the coffin is bespoke for the Queen, for popery is always in haste to kill when they are sure of taking possession.'[2] But on the other hand he nourished fantasies of the Whigs as 'phanatigs' awaiting the moment to revive the cry of 'No Bishops!'[3] In October 1717 he acceded to his Archbishop's promptings and delivered a furious charge to his own High Church clergy in Hampshire and Surrey; he found himself beset not only with 'phanatigs' and papists,[4] but with secret Jacobite sympathizers, 'a pestilent pernicious people . . . such as take the oaths to the Government, but underhand . . . labor its subversion'. These (and among them some of his own clergy) he denounced as 'a kind of Achans, who, to preserve the shekels & garments of their Order, shame & trouble our Israel'. There followed much odious rhetorical libation on the head of the illustrious House of Hanover.[5] He retained his electoral interests in Cornwall and, in 1720, explained to Archbishop Wake that he must change the time of the usual ordination Sunday since the elections of mayors in his home county clashed with the Church calendar, and he must post down to wait on and compliment the corporations:

1. Strickland, op. cit., p. 388; *DNB*. For Trelawny's substantial electoral interest and his shift from High Tory interests towards Whig dependency, see Geoffrey Holmes, *British Politics in the Age of Anne*, 1967, pp. 258, 323.

2. Archbishop William Wake's papers, Christ Church, Oxford: Trelawny to Wake, 3 March 1713, Arch. W. Epist. 17; and N. Sykes, *W. Wake, Archbishop of Canterbury*, Cambridge, 1957, II, p. 96.

3. Sykes, op. cit., II, p. 117.

4. For Trelawny's surveillance of Catholics, see Arch. W. Epist. 21, Trelawny to Wake, 28 April 1720; and Cranley to Trelawny, 14 April 1713, Hants Rec. Off. B/xivb/3/2 (13).

5. Arch. W. Parl. 7, Trelawny to Wake, October 1717.

I ask farther leave to prevent jealousies & unjust reflections, that if your Grace hears I visit some known or suspected Tories, you would not fear them converting me, but believe I am endeavouring to convert them. The persons under that character in the West are men of quality, & more sour'd against the Government by ill usage than any rancorous principle & I own to your Grace very freely that should the Ministers treat me with a high hand & brand of treason, I would do you all the despite and mischief I could though I resolved to cut the Pretender's throat the first moment I could come at him. Gentlemen may be won, but can't be frightened.[1]

They could also, it seems, cover their rear, with careful private apologies for their public actions.

Trelawny did not have an opportunity to cut the Pretender's throat. He did, however, have the opportunity, for fifteen years, to disturb the Church's relations with the customary tenants in his diocese. When he took office, in June 1707, he brought with him a most vigorous Steward, Dr Heron (or Herne), who had been in and out of his service for more than twenty years. Heron rode ceaselessly around the woods and lands of the bishopric, imposed his domineering presence at the various manorial courts, ransacked old deeds and tables of fees, and succeeded in treading on the corns of episcopal officers and tenants alike. He uncovered what were (in his view) atrocious goings-on; timber of the copyhold farms was wasted, farms were undervalued, officers of the courts were taking unwarranted fees. What Heron was uncovering might of course be viewed in another way. In Bishop Mews's senescence, the farmers and foresters of the bishopric had discovered that they could live very well without a bishop. The officers of the bishopric (mainly country attorneys and their clerks, with one or two small gentry and clergy) had also found ways of making themselves comfortable, taking a sufficiency of fees for themselves, allowing customary perquisites to enlarge (both for themselves and for the tenants), and winking at certain offences.

But these officers, who included the Woodward and his deputies, stewards of the lesser courts, the Clerk of the Lands, the Clerk of the Bailiwick, several bailiffs, etc., could not be disregarded so easily. Robert Kerby, the Woodward, was perhaps the most powerful among the bishopric's bureaucracy, holding his office for life, by patent, with perquisites enforceable at law (and with some five other lesser patent offices accumulated in his hands). He could not be dismissed by Trelawny, and was perhaps disappointed at not himself being chosen as the lord's Steward. In any case, after fifteen months of such provocations, Kerby made himself spokesman of the lesser officers and of the tenants in drawing

1. Arch. W. Epist. 21, Trelawny to Wake, 9 September 1720.

up a series of accusations against Heron, which survive, together with the Steward's replies.[1]

It is an extraordinary miscellany of complaint. Heron had clearly offended the entire bureaucracy, as well as the clergy and gentry with whom they associated. Some of the accusations are highly personal. He chose scandalous and ill-famed servants, making them his informers; he spread false stories about the Bishop's established officers; he was 'a very haughty imperious mann and of a rigid temper', used 'base and un-mannerly expressions' to the tenants, 'is a person that sweares and dams your Lordshipp's servants, officers and tenants',[2] is 'a frequent sabbath breaker' who spent his Sundays in searching records, 'is by fame a necessitous man and lives separate from his wife, and is very vicious', and (when invited to stay at Kerby's house) 'he behaved himself soe to his maid servant, by useing such violent temptations to her by way of de-bauchery, that she would not goe into his chamber . . .'[3]

A related group of accusations concerned his slighting of the existing officials: 'by his pride he's above advice of the antient officers of your Lordshipp's Bishoppricke who know the customes thereof.' He had threatened Wither, the Steward of the Land (a patent officer) with the forfeit of his office; he had refused to Wither's groom a customary allowance, and told Wither in public court that, if he did not like it, he could carry his portmanteau himself: 'What is your man to my Lord? Is my Lord to find him in pocket money?' He had told Kerby much the same. The affront was the worse, since these officers 'are gentlemen . . . and better men than Mr. Herne were he out of yr Lordshipp's service'.[4] He had defrauded the officers of their allowances for entertainment at manorial courts, and had usurped their functions (and their fees). 'Mr. Herne's intent is to breake them all, that he may be sole officer to your Lordship, and then he might be at liberty to make such accounts as he pleased, and not be detected . . .' Heron's reply to these articles was

1. Unless otherwise stated, material in the two paragraphs above, and in succeeding paragraphs, is drawn from the 'Articles against Heron' and 'Heron's Replies' in Hants Rec. Off. Eccles. II 415809 E/B12.

2. Heron's reply: 'Tis possible, I may at some time, within this year & a half, amidst the many oppositions I have met with, have bin provoked, but very rarely . . .' This accusation was not, in any case, likely to have bothered his master very much, since he was himself notorious for the same offence. Rebuked for it once by a fellow clergyman, as unbecoming in a bishop, he replied: 'I don't swear as a bishop. When I swear it is as Sir Jonathan Trelawny, a country gentleman and a baronet.' Strickland, op. cit., p. 389.

3. Heron's reply: 'I am so very innocent, that I cannot recollect what manner of person she is; tis possible I might offer to kisse her, it is an innocent liberty I have often taken, carelessly & without design . . .'

4. Heron's reply: 'Tis no new thing for country attorneys to ride with wallets, & tis to be supposed *these gentlemen* have done it before now.'

uniform: first, he was following Trelawny's prior instructions ('your Lordship can best answer, from whom I received my Orders'); second: 'Where I perceived either Officers or tenants negligent or incroaching, I assert yr Lordship's right & doe my duty . . . but where a man sets himself zealously to restore lost rights to the Bishoprick, after soe many years neglect, & discontinuance, it is impossible to preserve the good opinion of all.'

This was his case. Nevertheless, much custom remained unwritten, and could not be established simply by poring over old records on the Sabbath Day. A further group of accusations related to exactly this breach of custom. Some matters were trivial, some personal,[1] but taken together they added up to a formidable volume of grievance and psychic injury. Characteristic of the complaints is Article 19:

He breaks old customes and usages, in minute and small matters, which are of small value to your Lordshipp . . . he has denied to allow five shillinges att Waltham to the Jury att the Court, and two shillings and six att Droxford, to drinke your Lordshipp's health, a custome that has been used time out of mind, that he has denied your Lordshipp's Steward and Officers a small perquisite of haveing theire horses shoo'd att Waltham according to an antient usage which never exceeded above six or seaven shillinges, that he denied your Lordshipp's tenants timber for the repaire of severall bridges and common pounds where itt hath of right beene antiently allowed . . .

To this Heron replied:

I own, I affect sometimes to intermit those minute customs as he calls them, because I observe that your predecessors' favours are prescribed for against your Lordship & insisted on as rights, & then your Lordship is not thanked for them. Besides tho' they are minute, yet many minute expenses in a month's progress half-yearly amount to a sume at the end. As for the instance of shooing the horses at Waltham, that usage, as he calls it, was so far abused that even the woman who is Underkeeper of the Chase (& none of our fellow travellers) pre-scribed to have a set of shooes paid for, tho' she did not want them & I cannot conceive why Waltham should bee the place of rendezvous for shooing the Officer's horses round. . . What I doe with relation to allowances for timber, for repairs of bridges and pounds, your Lordship can answer for mee.

Against the cold breath of this economic rationalization, the flimsy protections of paternalist relations between Bishop and tenants could stand up no longer. The two critical points of conflict, which were to persist long after Heron's stewardship, were those of the terms of customary

1. Thus (Article 21) Heron had turned one James Robinson out of his place at Wolvesey Palace, after thirty years' service, to make room for one of his own favourites. Heron's reply: 'James Robinson was an old Mumper at Wolvesey in the last Bishop's time, and prescribed to be Butler . . . but having no occasion for him I dismissed him.'

tenure (and fines), and of rights to timber. Even Heron admitted that tenants on episcopal lands had unusual security of tenure: 'they have an interest in their estates almost as good as inheritance, because your Lordships the Bishops will always renew upon the known reasonable terms, & cannot grant a reversion over, as a lay Lord may . . .' The tenants at Farnham, rehearsing their customs in 1707, claimed to have the security of socagers, with absolute security of heritable tenure.[1] If the bishop wished to increase his rental, his steward had to have recourse either to raising fines upon death and renewals, or to breaking the old tenures (through actions for forfeit, for waste, debt, etc.) and re-leasing the land upon improving capitalist tenures.

Heron, and his successor Edward Forbes, had recourse to both means. In the bishop's manors, customary leases were normally for three lives (often renewed long before their expiry), with a 'reasonable' fine upon each renewal, and a herriot (or fine, of 'the best living good' such as a horse or cow) upon each death. Fines were being pressed upwards,[2] and Heron was accused of seizing herriots 'where none were due' on the death-bed of a tenant, with unseemly haste. Indeed, he presents a somewhat mean picture of episcopal zeal, riding post-haste to the death-bed, where 'the widow scrupled to show me her copyes', riding back to consult his books at Wolvesey, cantering back again to seize the five best beasts

---

1. 'The tenants of this manor are not meere tenants by court roule for then had they noe better estate (at the Common Law) than at the will of the Lord and soe might the Lord putt them out at his will . . . But the tenure of this manor is rather after the manner of sottage tenure . . .': Farnham Custom Roll, 1707, Winchester Cathedral Library.

2. Abundant materials exist in the Hampshire Record Office and the Cathedral Library, Winchester, from which the finances of the bishopric could be reconstructed. I have followed these only so far as they seemed relevant to my immediate inquiry. A cursory inspection suggests that customary rents remained stationary from the early eighteenth century to the 1730s. There was pressure to move up fines on deaths and renewals, but this was sometimes successfully resisted: at Farnham the homage presented that the fine on renewal could not be raised arbitrarily but was a 'fine certain' (of two years' rent): the Bishop's stewards (like lay stewards) were trying to break this custom, and calculated fines on the basis of 'improved' rents, or economic valuations. Leasehold rentals (and some tithes) were clearly being pressed upwards, sometimes by as much as 50 per cent. Receiver's Accounts, Winton Diocese, Hants Rec. Off. Trelawny MSS, I, Mis. 1; Dean and Chapter Records, Winchester Cathedral, Receptor's Books and Customs of Crondall (fine certain); Farnham Court presentments, 15 March 1709, Hants Rec. Off. 159,590 (fine certain – protested against by steward); W. Hearst to Trelawny, n.d. (1711?) protesting at increase of rent of South Farm, East Meon from £40 to £60: Hants Rec. Off. B/xivb/3/2 (10) and Receiver's Accounts show other Meon increases, 1703–11; and (for economic valuations and the ill will these caused) see Kerby to Trelawny, 19 October 1708, Hants Rec. Off. B/xivb/3/2 (35) and 'Articles against Heron'.

(compounded for at £20).[1] The patent officers took the widow's side, and: 'Afterwards at Waltham Court, without any previous notice, the son of the widow was brought into the room where we dined (with some clergymen and strangers of Mr. Kerby's acquaintance, all unknown to me) to challenge me publickly for this unjust seizure.'

The breaking of old tenures was probably pressed forward most vigorously at Farnham, the administrative heart of the bishopric.[2] Here actions were commenced for waste of timber which led to the forfeit of copyholds to the lord. The tenants at Farnham were acutely disturbed. They presented among their 'customs' that –

> Every new Lord brings in a new procurator, who for private gain racketh the custome and oftentime breaketh it, soe shifting that sometimes they have put the Steward [to the Farnham Court] out of his place, and sate themselves (which ought not to be) it being all one as if the Lord sat himselfe . . . for his owne profitt. Whereas a Steward who knoweth the customes ought to be judge, and not such procurators, seeing the Custome of the Mannor hath allways been that there was at all times a Man of Worship, faithful, honest, and true chosen (of the country) to doe justice and equity between the Lord and tenants . . .[3]

The proceedings at Farnham Court became bitter. When the nineteen jurors were required by the Steward to present seven further tenants as having forfeited their estates for cutting oak and elm on their copyholds without licence, 'they severally refused', and were amerced twenty shillings each by the Steward for this refusal. At the next Court a juror was fined 'for giving sawcy language to the Court'; there were disputes about cattle rescued from the pound, where they had been sent for trespassing in the lanes, and seven more jurors were fined for refusing to present the offenders. At the next Court the jury presented that, by their customs, no tenant could forfeit his estate except for felony or treason. Heron (himself now under a cloud) continued to urge Trelawny to press 'the business of the copyholders to a conclusion, & particularly to order executions against those who have forfeited since the fines'.[4]

1. Article 12 and Reply. Heron congratulated himself on having forestalled the servants of Lady Russell, who also sent to the same house for herriots due on an estate leased from her: had her men arrived first 'she would certainly have seized the best as we did, & then instead of Cattle compounded for £20 your Lordship must have taken so many sheep or pigs not worth 50s.'.

2. The diocese took in Surrey, Hampshire, the Isle of Wight and the Channel Islands. Trelawny commuted between Wolvesey Palace in Winchester, his Palace in Farnham, Chelsea Palace and his seat in Trelawne. The old Palace in Bishop's Waltham was ruined in the 1640s.

3. Farnham Custom Roll, 1707, Winchester Cathedral Library. This item was protested against by the Steward.

4. Farnham Court Presentments, 30 March 1708, 14 September 1708, 15 March

While the two dioceses referred to cannot be identified with certainty, there is little doubt that the comment of a contemporary pamphleteer is relevant to the general pressures within the Winchester bishopric:

> In this diocese and another . . . indefatigable pains are taken, and devices and pretexts hitherto unheard of, are used to levy money on tenants of Church and College lands. We are visited not for our manners, but our manors. Inquisitions and surveys are taken everywhere with the utmost rigour; valuations at pleasure are imposed upon our estates, and laid down as the measure and rule for renewals and fines. . . Attempts are made to break through and lay aside the customary tenure for three lives, and to convert the whole of these estates into leases for twenty-one years . . . that they are not compellable to renew with their lessees at the expiration of any life or term.[1]

The other critical issue was that of timber rights. All timber was in demand for building, and there had been a particular stimulus to shipbuilding in Hampshire during the 1690s which had increased the value of good oak timber.[2] The Bishop and his Steward looked to timber for a ready source of increased revenue. But two other interests were involved: not only the tenants, but also the interest of the Woodward, Robert Kerby. For the tenants, once again Farnham led the way: they presented that 'all woods and underwoods & tymber growing upon their tenements holden by fine . . . are their own . . . by payment of a certain wood rent'.[3] During the brief vacancy of the see they undoubtedly fell with vigour on timber. Farnham was an important and expanding centre of hop-growing,[4] and this required hop-poles – substantial posts of up to twenty-five feet

---

1709; Hants Rec. Off. 159,590. Heron to Trelawny, 13 December 1708: Hants Rec. Off. B/xivb/3/2.

1. 'Everard Fleetwood' [Burroughs S.], *An Enquiry into the Customary-Estates and Tenant-Rights of those who hold Lands of Church and other Foundations &c.*, 1731, p. 4. For the tenures of Church and College lands see also my paper in the proceedings of the Past and Present Conference for 1974 on *Inheritance and the Family*, ed. Jack Goody (forthcoming), and for the history of conflict over tenures see Christopher Hill, *Economic Problems of the Church*, Oxford, 1956, esp. chs. 1, 2 and 14.

2. See A. J. Holland, *Ships of British Oak: The Rise and Decline of Wooden Shipbuilding in Hampshire*, Newton Abbot, 1971, esp. chs. 2 and 5 (Holland notes that Richard Norton profited considerably from the sale of timber to the navy from his Southwick estates). For timber generally see also A. L. Cross, *Eighteenth Century Documents relating to the Royal Forests, the Sheriffs and Smuggling*, New York, 1928, and R. G. Albion, *Forests and Sea Power*, 1926.

3. Farnham Court Presentments, 15 March 1709: Hants Rec. Off. 159,590. The Steward protested against this claim. A similar claim was made by the tenants in the Farnham Customs Roll, 1707.

4. In 1670 there were 300 acres under hops at Farnham: R. N. Milford, *Farnham and its Borough*, 1859, p. 100. In 1724 there were 736 acres under hops in Surrey, much of which must have been in the Farnham district: returns in T1.271 (23).

in height and an eight-inch girth at the top.[1] In the view of a well-informed officer some Farnham tenants wished to be 'ridd of their timber and make room for the growth of hop poles instead of good oak, elm and ash'.[2]

A case was tried at Surrey Assizes, and decided against the tenants: they could not cut timber (unless for necessary repairs on their own lands) without licence.[3] But ambiguities remained (as well as ill feelings): what was 'timber'? What constituted 'repairs'? There was also the question of the licence, which was to be granted not by the lord's Steward but by Kerby, the Woodward. Upon each licence, the Woodward took a fee in bark and 'lops and tops'; Kerby claimed that this was not less than one third of the value of the timber, but Heron claimed that the deductions were 'unreasonable', as they amounted to two thirds – the loss sustained by the Bishop through the waste of his tenants was nothing to the loss sustained through the perquisites of the Woodward: 'the loyns of the tenants are not so heavy as his little finger.' Kerby, a patent officer, proved to be immovable.[4] To circumvent him the Bishop and his Stewards attempted to dispossess him of his functions. They tried to win the tenants to their side by permitting them to cut timber (but not oak or beech) upon their own lands, if strictly for their own repairs, without licence of the Woodward; no other cutting of any kind was permitted, either on their own lands or on the commons. Heron argued that the waste throughout the bishopric had already been taken so far that the tenants would perforce exercise the greatest care to nourish what was

1. See Edward Lisle, of Crux-Easton in Hampshire, *Observations in Husbandry*, 1757, p. 209. Lisle said that ash or withy was most suitable. But if deer cropped ash saplings they grew up bent and unusable for poles: see *The Letters of Daniel Eaton*, ed. J. Wake and D. C. Webster, Northamptonshire Record Society, 1971, p. 20.

2. E. Forbes to Trelawny, 7 April 1708; Hants Rec. Off. B/xivb/3/2 (48). Forbes himself was a substantial hop farmer (information from Mrs E. Manning of Farnham Museum Society).

3. The action was taken by two tenants, George and John Mills, who, it was alleged, had cut 239 trees, to the value of £400. The Mills appear to have been evicted from their tenancy, and left to pay the cost of the unsuccessful action. Petition of John and George Mills, and E. Forbes to Trelawny, 7 April 1708, both in Hants Rec. Off. B/xivb/3/2. But they were very probably readmitted to their tenures on payment of substantial indemnity, since the family endured and prospered as hop-farmers near Farnham (information from Mrs Elfrida Manning of Farnham Museum Society).

4. The failure to revoke, or buy in, Kerby's patent is referred to in Heron to Trelawny, 13 December 1708, and Thomas Cranley to Trelawny, 30 June 1713, ibid. The extreme difficulty of removing an officer who held his office for life (or lives) by patent, virtually as private property, is illustrated by the case of the Chapter-clerk at Bristol, described as 'a very lewd person, and having many bastards fathered upon him, and supposed to have two wives', in whose patent the lawyers could find no flaw, although they had attempted to do so through three years of unsuccessful trials: R. Boothe to Archbishop Wake, Bristol, 25 March 1721, Arch. W. Epist. 22.

left for their 'necessary occasions'; their tenure was secure, and 'it is absurd to imagine they would commit wast upon an estate which they propose should continue in their familyes for ever', 'because they know when all is gone your Lordship is not obliged to furnishe them from elsewhere, and they must be forced to buy (for the new-invented clause introduced in some leases, to furnish them out of the Chases in the case of deficiency, will not bind your Lordship)'. This policy had the added advantage that it would reduce the Woodward's business 'to a very narrow compasse – to look after the Chases & Woods in your Lordship's hands, & those few farms on which any quantity of timber happens to be remaining . . .'[1] To this policy a little guile could be added: the Bishop could conceal his own felling from the Woodward, and lay obstacles in the way of his asserting his perquisites.[2]

Heron did not himself remain in office to pursue these policies, being dismissed as Steward at some time between 1709 and 1713. His dismissal (it seems) did not arise from Kerby's 'articles' against him, but from two different offences: he had failed to gather in a sufficiently impressive rent-roll, and he had, through some negligence, failed to knock down the bills of the building tradesmen renovating the Bishop's Palace at Chelsea, and had occasioned a successful suit against the Bishop for debt. Heron's manner of exit from the scene is irrelevant to our theme, but provides a nice vignette as to the operation of the law. As to the matter of the unpaid bills (he wrote), if the Lord Treasurer did not sit on the Writs of Error the following Tuesday, then His Lordship would be safe for another six months. But if he did, then judgement would be affirmed, and the Bishop would then either be at the expense of Writs of Error in Parliament or have to pay the money in four days. The tradesmen, he was sure, could be broken: he had managed to persuade the painter and the glazier to settle at a 20 per cent discount, a saving of £50. But the others were holding out. Two recourses suggested themselves (although 'the misfortune I have of lying so long under your Lordship's displeasure upon this account makes me very fearful of offering my thoughts'). First, 'if your Lordship had any interest with Sir Christopher Wren or knew any body that had, you might certainly bring the tradesmen to comply, because he has an absolute command over Mr. Jackson, who is the great Incendiary . . .' Second, all turned on whether the Lord Treasurer would in fact sit in court on Tuesday: 'It is possible he may not sit, & if your Lordship should think

1. 'Articles against Heron': Article 24 and Reply.
2. Thus T. Cranley to Trelawny, 30 June 1713: '. . . as to pollards, I find Mr. Kerby hath had some knowledge or suggestion at some are to be cutt without him, & declared he will assert the right he pretends to s Woodward, which I fear will make people scrupulous in buying . . .': Hants Rec. Off. B/xivb/3/2.

proper to write to him . . . to be sure he would not, especially if Your Lordship tells him of the consequences, & that it would end in a Complyance.' Heron had (of course) the necessary money to meet the bills in his hands. The difficulty lay in the Bishop's scruples: he did not like to pay bills in full.[1]

Heron perhaps survived in the Bishop's service for a little longer. He disappears in the Bishop's records in 1712, arrested by a copyholder in a suit against him for the wrongful seizure of herriots. When the bailiffs arrived to apprehend him they 'found him delirious'.[2] That his exit did not signal any change in episcopal policies was indicated by the choice of Edward Forbes as his successor. Forbes, who was the Steward of the Farnham court, had been the officer most responsible for pressing the case against the Farnham copyholders. He was also their antagonist in another, and important, respect. In 1709–10 the Bishop had piloted through the House of Lords a bill authorizing the enclosure of Ropley Common (one of his Hampshire manors) to which was quietly tacked on authority to 'improve' Farnham Old Park. Some part of this ancient park had been disparked after the Restoration by Bishop Morley, and leased out in farms in order to repair his revenues. But some 500 acres (out of 1,000) it seems remained, over which the customary tenants claimed certain common rights. Some part of the tenants at Ropley petitioned the House of Commons fruitlessly against the bill, and, when it had passed, some of them petitioned again, against the Commissioners of Enclosure, claiming that these were partial, that some who 'always had right of common have no part allotted', while others had only half of their due.[3]

What took place at Farnham is less clear. But it is evident that the 'improvement', which took several years to complete, extinguished what remained of common rights in the Old Park. One could hazard that there may have been some ancient agreement with one of Bishop Trelawny's predecessors, under which the latter had been permitted to empark some land for his private use at the price of ceding all rights in other lands to his tenants.[4] If this had been so, they will have felt the enclosure to have been a cheat. The beneficiary of this improvement was none other than Edward Forbes, the incoming Steward to the Bishop, who rented the

1. Heron to Trelawny, 6 November 1708, ibid.

2. T. Cranley to Trelawny, 6 May 1712. Hants Rec. Off. Trelawny MSS, I misc. 12.

3. *Commons Journals*, XVI, 1709, pp. 381, 476, 509; *Lords Journals*, XIX, 1709, p. 50. The Ropley enclosure was still uncompleted in 1712: Cranley to Trelawny, 18 May 1712, Hants Rec. Off. Trelawny MSS, I misc. 12.

4. The Farnham Customs Roll of 1707 claimed that 'pastures in wastes appertains only to the tenants of the manor and the Lord ought not, nor useth not, common with the said tenants with no manner of cattell in any parts of the said manor . . .'; but it is not clear how far this claim extended to the parks.

entire park at the low sum of £70 p.a.[1] The attacks on deer in the
Bishop's other park (Little or New Park) appear to have become more
frequent at the moment when the Old Park was enclosed.

The common rights in dispute here probably included grazing, and
access to clay, marl, chalk, earth, stones, peat, turf and heath[2] There may
well have been divisions of interest here and at Ropley between the larger
farmers (who had some share or compensation in enclosure) and the
lesser inhabitants who could produce no legal title to prove their usages.[3]
But what was happening at Farnham sent a ripple of alarm throughout
the Bishop's other manors – an alarm which extended into forest areas
and into the manors of lay proprietors, some of whom held ancient
episcopal land governed by similar customs.[4] If the tenants' right to cut
timber on their own farms remained ambiguous (limited to wood for
repairs) and brought them under menace of forfeit, and if in any case this
timber was scarce, it was inevitable that they should assert more stubbornly
customary rights (or claims) over the common land and chases. Wood
was required for a hundred purposes; for barns, for hop-poles and
hurdles, for thick fences to keep out the infernal deer, which 'often get
into the meadows and corn fields, and do great mischief to the farmers, it
being almost impossible to keep them out after they have tasted the corn,
particularly wheat, in which they lie very much during the winter, and
also after the corn is in ear.'[5]

The concern for wood rights reappears in the presentments of the

1. Hants Rec. Off. 153,199, 14/15. Forbes's widow, Sarah, renewed the tenure (at the
same rental) from 1734 to 1768.
2. As presented in the Farnham Customs Roll of 1707 (and objected against by the
Steward).
3. At Ropley the tenants were clearly divided as to the benefits of enclosure: petition
and counter-petition in *Commons Journals*, XVI, pp. 476, 509. At Farnham the customs
emphasized at every point the favoured status of the customary tenants, and made no
reference to the inhabitants. Perhaps the freeholders and substantial tenants, in a period
when the Bishop was enlarging his claims, saw the benefit of an enclosure which gave
them freehold in their own. Cranley reported to Trelawny that the tenants at East Meon
had met to consider enclosing their common fields, 'and part of East Meon Park was
about to be burnt & broken up': 18 May 1712, Hants Rec. Off. Trelawny MSS, I misc.
12. At another episcopal manor, Woodhay, it was reported that the 'inhabitants' were
eager for enclosure: but these 'inhabitants' did not include the 'poor' – 'in consideration
of the damage that the poor . . . might receive thereby, 'twas agreed that a workhouse for
the benefit of the poor should be set up at the parish charge . . .' This solution was the
inspiration of the minister of the parish: memorial of John Osborne, 21 May 1725, Hants
Rec. Off. B/xivb/3/2.
4. See especially the interesting tract of Matthew Imber, *The Case, or an Abstract of
the Custom of the Manor of Merdon in the Parish of Hursley*, 1707.
5. *Commons Journals*, XLVII, 1792, pp. 1043–5.

juries at most of the Bishop's manors.[1] At Bishop's Waltham it was presented that all timber was the tenants' ('as part of our inheritance ... as formerly hath been by our forfathers time out of mind'); the claim was made in 1707, protested against by the Steward, reasserted several times, and then reiterated twice a year from 1713 until at least 1724. In 1709 the tenants threatened to try an action against the Bishop for denying to them customary timber to repair bridges and the pound. In 1710 there was added (against the Steward's protest) a claim to all 'the understuff and earbridge [herbage]' on Burseldon Common; in 1724 there was added (for the first time) a claim to the bushes and herbage of Wintershill Common, Srowd Wood and Waltham Chase.[2] The status of this Chase is unclear, but Bishop's Waltham shared one feature with Farnham: in both manors the large episcopal parks had been, at the Restoration, disparked and leased out as very substantial farms. Perhaps the Bishop had compensated for the loss of his Waltham park by stocking the Chase with more deer, to the deprivation of the ill-defined rights of the commoners.[3]

Thus across this belt of intermixed forest and Church land, stretching from Farnham to Bishop's Waltham, there were common anxieties about tenure and timber, kept alive by successive disputes and actions at law, and knitting together the tenantry in a common opposition to the Bishop and the forest officials. Not every case went against the tenants. In 1713 occupiers in Alice Holt won an important case, which in effect permitted them to cut bushes throughout the forest at will, on the grounds that this was essential to strengthen the hedges protecting their holdings against the deer. The case showed abundance of ill will between the borderers of the forest and the keepers. The former deposed that the keepers were selling timber on their own account, and that they were enclosing tracts of forest around their own lodges, fencing out the deer and thereby driving them to pasture on the borderers' crops. A yeoman from Kingsley, on the southern edge of the Holt, claimed that the keepers and their servants often rode over his standing corn; after harvest they threw down his

1. e.g. Bishop Stoke, Droxford (26 September 1715, 5 September 1720, etc.), Hambledon (19 March 1714, 24 March 1721): Hants Rec. Off. 159,657; 159,566; 159,613; and Customs of the Dean and Chapter manor of Crondall (Winchester Cathedral Library), VII: all customary tenants can 'fell carry away all manner of woods coppices hedgerows' etc. on their own lands (oak and ash for timber excepted): but in Crondall in 1718–19 one tenant was fined £3 'for cutting trees without licence': Winchester Cathedral Library, Receptor's Books.

2. Bishop's Waltham Court Presentments, Hants Rec. Off. 159,641–2. The Bishop's Steward did not protest at the claim to Waltham Chase on the first occasion when it was presented, but did protest in 1726. See also Frank H. Sargeant, *The Story of Bishop's Waltham*, Bishop's Waltham, 1961, p. 48.

3. As was to be suggested by 'King John', below, p. 146.

gates and broke down his fences, 'pretending to come a setting of partridges'. He had grown so 'weary' that he had thrown up his tenancy. Hammond, the victor of this law-suit, threatened to throw down the keepers' enclosures, saying that 'the forest was his common' and he had 'won it by Law'.[1]

In 1717 it was the turn of the Bishop to lose a case, relating to timber rights on tenants' lands in Hambledon. The cause, which was first tried at Winchester Assizes, turned upon whether beech was timber or not: if it was 'timber', it belonged to the Bishop, if 'wood', the tenants of Hambledon could cut it. Despite the Bishop's efforts to secure testimony in his favour from the naval shipyards,[2] the jury found that beech was *not* timber: 'the gentlemen who were nominated for the jury' (Forbes explained), 'not all attending, their places were taken by the tales men.'[3] The Bishop removed the case to the Court of Exchequer, but, once again, judgement went to the defendants.[4]

Even when victorious, such cases occasioned great anxiety and heavy costs to the defendants. The poorer farmers and foresters had their own forms of direct action for asserting their claims. 'It is very observable,' Charles Withers, the Surveyor-General of Woods reported in 1729,

that the country people everywhere think they have a sort of right to the wood & timber in the forests, and whether the notion may have been delivered down to them by tradition, from the times these forests were declared to be such by the Crown, when there were great struggles and contests about them, he is not able to determine. But it is certain they carefully conceal the spoils committed by each other, and are always jealous of everything that is done under the authority of the Crown . . .

If any timber was to be felled, no matter how formal the royal warrant, in the presence of the forest officials, at the wood sales 'many country people attend also officiously, out of this principle of jealousy, and express their uneasiness that any timber is sold from them'.[5] And they went beyond uneasiness: in Alice Holt, whenever timber was felled, the villagers of forest and contiguous villages, notably Frensham, asserted a claim to a share in the 'lops and tops', or offal wood, and asserted this time and again, in the teeth of the law, by main force.[6]

1. *Regina* v. *Hammond*, E134, 12 Anne Trinity 3, Southampton.
2. See Isaac Townshend, a Portsmouth Commissioner, assuring Trelawny, 10 November 1717, of 'all manner of assistance from my self & officers to prove that beech is timber . . . or any thing else in my power'. Hants Rec. Off. B/xivb/3/2.
3. Forbes to Trelawny, 2 August 1717, ibid.
4. *Bishop of Winton* v. *Culme*, E134, 5 Geo. I. Mich.
5. Memorial of Withers to the Lords Commissioners of the Treasury, in Walpole's papers, Cambridge University Library, C(H) 62/38/1.   6. See below, p. 244.

The Bishop's authority was hated, because it threatened security of tenure and encroached on old customs; but it was not a strong authority, having a cumbersome, remote, parasitic and divided bureaucracy.[1] The authority of the Crown in the forests was exceedingly weak. Alice Holt and Bere provided little or no revenue. The oak timber was not yet ready for naval use, whereas the comparatively well-governed New Forest had supplies in abundance. The King's table was never supplied with venison from them. They provided no field for ministerial patronage. Hence they were left, with little support from central Government, as a power vacuum over which different local interests contested.

If one interest was hated and the other weak, this did not ensure that they agreed well with each other. The Bishop's tenants raided Alice Holt for wood and deer, as did inhabitants of the Church manor of Crondall, to the west of Farnham. When the keepership of Waltham Chase became vacant, Richard Norton made urgent representations to the Lord Treasurer. The Chase was adjacent to the West Walk of Bere, and it was thus 'wholly in the power of the Bishop's Ranger, by laying in wait for them to cut off great numbers of her Majesty's deer passing over . . . to feed in the said Chase & grounds adjoining, & this the Rangers have formerly done.' He saw the Bishop's Ranger as an 'enemy' placed 'near our frontiers (& we have always found them enemies)'; hence the Wardenship of Bere and of the Chase should be in the same hands.[2] The Bishop's keepers, for their part, clung on to Havant Thicket, an enclave for the Bishop's deer within the Forest of Bere, and claimed the right to chase and rechase their deer from Havant or Waltham throughout the royal forest.[3] And within the forests there was friction, from time to time, between the Crown and private interests, and between the proprietors of the several royalties of Bere.

Thus in 1716 John Baker, one of Norton's keepers, encountered two men with guns on his royalty, 'soe he asket them what bisness they had there', and ordered them off the land. The gentlemen (as they turned out to be) told him he was 'an impedent fellow', 'if he did not hold his tongue one of them would brake his gun about his head for if he had ben a fellow of any manners he would a pulled of his hat . . . but Jack said he did not know whether they was gentlemen or not and therefore if they did not

---

1. According to a memorial to the Treasury of George Yeatts, a copyholder in the bishopric, Edward Forbes, the former Steward had himself become Woodward in 1726, and was committing greater waste of timber (to his own advantage) than Kerby was ever accused of: T1.255 (44).

2. Norton to Godolphin, 27 May 1707, Hants Rec. Off. B/xivb/3/2.

3. T. Service (?), Keeper of Havant Thicket, to Godolphin, 25 August 1709, T1.115 (44); State of the Case between the Queen and Bishop of Winton, 1711(?). T1.144 (28).

like his discors they mite mend there selves . . .' The suspect gentry turned out to be the son of Lord Dormer, the proprietor of the neighbouring royalty, and John Caryll, a friend of Alexander Pope. Norton jumped eagerly to his keeper's defence, the more eagerly perhaps because Lord Dormer and Caryll were Catholics and Norton a fervent anti-Papist. Caryll, in offering a half-apology, added that 'my father . . . never refuses any gentleman coming . . . nor was he yet ever refused the same privilege'. This would not satisfy Norton: there must be some 'catechise' between gentry; they must not allow 'common pochers . . . [to] borrow arguments from ourselves'. 'At the rate things go' it would be better if there were 'neither deer pheasant partridge or hare . . . unless there was a settled catechise'.[1]

The Forest of Bere, however, was still, in 1716, reasonably quiet and firmly governed.[2] It was in Alice Holt and Farnham that the trouble was breaking out most seriously. In 1711, 1714 and 1715 Ruperta Howe sent three fruitless memorials to the Treasury, complaining of the daily disorders and unlawful hunting in the forests, the cutting of bushes and lopping of timber, 'the offenders coming very often in the days, as well as night, disguised and armed with guns &c. in numbers too great for the few officers of the forest to oppose'. A private proprietor, Sir Simeon Stuart, had felled without licence an entire wood (Binswood) of 160 acres.[3] In supporting evidence it was said that 'both red and fallow deer will be destroyed in a very short time . . . they come in so great numbers that they carry them away on horseback in the day time'; the numbers of deer in the Holt had been reduced to around 150, 'the greatest parte of them rascald deer'. The tenants' successful verdict in the matter of bushes in 1713 had led to direct onslaught on parts of the Holt, where forty or fifty loads of bushes had been cut. The Hanoverian regime seemed to inspire less allegiance than that of Anne: 'since the Queen's death . . . the

1. John Hall to Norton, n.d. and various exchanges between Norton and John Caryll, 1716, in Hants Rec. Off. 5M50/921 and 5M50/833–9; Norton to Robert Dormer, 30 November 1716, Brit. Mus. Add. MSS 28,237.

2. See Hants Rec. Off. 5M50/1,111–16, for evidence as to Norton's activity in preserving game between 1698 and 1717. See also information against an innkeeper and wheelwright of Bishop's Waltham for killing a fallow deer in Waltham Chase, 1708: Portsmouth City Rec. Off. 11A/20/31; and Norton to Godolphin, 29 January 1705, T1.101 (30).

3. On this, a memorial of Ruperta Howe, 2 May 1712, T1.147 (26): 'the workmen he imploys lives remote from that place. Those who live in the adjacent parishes, and have a right of herbage and panage in Binswood as part of the forest, refuse to work for him as knowing he has no right to cut the same. And indeed the whole country is . . . much surprised at Sir Simeon's presumption . . .' For the Stuart family, see Hants Rec. Off. 4M51 (321).

country hath taken to shooteing and coming in the riotous manner that they now doe.'[1]

The assault upon deer was now a general occupation; the sale of venison and skins was perhaps becoming a trade. In March 1717 Edward Forbes wrote to Trelawny: 'I cannot forbear saying your Park is scandalously disturbed, and now the Holt is destroyed will suffer every day more & more, by a pack of beggarly thieves, not sportsmen, who kill for their skins more than the now unseasonable meat . . .' He had taken to intercepting the wagons that passed through Farnham, and had discovered in a covered wagon 'a greyhound dog, very promising for your park':

> Upon information that the concealed way of travelling . . . has been a practice (as well as those waggons carrying venison, hares, poultry & plunder of all sorts) I caus'd the dog immediately to be seiz'd for the Lord of the Manner. Some murmurings, but no owner appeared . . .
>
> I mention this to your Lordship because the Honorable Major-General your brother honour'd me with his commands to gett him a good grey-hound . . . therefore desire to know how this dog is to be despos'd of. His looks indicate speed and goodness . . .[2]

What happened after this is unclear. But what is clear, from two surviving letters of the Bishop, is that in 1718 the Farnham parks were coming under repeated armed attack. Trelawny, ageing and unwell, took steps to insert an advertisement in the *London Gazette* offering a pardon and reward to any informer whose evidence led to a conviction. He had scarcely initiated this action before he sought to retract it, writing to Serjeant Thomas Pengelly:

> My indisposition not letting me be get well, I have suffered a most dangerous passage in the King's pardon; for it is said there 'to any one of the offenders who shall discover two or more of his accomplice', whereas it ought to have been expressed 'to any two who should discover all their accomplices'. For what effect can I have if, among thirty, two beggarly rogues are produced? Whereas their number will make satisfaction, and I know too that there are persons of estate and quality among them. Pray rectify this.

But such rectification was more difficult than he supposed: for the King to offer a pardon conditional upon such large and indefinite premises went beyond the due forms. Pengelly evidently had to inform the Bishop that the terms of the pardon could not be revised, and Trelawny, choleric to the last, replied:

1. Memorials and supporting evidence in T1.182 and T1.199. Another reason given, in 1714, for the assault was 'the dispute . . . about the bushes and the taxing the lodges and the like'.

2. Forbes to Trelawny, 17 March 1717, Hants Rec. Off. B/xivb/3/2.

I never will consent to part with my money [the proffered reward for information]; it gives up my honour to the discovery only of two beggarly rogues, and therefore if the condition is to be so narrowed, I reject the publication in the Gazette and will think of other methods, and don't doubt 'em, to come at the deer-killers & pale-breakers without touching on the house burners and those who killed my horses and cows; in those cases the King's pardon is necessary, because man's life is concerned, but in the other, it being a civil action, and the Act of Parliament having found out rewards for those who only kill deer, &c, I will try their power, & I have already been successful enough to encourage my going on in that way only. The King is more concerned in interest than I am, the slaughter & insolence in the Holt being greater than in Farnham Park, and the cursing of the King being the usual word when they meet and begin their villanies & I had a letter sent me that they were more than 300 well armed, who scorned all opposition. I wish they might not have meant it farther than what they expected in defence of parks.

Trelawny concluded by positively forbidding the publication of his proclamation in the *Gazette*. He had signed it only 'through inadvertency': 'on my salvation . . . my full meaning from the first moment I hoped to have had a royal protection consistent with my honour.'[1]

The letters are significant, and they show how far all the components of Blacking were already fully assembled by 1718: deer-killing, pale-breaking, arson, attacks on horses and cows.[2] They are significant also in their illustration of the Bishop's notion of 'honour': to seek the protection of the King's proclamation of pardon was a loss of face, and a confession that he could not govern his own; he could suffer such a loss of 'honour' only if *all* the hunters were betrayed. Finally, we encounter a theme often present in the disturbances in Hampshire and in Surrey – the suggestion that 'persons of estate and quality' were involved. For neither the royal forests nor the emparkments of bishops or of courtiers were popular with the old-established resident gentry of the district, who perhaps shared some of the same attitudes to forest rights and to deer of their humbler tenants. When the royal forest had been forcibly expelled from Surrey in the time of James II, the dreaded Judge Jeffreys had been sent down with a Special Commission to try offenders; but he had been unable to proceed because the grand jury of local gentlemen proved to be

1. Trelawny to Sjt T. Pengelly, 23 November 1718 and 26 November 1718, Bodleian MSS Eng. Letters C 17: also published (with a few errors) in *Hist. MSS Comm. 7th Report*, Appendix, p. 684. I have not found the proclamation in the *London Gazette*; it seems that it was withdrawn. Perhaps Trelawny's 'other methods' were to induce informations by offering rewards privately around Farnham.

2. I have not come across evidence of arson; but it was stated in the Act which enclosed the Old Park (1709–10) that the old Lawday House had been 'recently accidentally burned down'. It is not known whether arson was suspected; see Elfrida Manning, *Farnham Parks*, Farnham, 1973, p. 3.

'of a complexion not likely to do the business'.[1] There were to be, in the years of Blacking, many rumours as to the sympathy of gentlemen of similar complexion.[2]

But, in 1718, the term Blacking does not yet appear to have been in use. In July 1721 Bishop Trelawny died. He was succeeded by Charles Trimnell, the Bishop of Norwich, a Whig polemicist, friend of Townshend, Clerk of the Closet to George I, and a clerical careerist after Walpole's own heart.[3] And it was probably in the autumn of 1721, at Farnham and also in the neighbouring corner of north-east Hampshire already described – at Crondall, Dogmersfield and Heckfield – that organized Blacking assumed a new, and even more highly organized, form.[4]

1. See Onslow MSS, *Hist. MSS Comm. 14th Report IX*, p. 486, and above, p. 55.

2. Such accounts were usually anecdotal: e.g. *Mist's Weekly Journal or Saturday's Post*, 26 January 1723: 'some weeks since the whole troop of these black foresters returning from their sport, went to a publick house on Bagshot Heath, and having made merry went away and forgot to pay the reckoning: a few days after, a gentleman of good figure light at the said house, and hearing the melancholy story . . . generously laid her down five guineas . . .'

3. *DNB*; Sykes, op. cit., II, pp. 99–100, 129–30, 140.

4. Before he died Trelawny had the satisfaction of seeing some deer-stealers arrested. Committals at Surrey quarter-sessions, Surrey Rec. Off. show three men (John Alexander, Stephen Phillips and Robert Bishop) arrested for killing deer in the Bishop's park in January 1721; and recognisances for a Farnham farmer (Richard Morris) for a similar offence in June 1721, roll 240.

5: King John

In October 1721 some sixteen deer-poachers broke into Farnham Park, carried off three deer and left two more dead on the ground, shooting and wounding a keeper.[1] Several suspects were arrested, two of whom were sentenced to the standard penalties of a day in the pillory, a year's imprisonment and a fine of £20. The comrades of the imprisoned men bound themselves to each other by oaths, and 'chose to be under a mock kingly government, and . . . elected a very robust, enterprizing, and substantial gentleman . . . for their King'. They broke once again into the Bishop's park at Farnham, in greater numbers, took eleven deer (and left as many dead on the spot) and rode through Farnham with them, at 7 a.m. on the market-day, in an open triumph.[2]

These riders were masked and wore black gloves. They were clearly something more than deer-stealers, and were more highly organized than the Windsor men. Their leader was known as 'King John', and he had an eye to public relations, 'giving out', from time to time, the objectives and apologies of his band. In 1720–22 the Bishop's park was attacked repeatedly, his herd of deer decimated, lodges burned, timber destroyed, and his cattle shot at.[3] At length troops were stationed at Farnham. The

1. *History of Blacks*, pp. 2–3. Apart from state papers, the main sources for Hampshire Blacking are this pamphlet and a series of reports in the *London Journal*. The author of the pamphlet drew upon the latter, and also upon the account of the Ordinary of Newgate (for biographical details of the executed men); but he also visited the condemned in prison and gained more information from them. See also Note on Sources.

2. ibid., pp. 3–4. Surrey QS records, roll 242, show a farmer accused of harbouring and concealing three Farnham men (one of them Francis Knight, Gent.) suspected of felony – probably Blacking (Surrey Rec. Off.).

3. ibid., pp. 5–6. Defoe in *A Tour through the Whole Island of Great Britain* of 1723 (1962 edn, I, p. 142) noted that 'some of the country folks' at Farnham, 'notwithstanding the liberality and bounty of the several bishops' have 'of late been very unkind to the

Blacks at this point diverted their attacks to the Bishop's other substantial deer ground, Waltham Chase, twenty-five miles to the south-west: 'where . . . large heads of deer were to be seen in droves before, scarce were to be seen in two months time two of those creatures grazing together'. 'All the adjacent country' was terrorized, and the men, who called themselves the 'Waltham Hunters', appear to have exacted some kind of blackmail through the forest districts – enforcing fines, supported by threats of arson or other punishment, upon those likely to discover them.[1]

The attacks on deer may be taken for granted. But once the nucleus of 'Hunters' had been formed, and the raids carried out with impunity, the objectives became more various. 'At their first appearance 'twas believed they only proposed to command the Chase'; well-mounted, and armed with carbines and pistols, the keepers with their quarter-staves were no match for them. Next, they extended their attentions to informers and forest officials. A substantial farmer near the Chase, who had informed upon them, found his fences beaten down, his field-gates thrown open, and cattle driven into his standing corn. The widow of the Ranger had received £10, a half-share of the fine of a convicted deer-stealer. 'King John' and some of his men rode up to the Lodge, and threatened to burn it if she did not refund the fine, adding 'that they were gentlemen, and were determined to do justice'. The Ranger's widow expressed disbelief and called them 'worthless fellows', whereupon 'the Captain immediately drew off his black glove, and exposed a fine white hand . . . asking her, Whether she thought it had ever been used to hard labour, or belong'd to a sorry fellow?' On this, the woman returned to him the money.[2]

From this, they extended their attentions to several of the substantial gentry in Hampshire, as well as interfering 'in most disputes that happen'. Gentry and professional men who refused to pay tradesmen's debts were visited; a doctor who had a reputation for 'frugal management', and who refused to pay for some hay, was visited by a Black, 'finely mounted, with pistols and a blunderbuss', with a letter from 'King John', advising

---

bishop, in pulling down the pale of his park, and plundering it of the deer, killing, wounding and disabling even those they could not carry away'. Recognisances among Surrey QS rolls against Richard Morris, yeoman, for entering the Bishop's park to steal deer and against Robert Sturt for shooting a cow of the Bishop's in the park: Surrey Rec. Off. QS rolls, 1721, bundles 239 and 240. One wonders whether Robert Sturt was an ancestor of George Sturt, Farnham's famous master wheelwright and author.

1. *History of Blacks*, pp. 5–6; R. Mudie, *Hampshire*, Winchester, 1838, p. 157.

2. *History of Blacks*, pp. 7–8 and *London Journal*, 10 November 1722 (the circumstantial accounts in this journal were supposedly sent in from a correspondent at Waltham Chase).

prompt payment. The doctor complied. A Farnham gentleman, named Blakely (following the example of the late Bishop), refused to pay a carpenter's bill for the building of a stable. The carpenter then boasted that he had received a 'summons' to appear before 'King John' in Waltham Chase, and that the Blacks had promised to force Blakely to comply, if necessary by burning his house. Blakely had the carpenter committed to Winchester gaol, whereupon he received a letter from 'King John', disowning any previous threats in this case, but warning Blakely that he would take a severe revenge upon him if he continued to imprison the carpenter in this way. Blakely bailed his prisoner out. At Wickham, on the borders of the Chase, there was a dispute about a pew in the parish church, which was decided in favour of a widow gentlewoman:

This the Blacks resented as an act of partiality and injustice, and King John summon'd the lady to resign; which she not doing . . . they cut down a fine walk, and defence of trees, before her house, and quite defac'd her flower garden, one of the nicest in the whole country. The parson, as a party concern'd was serv'd in like manner, and his bee-hives, for which he was very famous, were thrown into the highway.[1]

The Blacks of course also had an eye to disputes over timber, grazing and fishing rights. The steward of one Hampshire manor impounded two hogs, and made the owners pay a fine for their redemption, 'which hath been so resented by the blacks, that they have cut down & destroyed near 600 young heirs [growing trees] in his copices . . .'[2] A Mr Wingfield felled some timber on his estate near Farnham; the poor country people came for their customary faggots and offal wood and some 'carry'd off what was not allow'd' and were forced by Wingfield to pay:

Upon which, the blacks . . . stripp'd the bark off several of the standing trees, and notch'd the bodies of others . . . to prevent their growth; and left a note on one of the maim'd trees, to inform the gentleman that this was their first visit; and that if he did not return the money . . . he must expect a second from King John of the Blacks.

Wingfield complied, and saved the rest of his timber.[3]

For a few months the Robin Hood of legend was incarnated in 'King John'.[4] The resentments of decades sheltered him and his band, as he rode

1. *London Journal*, 10 November, 22 December 1722; *History of Blacks*, pp. 9–11.

2. E. Hooker to Sir John Cope, 8 October 1722, SP35.34 (ii), fo. 94. cf. *London Journal*, 22 December 1722.

3. *London Journal*, 10 November 1722; *History of Blacks*, pp. 8–9.

4. cf. *Mist's Weekly Journal or Saturday's Post*, 26 January 1723, describing the Blacks as 'a set of men who sometimes divert themselves with the manly exercises of deer-stealing, as Robin Hood and some other rustick heroes have done before them . . . rather out of a frolick than for the profit'.

openly about administering folk justice. His supporters seemed to be able to disappear as easily into the folds of popular concealment as did the Vietcong. Many of the incidents in north-east Hampshire, already discussed in our Windsor section, may very probably belong with the activities of this group, which may have been based near Farnham or Crondall.[1] Certainly the punishment of the zealous Sir John Cope by felling his young trees appears to fall in with the pattern of their actions. But if the Hampshire Blacks were in fact enrolled under oaths of fealty to 'King John', very few would have been of the actual fraternity: the correspondent of the *London Journal* guessed at anything from thirty to a hundred, but only twenty or so were ever seen in action at one time. These well-disciplined social rebels were however the precipitant of many other freelance actions, by poachers (and venison dealers), smugglers, fishermen and foresters. All of these actions were, of course, seen by the authorities, within one common blur, as outrages by the Blacks. 'King John', on at least one occasion, when smugglers smutted their faces and seized some wine, took pains to issue a disclaimer. The wine which they intercepted was on its way to the Prince of Wales, and the smugglers averred that they were delighted to have the means to make a loyal festival, and would be certain to drink the Prince's health. But 'King John' put it out that henceforth to circumvent the Proclamation and to distinguish themselves from imitators the Blacks would disguise their faces in *white*.[2]

'King John', in fact, knew well what he was doing, and took care to make it public. During the alarms of Jacobite conspiracy in the summer of 1722, he learned that it was being said that the Blacks were 'in the Pretender's interest' and were preparing for insurrection. It is said that he went as far as to counter this with a printed manifesto, sent to him from London, declaring his allegiance to the Hanoverian succession.[3] The accusation of Jacobitism continued to be put about, and in the first week of January 1723 'King John', learning that a proclamation against the Blacks was imminent, let it be known that he intended to answer it publicly near an inn on Waltham Chase: 'But fifteen of his smutty tribe appeared, some in coats made of skins, others with fur caps, &c. They were all well armed and mounted, and at least three hundred people assembled to see the Black Chief and his mock negroes . . .' Before this audience, 'King John' protested:

That they were well affected to King George; that they lov'd him, and would

1. See above, pp. 105–8.

2. *London Journal*, 30 March 1723; *History of Blacks*, p. 12. In November 1723 'a new order of Blacks' rescued five hogsheads of claret seized by an excise officer near Bishop's Waltham: *British Journal*, 9 November 1723.

3. *History of Blacks*, pp. 6–7. I have found no surviving copy of this 'manifesto'.

be ready to sacrifice their lives to maintain his right; that they had no other design than to do justice, and to see that the rich did not insult or oppress the poor; that they were determined not to leave a deer on the Chase, being well assured it was originally designed to feed cattle, and not fatten deer for the clergy, &c.

After this, the King's and other loyal healths were drunk, and the band rode off. 'I am apprehensive', the correspondent of the *London Journal* added, that 'you'll say that three hundred people might have easily secured sixteen, but no attempt of that kind was then made'. This 'shew'd the populace to be of their side'.[1]

At length, at the end of January, the expected Proclamation against the Blacks appeared, supplemented by a strict charge by Baron Page at the Winchester Assize.[2] There were one or two more forays at the Chase and at Farnham, but at the end of March 'King John' assembled his followers at Waltham Chase, announced that he would not 'concern himself with publick affairs' for several months, and the band then rode off with nine fat deer, taken 'in the very face of their keepers'. He intimated that he would, in due course, reappear with his whole posse. He did not. The events in Windsor, the Reading Special Commission and the Black Act supervened; and when Blacking resumed in Hampshire there is no evidence that it was conducted by the same people. Nor is there any evidence as to the identity of 'King John'. The ballads of Robin Hood still went their rounds, but this flesh-and-blood Robin Hood rode back, perhaps to some small forest estate, to be forgotten for 250 years, leaving behind him (so far as we can discover) no legend, no folk memory, not even a song.

1. *London Journal*, 12 January 1723; *History of Blacks*, pp. 6–7.
2. But even here something odd was going on: for the Assize sermon by the Reverend Knap was described by Baron Page in these terms: 'a more virulent Libel upon the Government he never heard'. Knap, the vicar of Bramdean, was presented for it by the grand jury the next day: *Northampton Mercury*, 18 March 1723.

6: Awful Examples

The trials at Reading put a 'damp' on Hampshire Blacking,[1] although a few incidents continued to be reported. Disguised raiders and keepers clashed in Ruperta Howe's own park near Farnham; a poacher and a keeper were wounded.[2] And in the surrounding countryside habitual poachers, emboldened by the exploits of the Blacks, continued their old trade, sometimes adding to it a new vigour of social protest. In Sussex the Justice in Eyre's son, the Earl of Tankerville, found the heads of his own fish-pond broken.[3] And in the same county we have a glimpse of the enlarging dimensions of disturbance in a case brought against Francis Riddall, a yeoman of Singleton. In the week before Easter a labourer, two yeomen, two carters and a tailor had been drinking in an alehouse in West Dean. The yeomen tried to persuade the labourer to go with them to catch a deer or some rabbits, offering him 2s. 6d. for his pains. When the yeomen were asked whether they had already been coursing that day, one of them (Riddall) replied that if they had, they had not been 'acoursing att my Lord Derby's again, for wee have paid enough allready, & I will never goe acoursing there, for I will pull his House down & I will burn down his windmill, that stands upon Halnaker Hill, & hee shan't stand a week longer . . .' But he also swore that he would first take 'the poor folkes grists' out of the mill, so that these would not be burned. Shortly afterwards the mill did indeed burn down, and – the labourer turning informer – Riddall was in serious trouble.[4]

1. *Post-Man*, 22 June 1723.

2. *London Journal*, 29 June 1723: *Weekly Journal*, 29 June 1723.

3. Recognisance against Antony Wakeford, '*molitor*', 1 December 1723, West Sussex Rec. Off. QR/W/325.

4. Examination of Henry Forster of Graffham, labourer, 5 June 1723: and recognisances against Francis Riddall, '*agricola*': West Sussex Rec. Off. QR/W/323.

Such freelance episodes illustrate the dimensions of agrarian grievance which supported Blacking, but not the activities of the Blacks themselves. The disturbances which (as we have already seen) continued on the Hampshire–Berkshire border were a different matter. This district lay along the escape route for Blacks on the run from Windsor. A surprising number of these escaped arrest, and melted into the forests; by the end of the year proceedings for outlawry were going forward against at least nineteen of them.[1] Undoubtedly, some of these moved down into Hampshire. On 3 June Baptist Nunn, who followed them like a bloodhound, 'went into Hampshire to find how affairs stood', and found 'five persons were together still'. Once again, he managed to place a spy among them, from whom he learned that William Shorter, the reputed leader of the Berkshire men, who had escaped from custody two months before, had joined the outlaws.[2]

At the end of July there was a small sortie in the Forest of Bere; in August attacks were resumed in Waltham Chase. Bishop Trimnell died in mid-August, and in the week of his death the 'insolence' of the Waltham Blacks was reported to have reached its former proportions.[3] On 1 September seven Blacks had a hard-fought encounter with six keepers, soon after dawn, in Alice Holt. A young man named Elliott, dismounted, was trying to catch a fawn, and was at a distance from his fellows. The keepers seized and bound him. The Blacks attempted a rescue. For some time the equal parties fought with quarter-staves. Then guns were presented. John Barber, a Black, fell with his thigh shattered by two balls; an under-keeper named Earwaker or Elleker was shot through the breast and killed. At this, three of the Blacks ran off, leaving two others – Kingshell and Marshall – to fight to the end for their companion. Both of them were overpowered, and the keepers held four prisoners.

They did not hold John Barber, the wounded man, for long. Kingshell, Marshall and Elliott were sent to Winchester gaol, but Barber was held in the house of the tithingman in Binstead, to the west of the forest, and attended by a surgeon who pronounced him too ill to be moved. Here, on the night of 12 September, he was rescued by about twenty fellows. Mrs Howe was of the opinion that he could not have been moved far, and the surgeon did not expect him to live. He was, in any case, never retaken.[4]

1. T1.249 (1), for the Treasury Solicitor's account of outstanding cases. Returns in Assi. 5.44 (2) shows 22 Blacks 'non sunt invent', and the Abingdon Assize (Assi. 5.46, 7 March 1726) shows 'exigi fac.' against William Cooke and 'divers others'.

2. Nunn Accounts, *passim*.

3. *London Journal*, 17 August 1723; *Northampton Mercury*, 26 August 1723.

4. Ellis St John, 22 September 1723: Delafaye to Townshend, 20 September 1723: both in SP43.67; A. Boyer, *The Political State of Great Britain*, XXVI, p. 315. I am indebted to Peter Linebaugh for drawing my attention to the *Ordinary of Newgate's*

These men were probably not of the original fraternity of 'King John'. (The gang at Farnham, it was reported, 'which has been formerly so much talk'd of, is quite dispersed'.)[1] Perhaps they had learned their trade, the previous year, from 'King John', and one or two may have served with him. Edward Elliott, only seventeen years old, is reported as saying that about a year before –

30 or 40 persons met him in Surrey, and hurry'd him away; the Captain of 'em saying, He enlisted him in the name of the King of Blacks, and he must disguise his face, and obey orders, whether it was to break down the heads of fishponds, to slaughter deer, to cut down woods, or the like and if he refused to enter himself among them, and to make a faithful oath to be true . . . they would turn him into a beast, he should eat only roots, and drink only water, and bear burdens as one of their horses, &c.

Elliott is also supposed to have said that he saw them bury two men, who had offended them, up to their chins, and then had tormented and teased them 'as befitted dogs'. He had at last made his 'escape' from the band. But all this, from a man under sentence of death, is worth little; if he had 'escaped' he had certainly proved willing to go on with the Blacking trade.

The men had come from several villages to the east of Woolmer Forest, on the Hampshire–Sussex border. The three who ran away were described as 'labourers' of Bramshot. John Barber was a lime-burner from Lurgashall across the Sussex border; he rode to Farnhurst where he knocked up Robert Kingshell, a cordwinder or shoemaker's apprentice. Barber put Kingshell on his horse, and they rode on to Liphook, where they found Marshall, a servant to a farmer and butcher, waiting in the street 'by appointment'. Marshall mounted his own horse, and they rode from there to collect Elliott and the three other Bramshot men. They then blacked their faces with gunpowder. These details indicate a ready communication over many miles of countryside; even labourers and servants were not as bound down to the boundaries of their own parishes as is sometimes supposed.[2]

Two days after the affray in the Holt, there was a raid in the Forest of Bere, in which ten or more were involved. After killing deer in the west Walk of the forest, they broke after midnight into Richard Norton's own park at Southwick, killing deer and shooting into the Lodge. An alarm

---

Account of the behaviour, confession, and last dying words of the seven Blacks, who were executed at Tyburn, on Wednesday, the 4th of December, 1723 (Ashbridge Collection, 920/SM, Westminster District Library) – hereafter cited as *ON*.

1. Boyer, op. cit., p. 316.

2. *ON, passim*; PC 2.88, fos. 335–40; Hants Rec. Off., QO 10, fos. 164–6. The relatives of the dead keeper, Earwaker or Elleker, received £50 under a clause in the Black Act, in compensation for his death: ibid., QM 5, 14 January 1724.

bell was rung, and three or four of Norton's servants sallied out, with some unarmed villagers. The Blacks cried out, 'Kill or be killed!', '. . . and so let flie at them, the poor villagers hearing the bullets whiz among them, & not being used to such serenading, retired . . .' The attack on Southwick Park was, from the point of view of the Blacks, a tactical error. This was (the well-informed correspondent of the *London Journal* noted) 'the first time of Mr. Norton's being insulted . . . although his ponds are well stock'd with fish, and his park with deer'. Norton was 'well beloved', and perhaps this made it easier to get information on the raiders. The silence of the countryside was broken, and the Southwick blacksmith was willing to swear a deposition against three Portsmouth men, 'reputed deer stealers', whom he 'believed' to have been in the attack. Deer-skins were found in the possession of two of the men; the trail led to two more, one of whom, Thomas Barton, became an evidence and named a number of others.[1]

Once again, it cannot be certain that these were Blacks of the 1722 kind. It was said that the original Waltham gang 'is . . . dwindled to nine or ten worthless fellows',[2] and several of this group may have been freelance hunters, venison traders, etc. The informer, Thomas Barton, was a yeoman from Swanmore.[3] The four men who were seized were John and Edward Pink, brothers, both Portsmouth carters; Richard Parvin, a Portsmouth innkeeper; and James Ansell, an ostler. It was discovered that only two of them (Ansell and John Pink) had been present at the attack on Southwick Park, and Edward Pink and Parvin were ultimately tried for appearing armed and disguised in an earlier affair (on 28 July) in the Forest of Bere. The case against them was, at the best, sketchy. Barton's evidence led to eight others being proclaimed, under the Black Act, for taking part in the affray on 3 September: these included a labourer from Portsea, a miller from Tichfield, two labourers, a miller and a gardener from Wickham (on the edge of Waltham Chase) and two labourers from Fareham. One of the accused had the Blackish pseudonym of 'Lyon', and three men (two millers and a labourer) were all named Hobbs and were presumably related. There is no record that any of them were tried or apprehended.[4]

1. Richard Norton, 14 September 1723, SP35.45, fo. 34; PC2.88, fos. 340–45; *London Journal*, 14 September 1723; deposition of Thomas Sutton, blacksmith, 5 September 1723, Portsmouth City Rec. Off. S3.81.

2. *London Journal*, 14 September 1723.

3. In a curious contemporary account, where he is given as James Barton, he is described as a young rake and ne'er-do-well, a former commoner of Winchester College, and the son of parents 'of good estate': 'Captain' Alexander Smith, *Memoirs of the Life and Times of Jonathan Wild*, 1726, pp. 99–115.

4. PC2.88, fos. 342–3; *ON, passim*; *British Journal*, 14 September 1723.

Thus by mid-September the authorities had seven prisoners in their hands; three from the Holt affair, and a mixed bunch of four from Bere. The local magistrates were anxious for examples. Norton wished to 'put an end to these arabs and banditti', and Ellis St John of Dogmersfield in the north of the county, declared, '. . . they were become an intollerable grievance, and nothing can suppress them but vigorously putting the Act in execution, which my brotherhood in these parts resolve to do.'[1] Nunn was sent down to assist St John and Cope, and he found that Shorter's gang was now lying 'about Shurville', had increased to twelve persons, and was 'very resolute'. He managed once more to place a spy among them: 'A person here out of the Holt acquainted with Shorter & gang is gone down to act with them under pretence of flying his home for the murder in the Holt, gave him £2.2.0.' But this was the last entry in his accounts, and there is no evidence that any of Shorter's band were ever caught.[2] The news of Shorter's continued liberty probably made the Lords Justices all the more anxious to convict the arrested men. 'These people grow in some places more outrageous since the Law made against them last session,' Delafaye informed Townshend, 'and they must feel the effects of it to make them quiet.'[3]

It was decided to employ the full rigours of the Black Act for the first time. Since the Holt affair involved murder, it would have been possible to obtain a conviction under the normal Assize procedures; or the authorities could have proceeded, as at Reading, by Special Commission. But the Black Act enabled the Lords Justices to instruct the Attorney-General to remove the trial to the Court of the King's Bench: 'the trying them in the King's Bench was judged a less expensive method' than a Special Commission, 'and rather more effectual; especially now we may depend upon having jurys of men of probity and well enclined towards their Kings and country's service & interest.'[4] No repetition of the fiasco at Wallingford, where the Assize juries had found 'contrary to evidence', was to be permitted. Since this was the first use of the Act, great precautions were taken to ensure that the requisite informations were taken in due form: the Assistant Treasury-Solicitor, Paxton, was sent into Hampshire to assist in preparing the cases; there were rumours of a rescue attempt at Winchester gaol, and troops were sent to prevent

1. Norton, 14 September 1723: St John, 29 September 1723: both in SP35.45.
2. Nunn Accounts, entries for 5, 8, 15, 17, 22, 24 September. Delafaye informed Townshend that 'Mr Nun . . . has been very active', and that he imputed the boldness of the Blacks to the fact that the soldiers had been drawn out of their quarters: Delafaye to Townshend, 20 September 1723, SP43.67.
3. 24 September 1723, SP43.67.
4. Delafaye to Townshend, 1 October 1723, SP43.67.

it.[1] Proclamations under the Black Act had now been issued against twelve other men involved in the Holt and Southwick Park affrays; under the terms of the Act, the failure of any proclaimed man to surrender himself by a given date made him guilty of felony, and liable (if caught) to execution without any form of trial.[2]

It was perhaps at this time that the Hampshire bench received an urgent memorial from the Keeper of the county gaol at Winchester:

> That he has now in his custody a very great number of people charged with doing many acts of violence under the disguise of black'd & painted faces, & as being guilty of many great & capital crimes; that he has many others likewise under the imputation of crimes not much less destructive to the estates interests & privileges of several of his Majesty's good subjects . . .

The prisoners 'appear to be a dangerous set of rogues, determined, if not confined to the strictest bondage, to do or dare anything against the common peace & to rescue themselves in defyance of & in opposition to all manner of law and justice'. The Keeper was also holding 'a great number of debtors'. His facilities were sadly inadequate to entertain these numbers: he was forced to crowd together all types of prisoner 'in a promiscuous manner', and many were sick (perhaps with smallpox). He feared that at any time the prison might be broken open by the prisoners, 'aided by other rogues without (of which there are doubtless very great numbers)'. Winchester scarcely seems to be, in this memorial, the retired cathedral city which we have come to expect. The Keeper asked for relief 'instantly': the gaol had to be enlarged, and the existing buildings strengthened in such a manner 'as may give it not only the name of a gaol, but answer the ends intended by that name . . .'[3]

On the last day of October the seven accused were brought in irons

---

1. Instructions of Lords Justices in SP44.289, fos. 184–5, 191–3; Paxton to Delafaye, 26 October 1723, SP34.122, fos. 196–7; Minutes of Lords Justices, SP44.291, and 17 October 1723. The accounts of Edward Wynn, steward to Richard Norton, for expenses incurred in the prosecution of four of the men, are in T1.246 (99): these are very much more modest than those of Baptist Nunn.

2. PC2.88, fos. 335–45.

3. This memorial of Thomas Skeat, keeper of the county gaol in Winchester, was kindly brought to my notice by Miss Hazel Aldred, Assistant Archivist at Hampshire Record Office. It is undated, and was found as a wrapper to a will in the Archdeaconry series, of 1729. Although I insert the memorial here, I am uncertain as to its date: Hants QS records show cases of smallpox among the prisoners in 1723, and money granted for repairs to the gaol in that year. But June 1726 (QO 11, p. 60) shows an extra payment of £5 to Skeat for his great charges in keeping secure 'several most dangerous rogues', who had attempted to break out. Miss Aldred prefers 1726 as a date for this memorandum: but if this is the case, then Blacks (of whom I have no record) were arrested and sentenced in that year.

from Winchester to Newgate, linked together by an iron chain, and guarded by a contingent of the Duke of Bolton's Blue Guards.[1] The prosecution was conducted by Raymond and Yorke, the Attorney and Solicitors-General, before Mr Justice Eyre. Since murder could only be tried in the county where the offence was committed, the three Holt offenders (Marshall, Elliott and Kingshell) were convicted for appearing armed and with faces blacked and killing the King's deer. Ansell and John Pink were convicted for the same, in Southwick Park and the Forest of Bere. Edward Pink and Richard Parvin were tried on a more doubtful charge. Edward Paford, the keeper of an alehouse on the edge of Waltham Chase, gave evidence that they belonged to a small party which, on 28 July, had killed a deer in Bere, brought it to his alehouse, dined on a haunch of venison, and then sallied out to kill more in the Chase. They had been accompanied by a personable young woman, Hannah Wright, who rode with them, pistols and dagger at her side, and who cut the throat of a wounded deer. Parvin (the Portsmouth innkeeper) claimed in his defence that Hannah was a maid in his service, 'admired by several gentlemen'; 'She happen'd in an ill mood to fly from him, over the Forest . . . Thinking that her leaving him might be prejudicial to his trade, he hasted after her, and in the search call'd to refresh himself at [Paford's] ale-house . . .' Here he found his maid, who had been captured by the Blacks and forced to slaughter their deer. His story was even less likely than that of the prosecution; Hannah was assumed to be 'one of the gang', and Parvin was, with the others, convicted. It is, perhaps, an upside-down world when a charge of poaching could be countered by the defence of pimping.[2]

On 19 November all were condemned to death. It was believed in Hampshire that strong attempts were being made to secure, for several of them, a pardon. Throughout the preparations for the trial, Sir John Cope had been restive at the lack of deference paid to him as Hampshire's leading Parliament man: 'The Sollicitor never shows me anything & the Advocat but a little now & then, so I am left to grope my way in the dark. 6 blank commissions sent the President will turn his head, disoblidge others, are too late. Let me know what I'm to do, I'm wearie of my situation . . .'[3] Richard Norton, who had received a note of particular

---

1. SP43.68.

2. 'List of those convicted at King's Bench, 13 November 1723', SP43.68; KB28.87 (16–19); T1.246 (99); *ON, passim*; *Gloucester Journal*, 18 November 1723; *Northampton Mercury*, 18 November 1723. For a discussion of Parvin's real motives, see below, pp. 157–8.

3. Cope (to Walpole?), n.d. (1723). Presumably the reference to the six blank commissions indicates that the Hampshire bench was to be strengthened – and Cope would have preferred to have nominated men in his own personal interest. The letter is annotated: 'A hint to Sir J. Cope to consult & give ass.[istance] to Ld J. Clerk.'

commendation from Walpole,[1] wrote anxiously on 23 November. It was rumoured in Portsmouth that his four Blacks were to be transported only. If so, they would soon return from transportation 'with revenge', '& every one able to head a new gang, and thus will it not be thought that honest men have not the time nor indulgence to avoid outrage & murther as villains to the King & Government, for so it is at bottom, to escape due punishment . . .'[2] Despite the inchoate grammar, his meaning was clear. Walpole was quick to reassure him[3] and the Lords Justices refused to consider a petition on behalf of Parvin and Kingshell.[4]

All seven were executed on Wednesday, 4 December, at Tyburn. Parvin, the innkeeper, professed his innocence to the last. He claimed that he had been unable to prepare his defence, and to pay for the summoning of witnesses, since the Mayor of Portsmouth had 'seized upon all his substance' upon his arrest. As he waited in the cart, 'with wishful eyes he look'd for a reprieve, which he continually expected to be riding up towards the Tree'. The two Portsmouth carters, Edward and John Pink, claimed that they had been convicted for their first offence against deer. The others made no attempt to deny that they were deer-poachers. Ansell regretted only that he had 'done any damage in Squire Norton's park, because he had heard that that gentleman, when his Majesty enquired of the nature of the people call'd Blacks, gave a very favourable account of them'.[5] The three Holt offenders were taciturn. Kingshell, the shoemaker, had recourse to religious devotions, but (recalling the affray in the Holt) he declared 'they had more honour than to go off with safety and leave their friend in danger'. Henry Marshall, a small, robust man in his thirties, distinguished by skill in 'rustic exercises' (he had once broken the arm of a highwayman whom he had caught in a robbery), appeared to think the death of the keeper was 'a trifling matter, and that he had a right to stand upon his own defence, and not to leave a companion among enemies'. When the Ordinary asked him, 'if he consider'd what a great

1. Walpole to Norton, 1 October 1723, SP44.81, fo. 313.

2. Norton to Walpole, 23 November 1723, SP35.46. Norton enclosed an anonymous letter which he had received, threatening a renewed attack on his park: below, p. 157 n. 2.

3. There was no intention to pardon any of the Blacks, and 'if there had been any thoughts of that kind, they would have been laid aside upon what you write, and a very great regard would have been paid to your opinion': Walpole to Norton, 26 November 1723, SP44.81, fo. 324.

4. Minutes of Lords Justices, 28 November 1723, SP44.291; Delafaye to Townshend, 29 November 1723 – the Lord Justices 'adhere to their resolution not to pardon any of the blacks . . . which is certainly the only way to quell those outlaws': SP43.68. Present at this meeting: Archbishop of Canterbury, Lord Chancellor, Lord President, Newcastle, Devonshire, Roxburgh, Cadogan, Walpole.

5. The King had visited Norton at Southwick in December 1722, see below, p. 204.

work it was to repent for the sin of murder, so as to save his soul from ruin?' His reply was, 'That to be sure he should take care of himself.'

All except for Parvin, Elliott and the Pinks were illiterate; but this did not prevent them from holding strong views as to the perversion of customary legal practice. They conceived it to be a hardship that they were tried in another county from that in which the facts were committed, and not 'by a jury of their own country'. Several of the men were, like those at Reading, too sick to stand in the cart before execution. No doubt they considered it a hardship also to be hanged before that alien crowd, in the midst of a metropolis which few of them can ever have visited. Their death (among so many London hanging-days) made little impression. A perfunctory account of their offences entered the various published Tyburn Calendars, but there is little suggestion that they appeared either as heroes or as monsters in the eyes of the London crowd. Jack Sheppard and Jonathan Wild were much better copy.[1]

1. *ON, passim*; *History of Blacks*, pp. 25-32.

7: The Hunters

We have already examined the social composition of the Berkshire Blacks. While the Berkshire sample stretches from gentry and substantial yeomen to labourers, the Hampshire sample is more plebeian:

HAMPSHIRE BLACKS: OCCUPATIONS[1]

Labourers and servants	15
Millers	2
Innkeepers	2
Carters	2
Farmers or yeomen	2
Blacksmith, butcher, carpenter, cordwainer, gardener, limeburner, ostler, shoemaker's apprentice, tailor, wheelwright	1 each

But this sample is small and may be unrepresentative. It is possible that none of 'King John's' Blacks were detected by the authorities; and local tradition, as well as fragmentary evidence, suggests that 'gentlemen', or at least yeomen of substance, were involved in Hampshire as in Berkshire.[2] Without such support, it is difficult to explain how so many of the affrays

1. Compiled from various sources in state papers, Assize records, press etc. Of thirty-five individuals tried, accused, proclaimed, or described by the authorities as Blacks, an occupation is given in no fewer than thirty-three cases – a very much higher percentage than in Berkshire.

2. The Reverend Frank Sargeant, for many years incumbent at Bishop's Waltham and author of *The Story of Bishop's Waltham* (1961), tells me in a private communication that family traditions as to the Blacks survived into this century, and he adds: 'I have always felt that the deer stealing was not the fundamental cause of the trouble but the Bishop's attitudes and actions (through his Stewards) encroaching on the traditional "rights" of the residents of Waltham Chase . . . for the benefit of his hunting parties.' See also Note on Sources, below, p. 300, for Harriet Martineau.

were led by mounted men with firearms. And in both counties there were gentlemen sufficiently at odds with the forest or episcopal authorities to have given the Blacks at least passive support.

Thus one of the lodges in Alice Holt had been twice sub-let (together with the office of deputy keeper of one of the Walks), and had come into the hands of a Colonel Frampton, who had made free with both deer and timber. Lady Howe complained that when Earwaker (or Elleker), who was under-keeper of this same lodge, had been killed in the encounter with the Blacks on 1 September 1723, 'no persons were sent to his assistance by Colonel Frampton'.[1] Since the Blacks had been coursing deer in the forest from midnight until 8 the next morning, it was a large omission. Such omissions might give colour to the assurance which Elliott had been given by Marshall and Kingshell (when they had pressed him to join the raid on the Holt on the previous evening) that ''twould be very beneficial to him, and so far from disobliging, that 'twould oblige Gentlemen, who would preserve him from danger'.[2]

As to the motives of individual Blacks, we have a little evidence, chiefly from statements made by the Hampshire condemned to the Ordinary of Newgate. Significant may be the fact that several of the accused were well-placed to operate a trade in stolen venison. Richard Fellows, the Maidenhead 'Jacobite', was a butcher. So was Eads of Hartley Row. Of the seven men executed in Hampshire, Henry Marshall was servant to a farmer and butcher, Ansell, an ostler, travelled the Portsmouth road, Richard Parvin was a Portsmouth innkeeper, and the Pink brothers were carters in the same city.

Parvin pleaded his innocence so tenaciously that one doubts whether he had either the record or the mettle of a deer-poacher. As the Hampshire men were brought down in irons to London, one of his comrades is said to have remarked, with ghoulish jocularity, that 'whatever happened they would not lose the company of their Landlord'.[3] Parvin pleaded on his

1. Petition to the Treasury of Ruperta Howe, 13 January 1724, T1.247 (6). There is an information in SP35.43, fo. 23, which appears well informed in other respects, and which identifies a 'Capt Clavered in Hampshire at the head of the blacks'. But I have no more information on any such man.

2. As reported to the Ordinary of Newgate, *ON*, 4 December 1723. Norton received, in the interval between the trial and execution of the Hampshire men, an anonymous letter warning that an attack upon his park was impending from 'about 40 hunters . . . bound in a strong ingagement': 'they ar all trusty Horse men and moast of them good Estates': some had bought themselves red coats made by 'three tayloars about Winchester', themselves 'hunters'. The attack did not take place, but Norton found the warning credible and sent it on to Walpole: enclosure with Norton, 23 November 1723 SP35.46.

3. *ON*. In another report Parvin was described as 'the Landlord of the house where

trial that 'he was master but of one poor horse . . . nor was able to carry such loads of venison as they were reported to bring from the forests'. But it is clear that the authorities thought otherwise. One is reminded that, in a number of accounts, the Hampshire Blacks were described as having been in origin 'owlers', who had formed gangs 'and by open force run their goods', and who had gathered around them poachers and other malcontents.[1] The Portsmouth road was an evident smugglers' route, and Ansell, who travelled it, the two carters, and Marshall who lived at Liphook, half-way on the road to London, seem a likely group of such 'owlers', with Parvin's inn as a base, and with an additional trade in venison as it came – or as they could make it come – available.[2]

Venison was certainly a valuable product. Its consumption was a sign of status, and the gift of game was one of the more delicate means by which the gentry expressed influence and solicited favour.[3] Venison was the most expressive of all such gifts.[4] A good haunch served as a centre-piece to a small dinner-party,[5] and from the other parts of the beast

they used to rendezvous': 'as he shared in their plunder, he is now likely to bear a part in their fate': *London Journal*, 23 November 1723.

1. See e.g. *Weekly Journal, or British Gazetteer*, 4 May 1723.

2. Parvin also claimed that a Portsmouth victualler hired a man to attend the trials in London, 'that he might give . . . immediate notice if his name was call'd in question': the victualler (Parvin claimed) could have cleared him 'and 'twould have been a Christian part to have done so': *ON*, 4 December 1723, p. 3. The Pink brothers, however, seem at least to have fancied themselves as Blacks, adopting the pseudonyms of 'Madok Lyon' and 'King'. (This gave the Ordinary of Newgate a nice text for the sermon before execution, from Ezekiel 19:6: 'He went up and down among the Lions, he became a young Lion, and learned to catch the Prey; and devoured Men': ibid., pp. 2, 6.) The attempt to distinguish between Blacks and venison-traders is perhaps foolish.

3. See the comments of Douglas Hay in D. Hay, P. Linebaugh and E. P. Thompson, eds., *Albion's Fatal Tree*, 1975, pp. 246–7.

4. Venison gifts were expressive of favour and continuing patronage: the correspondence of poets, scholars, clergy, lawyers, etc. with their lordly patrons is often punctuated with the details of such gifts, in terms which Marcel Mauss would have approved. The deer, however, may have approved these less. Sarah, Duchess of Marlborough's venison papers show, in 1723, no fewer than ninety-four bucks and fifty-four does slaughtered at Blenheim for gifts: Blenheim MSS, F1. 64. When Townshend retired to his Raynham estate, venison warrants soared in election years or in their aftermath. Thus in 1745 only fifteen bucks were killed as gifts, but after the 1747 election there were forty-nine – portions of which were sent to the Mayors of Norwich, Lynn, Yarmouth, to the Bishop and the Dean of Norwich, to the Recorder of Lynn, to the Gentlemen of the Norwich Constitutional Club, to aldermen and gentry, etc. The deer must have dreaded a general election, unless they were, as good Whigs, anxious to contribute to constitutional stability: Norfolk and Norwich Rec. Off. B-Lviib.

5. Swift, when attending the Court at Windsor in 1711, dined on venison frequently: 'Aug.1. We had for dinner the fellow of that haunch of venison I sent to London; 'twas mighty fat and good, and eight people at dinner, that was bad': *Journal to Stella*.

meat could be found for such fare as the venison patties to which people sat down at the Mayor of Reading's banquet in 1722.[1]

In the year of the Bubble the price of venison soared. Pope asked:

> What made directors cheat in South Sea year?
> To live on venison when it sold so dear.

And he obligingly provided a footnote: in this year the price of a haunch of venison had risen to between £3 and £5.[2] Two haunches at £4 apiece made the considerable sum of £8, and after that there was additional meat for patties etc., and also the skins.[3] Such prices, in 1720–21, might have served as a stimulus for the up-turn in poaching in that year. But these were retail prices in fashionable London. Defoe, in 1724, suggests 'a couple of guineas' a haunch.[4] The valuation of a fallow deer, in Assize cases, at 40s. each is, in any case, not unrealistic, as the price to the producer; the retail price could be much more.

Deer were thus an economic crop. And they combined this virtue with the superb and graceful emblemization of the status of their owner. These decades of ostentatious architectural aggrandisement and of landscape gardening are also singled out by the historian of deer-parks as the period in which many great gentry for the first time constructed parks contiguous to their seats; in place of the indeterminate extent of forest or woodland, easily poached, they strengthened their pales, or high brick walls, and employed a staff of keepers.[5] The park, so placed, provided the host and his guests with a sharp morning's entertainment – venison, like beef, tasted all the better for being well coursed.[6] In the owner's absence, the crop matured – to be dispensed as gifts or sold to a dealer.

1. *The Memorandum of John Watts Esq. (Mayor of Reading)*, ed. K. G. Burton, Reading, 1950, p. 23.

2. 'Epistle to Bathurst' (1732).

3. Matthew Prior, receiving a gift of venison from Lord Harley in 1719, reported that he had made a pie with the side and reserved the haunch *'pour être bien mortifié'*: *Hist. MSS Comm. Marquis of Bath III*, p. 58. The skin, offal and sometimes the rest of the beast (the haunches excepted) were often perquisites of the under-keepers: see e.g. *Commons Journals*, XLV, 1790, p. 169 (Alice Holt). Nor were such perquisites without value: venison accounts of Sarah, Duchess of Marlborough (Blenheim MSS, F1. 64) shows the 'price of the offald' of a buck running, in the 1720s, at around 14s. to 16s. Venison might also be salted down, or used to flavour the cottager's humble pease pottage: see Nottingham University, PW2. 366a, 368. Detailed recipes for treating different portions of the beast in Theodora Fitzgibbon, *Game Cooking*, 1963, p. 254.

4. D. Defoe, *The Great Law of Subordination Consider'd; or, the Insolence and Unsufferable Behaviour of Servants in England duly enquir'd into*, 1724, p. 272. De Saussure, in 1727, puts the sum as low as half a guinea to 15s., but he may have been treating of the smaller roe-deer: De Saussure, op. cit., p. 308.

5. See E. P. Shirley, *Some Account of English Deer Parks*, 1867, p. 50.

6. See W. Chafin, *Anecdotes and History of Cranbourn Chase*, 1818, p. 30.

De Saussure remarked that a deer-park, not too distant from London, brought in 'a very good revenue'.[1] And if the keepers were attentive, the deer did not need to compete with the timber. The land, thereby, could carry a double crop, the one slowly maturing, the other with a rapid turnover, as, each year, mature hinds and young bucks were culled – and both crops prestigious and ornamental.

Much must have depended upon the zeal of the keepers. It was commonly alleged that gamekeepers milked the spoils of office (in much the same way as statesmen or revenue collectors). Defoe, in 1724, singled out 'your Ranger, or park-keeper' as a worse offender than any 'Black': despite his many perquisites,

Unless you . . . give him leave to sell a fat buck for you, to some great feast, *and the like*, you shall feel the consequence of it; for you shall have the park never fail of being robb'd, three or four times in every season, and the best bucks carry'd off, four or five brace at a time. Then to solve his own credit, he has the impudence to accuse several of the young fellows round the country, who know nothing at all of the matter . . . when at the same time your keeper has horses sent to fetch the venison, by his own order, and as punctually as his master himself, from certain pastry-cooks, and sly merchants in *London*, who deal in such goods; and perhaps you chance, if come to *London*, to give a couple of guineas to some or other of them, for a haunch of your own venison.

If, on the other hand, you are in the country and want venison for your own table – 'Or to make a present to any neighbouring gentlemen, your park keeper shall tell you, there is very little fit for your use, and that if you kill any more 'till next season, you will spoil your park'.[2]

Defoe alleged that 'two or three park-keepers are, I think, at this very time in prison for such rogueries'. It is more than likely that some keepers traded regularly with venison dealers[3] and undoubtedly poachers would also have an illicit venison trade. Possibly the Portsmouth offenders took part in it. But the evidence does not allow us to make too much of this as an explanation of Blacking, except in the cases of attacks on Richmond Park and Enfield Chase.[4] In Berkshire, Hampshire and at Farnham other motives were dominant. The deer killed were often either eaten by the hunters, or their carcasses were left in the parks. Whereas there were distinct venison seasons, with the culling of bucks in mid-summer and of

1. De Saussure, op. cit., p. 308. Cadogan's deer-park at Caversham of 240 acres was valued at £180: the stock of deer upon it at £400 – perhaps 200 head at 40s. each?

2. Defoe, op. cit., pp. 271–3.

3. It is of interest that building work in this century revealed a great number of antlers beneath the keeper's lodge at Farnham (information from Mrs Elfrida Manning).

4. See below, Chapter 8.

hinds in mid-winter,[1] the attacks of the Blacks were at all seasons, at times when the meat would not only be poor, but its attempted sale would attract notice. Above all, the whole pattern of Black actions – the threatening letters, felling of young trees, blackmail of forest officers – disallows a simple economic explanation.

At one extreme, cash; at the other, love. Edward Elliott, aged only seventeen, went to the gallows because he had strayed from his fellows (during the raid on Alice Holt) trying to catch alive a young fawn as a present for his girl-friend.[2] By one account, John Guy was drawn into deer-stealing in the environs of London by much the same motive. Taking supper at an inn with his sweetheart: 'A discourse arose concerning the expeditions of the deer-stealers, which Guy's mistress took occasion to express great admiration of, and to regard them as so many heroes, who had behaved with courage enough to win the most obdurate heart, adding that she was very fond of venison, and she wished she had known some of them.'[3] What beautiful but obdurate young women admire, young men will soon be found to perform. Undoubtedly the sheer risk and ancient excitement of deer-poaching, and the melting obduracy which these adventures brought, must be counted among effective motives. John Hutchins, the historian of Dorset, describing this period, said that many gentlemen took part in hunting as 'a kind of knight errantry'. The hunters were formed into clubs, of from four to twenty men, armed with quarter-staffs and wearing defensive helmets; they had a watchword for the night, and an agreement whether to stand or run from the keepers. From about 1730 'this rude gothic amusement has been practised by the lower class only, and thereby the title of deer-hunters is sunk into deer-stealers'.[4] Gilbert White lived (at Selborne) within the affected district of Hampshire, and, while he was not a contemporary of the Blacks, he must have heard many tales of them from those who were. 'Though large herds of deer do much harm to the neighbourhood,' he wrote,

1. Townshend's own deer warrant book shows warrants to kill bucks issued in July to September, and doe warrants in November to January: Norfolk Rec. Off. B-Lviib (1740s). Warrants for the royal parks show bucks taken from 24 June to 14 September, does from 1 November to 2 February (old-style dating): Shirley, op. cit., pp. 251–2. According to the by-laws of venery buck-hunting commenced on Holyrood Day and closed on Michaelmas Day: J. P. Hare, *History of the Royal Buckhounds*, Newmarket, 1895, p. 224.

2. *ON*, 4 December 1723.

3. *Lives of the Most Remarkable Criminals*, ed. A. L. Hayward, 1927, pp. 216–17.

4. John Hutchins, *History and Antiquities of the County of Dorset*, 3rd edn, 1869, III, p. 411. For a contemporary picture of the hunters see Plate 13. The protective cap was made of straw, lined with wool, and was guarded with iron ribs and a pointed piece of iron at the top. The coat or 'jack' was of quilted canvas. In addition to the staff, these hunters carried a flail-like weapon called a 'swingel'.

yet the injury to the morals of the people is of more moment than the loss of their crops. The temptation is irresistible; for most men are sportsmen by constitution: and there is such an inherent spirit for hunting in human nature, as scarce any inhibitions can restrain. Hence, towards the beginning of this century, all this country was wild about deer-stealing. Unless he was a *hunter*, as they affected to call themselves, no young person was allowed to be possessed of manhood or gallantry.[1]

The park-owner, cultivating his prestigious antlered crop, no doubt wished to equate deer-stealing with horse- or sheep-stealing – to see them equally as thefts of his property and as felonies. Universally the 'country people' made a distinction. The taking of wild game was no felony, and if experience taught them that poaching was risky, nevertheless they were roused to indignation by the suggestion that the offence could merit death. It was said of the Hampshire condemned that they were 'not able to reconcile the greatness of such a punishment as death to the smallness of a crime, which was only making free with a few *deer*'. One of them, indeed, made a refined moral distinction. John Pink, the Portsmouth carter, said

he believed the Evidence [chief prosecution witness] was the severer against him and Ansell, because some time ago, they ran away with his wife, adding that he ought to owe them no ill-will because they had return'd his wife to him again. He acknowledg'd adultery to be a sin, but had not the same sentiments with regard to spoiling and wasting forests and public chaces.[2]

Of two offenders who were hanged subsequently in Middlesex, it was only some days after John Guy received sentence that he 'could be persuaded that he should really suffer'; and William Gates, the Edmonton blacksmith, confessed himself guilty of deer-stealing, 'but thought it too small a crime to suffer death for it'. Of the Reading condemned it was said, 'They could scarcely be persuaded that the crime for which they suffered merited death. They said the deer were wild beasts, and that the poor, as well as the rich, might lawfully use them . . .'[3]

Two questions remain. How far were the hunters associated with any organized criminal community? And was there any association between Blacking and Jacobitism? One may give a negative to the first inquiry, so

1. Gilbert White, *The Natural History of Selborne* in *Works*, 1802, Letter VII. White adds: 'Our old race of deer-stealers are hardly extinct yet: it was but a little while ago that, over their ale, they used to recount the exploits of their youth.'

2. *ON*, 4 December 1723. The 'evidence' was probably Edward Paford, the ale-house keeper by Waltham Chase, but might also have been Thomas Barton.

3. For Hampshire men, see *ON*, 4 December 1723; John Guy, Hayward, op. cit., p. 217; Gates, *ON*, 14 March 1726; Reading, C. Chenevix Trench, *The Poacher and the Squire*, 1967, p. 117.

far as the counties of Hampshire and Berkshire are concerned. Only one of those brought to trial in either county was accused of a previous criminal record. This was James Ansell, who had 'led an unsettled life' along the route of the Portsmouth–London road, and who was suspected of more than one highway robbery.[1] No doubt others, who were venison traders or were driven into outlawry, followed courses in congruence with a more structured criminal society.

But in 1723 we are at the height of Jonathan Wild's imperial reign. Wild's arm could reach far into the provinces, if there was blood-money worth collecting on any hunted head. And the Blacks, at £100 a time, were well worth hunting. Yet Wild and his fellow thief-takers took none of them; not even William Shorter, who, after he escaped from custody, must have sheltered for a time in London. It is true that Wild attended the hanging of the Blacks at Reading. He made a business of attending hangings, fairs and large concourses anywhere near London, since these were occasions of flourishing trade, in pick-pocketing and petty offences, and he might always recognize someone valuable enough to be worth turning in – as, indeed, he did on this occasion.[2]

Some of the men who hunted deer in Enfield Chase and Richmond Park (whom we have yet to discuss) may have been more integrated with London's structure of receivers, informers and thief-takers. After Wild's downfall one of his former employees, Aaron Maddocks, joined the Enfield poachers. A famous deer-stealer, Thomas James, was also in the horse-stealing trade. In 1725 an informant alleged that he had eavesdropped on seven or eight men, 'fuddled' with drink in a Hatfield inn; they belonged (he said) to a gang of some fifteen, bound by oaths, and they spoke of a surgeon–apothecary who lived near Shadwell Church on Ratcliffe Highway, and who had been factor and surgeon to the gang for many years.[3] But whenever any offence was committed in these years, someone testified that it was the work of a 'gang'. All we can say is that the scholar who has researched most closely into the actual membership of those groups who turned, like little cogs, around the master-wheel of Wild, has identified not one Black or habitual deer-stealer among them.[4]

The issue of Jacobitism is more complicated, and made immensely

1. *ON*, 4 December 1723.

2. Wild picked up (and collected blood-money on) Humphrey Angier whom he spotted at the Reading hangings: and his pick-pockets were plying their trade successfully at the execution of the Hampshire men: see *British Journal*, 22 June 1723; Gerald Howson, *Thief-Taker General: The Rise and Fall of Jonathan Wild*, 1970, pp. 197, 202; *St James Evening Post*, 13–15 June 1723.

3. Letter of 'G.L.' in SP35.57.

4. See Howson, op. cit., esp. Appendix III. For a further discussion of Blacking and 'crime', see below, pp. 192–5.

more so by the double-talk of the times, and by a press blanketed by censorship. And the picture is further confused in Berkshire by Parson Power, who certainly tried to involve Blacks in Jacobite sedition. In this he does not seem to have been notably successful. The three accused against whose names the suspicion of Jacobitism is noted (in surviving papers) are Fellows, Barlow and Rackett. None (it seems) was brought to trial. While the Crown had a number of depositions as to Fellows, the Maidenhead butcher, enlisting men for the Blacks, there is jotted against these facts at one point: 'Pretender not mentioned'.[1] Nor was the Crown prepared to trust its case against Barlow to a jury.[2] Possibly both these cases arose so clearly from Power's provocations that they were un-provable, just as Rackett may have been accused of Jacobitism (as would have been his brother-in-law, Alexander Pope, had he still been living near Windsor) as a necessary inference from his Catholicism. In Hampshire 'King John' was at pains to deny Jacobite sympathies, and in Berkshire the Jacobite Earl of Arran had his own park attacked.

So the association appears unlikely. But this evidence is not con-clusive. Undoubtedly the years after the Bubble saw a rise in Jacobite fortunes – or, at least, a decline in popular loyalty to the House of Hanover and to Hanoverian ministers – which sometimes found an outlet in whistling Jacobite airs or in adopting Jacobite symbolism. Walpole and his ministers were on edge. Military discipline was harsh,[3] and there was a rash of prosecutions or petty demonstrations of 'sedition'. A few of these came from the 'Black' counties. Thus a joiner was brought before Berkshire Assizes in the summer of 1723, who was accused by a soldier of saying 'God damn King George' at the Angel Inn, Hungerford; he was convicted, but let off with the light sentence of the pillory on market day.[4] A man from Alton, Hampshire – close to Alice Holt – got into similar trouble.[5]

And perhaps a little more may be inferred, from scattered and trivial fragments. Thus there appears to have been some polarization between a Whig Mayor and Corporation and a disaffected part of the population at Winchester, where two men had been imprisoned in 1720 for calling out 'God Bless King James the Third'. The City Chamberlain's accounts for

1. SP35.43, fo. 23.

2. Above, p. 79 n. 3.

3. e.g. Minutes of Lords Justices: 22 August 1723, sentence confirmed on Edward Welsh of Colonel Cadogan's regiment, to run the gauntlet through the regiment sixteen times and then to be drummed out with a halter around his neck (for cursing the King): 12 September 1723, death sentences, sentences of 600 lashes etc., for desertion: SP44.291.

4. Assi. 5.43: see also *Reading Mercury*, 5 and 12 August 1723.

5. For drinking a health to 'King James the Third and Eighth', Hants Rec. Off. QS B/xvib/2/5.

1722–3 show much corporate junketing in the name of Hanoverian loyalty: wine at the anniversary of the powder plot, wine at sessions dinners, wine on the anniversary of the King's accession, wine on the anniversary of the King's coronation, wine on the King's birthday. In August the King himself appeared on a brief progress through Hampshire. The Corporation celebrated by buying a new mace for the occasion: £90 4s. 3d. This was borne in solemn (and, no doubt, pompous) ceremony before the King. About an hour later, a mock processional went past the Town Hall, headed by a 'mace-bearer' – 'on his shoulders a large cabbage with the roots on to it . . . with an intent to ridicule the Mayor and Aldermen . . . who had just before carried the mace before his Majesty'. After inquiry, the Corporation decided that one Ambrose Tarleton, a butcher, had inspired this demonstration; he was indicted at Assizes.

But Tarleton reappears in 1723, when Guards were billeted in Winchester, mainly for use against the Blacks. The officer commanding complained that Tarleton was encouraging them to mutiny, and protecting a mutineer in his house; Tarleton was arrogant and insolent to the Mayor and the Justices of the Peace. Walpole advised caution. He would approve a successful prosecution but 'an unsuccessful attempt . . . would give him cause of triumph and make him more impudent'.[1]

There is not much here: a mock procession, a disloyal butcher, and, a few months later, unease at debtors and Blacks promiscuously mixed in gaol, rumours of rescue attempts, an anonymous letter.[2] This is the kind of insubstantial evidence with which one must deal. Nor is there much more in a curious episode at Hambledon in June 1723, which left traces only because it became a source of litigation in the Consistory Court. On 10 June, the Pretender's birthday, a churchwarden named Collins – who was described as 'a poor, tricking, shuffling fellow of no visible substance' – 'suffered the bells to be rung both morning and evening . . . and went after . . . to a public house and drunk plentifully with the ringers'. This outrageous peal 'occasioned a great clamour and discourse in the country'. Collins was also accused of having frequented the company of papists, of whom there were several of some substance in Hambledon and neighbouring villages. The cases which followed in the Church court suggest a deeply and bitterly divided community. Collins's fellow churchwarden

---

1. Cutting books of W. H. Jacobs (Winchester Public Reference Library), vol. I, pp. 44, 76, 79, and scrapbook SW09, p. 68. Tarleton was fined ten guineas and costs, but it is not clear whether it was for the incident in 1722 or that in 1723. Also Major Wyvill, 22 July 1723 and Delafaye, 25 July 1723, SP34.122, fos. 174–6.

2. See above, p. 157 n. 2. A Portsmouth correspondent of the *London Journal* (6 April 1723) reported that several Roman Catholics in the neighbourhood had been seized for drinking treasonable healths in clubs.

was a substantial yeoman named Thomas Land, who joined in the hue-and-cry after his fellow officer. A year later six piles of wood in Land's coppice were fired, and three men, including a local cordwainer and local blacksmith, were proclaimed under the Black Act for arson.[1]

Hambledon lay mid-way between Woolmer and Bere forests. A peal for the Pretender just after the Black Act was passed might indicate something. But not much can be made of it. Nor can we do better for the disturbed corner of Surrey. Here again there is the odd prosecution for sedition – in Easter 1721 Sarah Thatcher, a landlady, was charged on the oath of a soldier billeted on her with swearing 'God Damn the King and the Cloth and the Soldiers too!'[2] But from a Surrey market town 'about 20 miles from London' we can, in 1724, at last produce a genuine Jacobite handbill, hand-written and dropped in the street: 'I hope some patriot will rouze up the people to shake off this arbitrary Government, and animate them with the saying of the noble Roman who defended the Capitol . . . How long will you be ignorant of your strength? Count your numbers.'[3]

And that, in the present state of our knowledge, is the sum of our evidence. No single Black was proved in the courts to have Jacobite associations. (But did the Jacobites ever organize seriously among common people?) Walpole and Townshend, who were keen to prove such associations and who employed Power to obtain such proof, were left empty-handed. There is some sort of undercurrent of disaffection: a cabbage-processional here, a peal of bells there, a few taxed and terrorized Catholics, a handbill in the street. It is not much. But it is not quite nothing. If Parson Power had been a cleverer or more hard-working operator, he might have stirred up something which Walpole could have really put down with blood.

1. Consistory Court Cases, Hants Rec. Off. C/10/A (52) and (50); SP35.58, fo. 102. See also above, p. 122 n. 2. For Pope's Catholic friend, John Caryll of Ladyholt, see above, p. 138 and especially Howard Erskine-Hill, *The Social Milieu of Alexander Pope*, New Haven, 1975.

2. QS bundles, 2 March 1721, Surrey Rec. Off. Also William Brooks, for uttering a seditious ballad, county gaol calendar, 13 January 1719, QS Order Book.

3. Enclosure in 'I.S.', 12 October 1724, SP35.53, fo. 13.

1. Charles Withers, Surveyor-General for Woods and Forests

2. A detail from 'The Death of the Stag' by John Wootton

3. Windsor Castle, 1720

4. Survey map of Windsor Forest, 1734

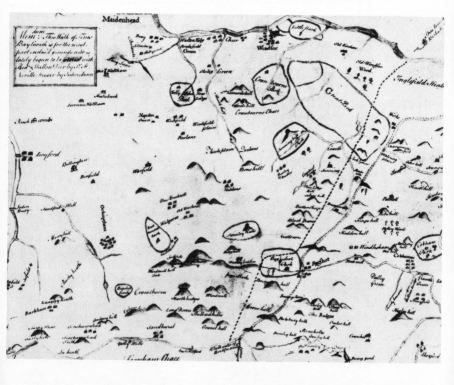

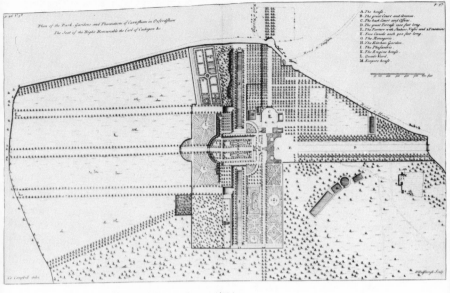

5. Plan of Caversham, 1721

6. Westminster Hall, 1733

Southwick in the County of Southampton. the Seat of Richard Norton Esq.

7. Richard Norton's seat at Southwick

8. The Lodge in Ashdowne Park

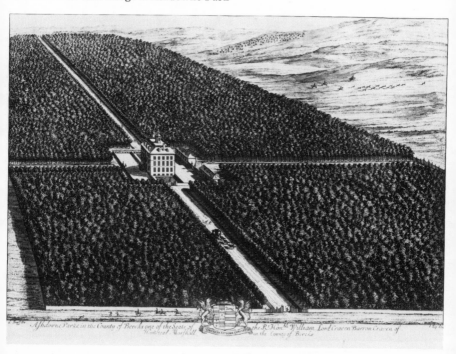

Ashdowne Parke in the County of Berks one of the Seats of the R.t Hon.ble William, Lord Craven Barron Craven of Hamsteed Marshall in the County of Berks.

9. A detail from 'The Forest of Bere' by J. M. W. Turner

10. A plan of Enfield Chase

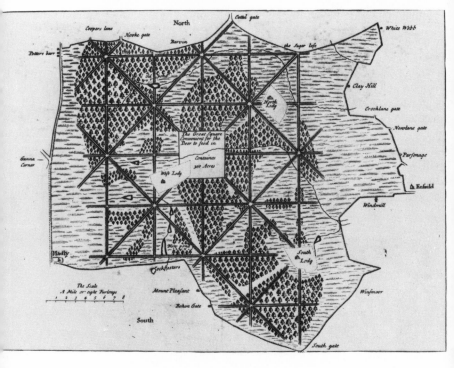

Richmond Park.

11. Breaking the wall of Richmond Park

12. Walpole as Ranger of Richmond Park

13. Deer hunters, 1720

14. Bobson, a famous running
   horse

15. Sir Francis and Lady Page at rest

16. Sir Jonathan Trelawny,
Bishop of Winchester, by
Sir Godfrey Kneller

Some of the Principal Inhabitants of ye MOON, as they
Were Perfectly Discover'd by a Telescope brought to ye Greatest
Perfection since ye last Eclipse, Exactly Engrav'd from the
Objects, whereby ye Curious may Guess at their Religion,
Manners, &c.

17. 'Royalty, Episcopacy,
and Law' by Hogarth

PART 3

Whigs

8: Enfield and Richmond

A consequence of the passing of the Black Act was to bring into prominence two other arenas of conflict between keepers and poachers, which had featured very little in the events leading up to the Act's passage. These were Enfield Chase and Richmond Park, both within easy distance, on horse or afoot, from hungry London.

John Evelyn found Enfield Chase, in 1676, 'a solitary desert, yet stored with not less than 3000 deer'. The Chase was only fourteen miles north of the centre of London, was twenty-seven miles in circumference, and contained above 13,500 acres. Evelyn had noted not a single building on the Chase, except for three lodges, but fifty years later a witness claimed that about a hundred houses had been 'long since built' by 'rich and able' persons within its borders, with plots of land.

But these householders were only a few of those interested in the use of the Chase. Four parishes – Enfield, South Mimms, Edmonton and Hadley – all claimed rights to firewood and to grazing for their horses and cows. An 'abundance of loose, idle and disorderly persons who live in other parishes' were also said to 'infest' the Chase, 'going in dark nights, with axes, saws, bills, carts and horses, and in going and coming rob honest people of their sheep, lambs and poultry, and make ... great strip, havock, and wast of your majesty's best timber and underwood ...' To the east nearly two miles of the Chase lay open to the Grand North Road through Barnet, making a wasteland of scrub and gravel-pits, where 'highwaymen and foot pads (who greatly infest the road)' could escape into the woods.[1]

The people of the Enfield parishes had a record of violent resistance to encroachment on their rights. In the 1650s parliamentary commissioners, anxious for revenue, sold off half of the Chase, mainly to army officers.

1. *Diary and Correspondence of John Evelyn*, ed. W. Bray, 1906, 2 June 1676; Memorial of John Hale, Clerk of Enfield Manor Court to George II, n.d., C(H) 45/40.

The commoners complained that they had lost most of their timber and much of their grazing rights, and the allocation of lands had been unfair. In 1659 there occurred one of the saddest and most confused episodes of the interregnum. The commoners gathered, armed with pitchforks, scythes and colours on poles; they threw down the fences and quicksets of the purchasers, turned cattle into their corn, burned wood-stacks and levelled a barn; by one account, they declared for Charles Stuart. The soldiers retaliated by shooting their sheep and cattle. Eventually there was an affray in which two or three of the commoners were killed, but the soldiers were overpowered, violently beaten, and carried off to Newgate.[1]

The Restoration of Charles Stuart did not dispel the commoners' grievances. There were successive encounters, not only between keepers and deer-poachers, but between the villagers and wealthy settlers (the commuters of those days) who laid waste to their rights. In 1701 the Ranger, the Earl of Stamford, was arraigned in the Commons for the wholesale felling and sale of timber.[2] The deer continued to be attacked, and the poachers continued to be punished.[3] Matters finally reached a crisis under the regime of Major-General John Pepper.

We have already encountered General Pepper, as the promoter of an Act against deer-stealers in 1719 (above, p. 59). King James had granted the Chase, in 1687, to Lord Lisburn for a fifty-year term. The grant changed hands more than once, and Pepper bought it up from Sir Basil Firebrace in 1716; there were then some twenty-one years to run.[4] Thereafter he lived a prosecuting, persecuted sort of life. The Chase was within the Duchy of Lancaster, but there was little pretence of its affording revenue to the Crown. King James's grant had been all-inclusive: the Ranger was also Forester, Steward of the Manor, Bailiff and Woodward,[5] and he had virtually the uncontrolled exploitation of its assets during his term of tenure. These assets included 'an extraordinary good house . . . fit for any gentleman', gardens, fish-ponds and orchards;

1. *A Relation of the Cruelties and Barbarous Murthers and other Misdemeanours, done and committed by some Foot-soldiers upon some of the Inhabitants of Enfield, Edmonton, South Myms and Hadley*, 29 July 1659, Brit. Mus. press-mark E 993 (10); *A Relation of the Riotous Insurrection of Divers Inhabitants of Enfield, &c.*, n.d. (1659), Brit. Mus. Thomason Tracts 669, fo. 21 (64); *Petition of Enfield Inhabitants*, Brit. Mus. 190 g12 (58); *Bloudy Newes from Enfield* etc., n.d. (1659), Brit. Mus. 579 c67.

2. *Commons Journals*, XIII, pp. 571–2, 26 May 1701.

3. See e.g. Simon Harcourt to Newcastle, 21 June 1711, discussing convictions of deer-stealers in Enfield Chase, in Nottingham University, Portland MSS, PW2.91 and 92.

4. Pleadings, 25 April 1724, DL 1/481; DL 39/5/17.

5. 'A brief account of the forests and chases within the Duchy of Lancaster', DL 39/5/17, which adds: 'it seems inconsistent with reason that all these offices should be in one person.'

two additional lodges; the use of timber and venison; and the opportunity (if supported by due 'interest') to enclose some part for private use – and General Pepper succeeded in enclosing at least ninety acres. In 1725 Pepper, ill and anxious to sell, valued the grant at £630 p.a.[1]

With these advantages came certain disadvantages. Pepper claimed to have found the Chase, on his entry, 'in a very ruinous condition', and he certainly left it more ruinous. Notwithstanding numerous prosecutions, 'Great numbers of people have come into the Chace in a hostile manner, who have destroyed his Majesty's timber & deer, attempted to murder the said Ranger at his own house, & severely wounded him, to the great impairing of his health.' He had been 'shot at in the Chase, his servants wounded, and his horses wounded and kill'd under them', all of which had led him to feel himself to be unloved.[2]

His prosecutions had, perhaps, been carried on in a somewhat military style, as befitted the man who had relieved Barcelona and thereby 'saved the Kingdom of Spain',[3] but not entirely in accord with the customs of north Middlesex. Undoubtedly the existing keepers, when he took over the Chase, were engaged in the usual rackets. He poked into their lodges, found deer-skins in one, a 'bullet gun' in another, concluded that they were engaged in a clandestine venison trade, turned them out of their lodges and their places, and prosecuted one for spoil of timber.[4] He busied himself with prosecutions against deer-stealers and timber-cutters.[5]

In 1720 he sent a keeper to ride around all the farms and houses bordering on the Chase, at Enfield, Clay Hill, Potter's Bar, Bentley Heath, Bush Fair, South Sheet, Winchmore Hill, to report on any wood found stacked in their yards. The wood (which the villagers claimed, in the form of 'lops and tops', as their right) was assumed to be stolen; and proceedings were instituted against no fewer than thirty-four of them in the Duchy Court.[6] By 1721 the Chase was in an uproar, and skirmishes

1. Chandos to the Earl of Dysart, 16 October 1725, Huntington Library, ST57, XXVII, 37–8.

2. 'Representation of John Pepper' (n.d., after 1721), Cambridge University Library, C(H) 376a.

3. Petition of Major-General John Pepper to George I; n.d., SP41.5.

4. Depositions in the case of *Rex* v. *Whitlock*, DL9/21 (Part I). It will be recalled that one of the purposes of Pepper's private bill against deer-stealers (above, p. 59) was to increase the penalties against keepers in league with them.

5. Charles Garrett, an Enfield baker, was fined £30 in 1719 for killing a fallow deer; his case was tried before General Pepper, J.P.: see KB33/13/6 (4), 5 Geo. I, Middlesex. Various depositions against timber-cutters in DL9/21.

6. Depositions of Mathew Colgan in DL9/21 (Part II). According to the customs of the Manor of Enfield, recited in the time of James II, every copyholder had the right to 'sufficient timber allowed him for his needful reparations out of the Chace': MS bound in *The Case of the Earl of Stamford*, 1701, Brit. Mus. 2267.

between keepers and deer-stealers frequent.[1] Three men were imprisoned for three months, and sentenced to monthly public whippings, for cutting boughs on the Chase for a bonfire in Enfield market-place on Guy Fawkes Day, 1721; John Pepper, in his alternating role as a Justice of the Peace, was one of those who passed sentence. They petitioned for release in the name of Hanoverian loyalty ('it has been customary ever since the Revolution to cut wood on our Chace . . . to make a bonfire'); their petition succeeded, and Pepper's credibility was injured.[2] In the same year he convicted three other men for deer-stealing; they received the standard sentence of a year's imprisonment and a day in the pillory (at Enfield). But having undergone their full sentence, they were confined by Pepper, without grounds, for a further term. In March 1723, when the men were brought from Newgate to Enfield for a further spell in the pillory, there were expectations of riot. Horse grenadiers guarded the pillory (Pepper could rely on the support of Earl Cadogan) and they remained stationed in the small town.[3] The wheel had come full circle, and the commoners had to turn to the Stuarts once again.

Poaching was endemic on the Chase. But no one attempted to associate this with any organization of Blacks. Some of the offenders were certainly local men to whom Pepper had given offence. George Ebbs, one of the three imprisoned in 1721, was a labourer of Edmonton, who had been prosecuted in 1715 for selling timber off the Chase to three Tottenham wheelwrights.[4] Minshull, proclaimed under the Black Act for an affray in October 1723, was probably a baker of Winchmore Hill who had been prosecuted for having wood in his yard in 1720.[5] William Gates (or Yates), the Edmonton blacksmith (known as 'Vulcan'), who had 'always from his youth delighted in deer-stealing', was another of the imprisoned of 1721, and was to return to the fray.[6] But others of the offenders were very probably agents in a considerable venison trade with London; one of them, Aaron Maddocks, was commonly known as 'Wild's man', having been a servant to Jonathan Wild, and no employee of that gentleman was likely to have put himself at risk without hope of a large financial return.[7] The King was still receiving for the royal table each year four brace of

1. See e.g. *Weekly Journal*, 29 July 1721, which records a skirmish in which 'four or five of General Pepper's servants were miserably wounded, and not one of the Gamesters taken'.

2. SP44.361, fo. 156; SP44.8, fo. 153.

3. SP35.77 (2), fo. 97; SP35.47, fo. 74; *British Journal*, 9 March 1723; *Gloucester Journal*, 11 March 1723; *London Journal*, 17 August 1723.

4. Deposition of John Hankin, 28 June 1715, in DL9/21 (Part II).

5. *London Gazette*, no. 6,249, 7–10 March 1724; DL9/21 (Part II).

6. See below, pp. 174–5.

7. Information of Thomas Gray, 26 July 1725, SP35.37. See also below, p. 233.

deer from the Chase;[1] one suspects that poachers were receiving much more.

In March 1724 three men were proclaimed under the Black Act, after an affray on the Chase the previous October in which a keeper was wounded. Two of these – a London wheelwright named John Berrisford (known as 'Jack the Wheeler'), and Thomas James, described as an Enfield labourer – were famous deer-stealers. There were further attacks on deer-parks around London in the next two or three years. In August 1724 there was a shoot-up between poachers and keepers at Richmond New Park; one poacher was shot dead, two were caught, and one (a baker's apprentice) escaped. Two weeks later the deer-stealers returned, led by Jack the Wheeler, who was mortally wounded and died in Kingston gaol. Several of these poachers on the environs of London were without horses: 'They went into the park on foot, sometimes with a crossbow, and sometimes with a couple of dogs, being armed always, however, with pistols for their defence. When they had killed a buck, they trussed him up and put him upon their backs and so walked off.' Such was John Guy, who eventually came to grief while poaching in the park of Anthony Duncombe, the heir to 'the richest commoner in England', at Teddington, near Kingston. Ambushed by keepers, his companion was killed, and he was captured; he was, perhaps, the first Londoner to be executed (in April 1725) under the Black Act.[2]

Meanwhile Thomas James, proclaimed in March 1724, remained at large. On 9 July 1725 William ('Vulcan') Gates and another man killed two deer in Enfield Chase, and exchanged shots with the keepers. For this they were proclaimed under the Black Act, on 20 July, on the sworn information of Henry Best, a keeper. News travelled fast, and on the same day four armed horsemen rode into the Chase, in search of Henry Best, whom they threatened to shoot. They failed to find him, but returned ten days later, sought him out and beat him up, breaking one of his legs. Vulcan Gates, Thomas James and Aaron Maddocks were among these four. They were, perhaps, members of a genuine London 'gang', bound by oaths, and with their own places of resort.[3] They were accused of

1. SP44.287, fo. 186.

2. *London Gazette*, no. 6,249, 7–10 March 1724; *Gloucester Journal*, 24 August and 7 September 1724; *Lives of the Most Remarkable Criminals*, A. L. Hayward, ed., 1927 pp. 216–17; *Northampton Mercury*, 7 September 1724. Guy's companion, sometimes named in the press as 'Biddisford', may in fact have been Berrisford, or Jack the Wheeler, in which case the Teddington affray took place on the same night as one of the attacks in August on Richmond Park. Guy took precedence as the first London victim of the Black Act over Bryan Smith; see below, p. 250. For Guy, see *ON*, 30 April 1725; *Mist's Weekly Journal*, 1 May 1725.

3. *London Gazette*, no. 6,392, 20–24 July 1725; ibid., no. 6,397, 7–10 August 1725;

being 'constantly' in the Chase, and had become so 'insolent' that the keepers could not appear 'without hazard of their lives'.[1]

Thomas James was picked up in February 1726, not, as it happens, for deer-stealing. He had stolen two mares at Hatfield, and was caught while trying to sell them at Bromley Fair. He was convicted at the next Kent Assizes, and executed, without recourse to the Black Act.[2] His comrade, Vulcan Gates, met with a more unusual legal termination. Under a clause in 9 George I c.22, if an accused man was formally proclaimed by the Privy Council (on the oaths of one or more 'credible' witnesses) for offences within the Act, and if the proclamation was published in the *Gazette*, read by the sheriff's officers in two market-towns on two market days in the county where the offence was committed, and affixed on some public place, then he must surrender himself, within forty days, for trial. If he failed to so surrender, then he was 'adjudged, deemed and taken to be convicted and attainted of felony, and shall suffer pains of death as in case of a person convicted and attainted by verdict and judgement of felony'.

Vulcan Gates had the privilege of trying out this surprising clause. It worked smoothly. He had been committed to Newgate under an alias and on another matter, and had talked too freely to the prison barber, who (mindful of the reward) gave him away. It was therefore necessary only to prove his identity and to prove him to be a proclaimed man. He was then sentenced to death early in 1726. The Edmonton blacksmith told the Ordinary of Newgate that 'when the proclamation was emitted he was out of town at fairs; and being ignorant, and not understanding to read, he did not consider the dangerous consequence of disobedience'. It was a vindictive prosecution, since it was never proven that Gates had hunted armed or disguised (and he denied the former); and if tried under 5 George I c.28, he could have been transported. He clearly resented the cursory and inglorious procedure and was reluctant to perform the accepted role, whether penitent or truculent, of the condemned. On the day of execution, he and some fellows 'took it into their heads that they would not be hang'd'. They obtained a crowbar, and while some drowned the noise by singing psalms, the others prised up the flagstones and erected a prodigious barrier against the door of the condemned cell. After all other persuasions failed, Sir Jeremiah Morden, Sheriff of London, was sent for, 'who spoke *seriously* to them' through a little hole in the ceiling, and who even deigned to dangle his gold chain through the

---

two informations of Thomas Gray, in SP35.37. The evidence as to an organized gang is in the letters of an informer, 'G.L.' in the same bundle.

1. Various papers in SP35.57; SP43.69, fo. 74; SP44.292, fo. 74; PC4.1.
2. Various papers (relating to claims for blood-money) in T1.257 (32); T53.32, p. 424.

hole as proof of his office. At length Vulcan Gates and his fellows agreed to play their appointed part at Tyburn.[1]

But there was yet one more clause in the Black Act, which we have so far overlooked. Under this, if any person did 'conceal, aid, abet or succour' any proclaimed person who had failed, after forty days, to surrender, knowing him to be such a proclaimed felon, then he also, 'being lawfully convicted thereof, shall be guilty of felony, and shall suffer death'. The difficulty in this clause, from the point of view of the Law Officers, was that the person so sheltering a proclaimed felon had to be 'lawfully convicted' and this presumably required bringing to a jury proof of two facts; first, that he did so shelter him, and second that he did so, knowing him to be a proclaimed man. The victim selected to try out the working of this interesting clause was one John Huntridge, who kept a 'noted inn' on the road between Putney and Kingston, and (it seems) on the wall of Richmond New Park: the Halfway House near to the Robin Hood Gate facing Wimbledon Common.[2]

We enter at this point a story which may always remain inscrutable, owing to the villainous motives of the chief actors and the opacity of the sources, and especially of a heavily censored press. It is clear, however, that the episode illustrates the workings of interest and dependency in an integrated paternalist society – the links between the Court and the alehouse, the Treasury Bench and Tyburn. And a digression is necessary, before we return to Huntridge. We may leave him safely, since he seems to have spent some part of 1725 in the custody of the King's Messenger or in Newgate awaiting trial.

After the Restoration, such royal or public lands as were available returned to the Crown, for the Crown's gift or sale to favourites; and grants of their use (in the form of Rangerships, etc.) could be made for life, or for several lives, or for a long term of years, or even in perpetuity. James II and William III had used this means of reward and influence, and the offices (and perquisites) of Ruperta Howe, Richard Norton, the

1. *ON*, 14 March 1726; KB33/12/1, 11 Geo. I, Surrey; T1.255 (33) and (55); SP35.60, fo. 4; Hayward, op. cit., pp. 305–6.

2. *Weekly Journal, or British Gazetteer*, 13 and 27 November 1725. The published *Extracts from the Court Rolls of the Manor of Wimbledon* (1866) show a John Huntridge on the 'great inquest' in 1715, 1719, and again at some point after 1726: pp. 276, 280, 299. When the Wimbledon warreners were beaten up in September 1723 (see below, p. 208) they sent to 'Huntridge's' for assistance: SP43.68. There is still a Robin Hood Gate from the Park onto the Kingston road. According to a 'Plan of Richmond New Park' drawn by Edward John Eyre, 1754 (Brit. Mus. maps KxLI/15/B1) The Halfway House (half-way between Kingston and Putney) was less than half a mile from the Robin Hood Gate, outside the park wall and on the edge of Wimbledon Heath Common. There was also a Robin Hood Alehouse on the wall by the Gate.

Earl of Arran, Mr Justice Baber and General Pepper had all descended from such grants. One of William's more lavish grants was that of the wardenship of Sherwood Forest to John Holles, Duke of Newcastle – an office which the Duke transformed into virtual ownership, in return for keeping for the King some hundreds of red deer (many of which were active in 'consuming and destroying' the cornfields of neighbouring farmers).[1] This claim on the use-rights of a whole forest was a large addition to the huge landed base from which his timid, fussy, unlovable nephew, Thomas Pelham Holles, purchased his dominating role as Whig manager for four decades.

Once an office had been granted for a term of lives, or the reversion to that office (when a previous grant should come to the end of its term), this grant became virtually a property, like a ground lease, which could be sold on the market. Since the power to effect grants had been somewhat curbed, and their length limited, by the Civil List Act (1 Anne c.7), the value of grants awarded before this limitation was in fact enhanced.[2] And such properties were in short supply. In the environs of London, Richmond Park and Enfield Chase were probably the most desirable parcels.

General Pepper was, as we have seen, a most vigorous Ranger. He rode ceaselessly about the Chase, prosecuting (at his own expense) deer-stealers and wood-spoilers, at hazard of his own life. He was an admirable public servant, a guardian of the King's interest, and his career is a useful corrective to the bias of those disaffected historians who suppose that all office-holders were intent only on milking their offices for their private advantage. Or so he would appear to be from one set of sources, the prosecutions and apologias of which he was himself author. But from another set of sources he appears in a different light, for in 1724–5 hell broke out, not only beneath his feet, but also above his head.

The first step in his downward glissade was perhaps the disclosure, in 1720, that he was one of the Members of Parliament who had been bribed by the South Sea Company. Thereafter favour seemed to slip from him. The Treasury Commissioners would not pay for his prosecutions; his bonfire burners were pardoned. In 1724 he found himself arraigned by 'the King' in the Court of the Duchy of Lancaster. The validity of his grant was called in question: he was referred to as 'the pretended' Ranger:

1. Papers Relating to Sherwood Forest, Nottingham University Library PW2.612–36 and 6/171/167.

2. See 12th Report of the Land Revenue Commissioners, *Commons Journal*, XLVII, 1792, esp. p. 846; 'B', 'The Office of Woods and Forests', *Law Magazine & Quarterly Review of Jurisprudence*, n.s., vol. 14 (1851), pp. 19–33.

John Pepper not only commits great spoyle and wast and permits others [to do so] . . . Every year since he entered without lawful warrant [he] did kill great numbers of His Majesty's game of pheasants, woodcocks, partridges . . . grubbed up cut maimed spoiled felled and destroyed vast quantities of . . . timber woods underwoods dotards . . . pollards oake elme ashe and maple . . . and by such practice hath almost ruined and destroyed His Majesty's Chase without having left 1000 head of deer whereas 4000 have been heretofore and ought and may be fed . . .

He had purloined for himself the rents and profits of the manor of Enfield. He had built himself a handsome new 'lodge', using 60,000 bricks (made on the Chase) and timber from the Chase, paying the workmen (in part) with allowances of wood and bushes. He had cut new ridings to the New Lodge – one of these forty feet wide and half a mile in length – clearing out all the timber in his way. He had sold timber wholesale to his toadies, granted timber and turfs to aristocratic neighbours, and sold tickets more generally to those who wanted turfs and firing. (Those who asserted common right and refused to buy his tickets he prosecuted.) He had manufactured and sold bricks as a private business. He had enclosed various parcels of land around the lodges without authority. He had not kept the proper local courts. He had 'fed great numbers of his own cattle' on the Chase, and had neglected to appoint an officer to regulate, mark and drive the commonable cattle. He had sacked the long-standing and capable Woodward and taken the office into his own hands. One witness deposed that, whereas there had been 1,000 deer in the Chase two years before, in 1724 there were 'not above 300 or 400, not above 4 bucks'; another witness thought there might still be as many as 600, but many of them 'rascally'. The General had been heard to swear that 'he cared not if there was not a deer in the Chase'. He had dismissed the proper keepers from one or two of the lodges, and rented them (at his own profit) to private persons. In one lodge he had installed a Mr Park Pepper ('who calls himself a sworn keeper') and in another a Mr George Pepper. Their degree of relationship to the General was not stated.[1]

If one half of these accusations were true (as seems very probable) we need speculate no further on the reasons for the assaults on the Chase, nor for 'the universal odium the present Ranger lies under' (as the Duke of Chandos noted in a private letter).[2] The prosecution of Pepper is instructive, and is a useful corrective to the views of those disaffected

1. Deposition of W. Sams, 20 May 1723, DL4/136; Pleadings, 25 April 1724, DL1/481; Proceedings in the Duchy Court, DL5/43, pp. 327, 344, 347, 357–8, 375; DL9/22 (1724). John Pepper to 'My Lord', 26 October 1724 (refuting, in general terms, these 'aspersions and calumnies') in Cambridge University Library, C(H) 1,177.

2. Chandos to Rogers, 10 September 1725, Huntington Library, ST57, XXVI 309.

historians who suppose that an impartial law could not intervene to protect the subject (and the public interest) against lofty predators. Or so it would seem from one set of sources, the protracted (and inconclusive) process in the Duchy Court of Lancaster. But there happens to survive, in this case, yet one more set of sources, which gives one yet another point of purchase from which to examine the confused affairs of Enfield Chase.

As we have noted, James II granted the rangership in 1687 to Lord Lisburn, from whom it had descended, in 1716, by purchase to John Pepper. In 1725 Pepper's grant still had twelve years to run. But in the reign of William and Mary Sir Robert Howard had secured a grant to the reversion of the rangership, for a term of a further fifty-six years. This piece of scrip had been bought up for £1,245 in 1714 by James Brydges, the Duke of Chandos, whose palace at Cannons, near Edgware, was a few miles from the Chase. Chandos was one of the wealthiest men in England. He had founded his fortune (as Ranelagh had done, and as Walpole was subsequently to do) on his tenure of the office of Paymaster General (1707–12). Vigilant and ruthless in his business ventures, he engaged ceaselessly in speculation in land and stocks. Although his greed and gullibility were soon to undermine his wealth, he remained, in the early 1720s, a plausible Midas, bribing and blowing bubbles, negotiating mercenary matches for his sons, speculating avariciously in the dirty trade of the slavers. In the aftermath of the bursting of the Bubble (he had extricated himself with a net gain of £200,000 although he could never get over the thought that if he had sold at the top of the market this would have been some £700,000 more) he invested heavily in the lands of bankrupt speculators; his interests extended into many counties – he even had a lease on Bishop's Waltham Park and may have contributed his portion of ill will to that story.[1] Moreover, he cultivated carefully his relations with the Whig oligarchs. Always obliging to Walpole (who no doubt needed his services to advance his own private fortune), he was one of those whose liberty and property Walpole's regime existed to preserve.[2]

Whatever cards were being stacked, Pepper's were at the bottom of the pack. This gallant and irascible gentleman, who was still petitioning for rewards for his military service, was an innocent in the more serious butchery of civil politics. He had probably crossed the Duke of Chandos as early as 1714 when he outbid him for the rangership.[3] Chandos knew

1. Hants Rec. Off. 154,501.

2. Chandos to Earl of Dysart, 16 October 1725, Huntington Library, ST57, XXVII, 37–8; C. H. C. and M. Baker, *The Life and Circumstances of James Brydges, First Duke of Chandos*, Oxford, 1949, *passim* and (for Enfield Chase) ch. XVI; Daniel Lysons, *The Environs of London*, 1795, II, p. 289.

3. Romney Sedgwick, *History of Parliament: The House of Commons 1715–54*, 1970,

how to bide his time. Pepper had probably not abused his office much more than similar office-holders, although Enfield was more in the public eye than, let us say, Alice Holt, and he had offended more gentry interests. But he had neglected his political lines of supply. He had attached himself, not to Walpole and Townshend, but to Cadogan and the King; and while Cadogan remained powerful, Walpole was jealous of him, and was happy to damage his creatures. There can be little doubt that Pepper would not have been arraigned before the Duchy Court if Walpole had not seen reason to withdraw ministerial protection – and if his prosecution had not been decidedly in the best interests of the Duke of Chandos.

Pepper's position became desperate. The Chase was in an uproar, his own character incurred 'universal odium', a former Steward of the manor of Enfield had fled to France with all the court rolls, he himself was ill, trying the Bath waters, and 'very desirous to part with his term'.[1] This was exactly the negotiating position which Chandos wished to achieve. In the Duchy Court Pepper could still bluster: the trial (one gossip noted), 'Is before Lord Leichmore, whose behaviour Pepper did not like, and, as they were going out of Westminster Hall, the latter said out aloud, that if Lord Leichmore did not mend his manners that he would send Lord Cadogan to him.'[2] But each episode of publicity lowered the cash-value of his remaining years of tenure. Chandos seized this moment to search for a customer for his own reversionary term, of fifty-six years. If Pepper's remaining years were added to this, it would amount (he argued) almost to a freehold of the Chase. Pepper, by now, would have been happy to sell his grant to Chandos, but Chandos exploited every ounce of his bargaining power. 'I must needs acquaint you with one circumstance,' he informed Pepper's intermediary (as if that gentleman did not already know!), 'that there is a prosecution carrying on against him to forfeit his grant, and should that happen, mine immediately takes place. This I think renders it pretty hazardous for anyone to meddle with, unless he can likewise purchase the grant I have, which if I can get a selling price for I shall not be unwilling to part with . . .'[3] Thus Chandos could wait happily, either for Pepper to forfeit his patent (which was, in the end, unlikely), or for a purchaser to come along willing to buy up both grants. Such a purchaser had once seemed likely in 'a very

---

II, p. 336. Chandos to Erle, 6 March 1728: 'Pepper step't in and took it out of my hands by giving a larger sum': Huntington Library, ST57, XXXI, 135.

1. Chandos to Walpole, 17 June 1725; to Earl of Dysart, 16 October 1725; to Rogers, 10 September 1725; all in Huntington Library, ST57, XXVI and XXVII. Memo of John Hale to George II, n.d., Cambridge University Library, C(H) 45/40; C(H) 1,177.

2. *Hist. MSS Comm. Var. Coll., VIII*, p. 393.

3. Chandos to Rogers, 10 September 1725, Huntington Library, ST57, XXVI, 309.

considerable person', who 'had a mind to it' and was prepared with 'a large sum of money', in the region of £16,000, for Chandos's term.[1]

This person was Sir Robert Walpole, a great huntsman, who had perhaps had his interest in such properties stimulated by his attention to the Blacks in the previous two years, and who, having already bled the charity of Chelsea Hospital, was looking for larger prey. Chandos offered him the Chase, in June 1725: 'if either yourself or Lord Townshend are willing to secure it for a second son, it shall be at your services. The situation and command it gives, you are sure to be well acquainted with.' In a shrewd sentence calculated to inflame Walpole's political jealousies, as an additional goad to his avarice, he added: 'Mr. Poultney and Lord Bolingbroke have both of them spoke to me about it.' As for Pepper's grant, he is 'very desirous to part with his term . . . it might be had a great pennyworth'.[2] Walpole did not, in the end, rise to the bait, and we will shortly see why.

Chandos in the next year or two tried other customers; the assets of the Chase were clearly of most value to those with the right political interest. The Chase could let at 20s. or 30s. an acre, and 'if ever the public should incline to inclose this ground, there is no doubt but that a large tract thereof would be assigned to the owner of this grant'. (Indeed, when dealing with one prospective purchase, he suggested reserving to himself 1,000 acres in the event that the purchaser should obtain an Act of Enclosure.) If total enclosure proved to be impracticable, any owner of the grant with 'interest enough' should be able to 'obtain licence from time to time, to inclose part of it', as Pepper, with only a paltry interest, had done by ninety or more acres. But this gentleman had by now made a flurried exit. He had sold his grant, for £4,000 (at least £2,000 under his asking price), and Pulteney (no doubt for some other 'service' rendered) had transferred it at the same price to Chandos. This was in September 1725; in October Pepper set off for France, dying on his way at Dover, 'unlamented'.[3]

The reason why Walpole failed to come up to Chandos's expectations was that he had already settled his interest upon an even more desirable property, quieter and very much more fashionable than Enfield Chase,

1. Chandos to Colonel Horsey, 10 September 1727, Huntington Library, ST57, XXX, 266.

2. Chandos to Walpole, 17 June 1725, Huntington Library, ST57, XXVI, 106.

3. Chandos to Earl of Dysart, 16 October 1725; Chandos to Colonel Horsey, 10 September and 29 October 1727, Huntington Library, ST57, XXVII, 37–8: XXX, 266, 331; Petition from Pepper and opinion, in Hardwicke Papers, Brit. Mus. 36,135, fo. 90; A. Boyer, *Political State of Great Britain*, 1725, XXX, p. 418, which notes Pepper's death as 'unlamented'; C. Dalton, *George I's Army*, 1910, I, pp. 112, 246. For the subsequent history of the Chase, see C. H. C. and M. Baker, op. cit., ch. XVI and below, pp. 232–3.

and nearer to London. In 1683 the office of Ranger of Richmond Park had been granted to the Hyde family, Earls of Rochester and of Clarendon, who made Petersham Lodge, within the New Park, their seat. In 1721 the Lodge burned down, and the Earl became reconciled to selling his grant, which had been renewed by Queen Anne for two further lives. His valuation of the assets of his property and office survives. The perquisites of the office of Ranger or Keeper were valued as follows:

The herbage and pannage of the Park over and besides what is necessary for the sustenation of the deer, and also three bucks and three does in every season & all the woods and underwoods called browsewood windfall wood dead trees mastage and chimage . . .

£200 per ann. which att 21 years purchase comes to . . . £4,200

The fee of 6s per diem as Keeper of the said parke which amounts yearly to the sume of £109.10s att 21 years purchase comes to . . . £2,299.10.

£6,499.10.[1]

The price was perhaps high and Walpole was content to wait; eventually he managed to buy out the Hydes at £5,000, and the King bestowed the office upon Walpole's son, Lord Robert. Effectively the honours and perquisites of the office fell upon the father, who rebuilt Hartleton or Old Lodge (at a cost of some £14,000), kept his mistress, Maria Skerrett, in a house in the park, hunted there regularly and was painted in the full regalia of the Ranger.[2]

Since Richmond occupies only a small place in the history of the Black Act, it would be tedious to attempt to reconstruct the social relations in that neighbourhood in 1725. The New Park had been unpopular with the inhabitants ever since it was first carved out of the local commons by Charles I. There was the usual history of deer-stealing.[3] There was an unusually bitter contest about rights to firewood, which was to continue for many decades. A resort of royalty and nobility, attempts were made to keep out the commoners, to lock the gates, to provide the favoured few with keys or tickets of entry.

When Walpole's regime was only a bad memory, and the censorship had relaxed, there was an outburst of controversy about all these matters. The commencement of the grievances of local inhabitants was dated to

1. C(H) 45/30 and 45/37, both valuations undated.

2. I am indebted for information on Richmond Park to two local historians, Mr E. E. Dodd and Mrs Pamela Fletcher-Jones, author of *Richmond Park* (1972). See also E. Beresford Chancellor, *History and Antiquities of Richmond &c.*, Richmond, 1894, p. 218, and J. H. Plumb, *Sir Robert Walpole*, 1960, II, p. 90, who notes that Walpole's son 'gave up all the Ranger's rights and perquisites to his father'; the son was appointed only to ensure that 'the office would remain in the family for a longer period'.

3. See T1.90 (40).

Walpole's rangership – 'the grand corrupter of the nation, the waster ... of his country's liberties, [who] made the management of the Park a part of his venal administration ...' Roads crossed the Park, and access was free: by ladders over the wall or through unlocked gates. The ladders were first removed on Walpole's order. Man-traps were set in their places. The gates were locked, and access was to be had only by ticket. The rights of the people of several neighbouring parishes to take firewood, furze and gravel from the Park were curtailed:

> All these rights and privileges were fully enjoyed, until the lord Walpole suc-
> ceeded to the rangership of the park, upon which there was a succession of new
> laws and customs; the old-established rights being changed into new-fangled
> obliging privileges, which the people were to enjoy no longer than during the
> good will and pleasure of the Ranger.

But (continued the fair-minded pamphleteer) 'to do justice to his lordship', although he was the nominal Ranger, it was his father who managed the affairs of the Park. 'The people were afraid to contend with a minister that had all the treasure of the kingdom at his command, and was never known to be niggardly, in supporting any of his arbitrary measures.'[1]

By these accounts, the conflict over rights in the Park became intense only after Walpole (through his son) assumed the rangership. But there are some indications that the conflicts commenced in 1723 at the end of Rochester's term, when the Treasury Commissioners ordered a wholesale fall of timber in the Park as a means of raising revenue.[2] Such a timber sale would certainly have been felt by the inhabitants as an encroachment on their rights, and, while the deer-stealers of the 1720s were not all local men, there is no reason to suppose that the local people wished them ill. And at Wimbledon, to the east of the Park, there was also unrest. The manor had been bought in 1717 by Sir Theodore M. Janssen, a director of the South Sea Company. When the Bubble burst, part of his estate was forfeit and the manor was sold off, being bought, in 1723, by Sarah, Duchess of Marlborough. The commoners, who were also in frequent dispute with their lords about rights to firing, turfs and gravel, can

1. *A Tract on the National Interest, and Depravity of the Times*, 1757, *passim*. The Earl of Rochester had perhaps commenced locking the gates before Walpole's time: see *Merlin's Life and Prophecies*, 1755, pp. 62–72, and (for the whole issue) *Two Historical Accounts of the Making of the New Forest and of Richmond New Park*, 1751.

2. Memorial of Henry Earl of Rochester, and report of Charles Withers, 23 October 1722 and 21 March 1723, T1.243 (28). It should be noted (a) that Rochester was of a famous Tory family, and a political opponent of Walpole's, and (b) that Walpole directed Treasury policy. Treasury orders to fell timber, not for the navy but simply to raise revenue, were highly unusual, and overrode the Ranger's perquisites. It is probable that Walpole was already easing Rochester out of the rangership.

scarcely have felt any feudal deference to the master who changed above their heads.[1]

We meet, yet again, alternative definitions of social reality. In polite historiography we should now see the Richmond area as coming to its climax of fashionability and grace. With the King, his mistress, and the First Minister in the Park; with Sarah, Duchess of Marlborough, very occasionally at Wimbledon; and with Pope and his friends near by at Twickenham, nothing was needed to add favour to the district. King George greatly preferred Richmond to Windsor: by 1725 he was stag-hunting frequently in the Park, where Lady Mary Wortley Montagu was one of 'the *beau monde* in his train'. For this *beau monde*, however, the Park still required some 'improvement'. In the recollections of Horace Walpole it was 'a bog, and a harbour for deer-stealers and vagabonds'.

But in the surly plebeian minds of such vagabonds alternative definitions must have been proposed. For example, a servant at Wimbledon's old Elizabethan manor house would have found the world changing literally, and not metaphorically, above her head, and doing so several times in as many years. For Sir Theodore Janssen pulled the old house down and rebuilt; when his new mansion was scarcely finished, Sarah pulled it down in its turn, rebuilt, and then, not liking the 'aspect', pulled her own creation down and built yet once more. As for Richmond Park, the 'bog' had been a source of turfs and kindling for the poor, and (for the daring) a source of rabbit, hare and venison. Moreover, the inhabitants of several parishes must have shared a common interest in lost rights within the Park, for when Charles I had first made it he had taken within the walls not only Richmond common, but also most of Mortlake, Petersham and Ham commons, and small parts of Kingston and of Putney with (possibly) a portion of Roehampton commons.[2]

The exact date at which Walpole's interest in Richmond Park became intense is uncertain. But he had succeeded in securing the rangership for his son by the summer of 1725.[3] From April 1725 to September 1730 very

1. Lord Eversley, *Commons Forests and Footpaths*, 1910, pp. 64–5; *Extracts from the Wimbledon Court Rolls*, 1866, *passim*.

2. Horace Walpole, *Memoirs of the Reign of King George the Second*, 1847, I, p. 402; *The Letters of Lady Mary Wortley Montagu*, 1893, I, p. 489; Mrs Arthur Colville, *Duchess Sarah*, 1904, p. 299; E. Beresford Chancellor, op. cit., pp. 214–15.

3. Lord Hardwicke in *Walpoliana* (1783, p. 10) says that George I, in the last year of his reign (1726–7), spent part of every week on Richmond Hill, where Walpole had hired a lodging; the King ordered the New Lodge to be built before he went to Hanover for the last time (June 1727). But there is a Treasury Warrant to do extensive work in Richmond Park dated 20 May 1725: LR4.3 (21), and Lord Robert Walpole's appointment to the Rangership was given as 21 July 1725 in Treasury papers: see T53.32, p. 294 and T29.25, p. 44 (e). I suggest that Walpole must have obtained from the King a promise of the rangership early in 1725, if not before.

great expenses were incurred by the Treasury in repairing, building and rebuilding lodges in the Park; breaches in the wall were repaired, new gates and horse gates were set up, new locks installed, new paddocks fenced and pheasant coops and deer pens built. The accounts for the carpenters and bricklayers alone, from 1 April 1725 to 14 January 1727, totalled £3,715 18s. 9¾d.[1] Walpole was enjoying the fruits of his royal favour to the full. Nor was his interest in deer and in deer-stealing theoretic. He kept deer at Houghton, where he was engaged in extensive emparkment (shifting the local village in the process), he was said to have opened letters from his huntsman before letters of state,[2] and he was to keep beagles and to hunt many weekends at Richmond. His prey in 1725, however, was John Huntridge, to whom, after this long detour, we may now return.

It is not clear how this man crossed Walpole's path, although it is probable that the path was the one which ran from Westminster to the rangership. We have only the scrap of gossip that Huntridge 'lived on the wall of New Park, and had some words with a great man'; if true, these 'words' with the innkeeper could have related to deer-stealers, to timber rights, to access (or closure of access) to the Park through the Robin Hood Gate, or even to the matter of lodgings for himself or Maria Skerrett. This is sheer speculation. All that we know is that between 1723 and 1725 the contest between keepers and deer-stealers became unusually intense. In the autumn of 1723 the inhabitants of Richmond were ordered by the High Constable of Kingston Hundred to keep watch and ward, with five armed men, on Court Park Hill.[3] In 1723, also, two 'gentlemen hunters alias deer stealers' were seized and imprisoned.[4] On 10 November 1724 Walter Moor was committed for 'carrying matches' to set a keeper's house on fire, and John Huntridge for aiding deer-stealers and for 'feloniously harbouring Thomas James knowing him as an outlawed person'.[5] At the Assizes at Kingston in March 1725, seven or eight men were indicted for taking or killing deer in the previous August and September in the Park.[6] At least two of these men were subsequently

---

1. Accounts of Charles Withers among the Earl St Aldwyn's unnumbered Hicks-Beach papers.

2. Lord Hardwicke, op. cit., p. 10.

3. The order, dated 18 October 1723, drew a complaint from some of the inhabitants (6 November 1723); there was a further order for Watch and Ward on 5 October 1725, as a result of 'diverse outrages and disorders': QS bundles (1723) and Order Book: Surrey Rec. Off.

4. Surrey QS bundles, Midsummer 1723, Surrey Rec. Off. Thomas Boxall and Peter Yates were in fact first taken up in December 1722.   5. ibid., Christmas 1724.

6. Assi. 35.165.9 (28), (29), (49), (50), (51), (52).

executed, under the provisions of the Black Act.[1] In the cases of six of the indicted men, John Huntridge was coupled with them, as having 'feloniously procured abetted and counselled' them, or having 'harboured comforted and maintained' them.

Not all of these men were necessarily in custody. Thomas James, as we know, was still at large on Enfield Chase in the summer of 1725, and was not taken up until February 1726. Hence, if Huntridge was to be proved to have harboured James (a proclaimed man) *knowing* him to be so (which was necessary for conviction under the Black Act) this could only be done on the evidence of an accomplice. The evidence was obtained from another of the indicted men, Richard Blackburn alias Thompson alias Evans. He had been sentenced, probably at the Kingston Lent Assizes (1725), to three months' imprisonment and a fine, for killing deer. But he then found himself to be in much worse trouble: his mare, it turned out, was stolen, and he was tried for horse-stealing and sentenced to death. At the end of July he was writing from Newgate:

> Since my sad misfortune of having been cast for my life for a mare, which I bought of Thomas James, one of those vile men who first persuaded me to the practice of deer stealing, I have used my most just and best endeavours to inform the Right Honourable the Earl of Rochester and the Right Honourable Robert Walpole Esq., of what I know concerning such men . . .

He desired to know 'what is further required of me to complete my information', and what his own fate was to be.[2] It seems that the outgoing and incoming Rangers of Richmond Park, Rochester and Walpole, were working on the case together.

The first sign of ministerial intervention in the Richmond affair comes in March 1725, when the Treasury Solicitor was instructed to ensure that the prosecutions at Kingston Assizes should be 'vigorously pursued' at the expense of the state.[3] It is probable that Blackburn turned informer immediately upon conviction, at the end of March, and that his informations were taken directly by Walpole. Huntridge was not tried at Kingston Assizes, and had probably evaded arrest; a warrant for his arrest was issued directly, on 16 April, by Townshend, who had received

---

1. Richard Minchin was indicted for killing a deer in Richmond Park, Kingston Assizes, March 1725, Assi. 35.165.9 (28) and (29). See also accounts of the Civil List (Brit. Mus. Add. MSS 29,464, fo. 235) which show, in 1725–6, rewards of £200 to persons who apprehended Richard Minchin and Samuel Kellett 'executed for killing deer in New Park'; also T53.32, p. 436.

2. Blackburn to 'Honoured Sir', 30 July 1725, SP35.57; indictments in Assi. 35.165.9 (50), (51), (52).

3. Scrope to Cracherode, 19 March 1725, T27.24, p. 65.

'information upon oath' that he had concealed, aided, abetted and suc-
coured Thomas James.[1] The King then went to Hanover (accompanied
by Townshend), and Walpole, with the Lords Justices of the Regency,
was, as in 1723, in undisputed command. On 5 August the Lords Justices
considered the case, and requested a promise of a pardon for Blackburn,
'that he may be an evidence against one Huntridge, a notorious deer
stealer and harbourer of such offenders'. The King (Townshend wrote
back) 'has approved of their Excy's Recommendation in favour of Richard
Thompson alias Blackburn' and a pardon would be granted in order that
he might be 'an Evidence against one Huntridge a Notorious Offender'.[2]
Great pains were taken in preparing the case: the Treasury Solicitor had
several consultations with the Attorney and Solicitors-General, and they
and Serjeant Pengelly were briefed for the prosecution; it was very much
the most costly state prosecution of that year.[3] The press, which reported
the case thriftily and cautiously, assumed that the outcome was a foregone
conclusion: Huntridge 'being outlawed there remains nothing but judgement of death to be awarded against him, which we hear will be done one
day this term'.[4] He could be dealt with with as much dispatch as was to
be the case with Vulcan Gates.

This was not how matters turned out. After a trial lasting eight or
nine hours, and perhaps longer – the Attorney and Solicitors-General and
Counsel were paid 'refreshers', the trial 'being very long'[5] – Huntridge
was acquitted. The reports in the press give nothing away, and once
again we owe to Dr Stratford's correspondence with Edward Harley our
only glimpse of what was going on:

> The trial of Huntridge, on Wednesday last, makes a great noise. He lived on
> the wall of New Park, and had some words with a great man. He was prosecuted
> for concealing deer stealers. He had many witnesses to depose that they heard
> those who swore against him own that they were to have money for swearing. A
> horse stealer had been pardoned, and came in as a witness against him. After
> a long trial he was acquitted, upon which there was a great shout quite through
> Westminster Hall. The mobility [i.e. 'mob'] will have it that a great man was
> concerned in the prosecution.[6]

The 'great man', in these years of guarded correspondence, always stood
for Walpole. The horse-stealer was of course Richard Blackburn, in fear

---

1. SP44.81, pp. 415–16; SP35.55 (3), fo. 125.   2. SP43.74; SP43.76.
3. Accounts of A. Cracherode, 22 December 1725, T1.253 (63). The costs of the
prosecution of Huntridge were £168 19s. 11d.; of prosecuting two seditious libellers,
E. Curll (£42 19s. for each of two prosecutions) M. Earbary (11 gs).
4. *Weekly Journal, or British Gazetteer*, 13 November 1725.
5. Cracherode's accounts, T1.253 (63).
6. Stratford to Harley, 17 November 1725, *Hist. MSS Comm. Portland, VII*, p. 404.

for his own life. Huntridge, almost alone of the accused of these years, was able to fee competent defence counsel, and they served him well. Their room for manoeuvre was slender. They were able to call a great number of witnesses who gave Huntridge 'an extraordinary good character'.[1] But they also battered away at the formal structure of the prosecution, to find any conceivable or inconceivable point of weakness; they made the prosecution produce the commissions by which Townshend and Walpole held office; fussed about proof of James's proclamation in the *Gazette*; and finally found the breaking-point they needed. Walpole, it seems, had taken Blackburn's information on oath in some irregular way, contrary to the exact terms of the Act.[2] It was the loophole which the jurors wanted, and through which a hunted man made his escape.[3]

The case of Huntridge has been examined with particular attention to its procedural details (or what can be discovered about these). It may be of interest to recapitulate these trivia. There are two unknown (and perhaps unknowable) allegations in the case. First, Huntridge was accused of aiding and harbouring Thomas James. This is perfectly possible; but the licensee of a 'well-known' inn on a busy road is in an unusual position – he must, half-knowingly, harbour a great many possible offenders, and if he was to inquire too closely into his customers he would have no custom. Second, Walpole was accused of having some personal grudge ('having words') with the accused. This is equally possible; but it rests only on reported gossip as to what 'the mobility' believed.

The rest of the case is clear. Sir Robert Walpole was (through his son) Ranger of the Park, and therefore had a personal interest in the conviction of the accused; Walpole was also Secretary of State (in Townshend's absence) and the decisive member of the Regency Council of Lords Justices. This body initiated the prosecution of the accused; Walpole himself extracted evidence from a condemned horse-thief; the Lords Justices solicited a pardon for this thief in order that he should be brought as an evidence against the accused (whom they had already adjudged guilty); and the King, to whom the accused, if convicted, had to appeal for mercy, concurred in their prejudgement. The entire resources of the Crown were thrown into the prosecution (Attorney and Solicitors-

---

1. *Weekly Journal, or British Gazetteer*, 27 November 1725.

2. This appears from Crown notes jotted on the back of a copy of the indictment, in KB33/12/1, 11 Geo. I Surrey; also T1.253 (63) and the fuss about procedure discussed below.

3. Richard Blackburn also made his escape, and got his pardon: SP44.124, fo. 228; T27.24, p. 140.

General, Treasury Solicitor, etc.). Conviction, under the procedures of the Black Act, was expected to be a mere matter of procedural form. Jurors in the Court of King's Bench were normally compliant and subject to influence: 'we may depend', Delafaye (the Secretary to the Lords Justices) had assured Townshend two years before, 'upon having juries . . . well enclined towards their Kings and country's service & interest.'[1] It was made manifest that it was in this 'interest' that the Richmond publican should swing. He was a very lucky man to escape.

The authorities regarded the acquittal of Huntridge as a set-back. Three weeks later a magistrate sent in some rather stale sworn informations against offenders in the Forest of Bere, and Delafaye replied morosely that 'a late experience' had 'shewn that prosecutions upon the Act against the Blacks &c. are liable to cavils & exceptions'. The informations (two months old) would not 'answer the directions of the Act . . . to return such informations *forthwith*', and they should be sent, not by post, but by hand.[2] Clearly Delafaye could only see Huntridge's escape from the gallows as having been caused by a regrettable inattention to the proper forms.

This episode of Enfield Chase and Richmond Park may seem tiresome, complex and inconclusive. But there is a point of importance somewhere within it. One seems to observe the parallel motions, in two very different elements, of two different sets of predators. Although having some notion of right, and some public support, the deer-stealers – Thomas James, 'Jonathan Wild's man', 'Jack the Wheeler' – were horse-thieves, venison traders and a rough enough lot. They were the petty predators, and above them, in the element of 'interest', Court favour, money and power, moved the great predators – Pepper, Chandos, Newcastle, Walpole – eager for office, perquisites, enclosure of Crown or public land. Their depredations were immeasurably larger and more injurious, both to a notional 'public' and to those who claimed use-rights in the disputed lands, than the depredations of deer-stealers.

At the level of affrays between poachers and keepers there was some equality in the contest. But at the point where the petty seriously inconvenienced the great, then the entire apparatus of power and law could be brought to the side of the latter. The Black Act put unprecedented legal power in the hands of men who had not a generalized, delegated interest, such as the maintenance of order, or even the maintenance of the

1. Delafaye to Townshend, 1 October 1723, SP43.67. See above, p. 151.
2. Delafaye to Stanyforth, 16 December 1725, SP44.124, fos. 247–8. The magistrate duly changed the date of the informations from 27 October to 27 December 1725, and the demands of form were satisfied: compare SP35.58, fo. 102 and *London Gazette*, no. 6,447, 29 January 1726: also SP35.60, fos. 9, 19.

privileges of their own class, but a direct and personal interest in the conviction of men who were a nuisance to them. The obtaining of sworn informations, followed by outlawry and – as in the case of Vulcan Gates – summary condemnation to death, was a power only too easily open to direct abuse in a society in which every office-holder was subject to immediate political influence. It was a power which made nonsense of a whole costly historical paraphernalia whose proclaimed object was to safeguard the liberty of the subject. One part only of the traditional procedures of inherited law remained as a safeguard for the accused – the jury system. The acquittal of John Huntridge by twelve men, who knew themselves to be exposed to the retribution of 'interest' and who were probably astounded at their own temerity, provided a salutary check to the growth of arbitrary power. Men will, on occasion, act not according to their own interests but according to the expectations and values attached to a certain role. The role of juror carried (and still carries) such an inheritance of expectations. The acquittal of Huntridge may have been more important than a score of more celebrated cases in defending the subject against the state.

9: The Politics of the Black Act

Did the emergency of 1723 constitute a necessary cause for the enactment of 9 George I c.22? We will take this as two distinct questions. First, in what sense was there an emergency? Second, if there was one, could the authorities have handled it without recourse to this sanguinary code?

The forest and episcopal officers, the gentry and magistrates exposed to attack, had no doubt that they faced an emergency. This is evident from their letters and reports. We cannot quantify this emergency in terms of blood shed, nor even of deer killed. Indeed, the balance-sheet looks paltry. In the crisis years of 1723–4, two keepers were killed (young Miles and Earwaker) and several injured.[1] No gentleman or magistrate was harmed. This was no Jacquerie. And very adequate retribution was visited on the offenders: four Windsor Blacks were hanged at Reading, seven Hampshire Blacks at Tyburn, and, by 1726, at least five of the Enfield and Richmond offenders had been caught and hanged. An unknown number died in Newgate and Reading gaols. More were transported or imprisoned, and an estimate (made hazardous by the inadequacy of the records) suggests that some forty who evaded arrest from the three disturbed districts must have become outlaws.

Such a balance-sheet makes nonsense. Comparable encounters between keepers and poachers, at least as bloody as any in the episode of Blacking (and sometimes very much bloodier), can be found in many counties and in most decades of the eighteenth or early nineteenth centuries. But this was not the point. What made the 'emergency' was the repeated public humiliation of the authorities; the simultaneous attacks upon royal and private property; the sense of a confederated movement which was

1. One Enfield keeper who was badly injured may possibly have died subsequently. And another was reported as killed by deer-stealers in August 1725: *Mist's Weekly Journal*, 7 August 1725.

enlarging its social demands, especially under 'King John'; the symptoms of something close to class warfare, with the loyalist gentry in the disturbed areas objects of attack and pitifully isolated in their attempts to enforce order. It was a sorry state of affairs when the King could not defend his own forests and parks, and when the acting Commander-in-Chief of the armed forces could not prevent his own park from being driven for deer. The Blacks had, for a year or two, the support of forest communities in much the same way as Luddites were later to have the support of textile ones. It was this community support which made it difficult to effect the arrest of William Shorter, which led to the fear of rescues when the heavily guarded convoys of prisoners moved to and from London, and which led Townshend to station troops in Maidenhead to safeguard the peace of the country 'which at this time is infected with a lawless, riotous kind of people generally known by the name of Blacks'.[1] It was this displacement of authority, and not the ancient offence of deer-stealing, which constituted, in the eyes of Government, an emergency.

We may allow that this was so, and that Government saw this as the necessary cause for some measures of repression, and perhaps for some new legislation. To say this is not the same thing as saying that we have found a sufficient (or even an insufficient) cause for the passing of the Black Act. There is no evidence that the victims or the forest authorities in the disturbed counties were pressing for an Act of any such scope; they were suggesting proclamations and rewards, the stationing of troops in the disturbed districts, heavier sentences upon deer-stealers. In 1723 neither sheep- nor cattle-stealing were capital offences (although horse-theft had long been so); to make deer-stealing (if armed and disguised, or if in royal preserves) a capital offence was to revert 200 years. The breaking of the heads of fish-ponds had never been a felony: it carried a fine under 37 Henry VIII c.6 and a fine and three months' imprisonment under 5 Elizabeth c.21, and neither Act (Radzinowicz has remarked) 'originated in a period of English history remarkable for leniency'.[2] The cutting-down of young trees and the maiming of cattle appear to be new offences; presumably they could have been dealt with under other heads of malicious damage, but certainly not (before 1723) as felonies. Extortion or blackmail were already high misdemeanours at common law, punishable by fine and imprisonment; the Black Act was the first to introduce the death penalty.[3] And so on. Both in its severity and in the

1. Townshend to Officer in Charge of troops at Maidenhead, 21 May 1723, SP44.81, fo. 251.

2. Leon Radzinowicz, *A History of English Criminal Law and its Administration from 1750*, 1948, I, p. 61.

3. The only punishment for cattle-maiming before 1723 appears to have been

loose and wholesale manner of its drafting, the Act was unprecedented. It provided a versatile armoury of death apt to the repression of many forms of social disturbance. It was neither necessary, nor especially effective, in dealing with the particular 'emergency' which served as its excuse. The men condemned at Reading were tried under statutes passed before the Black Act (four of them as accessories to murder). Three of the Hampshire condemned could equally well have been tried for the murder of Earwaker, the keeper, in Holt Forest. Thus only the Portsmouth men could not have been sent to the gallows without the aid of the Black Act. These men's offences were to appear 'armed and disguised' in the forest, and they were accused of none of the more serious offences – blackmail, arson, the cutting of trees or maiming of cattle – which were supposedly the occasion for the Act. Their execution was a plain act of terror.

Thus it is necessary to distinguish between a situation which might reasonably be provocative of some new measures of repression, and the unprecedented character of the Act which was in fact provided. Professor Pat Rogers has recently confused these questions, in the first scholarly article to appear on the origins of the Black Act.[1] I do not wish to quibble about minor disagreements in our accounts of events, although certain points require correction: thus Rogers states (wrongly) that the Reading offenders were tried under the Black Act, and (of the Hampshire offenders who were so tried) that 'it was only actual murders which led to a capital sentence'. But, narrative questions apart, what occasions surprise is the discrepancy between our two interpretations of these events. We appear to be describing the same episode, but within that episode we see different actors and different social relations. What Rogers sees is – following in the old-established *Newgate Calendar* tradition – the operation of 'gangs' of 'criminals'. The method of these 'gangsters at large' resemble those of 'the gangs of Wild and William Field in London'. The Blacks were engaged in 'a calculated form of crime', their members belong to 'the criminal subculture of Georgian England', they were 'extortionists and protection-racketeers', and 'bully-boys with a certain swagger and professional confidence'.

The confidence, and perhaps even the swagger, are (one feels) less those of the Blacks than those of Professor Rogers. He is able, from slender evidence, and from evidence which is assembled by the authorities and opponents of the Blacks, to pronounce with assurance upon the

---

treble damages: Blackstone, *Commentaries*, IV, 245. Blackmail was a felony by an Act of 1601 which was, however, limited in its operation to the counties bordering upon Scotland: Radzinowicz, op. cit., I, p. 641.

1. Pat Rogers, 'The Waltham Blacks and the Black Act', *Historical Journal*, XVII, 3, 1974. See also Appendix 2, below.

objectives, motivations, organization and moral worth of these elusive men. Although I think that I have shown some of the critical economic and social tensions aroused in the forests, I cannot share Rogers's confidence. We know something of the objectives of the Blacks from their actions, we can infer a little as to their motivations, we know almost nothing of their organization, and we should hesitate before we pronounce on their moral worth.

The danger lies, in part, in allowing a moral judgement to precede the full recovery of the evidence, and indeed to infect the categories of our own examination. This infection may be of more than one kind, and Rogers may help us when he reminds us that – according to the categories of England's rulers – the Blacks were no more than 'criminals'. Being defined as such would have helped to persuade them to act as such – and in most practically persuasive ways: thus, with spies around, with blood-money hanging over their heads, and with the constant knowledge that the information of a colleague could bring them to the gallows, they are likely to have been driven into an ungentle underground of violence and blackmail which it is easy to tidy up and categorize as 'a criminal sub-culture'. Because we can show that offenders were subject to economic and social oppression, and were defending certain rights, this does not make them instantly into good and worthy 'social' criminals, hermetically sealed off from other kinds of crime. Offences which may command our sympathy – poaching or smuggling – were not conducted in especially gentlemanly ways: when an exciseman was killed in Dorset, in 1723, 'the smugglers swore they did no more matter to kill him than they would a Tode'.[1] No doubt the Blacks had similar views of Baptist Nunn or of the informers who took them to the gallows, although as it happens there is no evidence as to any effective reprisals against them. The Blacks were, one presumes, rough; and after the Black Act was passed they may have become rougher.[2]

Thus Rogers may usefully correct a certain contemporary fashion of romanticizing crime, which, by viewing it only in its aspects of resistance to oppression on the part of the propertyless, refuses to acknowledge other evidence. And if we choose to look there is abundant evidence as to the brutalization and demoralization which often accompany the life-style of groups which live outside some social norms, whose livelihood is precarious and parasitic, and whose lives may be every day at risk. But

1. SP35.46, fo. 39. See also Cal Winslow on 'Smuggling in Sussex' in D. Hay, P. Linebaugh and E. P. Thompson, eds., *Albion's Fatal Tree*, 1975.

2. The evidence is unclear, but see below, pp. 235–6. It is even possible that the suppression of organized Blacking left a vacuum in which unorganized and random violence and criminality took over.

there is no evidence that the Blacks constituted a group of this kind, except in the last days when William Shorter and his fellows became outlaws: and even then it is probable that they were supported by the norms of their own forest community. And if we should be on our guard against accepting moralistic categories which offer a facile apologia for criminality, it must be said that Rogers's own categories are even more disabling.

'Crime' itself – when we simply take over the definitions of those who own property, control the state, and pass the laws which 'name' what shall be crimes – is the first of these categories. But since many people have now started to write the history of crime, often without careful preparation and without historical controls, this may be the occasion to object even more strongly to the categories 'gangs' and 'criminal subculture'. Eighteenth-century class prejudice unites here with the anachronistic employment of the (inadequate) terminology of some twentieth-century criminology. Thus Rogers cites the Ordinary of Newgate's account of the seven hanged Hampshire Blacks as 'an unusually full picture of the criminal subculture of Georgian England'.[1] The lamentable thing about this account – and many other accounts of the hanged by the Ordinary – is that they are nothing of the sort; they are simply accounts of the commonplace, mundane culture of plebeian England – notes on the lives of unremarkable people, distinguished from their fellows by little else except the fact that by bad luck or worse judgement they got caught up in the toils of the law. In the Hampshire case in question we have two carters, a publican who perhaps was a receiver of venison, an ostler who may have had a 'criminal record', a farm servant, a shoemaker's apprentice and a seventeen-year-old servant (a tailor's son). Alight anywhere in Hampshire in 1723 and take a random sample of seven men, and one would be likely to get much the same. If this is a 'criminal subculture' then the whole of plebeian England falls within the category.

What twentieth-century criminologists describe as subcultures eighteenth-century magistrates described as gangs. What is at issue is not whether there were any such gangs (there were) but the universality with which the authorities applied the term to any association of people, from a benefit society to a group of kin to a Fagin's den, which fell outside the law. This was partly self-delusion in the minds of the magistracy, and unwillingness to acknowledge the extent of disaffection with which they were faced: if, after enclosure, fences were thrown down – if turnpikes were attacked – if coal-heavers besieged their sub-contractors – if threatening letters were received, it was somehow comforting to assert that these outrages were the work of 'a gang'. And the category was self-fulfilling: if an offender was then picked up, and if information was

1. Rogers, op. cit., p. 481. For the Ordinary's *Account* see above, pp. 149–63.

extorted as to his associates, then it confirmed that the 'gang' had been 'run to earth'. In the silence of terror which might follow their punishment, the authorities would assume further confirmation of the theory of the gang. There had been a kill and the rest of the 'gang' (if any) had 'gone to ground'.

The categories of 'gang' and of 'subculture' might perhaps be rehabilitated if applied, with scrupulous care, to some activities in London, the great ports and the larger fairs, in which certain criminal procedures were professionalized and institutionalized. But we will be examining here less the 'subculture' (the characteristic attitudes, skills transmitted in families and prisons, and cant vocabulary) than the infrastructure *to* this 'subculture': that is, very specifically, the receivers, the brothels and the pimps, the employers of pick-pockets, the police or thief-takers in profitable symbiosis with these employers, the 'houses of resort', and so on. In the eighteenth century it is probable that only a fraction of those who were caught up in the law – or who were hanged or transported – belonged to this professionalized sector.[1] Until we know more, and unless we can relate offences to specific evidence of elaborated infrastructure, we would be well advised to avoid the notions of 'gangs' or of 'criminal subculture' altogether. For these notions will only introduce inapposite preconceptions into the very evidence which we should be examining.

I must apologize to Professor Rogers for hanging these lengthy reflections upon the hook of his article. But they remain relevant to the question of the Blacks and the Black Act. For the category 'criminal' can be a dehumanizing one: if a group of men are described as a 'gang', made up of 'bully-boys' who inhabit a 'criminal subculture', then they have been described in such a way as to disallow more careful examination. They are seen (as they were seen by the park owners and by Walpole) as a threat to authority, property and order. And the categories then prepare us for exactly the conclusions which Rogers comes to. The behaviour of the Blacks was 'a real danger to peaceable men', and therefore 'the provisions of the Black Act . . . had a justification at this time'. 'Something needed to be done: and one cannot reasonably condemn the legislature for taking the appropriate powers.'[2] But there is a fracture in this logic, between premise and conclusion. If we agree that 'something' needed to be done this does not entail the conclusion that *anything* might be done.

1. See especially P. Linebaugh in *Albion's Fatal Tree*. My generalizations at this point rely heavily on the systematic researches of Linebaugh and of Douglas Hay, and no doubt they will be confirmed or refuted when this evidence is published more fully. For genuine London 'gangs' and infrastructure, see Gerald Howson's study of Jonathan Wild.

2. Rogers, op. cit., p. 484.

We must still scramble through a thicket of non-sequiturs and leap a gulf of class alienation before we can gain the safety of that conclusion – that 'the provisions of the Black Act' were in fact 'the appropriate powers', the 'something' that was not only necessary but was justified. How do we get from the premise of poaching affrays and the death of one or two keepers (offences against which the law already had adequate resources) to the conclusion that a man's life was worth the head of a fish-pond or a young tree?

It is true – and this much in extenuation must be allowed to a compliant and partially corrupted House of Commons – that the Act was passed under colour of emergency. It was enacted in the first place for only three years. In whatever terms the bill was first introduced to the House, these were clearly lurid and alarmist, pointing to a combination of night-poaching, sedition and insubordination. The fragmentary parliamentary diary of Sir Edward Knatchbull records the terms of its introduction to the House by the Attorney and Solicitors-General – the Blacks of Waltham 'were come to that pass now as to 'list people in their gang and swear they would protect such even against King George'.[1] A House bemused by revelations of Jacobite conspiracy, but in which the Tory country gentry, who formed the only opposition, themselves had no love for poachers, was swept into consent. Moreover, if that unsatisfactory term 'crime wave' could ever be used with conviction, it might possibly be applied to the early 1720s. As Gerald Howson has shown in his painstaking study of Jonathan Wild, a combination of factors (the profound corruption of the enforcement authorities, the 'blood-money' system of rewards, the bankruptcies and poverty in the wake of the Bubble, an acute crisis of genuine gang warfare between Wild and his competitors) had led to a high incidence of crimes of robbery and violence and to a heightened awareness of the dangers from footpads and highwaymen.[2] For most Members of Parliament the Blacks no doubt appeared as just another set of highway robbers. And, seeing matters in this way, the historian also can become bemused by the seemingly inevitable sequence of contingencies, and the absence of articulate opposition. Since all took place as it did, the event was not only possible but natural, even inevitable: it may be condoned in the light of the 'accepted standards of the age'.

But when, and how, and by whom, did those standards become so debased that such an Act can seem natural? At the best, the Black Act was an astonishing example of legislative overkill. It became an original

---

1. *The Parliamentary Diary of Sir Edward Knatchbull, 1722–1730*, Camden Society, 3rd Series, XCIV, 1963, p. 21.
2. Gerald Howson, *Thief-Taker General: The Rise and Fall of Jonathan Wild*, 1970

charter of death for eighteenth-century legislators, against whose bulk successive capital statutes seemed more petty annexes – a dotting of i's and crossing of t's, a closing of bolt-holes neglected by Walpole's Law Officers. Together with the Riot Act, which inaugurated the Hanoverian accession (in 1715), it established an armoury of sanctions to be used, in times of necessity, against disturbance; and it also provided a model for subsequent terrorist legislation against disaffected Highlanders, Irish agrarian rebels and English smugglers.[1]

The Black Act could only have been drawn up and enacted by men who had formed habits of mental distance and moral levity towards human life – or, more particularly, towards the lives of the 'loose and disorderly sort of people'. We must explain, not an emergency alone, but an emergency acting upon the sensibility of such men, for whom property and the privileged status of the propertied were assuming, every year, a greater weight in the scales of justice, until justice itself was seen as no more than the outworks and defences of property and of its attendant status. In some respects the eighteenth century showed toleration: men and women were no longer killed or tormented for their opinions or their religious beliefs, as witches or as heretics; cashiered politicians did not mount the scaffold. But in every decade more intrusions upon property were defined as capital matters. If in practice the operation of the laws was modified, this did not alter the definition. While no doubt the majority of the gentry approved of this definition, there is a sense in which this elevation of property above all other values was a Whig state of mind. The Black Act came as much out of the mind and sensibility of Walpole and of his associates as it did out of an emergency in two counties. If the forest disturbances had not precipitated it in 1723, it is probable that some other 'emergency' (turnpike or food riot or highway robbery) would have occasioned it, perhaps in more piecemeal form, in the same decade. The escalation of the death penalty did perhaps emerge out of a 'subculture' which we can clearly identify: that of the Hanoverian Whigs.

Political life in England in the 1720s had something of the sick quality of a 'banana republic'. This is a recognized phase of commercial capitalism when predators fight for the spoils of power and have not yet agreed to submit to rational or bureaucratic rules and forms. Each politician, by nepotism, interest and purchase, gathered around him a following of loyal dependants. The aim was to reward them by giving them some post in which they could milk some part of the public revenue: army finances, the Church, excise. Every post carried its perquisites, percentages,

---

1. See *Albion's Fatal Tree*, pp. 134–5.

commissions, receipt of bribes, its hidden spoils. The plum jobs of political office – notably that of Paymaster-General, upon the tenure of which the Earl of Ranelagh, the Duke of Chandos and Sir Robert Walpole all founded their wealth – were worth fortunes. The great commercial interests (whether in merchanting or finance) depended also upon political and military favours, and these could be paid for at a high rate. The great gentry, speculators and politicians were men of huge wealth, whose income towered like the Andes above the rain-forests of the common man's poverty. Status and influence demanded ostentatious display, the visible evidence of wealth and power: Blenheim, Caversham, Cannons, Stowe, Houghton. Deer-parks were part of this display.

The Whigs, in the 1720s, were a curious junta of political speculators and speculative politicians, stock-jobbers, officers grown fat on Marlborough's wars, time-serving dependants in the law and the Church, and great landed magnates. They were the inheritors, not of the Puritan Revolution, but of the canny and controlled Settlement of 1688. The libertarian rhetoric passed down from their forefathers they wore awkwardly, like fancy-dress. They derived what political strength they had in the country from the fact that they offered themselves as the only alternative to civil war or to a Stuart and Catholic repossession of the island.

But the rhetoric of 'the Protestant succession' meant different things to different people. To the great Whigs it was a convenient catch-cry, a stick to beat the small Tory gentry with, and an excuse to limit such powers of the King or of bureaucratic state as might have interfered with their predatory activities. It had no other democratic significance, whether electoral or economic or religious.[1] The English and Irish churches were subdued by Walpole to an erastian dependence upon opportunist political preferment which would have sickened Archbishop Laud.

In 1723 Walpole was still entering uncertainly into supreme power. Nor did this power (which he shared with his brother-in-law Townshend, and also, to some degree, with his rival Carteret) seem secure. No contemporary could have had the foresight to predict that he was to establish his power for twenty years, and become England's first and least lovely prime minister. He attained office by industry and exceptional attention to detail, ruthlessness, but chiefly through the luck of the survivor. In 1720–21 the South Sea Bubble crisis had, in blowing up the Whig hierarchy, blown him towards power. Stanhope and the two Craggs had all died; other rivals, like Aislabie, had been discredited and driven from political

1. For a fuller substantiation of this somewhat assertive argument, see my 'Paternalism' in *Customs in Common* (forthcoming), and also 'The Peculiarities of the English', *Socialist Register*, 1965.

life. As one of the senior Whig politicians unbribed by the South Sea Company (or whose bribes did not come to light) Walpole inherited power. Since the King's mistresses, and also very possibly the King, were among those bribed by the Company, office could not be allowed to fall into the hands of intemperate men, who would press inquiry too far or give way to the public outcry for vengeance. Walpole came forward as 'Screen-Master General'; so far from being seen as a popular saviour, he was, at that time, 'the most execrated and despised man in public life, hated, indeed far more intensely than Sunderland or the South Sea Directors'.[1] Having saved the Government, and saved the most prominent offenders from popular wrath, Walpole's business was over; the Whig peer, Sunderland, irritated by his presumption and (rightly) alarmed by his ruthless pursuit of power, took steps to get rid of him, and the general election of the spring of 1722 was complicated by obscure intrigues between the Sunderland and Walpole factions, in which Sunderland made a bid for Tory, and even Jacobite, support. On 19 April 1722, miraculously, the Earl of Sunderland died.

Less than a month later Walpole made public the first of successive Jacobite conspiracies, which were to keep Parliament and the public transfixed for a year, and which served as an excuse for stationing troops in Hyde Park through the summer of 1722, and suspending (in October) *habeas corpus* for a year. (More suspected Blacks were in fact arrested, on Townshend's or Walpole's warrant, during this year's suspension than were Jacobite suspects.) A punitive tax was imposed upon Catholics and non-jurors, and 1723 witnessed absurd processions of anxious yeomen and smallholders, on horseback and in carts, to the nearest market-town where they could swear the oath of allegiance. Dr Stratford, of Little Shefford in Berkshire, found 'great confusion' among his neighbours as to the oaths:

> Many women as well as men, who have forty shillings or three pounds *per annum*, who never heard of a state oath in their lives, and scarce knew who was King in Israel, are told they must leave their harvest work and trot a foot fifteen or sixteen miles, to take oaths or register. The poor creatures are frightened out of their wits, and think their copyholds are to be taken from them . . .[2]

'I saw a great deal of it,' Mr Speaker Onslow recalled,

> and it was a strange as well as ridiculous sight to see people crowding to give a testimony of their allegiance to a Government, and cursing it at the same time for giving them the trouble of so doing, and for the fright they were put into by

---

1. Plumb, *Sir Robert Walpole*, 1960, I, pp. 379–80.
2. *Hist. MSS Comm. Portland*, *VIII*, p. 364 (3 August 1723).

it, and I am satisfied more real disaffection to the King and his family arose from it than from anything which happened in that time.[1]

It is fruitless, in the present state of historical research, to speculate far upon the extent of real political disaffection in 1722–3. The press was muzzled, subject to prosecutions, and the thin surviving organs of opposition such as the Tory (subsequently Jacobite) Duke of Wharton's *True Briton* wrote mainly in riddles.[2] In few periods do the published contemporary sources give less away: on the surface (including the surface of known Jacobites) all is professions of loyalty to King George and the Protestant Succession. All, that is, except the savage cartoons, political ballads and innuendos which survive here and there. There was plenty of enduring rancour about the South Sea affair; there were certainly Jacobite sympathies among sections of the London crowd. A servile dissenting minister, Edmund Calamy, recalled in the London of these years 'a furious enmity to the happy Government we are under', and lamented 'the mutinous disposition of the mobbish crew'.[3] But the expression of people's political sympathies was more often oblique, symbolic and too indefinite to incur prosecution. At the most we are left with the evidence of rival bonfires upon the occasion of Stuart or Hanoverian birthdays; of theatrical episodes, like the Hambledon bell-ringing or the Winchester cabbage-processional; of anonymous letters, airs whistled in the street, or ballads in London taverns:

> Potatoes is a dainty dish, and turnips is a-springing,
> And when that Jemmy does come o'er, we'll set the bells a-ringing,
> We'll take the cuckold by the horns and lead him unto Dover,
> And put him in a leather boat and send him to Hanover.[4]

1. Onslow MSS, *Hist. MSS Comm. 14th Report, App. IX*, p. 464. See also *True Briton*, 34, 27 September 1723, and 62, 3 January 1724.

2. For a useful summary of official warrants for prosecutions of the press, 1721–3, see *Copies taken from the Records of the Court of King's Bench*, 1763, pp. 23–9 (Cambridge University Library, press-mark Syn. 5.76.14).

3. E. Calamy, *An Historical Account of My Own Life*, 1829, II, pp. 453–4. See also John Doran, *London in Jacobite Times*, 1877, I, esp. pp. 360–408; Norman Sykes, *Church and State in the XVIIIth Century*, Cambridge, 1934, p. 71; and H. T. Dickinson, *Walpole and the Whig Supremacy*, 1973, p. 62, for the aftermath of the South Sea Bubble: 'The King and his Whig ministers were more unpopular throughout the country than at any time since the Jacobite rebellion of 1715 and the Opposition in Parliament was more dangerous than at any time since the Hanoverian Succession.'

4. SP35.55 (3) (Information of William Preston, tailor, of 4 January 1725). Jacobite balladry at this time combined traditional ribaldry against cuckolds with hostility to the House of Hanover: King George was supposed to have been cuckolded early in his marriage, to have kept his wife locked up ever since, transferred his affection to mistresses, and to have disowned his eldest son, the Prince of Wales: he was at the same time a

Undoubtedly many would have been happy to see the Whig caucus overthrown by some coup; but very few of these would have been willing to put their own lives at risk, or to have aided a Jacobite invasion supported by the Catholic powers of Europe.

Equally, historians find it difficult to measure the seriousness of the Jacobite conspiracies involving Christopher Layer, Kelly and Francis Atterbury, the Bishop of Rochester. In themselves, they were of little substance; similar intrigues might be detected at other points of the first four decades of the century.[1] Supported by general popular disaffection, they could be seen as more significant. But what is most evident is that these plots were seized upon by Walpole as a heaven-sent opportunity to consolidate his power, and, with it, that 'stability' which has been celebrated as his major contribution to British history.[2] Mr Speaker Onslow, who had opportunities to observe Walpole closely, noted that the conspiracy

had the usual effect of matters of this kind, by a new and firmer establishment that it gave to the Government effacing in a good measure the prejudices that many things besides the South Sea project had raised against the King and his family. It so thoroughly broke all the measures of the party for the Pretender that they have never since been able to recover them . . . and ought therefore to be reckoned one of, if not the, most fortunate and the greatest circumstance of Mr. Walpole's life. It fixed him with the King, and united for a time the whole body of Whigs to him, and gave him the universal credit of an able and vigilant Minister.[3]

In such a context the episode of the Blacks may be seen as another 'fortunate circumstance'. It is doubtful whether Townshend or Walpole credited for long the tall stories which Parson Power told them as to Blacks and Jacobite conspirators in July 1722.[4] But in time of popular

---

'cuckold' or illegitimate King. See e.g. SP35.29, fos. 62 and 60 (1): 'The Highland Lass's Wish', where Jemmy '. . . looks not like a country clown, Nor there grows no thorns upon his ground, Nor keeps no whore of forty stone, For he is brisk and lordly.'

A Hertfordshire yeoman got into trouble for saying 'King George was a damned cuckoldy Rogue and Dogg and that he (the King) had banished his wife for making him a cuckold': *Herts County Records: Sessions Books 1700–52*, ed. W. Le Hardy, Hertford, 1931, p. 197.

1. Recent scholarship, however, takes seriously the threat of a Jacobite rising in 1721, planned to commence with riots in London, culminating in the seizure of the Tower, Bank and Exchequer: and confirms that Sunderland may have been negotiating with the Pretender in 1722: see Romney Sedgwick, *History of Parliament: The House of Commons 1715–1754*, 1970, I, pp. 65, 108–9.

2. See J. H. Plumb, *The Growth of Political Stability in England, 1675–1725*, 1967.

3. *Onslow MSS*, op. cit., p. 513.

4. However, they were anxious to obtain incriminating evidence against Atterbury,

disaffection, armed horsemen could not be permitted to attack the parks of gentry with impunity. To deal firmly with them was yet one more proof of 'an able and vigilant Minister', and no respectable voice of opposition was likely to give support to poaching or Blacking.[1] The episode provided a most fortunate pretext to strengthen the resources of 'stability'.

But the texture of interest was closer than that. There is a remarkable coincidence between the enemies of the Blacks and the Hanoverian interest. The first victim was no less than the King himself, and his deputies in the royal forests. It no doubt fixed Walpole even closer with the King to make Windsor safe for royalty. Sir Richard Temple, Viscount Cobham, had served with Marlborough in his wars, and, like his chief, fell out of favour in the last years of Anne. On the accession of George I he was showered with favours, culminating in his appointment as Constable of Windsor. He was, without doubt, a committed Hanoverian, at that time of Walpole's faction (and a counterweight among the military to Cadogan), and he was described by Swift as 'the greatest Whig in the Army'.[2]

Cadogan, whose park was twice driven for deer, we have already discussed (above, pp. 100–101). He had played an important part in engineering the difficult transition from Anne to George, and while he was a notable Whig there was little love lost between him and Walpole.[3] The latter was jealous of his command of German, his knowledge of continental politics, and his considerable influence with the King, who thought him to be 'the best officer in England, and the most capable of commanding the army'.

Cadogan was hated, not only by the people of Reading, but throughout the country; a malicious rhyme, attributed to the Bishop of Rochester, went its rounds:

---

and may have thought Power a possible channel; see G. V. Bennett's definitive 'Jacobitism and the Rise of Walpole', *Historical Perspectives*, ed. N. McKendrick, 1974.

1. The nearest to any public defence of the Blacks was perhaps a letter in the *True Briton*, 25 November 1723, attacking '*base* and *false informers*' who 'deserve to be included under the name of THE BLACKS, and to have the same punishment assigned to them. They are downright man-hunters . . .' The *True Briton* was addressed mainly to Londoners, and this number appeared ten days after the trial of the Hampshire Blacks before King's Bench, and shortly before their execution.

2. *DNB*; C. Dalton, *George I's Army*, 1910, pp. 2–8; W. Coxe, *Memoirs of the Life and Administration of Sir Robert Walpole*, 1798, I, p. 189. Cobham, like Walpole and, one suspects, Cadogan, is alleged to have removed a village while enlarging the parks at Stowe: information from Mr G. B. Clarke.

3. When Townshend and Walpole were driven into opposition in 1717, they had, for factional reasons, joined forces with the Tories to attack Cadogan for lining his own pockets out of moneys allocated to the transport of his forces: see Sedgwick, op. cit., I, pp. 26–7; Plumb, op. cit., I, pp. 253–6.

> Unmoved by Mercy and by Shame unaw'd,
> Th' undoubted spawn of Hangman and of Bawd:
> Ungrateful to the person that he grew by,
> A bawling blustering boystrous bloody booby.[1]

Cadogan also (a contemporary gossip affirmed) 'is not at all beloved by the officers'. But the royal favour protected him from his own officers, from public opinion and from Walpole. He was, indeed, in 1723 perhaps the closest ally (among the Whig oligarchy) of the German faction in the Court, and his followers made up a remnant of the old Sunderland group. He was Master of Robes to the King, commander of the troops encamped in Hyde Park through the summer and autumn of 1722, and a member of the Regency Council during the King's absence in Hanover in 1723. However much Walpole wished to be rid of him, he was certainly a man whose park it was well to protect.[2]

Cobham's deputy at Windsor, Colonel Francis Negus, was also, in a small way, a man of political influence in his own right. He appears to have owed his early preferment to the Townshend and Walpole families;[3] he was in effect Master of Horse (a court office which could have carried with it Cabinet rank) and was Member of Parliament for Ipswich, and firmly affixed to Walpole.[4]

1. This is the version noted by Sarah, Duchess of Marlborough (Blenheim MSS, Box XII (39)), and she adds: 'it is some part of my Lord Cadogan's character: it would be too long to make it compleat, & would swell to as large a bulk as his person.' Cadogan had 'borrowed' a large sum from Marlborough, invested it profitably, and refused to return either interest or principal, out of which a long, bitter feud at law grew. But Sarah neglects to mention a more common version of the rhyme, whose third line ran: 'Ungrateful to th'ungrateful man he grew by' (i.e. Marlborough himself). In November 1722 a friend informed Sarah that Cadogan's 'great passion for Mrs. Pulteney is . . . the Joke of the Town . . . He is the most ridiculous sight imaginable in all publick places': Blenheim MSS, E44.

2. *Hist. MSS Comm. Var. Colls. VIII*, p. 393; *DNB*; Plumb, op. cit., I, p. 282, II, pp. 23, 37, 42, 50–55; J. M. Beattie, *The English Court in the Reign of George I*, Cambridge, 1967, pp. 33, 150. Cadogan was officially Master General of the Ordinance, and not quite Commander-in-Chief; Walpole and Townshend stretched their influence with the King to its limit in the summer of 1723, in preventing Cadogan from taking on the formal Command: see *Hist. MSS Comm. Polwarth III*, p. 284; SP43.66 (where the King's warrant of 30 May 1723 appointing Cadogan Commander-in-Chief appears to be crossed out).

3. Papers in the Norfolk Rec. Off. HOW 603 and 783 show that Negus had been in the service of the Duke of Norfolk until about 1690, and was employed in some affairs by Colonel Robert Walpole in 1693, when, as a good Revolution Whig, he was much concerned at 'some disaffected' at Uxbridge 'drinking saucie healths'.

4. The Master of Horse was the third officer in the court hierarchy. The perquisites were normally enormous, but for reasons of economy George I put the post 'in commission' and Negus held it at the fixed salary of £800 p.a. A note in the Townshend papers (*Hist. MSS Comm. 11th Report, App. IV*, p. 102) shows that when Townshend

Major-General John Pepper, the Ranger of Enfield Chase, was another Member of Parliament, for the pocket borough of Steyning, Sussex. He was an unskilful member of the Cadogan faction. By his own account he resigned a sinecure as Governor of Kinsale in Ireland upon receiving a message (through Cadogan) from the King, asking him to secure his own election at Steyning 'rather than a person no way attached to your Majesty's interest should come into his seat in Parliament, as was then most probable':

> Your petitioner having the honour to be told that his serving in Parliament would be agreeable to your Majesty notwithstanding his great expenses on the former election, did attempt being chosen into this present House of Commons, & by his own strength without other assistance was returned against the opposition made by Sir Henry Goring & others, in both which elections your petitioner expended upwards of £5,000 pounds.

Cadogan had promised a compensation, directly from the King, for these services, but this had not, at the time of petitioning, materialized. Pepper felt hard done by, which may have encouraged him to recoup his losses by accepting bribes from the South Sea Company. It has already been suggested (above, p. 178) that Pepper's eviction from the rangership, in 1724–5, was hastened on by the Duke of Chandos, whose methods of touching the royal favour were more summary and more effective than Pepper's petitions: Chandos simply bribed the King's mistresses.[1] And Walpole left Pepper to flounder, since he had no interest in protecting one of Cadogan's unpopular creatures. But in 1723 Pepper remained (as a Whig Member of Parliament who might *possibly* have the ear of the King) a man whose interests were worth a little attention.[2]

Several of the lesser men who suffered at the hands of the Blacks were also tied closely by interest to the ruling Whigs. In Hampshire Richard Norton came from a family famous for its 'whiggery'. When, in December 1722, the King made one of his rare progresses out of London, he paid Norton the compliment of a visit. Walpole, ever-attentive to such details,

---

and Walpole were negotiating with Stanhope for a greater influence for their faction early in 1716, Cobham, as Constable (a counterweight to Cadogan) and Negus, as Master of Horse, were both to be in the Cabinet. Plumb, op. cit., II, p. 170 identifies Negus as a dependant of Walpole's. See also above, p. 44.

1. See Beattie, op. cit., pp. 164, 145, 245 n. 3.
2. Pepper's sad petition is in SP41.5. It is undated, and the fact that it remains in a bundle of miscellaneous War Office Papers suggests that it may never have reached the King; the recompense he was asking for was the gift of a regiment or a pension on the English or Irish establishment. In 1720 Pepper was still petitioning Parliament for a reward for his services in the relief of Barcelona, and for saving the King and kingdom of Spain: see *Commons Journals*, XIV, p. 360. For Pepper and the South Sea affair, see John Carswell, *The South Sea Bubble*, 1960, p. 116n.

would not have overlooked that he had influence in the useful Admiralty borough of Portsmouth.[1] Sir John Cope was Member for Tavistock – subsequently he sat for Hampshire; his son, Monoux Cope, was Member for Banbury. Sir John, in 1723, still had a little reputation for independence among Whig country Members of Parliament; he had seriously embarrassed Walpole, early in 1722, by accusing Baron Page (who was to preside over the trials of the Blacks at Reading) of excessive corruption in the Banbury election which Cope's son was also contesting. He had possibly done this at the instigation of Sunderland; and on the latter's death he attached himself firmly to Walpole, seconded the resolutions of the House against the Bishop of Rochester, and became one of Walpole's closer confidants.[2] He was clearly a man whose representations would be attended to. So also was Bishop Trimnell, Trelawny's successor at Winchester, who was Clerk of the Closet to the King, an undistinguished Whig polemicist who, translated from Norwich in July 1721, was one of the first of Walpole's episcopal pawns.[3]

There were, in plain terms, some useful votes to be attended to here, both in the Lords and in the Commons. In the Commons there was a significant small pressure-group of Members who had suffered in their own parks, their deer, their fish or their family dignity at the hands of the Blacks: Negus, Pepper, two Copes, the little family of Pitts, Sir Robert Rich, the Onslow family in Surrey and Charles Cadogan, brother to the Earl, who – expelled by the electors from Reading (in 1722) – found a safe seat at Newport, Isle of Wight (of which his brother was Governor). Other victims were well connected: Sir Anthony Sturt and Brigadier Philip Honeywood (whose brother Robert was county Member for Essex) held posts at Court. And one or two others, if not yet in Walpole's bag, might be beckoned in that direction: thus Thomas Lewis of Soberton, 'one of the richest commoners in England', was Member for Southampton; he was a Tory, and the Pretender was even informed that he was a Jacobite; but his parks received attention from the Blacks. In 1726 he was to cross the floor of the House, after a marriage had been arranged

---

1. See *The Journal of James Yonge*, 1963, p. 211; T. Pennant, *A Journey from London to the Isle of Wight*, 1801, II, p. 121; *St James's Journal*, 6 September 1722. Norton's grandfather had been one of Cromwell's colonels; Norton himself was an ardent Revolution Whig, who treasured until his death 'the true hair of my dearly beloved Sovereign King William III', preserved in a japan box with his small jewels (Norton's will, see below, p. 222), and who, when George I visited him at Southwick, received him with sixty 'keepers' specially provided with new green livery.

2. See Plumb, *Sir Robert Walpole*, 1960, I, p. 371, II, pp. 126, 246; Sedgwick, op. cit., II (entries for Sir John and Monoux Cope).

3. The *DNB* notes of Trimnell: 'as bishop he distinguished himself by the emphasis with which he urged the doctrine of the subordination of the church to the state . . .'

between his daughter and Walpole's second son; he said later, in a debate on the standing army, that 'in 1715 he was warm for reducing the army but has since seen the ill consequences of it'. No doubt the Blacks, and Walpole's firm handling of them, helped to extend his vision.[1]

In this context we can see the passage of the Black Act as a severe measure of Government business, serving first of all the interest of Government's own closest supporters. It was a step upwards in the ascendancy of the hard Hanoverian Whigs, and in particular in Walpole's own career.[2] This is to see it in its contingent evolution. But such an Act would not have been possible without a prior consensus as to the values of property in the minds of those who drafted it – indeed, a consensus which gained on the minds of the ruling class as a whole. As Radzinowicz has pointed out, the passing of the Black Act coincided with the ascendancy of 'the doctrine of undifferentiated and crude retribution'. Walpole or no Walpole, the Act was successively renewed, extended and enlarged, both legislatively and in case-law. It was renewed in 1725 for five years, in 1733 for a further three (with the addition of death-clauses for the cutting of rivers, sea-banks, and the cutting of hop-binds). In 1737 there were added clauses against setting fire to coal-mines, and destroying sea-marks and sea-walls. The Act was further renewed in 1744 and 1751 and made perpetual in 1758. As Radzinowicz remarks, 'The fact that the struggle for the repeal of this extraordinary statute was both intense and prolonged further enhances the symptomatic importance of the Act, which might otherwise be seen to be but an obscure enactment designed to meet a purely local emergency.' It was, on the contrary, an 'ideological index' to a large body of laws based on the death penalty which remained in force into the early years of the nineteenth century.[3]

The Act registered the long decline in the effectiveness of old methods of class control and discipline and their replacement by one standard recourse of authority: the example of terror. In place of the whipping-post and the stocks, manorial and corporate controls and the physical harrying

---

1. *History of Blacks*, p. 6; Sedgwick, op. cit., II (entry for Thomas Lewis); Royal Archives (Windsor), SP65.16.

2. In August 1723 Walpole was able to write with self-congratulation, 'we are in a state of tranquillity and satisfaction beyond what I have ever known': See C. B. Realey, *The Early Opposition to Sir Robert Walpole, 1720-27*, Kansas City, 1931, p. 126.

3. The continuing Acts were: 11 George I c.30 (1725); 6 George II c.37 (1733); 10 George II c.32 (1737) – this Act added a death clause for setting fire to coal-mines, but lesser punishments for destroying sea-marks and sea-walls: unenclosed forests and chases were brought within the terms of the Black Act, but in the latter deer-stealers might only be transported; 17 George II c.40 (1744); 24 George II c.57 (1751); and 31 George II c.42 (1758) – an 'Act for making perpetual several Acts therein mentioned . . .'

of vagabonds, economists advocated the discipline of low wages and starvation, and lawyers the sanction of death. Both indicated an increasing impersonality in the mediation of class relations, and a change, not so much in the 'facts' of crime as in the *category* – 'crime' – itself, as it was defined by the propertied. What was now to be punished was not an offence between men (a breach of fealty or deference, a 'waste' of agrarian use-values, an offence to one's own corporate community and its ethos, a violation of trust and function) but an offence against property. Since property was a thing, it became possible to define offences as crimes against things, rather than as injuries to men. This enabled the law to assume, with its robes, the postures of impartiality: it was neutral as between every degree of man, and defended only the inviolability of the ownership of things. In the seventeenth century labour had been only partly free, but the labourer still asserted large claims (sometimes as perquisites) to his own labour's product. As, in the eighteenth century, labour became more and more free, so labour's product came to be seen as something totally distinct, the property of landowner or employer, and to be defended by the threat of the gallows.

This thinking, which we have described as the Whig state of mind (although it was rapidly to permeate the gentry and employers as a whole), was maturing throughout the previous century, is well formed in Locke, and was influencing the criminal law well before the Black Act. We do not have to suppose, in the lawyers and judges of Walpole's time, a new race of men. But the drafters and executants of the Black Act were men of the times. The Attorney-General, Lord Raymond, was a careerist whose opportunism made him offensive even to the House of Commons of that opportunist time. Solicitor-General in the Tory administration of 1710, he had been brought, or bought, over to the Whigs, who found him a Government seat in 1719, and appointed him Attorney-General in the next year. In this post he was responsible for pressing proceedings against the Jacobite conspirators of 1722, including his former ally the Bishop of Rochester: 'branded as an apostate, his position in the Commons became so untenable that he abandoned politics for the bench', becoming, in due course, Lord Chief Justice of the King's Bench.[1]

1. *DNB*; John, Lord Campbell, *The Lives of the Chief Justices of England*, 1849, II, p. 194. Raymond later distinguished himself by leading the opposition in the Lords to the English Language Law Bill of 1731, observing that, if records were to be kept in the vernacular, then 'upon this principle, in an action to be tried at Pembroke or Caernarvon, the declaration and plea ought to be in Welsh'. The Duke of Argyll courteously answered that 'he was glad to perceive that the noble and learned lord, perhaps as wise and learned as any that ever sat in that House, had nothing to bring against the bill but a joke': see R. E. Latham, 'The Banishment of Latin from the Public Records', *Archives*, IV, no. 23 (1960).

Philip Yorke, the Solicitor-General, was foremost among Walpole's bright young men. The son of a Dover attorney, he owed his early advancement in the profession to the patronage of Lord Macclesfield, the Lord Chancellor (who was to be impeached for corruption in his office in 1724). His political stance was 'the quintessence of whiggism',[1] he was found a Government seat (in the Pelham interest) in 1719, and the next year was appointed Solicitor-General, at the age of twenty-nine. Thereafter, he served Walpole and the Pelhams to his utmost capacity, acquired, by the usual mysterious means, both a fortune and a reputation for probity, and moved by way of the offices of Attorney-General and Lord Chief Justice to the chancellorship. His entire career was marked by a contempt for the rabble, severity in handling rioters and rebels (whether turnpike protests in the West of England or Highland clansmen), 'and for the liberty of the press he can hardly be said to have had any respect whatsoever'. 'In his Chief Justiceship,' Horace Walpole remarked, 'he had gained the reputation for humanity, by some solemn speeches made on the Circuit, at the condemnation of wretches for low crimes.'[2]

It appears that the papers on the Black Act of neither Raymond nor of Lord Hardwicke (as Philip Yorke became) have survived. But it is certain that neither of them regarded the Act as an emergency measure, applicable only to deer-stealers in Berkshire and Hampshire; and it is abundantly clear that Philip Yorke never suffered, for his part in drafting it, a moment's remorse. In the autumn of 1723, two cases rose to the attention of the Law Officers which could perfectly well have been prosecuted under pre-existent law. The first was an affray about common rights and poaching on Wimbledon Common. On the night of 8 September 1723 several armed men (in revenge, it seems, at the prosecution of one of their fellows) waylaid two Wimbledon warreners, beat them up and left them tied to a tree, and then visited one of the warrener's houses, broke its windows, and fired twice (without injury) at a chamber window from which a woman had shouted at them. The case was referred by the Lords Justices of the Regency to the Attorney-General for an opinion. He advised that the offences could only with difficulty be prosecuted as felonies, 'for burglary is when a person . . . breaks and *enters* a mansion

---

1. See *DNB* entry. Yorke may first have caught the eye of Walpole by the vigour with which he argued for the death of the Jacobite lords, convicted of complicity in the '1715': see Plumb, *Sir Robert Walpole*, I, p. 219.

2. *DNB*; George Harris, *Life of Lord Chancellor Hardwicke*, 1857, 3 vols.; P. C. Yorke, *The Life and Correspondence of Philip Yorke, Earl of Hardwicke*, Cambridge, 1913, 3 vols.; Richard Cooksey, *Essay on the life and character of John Lord Somers . . . also Sketches of an Essay on the life and character of Philip Earl of Hardwicke*, Worcester, 1791, esp. p. 74; John, Lord Campbell, *Lives of the Lord Chancellors*, 1846, vol. v; Horace Walpole, *Memoirs of the Reign of King George the Second*, I, p. 159.

house to the intent to commit some felony', but since 'it don't appear they put their guns in at the window . . . here does not appear to me to have been such entry in the house as the law requires . . .' But he concluded that the shooting incident could be found as 'a felony without benefit of clergy (the punishment of which is death) by the late Act of Parliament', i.e. the Black Act. Thus already, in November 1723, and *before* the conviction of any Waltham Blacks, the Attorney-General was recommending the application of the Act to other offences, unrelated to that Act's preamble.[1] The Law Officers had found a useful new toy.

The other case was the attempted assassination, late in August 1723, of Lord Onslow. Onslow had been fox-hunting near his seat at Guildford when a yeoman farmer, Edward Arnold, fired at him, wounding him in the shoulder and neck. Since Onslow was a staunch Whig local magnate,[2] there was a moment of panic at this, until it was discovered that it was well known in the neighbourhood that Arnold was crazed. His mental confusion was not, perhaps, as strange as all that. By one report, Arnold, 'a most notorious Jacobite', did not 'pretend the least private pique' to Onslow: 'All that he says is that many persons having complained of My Lord's zeal and activeness in public matters in the country, and that he was the occasion of all disturbances there, he thought if My Lord was out of the way all things would be quiet . . .' By another report he had said: 'Lord Onslow and King George had got all the money, so that he could get none.' Onslow recovered; and, once again, it was thought that a death sentence would be most certain if Arnold was prosecuted under the Black Act. The case is remembered chiefly for its bearing on the insanity plea; but it also brought an enlargement in the interpretation of the Black Act.

The defence raised, in a half-hearted way, the question as to whether Arnold's offence came within the Black Act, which was entitled 'An Act for the more effectual punishing wicked and evil-disposed persons going armed in disguise &c', and in which arming and disguising appeared in the preamble, 'runs through the whole', and 'governs the rest'. The

1. The Preamble to 9 George I c.22 refers specifically to 'ill-designing and disorderly persons . . . under the name of Blacks'. For the Wimbledon case, see memo of Raymond to Lord Justices, 9 November 1723, SP43.68; *British Journal*, 14 September 1723; *London Gazette*, no. 6,216, 12 November 1723.

2. For the Onslow interest in Surrey and its important place in the Whig ascendancy see J. S. T. Turner, 'An Augustan Election (1710)', *Surrey Archaeological Collections*, LXVIII (1971). Onslow was credited with having blown a Bubble all of his own (the Royal Exchange Assurance), and his cousin, Onslow the Speaker, noted of his character that he had 'so much of pride and covetousness . . . that his behaviour, conversation and dealings with people were generally distasteful and sometimes shocking, and [he] had many bitter enemies and but with very few friends': Sedgwick, op. cit., II, p. 311.

matter was decided peremptorily by Tracy, the presiding judge, in the following exchange:

Just. Tracy. Because I knew I was to have this cause come before me, I have had a meeting of my brethren, to have their opinion in relation to this clause in the act. . . Every judge was of opinion, it is an entire clause of itself, and it had no relation to the former clause of being in disguise &c. So that there is nothing in this objection. I was under no manner of doubt myself before, but I was willing to have my brothers' opinion.[1]

Mr. Bains. It would be presumptious in me to offer any thing further, if it is the opinion of all the judges.

Just. Tracy. It is indeed; I did intimate it to Mr. Hungerford.

Mr. Hungerford. I humbly thank your lordship for the indulgence you have given me, and I wave it.

Hungerford, in waving out his client's defence, thus waved in a large addition to the Act's scope, whereby every offence in the Act became felony, whether committed by men armed and disguised, whether in royal forests or parks or elsewhere, whether or not it had anything to do with Blacking or deer.[2]

This decision made some later legal authorities uneasy; but Philip Yorke, who must have helped to draft the Act, was not among them. Ten years later he presided over the trial of two Herefordshire turnpike rioters, in his brief tenure of office as Lord Chief Justice. The offenders, two colliers named Baylis and Reynolds, were prosecuted under the Black Act, and the trial was removed from Herefordshire to the Court of King's Bench. At the close of the trial, Yorke, now Lord Hardwicke, C.J., directed the jury thus:

The several facts mentioned in this Act are not to be taken as being parts of the same offence, but are every of them several offences; and this . . . is a single crime, and is for appearing in the high road with faces blacked, and being otherwise disguised . . . If, upon the evidence, you believe that the prisoners did appear in the high road with their faces blacked, that is sufficient within the Act. . .

In the Hardwicke Papers notes survive of several charges made by him when he was Lord Chief Justice (1733–7); in one he refers to the Black Act as 'a very useful Act', in another he explained – 'The degeneracy of the present times, fruitful in the inventions of wickedness, hath produced

1. According to *Fortesc. Rep.* p. 388, seven or eight judges met on 27 February 1724 to decide the point.

2. *State Trials*, XVI, pp. 743–5; *Hist. MSS Comm. Var. Coll. VIII*, p. 365; *Gloucester Journal*, 2 September 1723. For the Arnold case in its bearing on the insanity plea, see Nigel Walker, *Crime and Insanity in England*, Edinburgh, 1968, pp. 53–7. Arnold was very probably 'insane', and he was, in the end, reprieved.

many new laws necessary for the present state and condition of things and to suppress mischiefs, which were growing frequent among us.' His Lordship had originally written 'many good new laws', but had thoughtfully scored out 'good', considering, perhaps, that it would be immodest in himself to praise too highly the work of his own pen.[1]

Thus within a year of its passage the Black Act had been divorced from the 'emergency' which supposedly occasioned it, and had entered the general armoury of repressive law. Of the other executants of the Act there is less to be said, although all of them consort well with the same careerist and Whiggish circles which had conspired to secure the bill's passage. Sir Francis Page, who presided over the Special Commission at Reading which sentenced the Berkshire Blacks, had been a Member of Parliament in the Whig interest and was the same Baron Page whom Cope had accused in February 1722 of corruption in a Banbury election. Walpole saved him on that occasion, by a margin of four votes. He was already known to contemporaries as 'the hanging judge', and he went down in literary tradition with a reputation only a little more salubrious than that of Jeffreys:

> Morality, by her false Guardians drawn,
> (Chicane in furs, and Casuistry in lawn),
> Gasps, as they straiten at each end the cord,
> And dies when Dulness gives her Page the word –

So wrote Pope, in the *Dunciad*, and he added, for the benefit of posterity, a footnote: 'There was a judge of this name always ready to hang any man that came in his way, of which he was suffered to give a hundred miserable examples during a long life . . .'

When Fielding gave Partridge a tale about a horse-thief, the judge who came at once to his mind was Page (and Fielding knew more than a little of the history and practice of the courts). When the thief claimed he had 'found' the horse, Judge Page is made to exclaim: 'Thou art a lucky fellow: I have travelled the circuit these forty years, and never found a horse in my life: but I'll tell thee what, friend, thou was more lucky than thou didst know of; for thou didst not only find a horse, but a halter too, I promise thee.' Upon which (Partridge relates):

Everybody fell a-laughing, as how could they help it? Nay, and twenty other jests he made, which I can't remember now. . . To be certain, the judge must have been a very brave man, as well as a man of much learning. It is indeed charming sport to hear trials upon life and death. One thing I own I thought a little hard, that the prisoner's counsel was not suffered to speak for him, though he desired to be heard one very short word . . . I thought it hard,

1. Cas. T. Hard. 292–3; Brit. Mus. Add. MSS 36,115, fos. 80, 102; Yorke, op. cit., i, p. 135. For the Herefordshire turnpike case see also below, p. 257.

I own, that there should be so many of them; my lord, and the court, and the jury, and the counsellors, and the witnesses, all upon one poor man, and he too in chains. Well, the poor fellow was hanged, as to be sure it could be no other-wise . . .

We are very close to the charming sport of the Reading Special Com-mission. Page was said also to have taken bribes, but this is one area of early-eighteenth-century legal practice which will probably never give up its secrets. Like other great Whig politicians and lawyers, he built himself a sumptuous seat, in Oxfordshire, leaving a huge monument in the local church of himself and his wife, in the postures of Romans lying at a banquet.[1]

The case against the Hampshire Blacks was conducted by Lord Raymond and Philip Yorke, before Baron Eyre. Sir Robert Eyre has not left as large a reputation behind as that of Baron Page. He also was a Whig politician–lawyer, had managed the Sacheverell impeachment, was a friend of Walpole's, and (according to the *Dictionary of National Biography*) 'appears to have been a peculiarly haughty man'. It may also be thought peculiar that the Hampshire Blacks came before him for trial (and were found guilty) on 13 November 1723; Eyre was promoted from a judgeship to be Lord Chief Baron on 16 November; and the prisoners were brought before him to receive sentence on 19 November. A coin-cidence, no doubt: 'In the Tryal of Persons accused for Crimes against the State, the Method is . . . short and commendable: The Judge first sends to sound the Disposition of those in Power; after which he can easily hang or save the Criminal, strictly preserving all the Forms of Law.'[2]

But it cannot be coincidence that the same Whiggish trail can be found wherever we look. It was not Cracherode, the Treasury Solicitor, who took on the most active work of assembling informations and preparing the arrests and trials of Blacks, but his assistant, Nicholas Paxton, who was subsequently to succeed him in office. Paxton had won his spurs and had established a claim to government employment when he had been hired as the leading solicitor preparing the Crown's evidence against rebels of the '1715' in the subsequent trials at Carlisle and Edinburgh. While this was, no doubt, legitimate professional work, he may have shown excessive zeal. At Carlisle, 'contrary to all expectations I convicted two and thirty . . . who were gentlemen of as considerable estates as any in the rebellion

1. *DNB*; W. Wing, *Annals of Steeple Aston*, Oxford, 1875, *passim*, and Richard Savage in Johnson's *Poets* (1779 edn), vol. XLV, p. 180: 'All, all, shall stand condemned who stand arraigned . . . Must hang to please him when of spleen possesst – Must hang to bring forth an abortive jest.'

2. *Gulliver's Travels*, Part IV, ch. 5. The Lord Chancellor had in fact recommended Eyre's promotion on 31 October, but Townshend explained that the King's absence had delayed approval: SP35.75 (40).

in Scotland'. He procured 'Several who had no estates to forfeit to become witnesses against others by whose attainder of high treason many considerable estates became forfeited to the Crown'. (This experience of turning some of the accused into evidences against the others was to prove invaluable when he came to prepare cases against the Blacks.) In two whining petitions for some place of profit under the Crown (he fingered two nominees of the Harley Ministry, still holding their sinecures, who might be displaced to make way for him[1]), he managed to hint that he was a dangerous man to leave unrewarded: if at Carlisle or Edinburgh 'I . . . would have been corrupted, I neede not now to have troubled your Lordship for a provision'. His service in the trials had lost him clients, who had 'taken a distaste to your petitioner', 'a great many of them having taken offence at my zeal for his Majesty's service, became my greatest enemies', so that 'my ruin would occasion the greatest joy in the disaffected'.[2]

Paxton, as Walpole's Treasury Solicitor, was an expert piece of casting. He went on to become Walpole's manager of the means of corruption, the only man fully apprised as to the disposition of Secret Service and other privy funds. When his master at length fell from power, Paxton showed the loyalty, or discretion, of an accomplice, in refusing to divulge to the House of Commons how these funds had been disposed.[3]

Even Baptist Nunn, the humblest – and also the most energetic and effective – agent of the campaign against the Blacks, may be seen in the same light, as a dependant upon the thin crust of Hanoverian adventurers, placemen and politicians. Indeed, it was in exactly this light that he was seen by the antiquary, Thomas Hearne, who had been born and educated in Windsor Forest:

> When I was a school boy at Bray, among others was my school-fellow one Baptista Nunn. . . . This Bapt. Nunn was a boy of good parts, & very forward to learn & show'd much respect for me, but he was sadly rude, & unlucky, & makes a vile man, being now living in Windsor Forest, a great informer, & a mighty cringer to the D. of Brunswick's Courtiers.[4]

1. The Secretary to the Wine Licence Office and the Solicitor to the Salt Duty.

2. Petition of Paxton, n.d., to Treasury Commissioners, T1.211 (14); Paxton to 'My Lord' [Sunderland], 18 November 1721, SP35.29.

3. Paxton was another who succeeded in having his name immortalized by Pope, whose windows were broken when Bolingbroke and Bathurst dined with him. Pope believed that Whig hooligans had been paid by the Treasury Solicitor: 'What! shall each spur-galled hackney of the day, When Paxton gives him double pots and pay, Or each new-pensioned sycophant, pretend To break my windows if I treat a friend . . . ?' (*Epilogue to the Satires*, 11, 140–43).

4. *Remarks and Collections of Thomas Hearne*, Oxford Historical Society, 1907, VIII, p. 215 (entry for 22 May 1724).

We have proposed an answer to the question of the causation of
the Black Act in two parts. In the first part we examined contingencies:
the particular 'emergency' which called forth a measure in the interests
of Government's own supporters. In the second part we have noted the
ideology, interests and sensibility of those who responded to these
contingencies: those who drafted, executed, perpetuated and enlarged
the Act. To forestall the accusation of a 'conspiratorial' interpretation of
history which is commonly visited upon my work, I must make clear that
I do not suppose that Walpole, Yorke or Paxton had the prophetic powers
to foresee all the uses to which this Act might subsequently be put in
terrorizing the disorderly kind of people. I do not suppose that the episode
of Blacking was eagerly seized upon by them as an excuse to enact a code
of terror which they had already meditated and which they had prepared
in draft in a drawer, for exactly such an opportunity. The contingency
arose in an unpremeditated way, and exactly as this study has described.
But the kind of response made to this contingency was determined by the
ideology and sensibility of the kind of men who were in power; and
scarcely had the Act received the royal assent before these men saw the
useful powers which they had taken into their hands, and looked around
for opportunities to use and to prolong them. This is not conspiracy but
consequence.

The defence commonly offered by historians on behalf of 'the Duke of
Brunswick's Courtiers' is that their actions conformed to 'the accepted
standards of the age'. For 'the age', in such apologetics, one should
normally read 'the ruling political élites', since on many occasions it is
apparent that those who were ruled regarded those standards with
derision.[1] With this proviso, it is true that for most of Walpole's measures
and means of corruption there were precedents; and (if we leave 'honest
Shippen' and his small Jacobite following aside) the political morality
evinced by his leading political opponents, such as Bolingbroke and
Pulteney, gives one small grounds for supposing that, if they had achieved
power, they would have behaved better. High politics was a predatory
game, with recognized spoils, and Walpole is to be distinguished chiefly
by his systematizing of the means of corruption, with unusual blatancy.

But we should be careful as to the employment of double standards. A
certain style of historical apologetics has become commonplace in which
the Hanoverian Whigs are justified as realists acting according to the

1. Thus a contemporary judgement of Walpole, in *A Copy of the Paper Drop'd in
St. James's Park, or a Hue and Cry after a Coachman*, 5 January 1725, advertising for the
apprehension of a felon of 'a heavy, clumsy, slouching, wadling gate . . . a supercillious,
sneering, grinning look; of a malicious, vindictive, sanguinary nature . . .' Brit. Mus.
press-mark 816 m 19 (82).

'standards of the age', while every criticism of these 'standards' is disallowed as coming from interested sources.[1] Bolingbroke, Pope or Thomas Hearne, the antiquary, and lesser critics, are dismissed as disappointed factionalists or Jacobite sympathizers. Such 'factionalists', however, sometimes put their careers or lands at risk, or in a time of overwhelming ministerial 'interest' put themselves outside the bounds of favour. We may be disinclined to attend with any sympathy to the politics of the Pretender or to the dubious opportunism and nostalgic patriarchalism of Bolingbroke. But we cannot stop complacently at this point; we are bound also to go further, and inquire why some men were attracted to these positions, and we must include their critique of 'the age' among that age's standards. Francis Atterbury, the exiled Bishop of Rochester, may have been foolish or ambitious: but his critique of Walpole (in 1726 or 1727) was sober enough: 'His whole administration is built on corruption and bribery, which he has carried to a greater height than any of his worst predecessors ever did . . .' He had obtained his parliamentary majorities in this way 'at the expence of the morals of a people, who were remarkable for their honor and probity, and who had some share of it left till they came under his administration'. By these methods he had poisoned both Houses of Parliament; and the Whigs had further supplemented their powers and limited democratic process by the Septennial Act, the liberal suspension of *habeas corpus*, and the recourse to a standing army. Atterbury's remedies may have been folly or worse, but the critique commands as much attention as do Whig apologetics.[2]

For if historical judgement were to be governed always by the search for precedents, then one would never be able to distinguish any age from any

---

1. Thus successive Paymaster-Generals had preceded Walpole in milking the public revenues. Professor Plumb discusses this point (*Sir Robert Walpole*, I, p. 209), and adds: 'These sharp practices by our standards were legitimate enough by the standards of Walpole's day, although these methods, when employed by former Paymasters – Ranelagh and Brydges – had caused a great outcry.' Which is it to be? How can we explain that 'a great outcry' was provoked by practices which were 'legitimate enough' by 'the standards of Walpole's day'? In fact, Ranelagh was disgraced and harried in his accounts until his death: Chandos (or Brydges) was like a cat on hot bricks for a decade after leaving office, expecting exposure and disgrace: Walpole could save him from this but could not allow so scandalous a man back into public office. The difference is that Walpole, and several of his successors in this office, got away with it, not because 'standards' had changed but because the administration had greater power to silence opposition and manipulate opinion.

2. For Atterbury's critique, see William Coxe, *Memoirs of the Life and Administration of Sir Robert Walpole*, 1798, II, pp. 229–32. For important new evidence and interpretation of oppositional politics and values, see H. T. Dickinson, *Bolingbroke*, 1970; Isaac Kramnick, *Bolingbroke and his Circle*, Oxford, 1968; Howard Erskine-Hill, *The Social Milieu of Alexander Pope*, New Haven, 1975.

other. It is not true, unless in the eye of the mystic, that the political morality of one age is much the same as any other; precedents of corruption do not add up to a system of corruption. It is not true that the Walpole and Newcastle system – of nepotism, of the brutal imposition on every branch of public service of the Whig interest, of the purchase and intimidation of electors, of diverting public money into private pockets, of bribes and pensions, of death bills, press prosecutions and taxes on the means of life, of the Riot Act and the Black Act, and of religious cynicism combined with the subordination of the Church to factional interest – was identical with that of twenty or of fifty years before, even if it is true that the system was to be inherited, with little modification, by George III and the Tories.

Somewhere between the Puritan gentry and officers of the Commonwealth and the great Whig managers of the 1720s some lapse had taken place. It is a historical problem which demands more serious research than solecisms as to the 'standards of the age'. And 'the age' turns out, on the most cursory inspection of enduring evidence, not to have had any such homogeneous standards. With the exception of Defoe, the most gifted writers, almost to a man, took refuge from these standards of Whig politicians in Tory humanism. There was no other place to which to go, and what these writers have left us is not concurrence in the 'accepted standards' but page after page of some of the most sustained and savage satire in our history against them. The *Beggar's Opera* and Pope's *Epistles* and *Gulliver's Travels* have an authenticity of feeling which disallows their being explained away as expressions of envy and political faction.

The years 1720–24, from the South Sea Bubble through the Jacobite conspiracies to the consolidation of Walpole's power (and the fall of Carteret), were critical and formative ones. The Black Act was a significant episode in these years. An understanding of it may at least help one to see that the satire of these years was less hyperbolic or misanthropic and more precisely aimed than is supposed. Men did not have to sympathize with the Blacks to take note of the Act as an example of the style of Walpole's rule. Swift certainly knew about the story of Parson Power, and very probably a great deal more gossip and information went round by word of mouth than has survived.[1] Pope must have learned more, from his nephews and brother-in-law, the Racketts.

It was in these years that the comparison of statesmanship with

1. Thus the whole episode of Thomas Power would remain meaningless were it not for the fortunate survival of Stratford's private letters to Lord Harley, the veracity of which can be confirmed at many points. But Stratford was clearly only reporting what was common knowledge among Berkshire gentry and clergy, and he adds at one point: 'If you know Mr Kent, the member for Reading, he perhaps can give you a fuller account

criminality became common coinage. In the summer of 1723 the Duke of Wharton's *True Briton* asked why a highway robber 'committed, perhaps, for a trifle, or the mere relief of his necessities' should be executed, 'whilst another, who has inriched himself by continual depredations, for a course of some years, at the expence of his country, shall not only escape with impunity, but, by a servile herd of flatterers and sycophants, have all his actions crowned with applause.'[1] John Gay, in a private letter a month or two before, had made much the same point: 'I cannot but wonder that the talents requisite for a great statesman are so scarce in the world, since so many of those who possess them are every month cut off in the prime of their age at the Old-Baily.'[2] If Lord Hardwicke was to explain the need for the Black Act in terms of 'the degeneracy of the present times, fruitful in the inventions of wickedness', there were contemporaries who saw the authors of the Act as the most flagrant exemplars of this degeneracy.

The comparisons with the 'statesman' and the criminal rose to their climax in 1725, with the impeachment of Thomas Parker, the Earl of Macclesfield, for taking – as Lord Chancellor – bribes to the tune of £100,000, and with the coincident exposure and execution of Jonathan Wild, the great 'thief-taker'. But we need not suppose that Walpole's administration, which allowed the impeachment of Macclesfield to follow its course, had suffered an agonizing change of heart. Macclesfield had committed two indiscretions, which made him expendable – indeed, quite a serviceable sop to throw to critics in the House and in the country. First, he was attached to the wrong faction and was heartily disliked by Walpole;[3] second, his corruption had operated in an impermissible area – the adjudication of property-rights in the Court of Chancery. But not all of the administration's critics allowed themselves to be distracted so easily. Nathaniel Mist, in his editorials on Wild's career – 'that celebrated statesman and politician' – was already elaborating the Walpole–Wild analogy which Fielding was later to build into the structure of his novel. For Jonathan Wild was 'In Principle and Practice a right Modern Whig,

---

of it' – and Kent was likely to have spread his knowledge more widely in Westminster. In the case of Huntridge also Stratford is our only informant as to matters which never broke the surface of the press but were clearly talked about very widely: see above, pp. 70–71 and 186.

1. *True Briton*, 26 August 1723.

2. *Letters of John Gay*, ed. C. F. Burgess, Oxford, 1966, p. 45.

3. See Plumb, *Sir Robert Walpole*, II, p. 110: 'Even the impeachment of Lord Chancellor Macclesfield . . . strengthened rather than weakened [Walpole's] ministry. Walpole had never liked Macclesfield and was particularly glad to see him go . . .' Macclesfield was of the old Sunderland faction: Walpole replaced him with 'an old, loyal friend', Sir Peter King.

according to the Definition of those Gentlemen – *Keep what you get, and get what you can . . .*'[1] From the *Beggar's Opera* to Nathaniel Mist to the ballad-vendors, the moral which resounded throughout the decade -

> Little Villains must submit to Fate,
> While Great Ones do enjoy the World in State -

was a good deal more accurate than some historians and critics have supposed. For an examination of the practices of the administration in these years reveals the same use of informers and evidences, employment of blood-money, the same casual sacrifice of colleagues who had outlived their utility, and a similar parasitism upon the public, as that exemplified in the career of Wild. The 'subculture' of the Hanoverian Whig and the 'subculture' of Jonathan Wild were mirror-images of each other. As one examines the circumstances surrounding the origin of the Black Act one is repeatedly reminded that it was exactly in these years that Swift completed his *Gulliver's Travels*, with its description of the 'Discoverers, Witnesses, Informers, Accusers, Prosecutors, Evidences, Swearers' who made up the bulk of the people of the Kingdom of Tribnia.

1. *Mist's Weekly Journal*, 12 and 19 June 1725. See also Howson, op. cit., pp. 223-4, 280-81, 284, and William Irwin, *The Making of Jonathan Wild*, New Haven, 1966.

10: Consequences and Conclusions

i. People

We may look briefly at some of the consequences. And, first, for a few of the actors.

It's an ill wind that blows no good. Some humble men profited a little from the episode of the Blacks. Walpole's ascendancy in 1723 finds an apt quantitative expression in the accounts of money impressed to the Treasury Solicitor for the prosecution of law suits, etc.:

1721	£4,000
1722	£4,300
1723	£11,150
1724	£3,500[1]

While the bulge was partly accounted for by the Jacobite trials of 1722–3, Cracherode's own accounts of causes under prosecution makes it clear that as much went on hunting Blacks.[1] Thus some largesse was extended, not only to lawyers, but to clerks, King's Messengers, jurors, witnesses and others. For example, one or two of the Berkshire evidences may have received, on Walpole's order, a weekly cash income in excess of their customary standard.[3] In addition, a number of loyal citizens received the King's money for their share of rewards in securing the conviction of Blacks. The seven Hampshire Blacks were worth £100 a head (although

1. Accounts in C(H) MSS 63.36.

2. In T1.243 and 249, etc. This would not include secret service payments for services such as those of Parson Power: between March 1721 and March 1725 £339,100 was recorded in secret service payments: C(H) MSS 63.68.

3. After the failure of the Wallingford Assize, Walpole ordered that the chief Crown evidences be held for further trials: Terry and Stedman were subsisted at 10s. a week from June until December 1723, and Cox at 3s. a day: T27.23, p. 404; SP44.81, fo. 304.

a good many hands were outstretched to receive it). The two executed Richmond hunters were worth the same. Vulcan Gates and Thomas James, however, were worth only £40 each; Thomas Archer, the Newgate barber who 'grassed' on Gates, got £10 out of this. Thus not only Luxury but also the Law performed a function of distributing wealth among those in most need. The Treasury, parsimonious as ever, complained that too much was being allowed to escape from its coffers.[1]

Baptist Nunn was not only reimbursed in full for his expenses, but was further rewarded. 'Your Lordship will remember Baptist Nunn who was so active against the Blacks,' Delafaye wrote to Townshend at the end of June 1723. 'I cannot help thinking he deserves at least twice the salary to his office of porter.' This office – newly added to his existing offices – was that of Porter of the Outward Gate and Janitor of Windsor Castle, at £25 p.a. As part of his perquisites of office there went a set of rooms in the Castle. But Owen, the Steward of the forest courts, who (we remember) had never shown any liking for Nunn, was already in occupation of this suite and refused to budge. Not even the new Governor, the Earl of Carlisle, could persuade him to move.

We must sympathize with Nunn's plight. But Delafaye was misinformed if he thought that the gallant gamekeeper–janitor was subsisting, houseless, on £25 p.a.[2] In addition to those perquisites which we have already noted (above, p. 98), he was awarded, in December 1726, the under-keepership of Linchford Walk, with a salary of £20 p.a. and the use of the Lodge. But something greater was added to this: 'reposing especial trust and confidence in the care, fidelity and circumspection of Baptist Nunn, *Gent.*' And even more was to follow, for a Survey of 1734 shows Nunn, not as under-keeper of Linchford Walk but as Keeper ('by Lord Warden's Warrant'), in the company of such notabilities as Lady Rich, General Honeywood, Sir Henry Neville and Sir Charles Howard. The gamekeeper had made the most difficult of eighteenth-century transitions. If the Blacks had had one quarter of the organization ascribed to them it is difficult to see how he could have remained alive.

1. Civil List accounts, Brit. Mus. Add. MSS 29,464, fos. 182, 207, 208, 235; Gates, T1.255 (33); James, T1.257 (32), T53.32, pp. 424–5, 436–7. For the Treasury's complaints, that £5,000 p.a. were being spent each year in rewards, see C(H) MSS 46.25; and T27.24, p. 130. The complaint, however, which presumably arose from the notoriety of Jonathan Wild, was that the rewards were being paid 'for the crafts and doings of pick-pockets, and such slight dexterities', and not for the conviction of more dangerous felons. Money for hanging Blacks was not under scrutiny.

2. Nunn's expenses claim for hunting Blacks totalled £468 7s. 6½d. of which he had been paid some part on account by Walpole: hence he was claiming £377. An annotation to the accounts suggests that the claim was met handsomely, with £600: Nunn Accounts, T1.244 (63), and T27.24, p. 79. For other matter in this paragraph,

The former Christ Church commoner and clerical *agent provocateur*, Thomas Power, returned to his cure of souls. But Townshend and Walpole must have decided that his usefulness was at an end in England.[1] In the summer of 1724 they nominated one of their clerical favourites, Hugh Boulter, to be Archbishop of Armagh and Lord Primate of All Ireland. His Primacy was glad to oblige Townshend by providing – as one of his first actions – for Power 'whom your Lordship was pleased to recommend to my care, before I left England. I have given him a living of about £150 p.a.' In fact, he did better than this, preferring him both to the curacy of Ballymore (February 1725) and to the Rectorship of Ballinderry and Tamlaght (July 1725). But Boulter found Power to be an embarrassment, and it proved to be necessary to address him in tones of marked displeasure: 'You are represented as a person who have neither discretion in your words and conversation, nor proper decency in your actions and conduct, nor a due regard to the offices of your function . . .' It is not recorded whether his wife accompanied him, nor whether he still had plans to hang her by a leg from the window. The preferment came in a time when national sensibilities were exasperated by the affair of 'Wood's Halfpence', and it did not pass unnoticed. Archbishop King of Dublin was enraged that the Lord Primate (Boulter), who had (after a year in office) had only two livings vacant, had given one 'to one of his Walton Blacks', the other to a 'Hottentot'. To Dean Swift, still smoking from the 'Draper's Letters', who had noted this as a scandalous example of the preferment of servile English Whigs above the heads of Irish churchmen, may be left the appropriate comment:

> The Archbishop of Dublin attacked the Primate [Archbishop Boulter] in the Castle for giving a good living to a certain animal called a Walsh Black, which the other excused, alleging he was preferred to it by Lord Townshend. It is a cant word for a deer stealer. This fellow was leader of a gang, and had the honour of hanging half a dozen of his fellows in quality of informer, which was his merit. If you cannot match me that in Italy, step to Muscovy, and from thence to the Hottentots.[2]

---

see SP44.286, fos. 86–7; SP43.66; SP44.290, fo. 21; Constable's Warrant Books, II, fos. 24, 25 *verso*, 90 *verso*–93; T1.265 (40); MPE348. A further indication as to Nunn's new status is to be found in the fact that he was a witness, along with Paxton, of the will of Charles Withers: Earl St Aldwyn's MSS, Hicks-Beach unnumbered papers.

1. In the Secretary of State's Warrant Book there is a warrant, dated 18 April 1724, for the arrest of Thomas Power for publishing a scandalous and seditious libel entitled 'Heydegger's Letter to the Bishop of London' (SP44.80). I do not know if this was the same Power, nor what the case was about.

2. *Letters written by His Excellency Hugh Boulter, D.D., Lord Primate of All Ireland*, Oxford, 1769, I, Boulter to Townshend, 4 September 1725, to Power, 24 February 1726, pp. 37, 65; R. Mant, *History of the Church of Ireland*, 1840, II, pp. 444–5; *Notes and*

The actors, so far, have spoken their final lines in character. But there was one who broke decisively from the conformism of class avarice. Richard Norton, the Warden of Bere Forest, fully lived up to his local reputation as an eccentric. Possessed of estates worth at least £60,000,[1] as well as the choicest furnishings, paintings, jewellery and silver at Southwick Park, he had early become reconciled to the fact that (having expelled his wife) he would die without a direct heir. When he died, in 1732, it was found, to the consternation of his relatives, that he had left a lengthy will – unambiguous and reaffirmed over many years in several codicils – bequeathing his estate to the poor: 'That is to say, the poor, hungry, and thirsty, naked, and strangers, sick and wounded, and prisoners, and to and for no other use, or uses whatsoever.' He requested Parliament to act as executor, and, should it refuse, the bishops of England.

To leave some dole, or some modest parcel of land as charity, was one thing; it was seemly, although not perhaps felt so often to be seemly as in the sixteenth and seventeenth centuries. But the alienation of property on this scale offended against the capitalist law of nature. On the night that Norton died, his Steward – and probably his closest friend – Edward Wynn was found by a neighbour in tears, and unable to read the funeral instructions through his grief:

> Mr. Smith said to him, 'Mr. Winn, you have great people to do with, no less than the legislative power of England, and if they refuses to act, then the bishops, which are great people' and Winn answered him, 'I do not know how I shall go through it', and then we went to sealing up the doors and chestes.

It was inevitable that Norton's relatives should contest the will, and every available source of gossip about 'crazy Norton' was turned to account. A cottager was found who testified that Norton had made 'many offers to exchange Southwick house for [his father's] cottage, for that he was tired of living at Southwick, the Devil would not let him be quiet'. In or about 1724, when Norton was going by chaise towards Bishop's Waltham, he was stopped by some beggars who solicited him for alms. Norton 'started

---

Queries, 5th Series, III, 3 April 1875; *Correspondence of Jonathan Swift*, ed. F. E. Ball, 1912, III, pp. 290–91; J. B. Leslie, *Armagh Clergy and Parishes*, Dundalk, 1911, pp. 122, 137; Charles S. King, *A Great Archbishop of Dublin*, 1906, pp. 252–3: King complains that the Lord Primate (Boulter) has given one of his livings 'to one of his Walton blacks, whom he since ordained priest, & the other to one Mr. Blennerhessett whom they commonly call an Hottentot; I know not for what reason'.

1. Affidavits in Hants Rec. Off. 5M50.397 suggest that in addition there was between £20,000 and £30,000 worth of standing timber on the Norton Estate. In 1736 the rents and profits of the Norton Estate were given as £9,000 p.a.: *Commons Journal*, XXII, 1736, p. 778.

up in his chair, and said he was mad enough before, but was then now more mad than ever'. He dropped his hat and wig, 'took no manner of care to get them again, but went on his way to Waltham on foot'. Conduct which might have marked him out, in medieval times, as a saint was cited – according to the 'accepted standards of the age' – to prove him a madman. In 1739 a special jury of Hampshire gentlemen had no difficulty in upsetting the will, pronouncing that Norton had made it while of unsound mind.[1]

Our faith in capitalist nature is restored by an anecdote from the later life of Viscount Cobham, the Constable of Windsor Castle during the episode of the Blacks. Cobham, like Cadogan, had emerged with a fortune from the wars, which he employed upon the lavish buildings and gardens at Stowe. In 1748 two young men from near-by Salcey Forest were caught while raiding his deer-park. According to a firm local tradition, the wives of the men sought an interview at Stowe and begged for their husbands' lives. It seemed that old Cobham, now in his eightieth year, was moved by their tears. He promised that their husbands would be returned to them by a certain day – and so they were, for on that day their corpses were brought to the cottage doors on a cart. Cobham celebrated the occasion by striking statues of the dead men in his park, a deer across their shoulders.[2]

As for Sir Francis Page, he also remained active until his eightieth year. 'When phthisicky and decrepid, as he passed along from court, a gentleman enquired particularly of the state of his health. "My dear sir, you see I keep hanging on, hanging on." '[3]

ii. Forests

As for the forests, the Black Act did not bring to them instant security for their timber and deer. Although I have found no further references to Farmer William Shorter and his band of outlaws[4] nor to 'King John', in

1. *Gentleman's Magazine*, December 1732, February 1733, pp. 57–62, and May 1739; Hants Rec. Off. Daly MSS, 5M50/397.

2. J. E. Linnell, *Old Oak*, 1932, ch. 1.

3. William Hone's *Year Book*, 1832, p. 614. W. Wing in the *Annals of Steeple Aston* (Oxford, 1875, p. 53) has another characteristic Page joke: Barrister (entering court) – 'I suppose the judge is just behind?' Second Barrister: 'I hope so, for he never was *just* before.'

4. Nunn's accounts end in September 1723. At that point his informants told him that Shorter and his gang were lying 'about Shurville', Hampshire: 'they are numerous and very resolute' (perhaps twelve men); and the last entry (24 September) is: 'A person here out of the Holt acquainted with Shorter & gang is gone down to act with them under the pretence of flying his home for the murder in the Holt' (i.e. the death of Earwaker, the Alice Holt keeper; above, p. 148): 'Gave him £2.2.0.' Thereafter there is silence. 'Shurville' was an old variant of Sherfield English, four miles west of Romsey, on the

most other respects matters went on in the forests much as they had done before the passage of the Act.

Just as the trouble may have started first in the Crondall–Dogmersfield–Farnham corner where Berkshire, Hampshire and Surrey met, so disturbance appears to have persisted in this corner longest. At Crondall, in 1724, a gentleman had his young oaks cut and his horses stabbed. Later in the same year, some Crondall labourers, armed and disguised, were out killing deer again in the Bishop's park at Farnham: five of them were proclaimed under the Black Act. Farnham Park continued to receive raids in 1725 and 1726, and the game was still going on in 1730.[1] In July 1727 James Over, of Dogmersfield, and a man from Crondall were proclaimed under the Black Act for entering, with arms, the park of Ellis St John, and taking one fallow deer. There was some close family connection with Blacking in this parish: an Over had lost his copyhold through the manipulations of Ellis St John, an Over was among those who became outlaws with William Shorter, and James Over was proclaimed on the information of Henry Over, a Dogmersfield labourer who had taken part in the same raid and was presumably related. But James, who had taken refuge in Kent, was unlucky enough to get into gaol, where he was recognized. He disappears from the records in the same direction as Vulcan Gates, awaiting formal identification and summary execution as a proclaimed man.[2]

Lord Craven also received attention at two of his seats – at one (Dummer, near Basingstoke) his deer were carried off from the park, his stables broken and horses stolen. At another seat, at Hampstead Marshall,

---

Hampshire–Dorset border, and not too far from either the New Forest or Cranbourne Chase: see Grundy, 'Hampshire Charters and Place Names', Hants Rec. Off. Typescript. But there were other Sherfields in north Hampshire (e.g. Sherfield-on-Lodden), close to the old disturbed district of Heckfield, Bramshill, etc.

1. *London Gazette*, no. 6,289, 25 July 1724 and no. 6,328, 8 December 1724. PC1.4.7, proclaiming James 'Batt' Heath and others. (It appears that 'Batt' Heath was caught in 1727, and convicted under the Act: see Delafaye to Paxton, 31 May 1727, SP44.125, fo. 121.) *Northampton Mercury*, 16 August 1725, 30 May 1726. Memorandum of William Field in Hants Rec. Off. (Farnham Castle, unnumbered papers), relating to the activities of one 'Black Will', an intrepid and boisterous poacher, in 1730.

2. Ellis St John appears to have foreclosed upon a £100 mortgage (at 5 per cent) on the Over copyhold, made in 1721: Hants Rec. Off. 15M50/72/10, 15M50/712 and 15M50/959–63. But that was John Over. William Over was a very active Black, and he and his son took refuge 'about Shurville' with William Shorter; Nunn negotiated unsuccessfully with them to turn evidence: Nunn Accounts, August and September 1723. We do not know what relation, if any, William was to James, whose proclamation under the Black Act is entered in PC 2.90, fo. 332 (19 June 1728), nor what relationship either bore to the informant, Henry Over. For the arrest of James Over in Kent in 1730, KB33/13/6, Hants, Trinity 5 Geo. II.

a keeper named Coats was committed to Newgate for 'disposing of every buck' in the park, and for

procuring several persons, many times, to kill and destroy the deer, when with young . . . for hire; and hanging the same on the park pales and stiles, and also requesting the Waltham Blacks and others to burn his Lordship's houses, barns, reeks, &c. . . aiding and assisting them with money, fire-arms and apparel to disguise. And also procuring the said blacks to kill his Lordship's keeper, and maim, wound and kill his cattle.

I do not know what may lie behind these sensational accusations. For Coats, after a trial of four hours, was acquitted. Whether he was innocent or not, it is likely that someone committed at least some of the offences for which he was tried.[1]

The evidence confirms what one would expect – that a degeneration of relations followed upon the Black Act. In place of the gentlemanly 'King John' we have reports of arson, the stabbing and maiming of beasts, terror and counter-terror. Gamekeepers were at the vortex of this conflict: sometimes they were terrorized into aiding the poachers, sometimes they were agents of terror and freebooters on their own account. In 1731 the manor of Mortimer, one of the seats of the Lady Dowager Ann Powlett (Mrs Nathan Wright, the old enemy of Sir Charles Englefield), was under attack: gates were smashed, young trees cut down, and the gamekeeper threatened with death.[2] But the extraordinary complexity which this agrarian warfare could now assume is best illustrated in the case of Lewis Gunner.

Gunner's case would appear, at first sight, to be that of 'the biter bit'. He was gamekeeper to the lord of the manor of Bentworth, 'in which station he acted with great severity, by shooting the gentlemen and farmers' dogs, taking guns [and] nets from such as were not qualified', and so on. This had rendered him 'very obnoxious' to the local people, including (it would seem) many of the gentry. Dislike of Lewis Gunner spread to near-by Alton and to Alice Holt. But Gunner, faced with this hostility, appears to have built up his own organization of subalterns, dependants and loyal associates – or, in the terminology of the time, his own 'gang'. Finding his legal powers ineffective, he supplemented them with the same kinds of extra-legal terror of which the Blacks were accused: he or his gang were accused of incendiarism, of stabbing all the horses and cows of a farmer in the Holt, and of sending threatening letters; and

1. *Northampton Mercury*, 20 June 1726 (Hampstead Marshall is in the south-west corner of Berkshire). Also *Mist's Weekly Journal*, 8 January 1726 (arrest of several deer-stealers at Dummer), 12 March 1726, 23 July 1726.
2. *London Gazette*, no. 6,975, 3 April 1731.

Gunner certainly always carried loaded pistols and discharged them, more than once, to terrify opponents.

This brought about his downfall. 'Undisguised (except in liquor)' Gunner had fired his pistol, in a public house, at one of his opponents; the bullet missed, and Gunner pleaded that he had never intended it to find its mark. But the man at whom he fired was able to initiate a prosecution under the Black Act – a prosecution fully supported by local opinion, and resulting in a conviction. Sir John Fortescue, at the Winchester Assizes, duly sentenced Gunner to death, but recommended his reprieve on the grounds that the shooting was under 'doubtful circumstances' and did not appear to the judge to be 'a malitious act'. (No Black could have expected so favourable a construction to be placed on the Act.)

Fortescue's reprieve of Gunner divided the community even more bitterly and led on to even greater complexities. His reprieve was (it seems) conditional upon the recommendation that he 'transport himself' for fourteen years. But each stage in these proceedings was accompanied by incendiarism in Bentworth and in Alton, together with menacing messages 'drop't about'. Two barns and three houses were burned down. The local people, headed by their Rector, had no doubt that these fires were the work of Gunner's 'gang'. There was no firm evidence of this, but much inference and hearsay. The first fire came on the night after Gunner had been sent to gaol; the second shortly after his condemnation; the third on the morning when he should have been hanged. A woman of Alton had been heard to say that 'if Lewis Gunner were hanged, Bentworth would come into more trouble than ever it did and Alton too'. Petitions were drawn up on both sides, supported by people of substance and influence. At first general feeling wanted Gunner to be hanged; then, when he was reprieved, it was determined upon his transportation. So long as he remained in Winchester gaol, the villagers of Bentworth nightly expected further conflagrations: 'our farmers, labourers, and servants,' wrote the Rector, 'are all worn out with toil, fear, & watching.' But when Gunner succeeded in obtaining bail, on condition that he 'transport himself', consternation grew even higher. So far from leaving the country, Gunner remained in Hampshire 'to the great Terror of us all', assembling signatures to a petition for his free pardon, and (by one account) threatening arson, stabbing the beasts, and firing through the clothes of any who dared to oppose him. 'No doubt he will add Names enough . . . for very few would have the Courage to deny him. Our thatcht buildings and inclosed country, My Lord! lay both our Lives and Fortunes at the Mercy of Such Desperate Villains.' Should he obtain his pardon 'he may put us all under Contribution and we shall be glad to purchase our Safety on his Terms'.

This is the best evidence to come to hand, at any point in this book, as to a 'gang' and a 'protection-racket'. But it emerges, in a very complex way, from the side of the park-keepers and not from that of the farmers or foresters. The evidence is everywhere difficult to evaluate. The soberest account came early on in the affair, shortly after Gunner's condemnation, in a report from a Hampshire magistrate, Thomas Bates, to Judge Fortescue. Bates had taken the depositions at Gunner's first arrest, but had never seen him before. Bates was willing to credit the view of 'the generality in this neighbourhood' that Gunner, though poor, was 'of a proud, insulting and revengefull temper'. But he could find no evidence to prove that the arson was the work of his 'gang'. In the neighbourhood itself 'they are all of them unwilling to have him executed, believing that punishment not adequate [i.e. excessive] to his crime'. Yet at the same time no one would feel himself safe if Gunner was let free again among them. And from beyond the village there were 'popular clamours' that Gunner should be hanged: 'I have been applyed to by persons of credit remote from his neighbourhood to hasten his execution.' Concluding his appraisal of the facts of the case, Bates added: 'My Lord, this Gunner is without a friend, therefore justice requires this of me.' In the face of so much outcry, the magistrate's careful attention to evidence does him honour, and reminds one of values of justice more exalted than those commonly exhibited in this study. But, at the same time, Gunner was a gamekeeper; we have nowhere found any similar impartial assessment on behalf of a condemned, and even more friendless, Black.[1]

We have followed this complex case in detail, because the evidence happens to survive, and one must put to use whatever does. It reveals a deeply divided community, subject to arson and violence, and the divisions not according to any regular socio-economic stratification, but between the park owner and the keepers on one side, and most of the rest of the village (including its Rector) on the other. This division sustained, on both sides, structured hostilities and organization which could be seen as 'gangs'. Nor is there any reason to assume that these hostilities died away in other parts of north-east Hampshire. I have not investigated why, in 1733, a clause was added to the Black Act making it a capital offence to cut hop-binds. But Farnham was a hop-growing centre, and that much-hated man, Edward Forbes, Steward and subsequently Woodward to the Bishop, and tenant of Farnham Old Park, was a substantial hop-farmer: and it is tempting to suggest that this death clause also may have arisen from an episcopal nexus. After 1733 there may have been a lull of sorts.

1. Papers on the Gunner case are in SP36.14 (1), items 29, 124, 125; SP36.15, items 68, 71; SP36.22, items 155–6, 158–9.

But in 1746 something like a revival of Blacking was reported in Hampshire:

A gang of desperate ruffians, call'd *The Blacks*, are again got together in that country, living in a retir'd house, in a forest; from whence they have issued out disguis'd by night, with a woman in their company, and . . . committed innumerable outrages, robbing gentlemen's parks, fishponds, and stealing fat sheep.

The Bishop's park at Farnham was among the parks attacked.[1]

Nor did the Black Act bring peace to the central and southern forests of Hampshire. At Hambledon in the Forest of Bere, after the arson of some wood-piles, a cordwainer, a tailor and a blacksmith – one of them a Bishop's Waltham man – were proclaimed under the Act.[2] There were also incidents of robbery and violence which were not associated with Blacking, but which took place in the same district. Surviving Blacks were no doubt satisfied to see in 1725 the chief informer against the Portsmouth men, Thomas Barton, himself cast for death, for highway robbery, at Winchester Assizes. Not even Richard Norton's representations could save him.[3] The next year the authorities succeeded in rounding up at least one of their hunted Blacks, and Benjamin Rivers was convicted under the Black Act. At the same Winchester Assizes three offenders were convicted for the robbery and murder of a farmer near Bishop's

---

1. *Northampton Mercury*, 17 March 1746.

2. SP35.38, fo. 102; SP44.124, fos. 247–8; *London Gazette*, no. 6,447, 29 January 1726; Hants Rec. Off. QM/5 (October 1725); Portsmouth Rec. Off. 11A/16/360. In December 1725 it was said that 'the Blacks of Waltham' were active again, after farmers in the neighbourhood found their horses stabbed: *Northampton Mercury*, 13 December 1725.

3. Procedures in this case are interesting. Norton first wrote to Paxton asking that Baron Page and Serjeant Reynolds be told that Barton's father 'and other substantial relations & even my poor self beseech you that Mr. Thomas Barton, whom you know was so useful for his Majesty's service against the 4 Blacks, being in Winton Gaol for some petty robberies, if he should be convicted might have the grace of transportation'. Paxton passed the letter to Townshend, who wrote at once to the Justices of Assize for the Western Circuit (25 February 1725): Barton had been 'particularly serviceable to the Government in detecting the Blacks': 'I desire that . . . if found guilty you will allow him the favour of transportation.' Townshend underestimated Page, who might have been willing to be instructed to hang, but not to reprieve: he left it to his junior, Serjeant Reynolds, to reply. His letter does not survive; but on 9 March Townshend answered that he knew nothing of the circumstances of the case, and had only written at the desire of Norton: 'You certainly did right to pass sentence of death, as you found his crime; and as he appears to be another sort of malefactor than I imagined, I have nothing further to say on his behalf, nor will I move the King any further upon it.' SP44.81, fos. 395, 401. Thus the independence of the judiciary was vindicated.

Waltham; the bodies of two of them were left to rot in chains on Waltham Chase, as a reminder of the resources of order.[1]

In Alice Holt and Woolmer forests Ruperta Howe continued for many years to exercise her office of Ranger. In 1740 she was writing to the Treasury very much as she had been writing twenty years before: 'in defiance of my endeavours, and the vigilance of the keepers, the deer & timber is dayly destroy'd.'[2] In 1741 the heads of several fish-ponds in Alice Holt and Woolmer were broken down by rioters.[3] Several years before there had been reports that Blacking had crossed the Solent:

About six months ago, a paper was affixed to the house of Mr Ridge, Keeper of the Forest in the Isle of Wight, threatening that if he should take away any gun, or hurt any man killing deer [on] their own grounds or corn, his horse would be shot under him, and his habitation laid low about his ears, and to remember the Walton Blacks.

This warning was followed up by the killing of deer, and the firing of a gun at the Keeper's chamber window.[4]

Some documents survive from West Meon, on the north-west border of the Forest of Bere, which (as in the case of Lewis Gunner) give a momentary insight into the continuity of these forms of agrarian protest. In April 1748 Henry Foxcroft – perhaps the same Foxcroft who had been visited, twenty-five years before, by the Blacks in Berkshire (above, p. 150) – received an 'incendiary letter' whose force was underlined by the cutting down of a plantation of more than 600 young trees (elm, walnut, apple and cherry) in front of his manor house at West Meon. (This seems a large operation to have been conducted swiftly and without detection.) When Foxcroft issued advertisements promising a reward for the detection of the culprit, these were answered by the burning of a summerhouse, the cutting-down of more fruit trees, the cutting of gaps in his hedges, the poisoning of one of his fish-ponds and the cutting of the head of another. The offences were tracked down to Henry Aburrow, a local blacksmith, recently sacked from Foxcroft's employment. Aburrow was duly convicted at Winchester Assizes under the Black Act, for breaking the head of a fish-pond; when the prosecution attempted to proceed with two other

1. *British Journal*, 5 and 19 March 1726. For Barton see also 'Captain' Alexander Smith, *Memoirs of the Life and Times of Jonathan Wild*, 1726, pp. 99–110; he was hanged for robbing a woman of 12s.

2. Ruperta Howe to Treasury Commissioners, C(H) 62.60.

3. *Calendar of Treasury Books and Papers, 1739–1741*, p. 542. Also in 1741 a Hambledon man who was probably innocent was transported for an assault on a keeper in Bere, provoking a wave of local indignation: Newcastle papers, Brit. Mus. Add. MSS 32,695 fos. 267, 277, 339.

4. *Weekly Miscellany*, no. 224, 8 April 1737. I owe this reference to Mr John Walsh.

indictments (for cutting the trees and burning the summerhouse) the judge courteously interposed and said that 'he thought that would be only losing of time; because as the prisoner had been already convicted capitally he could only hang him but once'. What Aburrow's grievance may have been – apart from dismissal – is unclear, but he appears to have had some local support: 'nobody within five mile' (said Foxcroft) dared to come forward against him at his prosecution 'for fear of revenge'; and there were influential applications for his reprieve. The Duke of Richmond, who was at this time busy with his campaign against smugglers, was enraged by these applications. He wrote in haste to the Duke of Newcastle urging Aburrow's execution:

> 'Tis certain that the fellow is a most notorious villain, a poacher, & a smugler, & so are his whole family, one of his brothers was evidence against him to save himself, & another of his brothers who is a famous bowler at crickett & goes by the name of *Curry* I committed some time ago to Horsham jayle for smugling with fire arms . . . Your grace sees what a family they are, & indeed if cutting down plantations, heads of ponds, & burning houses are not punish'd to the utmost rigour of the Law, there will be no living in the country . . .

He enclosed a letter from Henry Foxcroft which made much the same point. The case was one which 'Concerns all People, of Any Property in the Kingdom':

> I should be very unwilling to make the least Objection against Mercy did not Self Preservation tell me that my Life & Fortune must Run the Uttermost Hazard if this Offender is ever set at Liberty or Returns. . . . As Fireing of Houses & Doing such sorts of Mischiefs . . . are very much in Fashion in this Neighbourhood, & we are Unfortunately plac'd in a Nest of Smugglers, I hope Your Lordship will think this Man a Proper Person to make an example of . . .[1]

Investigation of this and other cases might well lead on into further avenues of research, stretching forward across the eighteenth century, and beyond our present inquiry. We have shown only that Blacking was not confined to the 1720s; that it comprised methods of agrarian warfare well remembered and from time to time 'very much in Fashion'; and also, perhaps, that this was scarcely the society of consensus and of deference which is sometimes supposed. We must hope that local historians will find out how, over the years, the battle swayed this way and that between commoners and keepers. But in eastern Hampshire, by the mid-century, one cause of conflict at least was being removed. Deer-stealing

---

1. Papers on Aburrow's case are in the Newcastle papers, Brit. Mus. Add. MSS 32,718. Cal Winslow, who drew them to my attention, discusses the Duke of Richmond's campaign against smugglers in D. Hay, P. Linebaugh and E. P. Thompson, eds., *Albion's Fatal Tree*, 1975.

was falling off in the old forest areas, not out of terror at the Black Act, but simply because there were fewer deer to steal. In 1750 a keeper was killed in a battle with poachers in Woolmer Forest.[1] He must have been one of the last victims of the age-old contest over this 'hungry, sandy, barren waste'. For Gilbert White, who described Woolmer Forest thus, goes on to say that where Queen Anne had once reposed on a bank and had watched the keepers drive 500 head of red deer before her, there was now not one straggler left. An old keeper told him that 'as soon as they began blacking, they were reduced to about fifty head', until the Duke of Cumberland 'sent down an huntsman, and six yeoman prickers, in scarlet jackets laced with gold, attended by the stag-hounds; ordering them to take every deer in this forest alive, and to convey them in carts to Windsor'. White himself witnessed the 'gallant scenes' as stags and hinds were rounded up.[2]

This was in the 1750s, and in the same years the fallow deer of Alice Holt had been reduced to seven or eight head.[3] An observer of Woolmer in the early nineteenth century wrote:

There is little life to be seen in the forest now. A few cattle crop the heather, and perhaps the wild-looking inmate of one of the few cottages in the forest may be encountered, while the 'chip' of the hatchet is heard from one of the plantations. But stillness and loneliness are the prevailing characteristics . . .[4]

The economy of the foresters, it seems, was in symbiotic relationship with that of the deer; when the latter left – and the sands of Woolmer could not be 'improved' – the people followed.

In the Bishop of Winchester's park at Farnham it is probable that the number of deer had been equally reduced. The bishops preferred their palaces at Chelsea and Winchester to Farnham Castle, and at the end of the century a traveller found the park neglected, 'cut with unlicensed paths', the trees mangled by deer (which had somehow survived), and a cricket ground with stands for selling liquor pitched beneath the castle windows, which 'had so long been suffered that the people conceived

1. TS23.19 – brief against the brothers Mayhew, husbandmen, for the death of Thomas Bridges.

2. Gilbert White, *The Natural History of Selborne* in *Works*, 1802, Letter VI. Compare the testimony of an old keeper, John Adams, in 6th Report of the Land Revenue Commissioners, *Commons Journals*, 1790, p. 162. Adams deposed that in the course of the hunting 'many were driven out into the country and destroyed', and that the last two or three brace were given by the Ranger to a neighbouring gentleman.

3. Information of Lord Stawell (Ranger) and William Moore (keeper) in ibid., pp. 127, 164, 169. Lord Stawell's father, however, re-stocked Alice Holt with fallow deer, which fluctuated in numbers between 300 and 1,500 head between 1760 and 1790.

4. *Journal of Forestry*, vol. I (1878), p. 43.

they had now a right to it'.[1] In the Forest of Bere the deer survived, although in hundreds rather than in thousands, and the old war between keepers and local farmers was going on at the end of the century much as it had been in the 1720s.[2] As late as 1770 the forest courts still met occasionally, with 'all the pomp and parade' of Verderer and Regarders, but offenders were seldom prosecuted 'so the poor fell the Hollies and Thorns, and lopp the Timber with impunity, and when the keepers forbid them, they only laugh . . .' A large part of the forest was felled at this time to pay for repairs to Buckingham Palace. The King also was served, grudgingly, with one brace of deer out of the forest each year; another seventeen brace went as perquisites to office holders, and poachers probably accounted for as many more.[3] But Waltham Chase remained, at least in the middle years of the century, a deer-free zone. When Benjamin Hoadly, Bishop of Winchester between 1734 and 1762, was urged to re-stock the Chase, he refused on the grounds that 'it had done mischief enough already'. It was a sentiment almost Christian in its implication, and scarcely to be expected in the mouth of a Whig bishop. But, then, Hoadly was a cripple, unable to perform minimal episcopal duties, and certainly unable to enjoy the pleasures of the hunt.[4]

Enfield Chase was of course too near to London, too much within the view of the great predators like Chandos, to survive as any kind of forest. The old game went on for a few more years. Francis Medlicott, General Pepper's Deputy, was left for a while in charge of the Chase, and found it a heavy care. In January 1727, while riding on his rounds, he encountered two villagers carrying off furzes on poles. He tried to arrest them and seized one man's bill-hook; this man, John Cogdall, retaliated by beating Medlicott and his horse with his pole, whereupon the Deputy Ranger slashed Cogdall's arm with his own hook. To Medlicott's astonishment, Cogdall, instead of showing deferential resignation, entered an indictment against him for assault and battery; moreover, he had a cast-iron case – a wound, which a doctor had dressed, and a fellow witness (while Medlicott had neither). It was therefore necessary to get 'the King' to quash the case, by ordering the Attorney-General to order a *noli prosequi*.[5] (Such

1. W. Gilpin, *Observations on the Western Parts of England*, 1808, p. 39.

2. 13th Report of the Land Revenue Commissioners, *Commons Journals*, 1792, pp. 1044–5. A memorial of Robert Thistlethwayte, *circa* 1793, recommending disafforestation and enclosure, claimed that there were fewer than 150 deer left in the forest: Hants Rec. Off. unnumbered papers.

3. 'A State of His Majesty's Forest of South Bere', n.d. (probably drawn up by South, the Surveyor, in about 1773); Crest.2.1672.

4. White, op. cit., Letter VII. For Hoadly's disabilities, see N. Sykes, *Church and State in the XVIIIth Century*, Cambridge, 1934, pp. 361–2.

5. Memorial of Cracherode (with accompanying papers) to Treasury Commissioners,

affrays were everyday: we mention this one only because it illustrates the flexibility of the law.) In 1729 the last of the old guard of Enfield deer stealers, Aaron Maddocks ('Jonathan Wild's man') came to his end: he was caught by a keeper while on a poaching expedition on the Chase, and carried, desperately wounded from the struggle, to Newgate where he died.[1] It was perhaps a better death than that of his old companions, Thomas James and Vulcan Gates; and, then, again (when one remembers what Newgate was like) perhaps it was not.

Enfield Chase turned out to be a somewhat less successful speculation than the Duke of Chandos had anticipated. He failed to find a customer for it, and settled down to exploit its resources himself. He was no longer the man he had been, having frittered away much of his fortune in unsuccessful ventures and in astonishingly conspicuous expenditure, at Cannons and elsewhere. He had run through, accordingly, his political capital also, and he experienced the vexations of being prosecuted in the Duchy Court of Lancaster in his turn. He found himself beset, as Pepper had been, on all sides: by wood-stealers (or villagers who claimed wood-rights), by deer-stealers, by under-keepers dealing in the timber and venison trades, by superior keepers who engaged in the same trade more flagrantly, and by the gamekeepers and packs of hounds of neighbouring noblemen (including the Lord Mayor). So bad did the situation become that his under-keepers were unable to serve the venison warrants of the King. In 1743 (as twenty years before) there were complaints of poachers who 'come in open day to kill the deer & cut down all the timber'. What predatory activities Chandos was carrying on on his own account are not disclosed in these sources, which give only his side of the story.[2] After Chandos's death the Chase was eventually enclosed, although it took longer than the first Duke had expected. Meanwhile it was nibbled at: by the time of enclosure, in 1777, Chandos's perhaps overgenerous estimate (in the 1720s) of 14,000 acres had been reduced to 8,000.[3] When enclosure

8 February 1727, T1.258 (16). Also in 1727 one Gibbs was proclaimed under the Black Act for killing deer on the Chase and shooting at the keepers: T1.260 (20).

1. Memorial of Cracherode (concerning reward) in T53.36 (21 January 1730).

2. C. H. C. and M. I. Baker, *Life and Circumstances of James Brydges, first Duke of Chandos*, Oxford, 1949, ch. XVI, 'Enfield Chase'. The full story of Chandos's rangership may be found in the Stowe correspondence in the Huntington Library and in the records of the Duchy Court of Lancaster, neither of which have I consulted for these years.

3. Chandos to Earl of Dysart, 16 October 1725, Huntington Library, ST57, XXVII, 37–8; W. Robinson, *History and Antiquities of Enfield*, 1823, pp. 108–10. But the size of the Chase is problematic, and perhaps fluctuated according to the interest (and claims) of the informant: John Hale, steward of Enfield manor under Chandos, estimated *circa* 1730 the Chase to be of 13,573 acres: C(H) 45.50; but a document dated *circa* 1766 gives only 6,740 acres: A. L. Cross, *18th century documents relating to the Royal Forests,*

finally came there were no set battles, as in the last days of the Common-wealth. Times and people had changed: the eighteenth century provided *francs-tireurs* of pale-breakers, wood-stealers and poachers, but very rarely any *levée en masse* of the peasantry.

So much for Hampshire and for Enfield. As for the rest of England, the years immediately after the passage of the Black Act may have witnessed an extension of serious attacks upon forests and parks in districts which hitherto may have been quieter. Thus in July 1726 as many as eighteen horsemen (one of them 'on a grey hunting-like horse, with a very long switch tail'), entered, with three or four brace of greyhounds, the Forest of Whittlewood (Northamptonshire), carried off deer and beat two keepers.[1] In these years there were attacks on deer in Sussex, Oxfordshire and in Hertfordshire, where eight labourers had driven the park of a gentleman at Tring; one of these was proclaimed under the Black Act.[2] The same episodes recur, in various areas, through the 1730s, and no doubt beyond.[3] In the true forest of Waltham, in Essex, the Warden and keepers were facing, in the 1730s, attacks quite as serious as those faced by Cobham, Negus and Nunn in Windsor Forest in 1721-3. Fourteen guns had been fired into the house of one keeper, seven armed men had visited another keeper and demanded brandy and beer; the poachers had 'within a very small space of time' killed in one walk 'near one hundred head of red and fallow deer'.[4]

As for the Forest of Windsor, it kept its deer, not through the for-bearance of the local population, but because the royal princes and their guests did actually hunt in the forest, and there were reserves elsewhere in the kingdom (as at Woolmer) from which it could be re-stocked. Immediately after the Reading executions it seems that the calm of terror descended on the forest. It was thought safe for the King to hunt in Windsor in the summer of 1724, and great preparations were made for

the Sheriffs and Smuggling, New York, 1929, p. 40. The survey at the 1777 enclosure gave 8,349 acres: E. Ford, *The History of Enfield*, Enfield, 1873, p. 42.

1. *London Gazette*, no. 6,508, 30 August 1726.

2. Sussex, *Worcester Post*, 13 December 1723; Oxfordshire, Oxon. Rec. Off. Type-script Calendar, quarter-sessions, VIII, p. 116 (Trinity 1726), p. 119 (Epiphany 1727); Herts, Proclamation of William Cooke of Wing, Bucks, April 1727, PC1.4.22 and *London Gazette*, no. 6,574, 18 April 1727; *Mist's Weekly Journal*, 30 July, 13 and 27 August 1726.

3. Thus in the Northamptonshire forests of Salcey and Whittlewood, 1733 and 1734: T53.37, pp. 490–2; T53.38, pp. 199–201. No systematic research has been attempted into the press and manuscript sources after 1724; the evidence in the preceding para-graphs has come to hand, but further inquiry might well reveal more substantial and continuous disturbances.

4. Memorial of Richard, Earl Tylney of Castlemain, Warden of Waltham Forest to George II, n.d. (but *circa* 1732), in Cholmondeley (Houghton) papers.

his reception.[1] The King had 'much diversion', slaughtered some pheasant and partridge, and pronounced himself 'much delighted with the place'. There was 'constantly a great concourse of country people', coming to gawp at their monarch and manorial lord. The King was 'perfectly well pleased' with Windsor, Townshend reported, 'And I believe likes it beyond any other palace he has. If anything could make it more agreeable to him, it would be a greater plenty of game, which indeed is pretty much wanting in the country thereabout.' The Earl of Carlisle promised to furnish him with more game the next time he came. He placed Colonel Negus at Swinley Walk 'by whose care and the late King's directions' (he informed George II on his accession) 'the game of all kinds is very much increased'.[2] The place, after all, had been well fertilized with blood.

Some troubles in the forest went on. The trees on the Trumbull estate at Easthampstead were cut and barked.[4] The conflict seems to have switched from deer and turfs to timber. William Lorwen, who had now succeeded his father as keeper of New Lodge, was involved in several brawls, when he attempted to prevent commoners from carrying away wood.[4] In 1726 the house, barns and stables of the keeper of Bearwood Walk, in the forest, were consumed by arson, 'there being reason to believe that the same was done by some wicked persons, for his endeavouring to preserve the herbage, timber and covert' in that Walk.[5]

It is difficult to read the evidence. On one hand, as organized Blacking receded, there is some suggestion that unorganized, random criminality may have increased.[6] In 1731 a servant came forward with an extraordinary confession in which he said that he and a 'gang' had planned to rob and fire half the gentry houses in the forest (including those of Colonel Negus and of the Duchess of Marlborough), and to end up by carrying coffins filled with gunpowder into three forest churches, to be

1. Although not, perhaps, as great as those made the previous year in the Forest of St Germain where, it was reported, all bushes and shrubs were cleared, and all holes filled in preparation for His Royal Highness. *Gloucester Journal*, 29 July 1723.

2. *Gloucester Journal*, 31 August and 7 September 1724; *Hist. MSS Comm. 15th Report, App. VI (Carlisle)*, Series 42, p. 49; *London Gazette*, no. 6,296, 18 August 1724.

3. ibid., no. 6,426, 26 October 1725.

4. A William Terry was involved in the first affair, in July 1724; it would be interesting if he was the same William Terry, master fisherman of Bray, who had turned evidence on the Blacks: above, p. 86 and SP44.81, fo. 356. Two other offenders, who had beaten up Lorwen, were prosecuted by the Treasury Solicitor in 1726: T27.24, p. 186 and T1.260 (20). Withers, the Surveyor-General for Woods, estimated in 1729 that 500 loads of wood were stolen annually from the forest: memorial of 10 April 1729, C(H) 62.38.1.

5. *London Gazette*, no. 6,483, 4 June 1726.

6. Recognisances in Assi. 5.45 relate to the deaths of one forest official and of the wife of another (John Sawyer of New Windsor); but the circumstances are unclear and I have found no supporting papers.

ignited by a 'clockwork machine' during divine service. But none of the names in the 'gang' is that of a former Black, and the 'confession' is probably a rambling drunken fantasy which throws light on nothing but the ugly human relations in the forest.[1]

The ugliness of these relations may indeed have found a climactic ceremonial expression in this year, 1731. By this time great progress had been made in making the forest more congenial for the sport of kings. There had been expenditure on the repair and improvement of Swinley Lodge, for the comfort and security of Colonel Negus. On the 'preserved grounds' new plantations of oak and underwood had been set as covert for the red deer; corn had been planted for their fattening; pheasants were being bred for the guns; the keepers' lodges in Bisghot Rails in Sandhurst were also being improved.[2] But it would no doubt have further embittered the last years of George I to know that it was his unloved son, George II, who was to have the enjoyment of this careful provision.

The new king killed more animals and birds in his forest at Windsor than his father had done. It is difficult for the impoverished imagination of a historian to envisage this royal sport in exactly the terms passed down to us in the idealizations of court painters and court poets and in the memoirs of hunting men. Well-fed pheasants, scarcely able to rise into the air, were carefully introduced to the muzzles of the least-skilfully-carried gun. Stags were kept fat and secure in their known covets, to be 'flushed' for the royal hunting party; after a jostling, quarrelsome gallop of half-drunken men the stag was run to bay and, as it panted in exhausted terror surrounded by wet-mouthed hounds, a liveried huntsman or an exhibitionist courtier darted beneath its horns to cut its throat. Nor were these courtiers, statesmen and princes all gallant and well-seated riders. The paragraphs of court news in the press reported to the public the weekly accidents and casualties of the field. In 1731 Sir Robert Walpole himself fell full-face in the mud of Richmond Park, to the delight of half the nation. In October the royal hunt was out twice a week in Windsor: on one occasion 'Major Selwyn, Equerry to her Majesty, and Mr Acourt, Page of Honour to her Majesty, fell from their Horses . . . Many others of lesser Note had also Falls.' The liveried huntsmen and yeomen prickers did the serious business of the day, while the courtiers toadied to the royal party or bickered among the bushes. On occasion the bickering became more obsessional than the toadying and the royal quarry itself was for-

1. Papers in SP36.25, fos. 122–30.
2. Memorials of Withers to Treasury, 3 May 1726, Negus to Treasury, 9 April 1728, Negus to Withers, 1 May 1728: all in Earl St Aldwyn's unclassified Hicks-Beach MSS; Withers to Treasury concerning Bigshot Rails, 6 October 1730, T54.31, p. 299.

gotten, as on the occasion when the Duke of Lorraine was being enter-
tained in the field:

> Saturday, the King, Queen, Prince, Duke, the three eldest Princesses,
> together with the Duke of Lorrain, and a great Number of Persons of Quality
> and Distinction, went to Swinly Rails in Windsor Forest, where a Stag was
> unharbour'd, and ran a Chace of about 25 Miles. The Duke of Lorrain came in
> at the Death, having twice changed his Horses. The Earl of Albemarle was
> ordered by the King to attend his Highness in the Field; but a Person having
> given his Lordship a violent Blow on the Head with the Handle End of his Whip,
> in Return for one he had received from his Lordship in the Course of the Chace,
> the Earl pursued the Man on a full Speed, for about four Miles, and coming up
> with him near Caesar's Camp, they attacked each other very briskly. . .[1]

Baptist Nunn was also in at two deaths that year, for in August at the
Abingdon Assizes William Marlow and William Bristow had been found
guilty under the Black Act of hunting, wounding and killing deer in
Windsor Park. Although cast for death there was general expectation of a
reprieve, 'through the intercession of a nobleman'. Foolishly the condemned men talked largely in prison about their expected reprieve and
about the revenge they would then take upon Baptist Nunn and his
brother, John. The two keepers rode up to Hampton Court to present
directly to the King a plea for the men's early execution. Their petition
was granted, for Baptist Nunn, in such a matter, had an interest which
weighed as palpably as that of 'a nobleman'. Both deer-hunters were
hanged in the evening, early in October, not far from Reading. Their
bodies were, no doubt, a palpable demonstration of the restoration of
stability to the forest, and yet one more trophy of the royal chase.[2]

On the other hand, there is a little contrary evidence which suggests
that the tissues of the forest community were beginning to heal after
1728. In this year the Earl of Carlisle gave way to the Duke of St Albans
as Lord Warden, Constable and Governor.[3] The Duke was the greatest
local magnate, Lord-Lieutenant of the county, and controlled the parliamentary borough of Windsor. He perhaps was more closely informed on

1. *Gloucester Journal*, 19 and 26 October 1731.

2. *Gloucester Journal*, 24 August and 12 October 1731; *Fog's Weekly Journal*, 7 August
and 9 October 1731. 1731 seems to have been a good year for the Black Act: at the Lewes
Assizes in August Daniel Izard and William Stacey were capitally convicted for cutting
down the head of a pond: *Read's Weekly Journal*, 14 August 1731. I do not know whether
they were executed.

3. Carlisle was an absentee Constable, and left the work to Colonel Negus. The value
of his sinecure can be estimated from the fact that, when he gave way to the Duke of
St Albans, Walpole compensated him by appointing him to the obsolete post of Master
of the Harriers (redesignated as Master of the King's Foxhounds) at £2,000 p.a.: *Hist.
MSS Comm. 15th Report, App. VI (Carlisle)*, pp. 74–7.

forest affairs than his predecessors. His appointment coincided with that of a new panel of Regarders; a surprising nominee was John Perryman of Bray. Even more surprising was the appointment, in November 1730, of a Robert Shorter as under-keeper of Billingbear Walk – almost certainly the (outlawed) son of a Black, and the probable nephew of William. He was to thrive in the King's service, and become a yeoman pricker.[1]

In 1734 the last identifiable Black passes through the state papers, in an episode of reconciliation appropriate to the final instalment of a soap-opera. Edward Collier, the Wokingham felt-maker, had been found guilty at the Special Commission in Reading in 1723 of killing a 'tame deer' of Sir Robert Rich, and had been sentenced to seven years' transportation. But Collier had not gone to America after all; soon after being sentenced he had escaped from prison 'and hath been obliged ever since to secreet himself and live from his wife and poor family', who had been reduced 'to great poverty and want'. Lurking somewhere in the forest neighbour-hood, Collier had learned of the death of his prosecutor, Sir Robert Rich. At first through intermediaries and finally in person he had thrown himself upon the mercy of Sir Robert's widow, Dame Mary. At last she proved forgiving and, through her intercession, Collier received the King's pardon.[2]

If there was a relaxation of tension a clue to it may be found in a general letter of instruction sent by the Duke of St Albans's secretary in 1733, which indicates clearly enough where the pressure of enforcement was intended to fall:

> The notion of the want of power to punish &c ought not to prevaile among the keepers, & the common people. His Grace would not be understood that the harassing and vexing gentlemen & farmers is meant hereby, unless such as are guilty of offences that must have cognizance taken of them, it is certainly best to live well with gentlemen, and look over little offences, but the loose idle people, who generally are the greatest offenders, his Grace would have restrained as much as possible from doing any prejudice to the vert & venison of his Majesty's forest.[3]

The Duke was perhaps enough of a forest man to know that policies which enraged very substantial farmers (like Perryman), professional men (like Will Waterson) and even some gentry, and which brought advantage only to the petty officialdom of the forest, were costly in time and pro-vocative of disturbance. If he was to control the 'loose idle people' he had to keep the gentry and farmers on his side. Accordingly, he let the

1. Perryman – Verderers' Book, LR3.3: also above, pp. 86–7. Shorter – Constable's Warrant Books, III, fo. 42: also above, p. 89 n. 2.
2. Papers in SP36.31, fos. 147, 175–8.
3. Constable's Warrant Books, III, fo. 120.

Swanimote Court drift into desuetude, while the Courts of Attachment sank into routine meetings.[1] He allowed capital, supplemented by interest and influence, and supported where necessary by the Justices of the Peace, to work out its 'natural' way. Will Waterson was pleased to note the difference; more gentlemen were settling in Winkfield parish: 'The great inducement of late years to purchasing and building in the Forest has been the relaxation or rather annihilation of the Forest Laws . . .'[2]

There was, however, one 'loose idle' person whom the Duke failed to control: Walpole's younger brother, Horatio. It had been the custom of Sarah, Duchess of Marlborough, as Ranger of the Windsor Parks, to serve venison warrants for the King's use on application to her from the Cofferer of the King's Household. When Horatio became Cofferer, in about 1730, he insisted upon serving the warrants directly to the keepers himself, and Sarah, who was having a quarrel with Queen Caroline, could do nothing to stop him. The consumption of 'the King's table' enlarged in an astonishing way: 'Mr. Horatio,' Sarah remarked, 'I have good reason to believe sold a good deal of the venison.' He is, she added, 'the most ingenious man in the world for getting money'. He was also, if Sarah's report is true, the most successful deer-stealer within the covers of this book. He died in bed of the stone.[3]

But despite the efforts of Horatio Walpole and of the whole Hanoverian clan, the repeated resistance which had been offered by the foresters of Windsor had not been without effect. When Commissioners came to inquire into the state of Windsor Forest in 1809, they were in little doubt that in the matter of common rights the foresters had held onto – and perhaps even extended – their own. The inhabitants of nearly all parishes (they found) had proved the actual enjoyment of the right to turn cows, horses, sheep and pigs on the forest without limitation as to numbers, and without reference to the nature or tenure of their possessions. They had maintained their right to cut turf, fern and heath, and to take gravel and sand, with little restraint. They had not only maintained but enlarged their claims upon browse wood, fallen timber, 'lops and tops' and rootage. The absence of compact villages, and the dispersal of foresters, made social discipline impossible: 'nothing more favours irregular and lawless habits of life among the inferior class . . . than scattered and

1. The last Swanimote Court seems to have been in 1728: LR3.3. But the Duke of Cumberland was considering holding one in 1754: Royal Archives, Cumberland Papers, 70/93.

2. Waterson (Ranelagh) 1. However, in 1773, long after Waterson's death, there was renewed conflict and the prosecution of offenders for cutting turfs in the 'preserved grounds' near Swinley Lodge: see TS11.390.1216.

3. Sarah to 'My Lord' (Earl of Wilmington), 9 October 1742, Brit. Mus. Add. MSS 9,120; W. Menzies, *The History of Windsor Great Park and Windsor Forest*, 1864, p. 23.

sequestered habitations.' The gentry, also in their scattered and sequestered habitations, had decided over the previous century that enclosure was the best resource for agrarian class control. This remedy was advocated by the Land Revenue Commissioners in the 1790s for Alice Holt, Woolmer, and for part of Bere. It was now recommended that it be applied to parts of Windsor also; the 'inferior class' could then be brought together in collected villages, each with a constable on patrol.[1]

But we run on too fast. It would seem, from this evidence, that in the long run the deer were the only absolute losers, and the foresters the gainers in the forest war. The first proposition is true. The second is not. It is true that the foresters in Windsor seem to have weathered the eighteenth century well, as perhaps they did also in one or two other great forests – the New Forest and the Forest of Dean. The unrestricted grazing rights they enjoyed were exceptional. But they had gained only a stay of execution, and they had gained this precisely because in these great forests concepts of property remained archaic, and out of step with the spirit of the age. The foresters clung still to the lowest rungs of a hierarchy of use-rights. While their own rights were inconsequential beside those of the greater users, they were more numerous than the great; they knew every pathway and spinney in the forest, and they exploited each faggot, turf, and hare until these added up into a livelihood. 'With its tree-fellers and hewers, its sawyers and hurdlers, its spoke-choppers and faggoters, its lath-renders, rake-and-ladder makers, and what not, the forest found food for hundreds of families.'[2] Little money passed among foresters; they did not go to a butcher for their meat. It was because they pursued not a luxury but a livelihood that encounters between them and the keepers were so grim.

But this livelihood depended upon the survival of precapitalist use-rights over the land, and upon some form of social organization (as with the old forest courts and the Verderers and Regarders) by which conflicting claims to use-rights over the same land and timber could be reconciled. Without such forms, however inequitable their operation might be, those on the lowest rungs of the hierarchy could only defend their claims by force or stealth. This they might do, and over some decades, with some success; according to times and circumstances, the battle between poachers and keepers, turf-cutters and stewards, might sway

1. See 1st and 2nd Reports of the Commissioners on the State of Windsor Forest, *PP* 1809, IV, *passim*, esp. pp. 264, 281–2, 292. Enclosure took place in 1813: 53 George III c.158.

2. Rev. J. E. Linnell, *Old Oak*, p. 3, which gives a sympathetic view of foresters in Salcey, Northamptonshire, in the early nineteenth century. And see also other closely observed accounts of the social economy of foresters and borderers: Thomas Hardy's *The Woodlanders* and *Under the Greenwood Tree*.

this way or that. Meanwhile, the very roof-beams which housed their practical economy were being eaten away, by money and by law, above their heads. During the eighteenth century one legal decision after another signalled that the lawyers had become converted to the notions of absolute property ownership, and that (wherever the least doubt could be found) the law abhorred the messy complexities of coincident use-right. And capitalist modes transmuted offices, rights and perquisites into round monetary sums, which could be bought and sold like any other property. Or, rather, the offices and rights of the great were transmuted in this way – those of the Rangers, bishops, manorial lords. The rights and claims of the poor, if inquired into at all, received more perfunctory compensation, smeared over with condescension and poisoned with charity. Very often they were simply redefined as crimes: poaching, wood-theft, trespass.[1]

Nowhere was this process more clearly at work than in certain royal forests and chases. The Revolution Settlement, supplemented by the Civil List Act (1 Anne c.5), had brought to an end the old supposition that the King should live off 'his own'. In place of this, the monarch received through Parliament an annual revenue (the Civil List) intended to meet his public expenses. In return, the royal lands (with important exceptions) came to be seen as lands of 'the public'; the King might no longer sell them or grant them away in perpetuity, and their revenue was governed through the Treasury and to be applied to reducing the cost to Parliament of the Civil List. Windsor was a special case, its prime function being to provide recreation for the King and his family. The prime function of other royal forests was to provide cheap timber for the navy.

In the 1780s and 1790s, under the impulse of new winds of economical reform and public accountability, Land Revenue Commissioners investigated the actual history. In Alice Holt and Woolmer they uncovered the following story. The office of Lieutenant or Ranger of the forest was held, by successive grantees, under a lease which awarded them £31 2s. 11d. per annum, secured on the rent of a Hampshire farm. Out of this they were to pay all fees and salaries to under-keepers. In addition, they were granted certain perquisites: dead wood and 'all manner of wood blown or thrown down by the wind'; wood for firing and repairs; pasture for some horses; fishing-rights; four fee deer; and lesser 'perks'. In

1. This is argued more fully in my 'Common Right and Enclosure', in *Customs in Common* (forthcoming). Marx wrote in 1842 that 'the customs which are customs of the entire poor class are based with a sure instinct on the *indeterminate* aspect of property': K. Marx and F. Engels, *Collected Works*, I (1975), p. 233. These early articles on 'Debates on the Law of Thefts of Wood', in which Marx first attempted an analysis of the nature of capitalist property-ownership, turn upon many of the issues disclosed also in the English forests of the eighteenth century.

return they were to preserve the deer and timber and repair the lodges and fences at their own expense.

Such terms were impractical in a monetary economy, and it was reasonable that (in 1701) the Treasury should have agreed to pay, from its own resources, the wages of five under-keepers (at £25 p.a. each, with an additional £5 p.a. for their servants). A Treasury memorandum of 1723 (perhaps drafted by Charles Withers, the Surveyor-General of Woods) argued that if the 'Crown' paid the wages, then the keepers should be under the orders of the Surveyor: 'For if the keepers have not wages, they must live on the destruction of the forest; and if they have the King's wages and are not to be subject to the King's Officer's orders . . . the King may be said to give his money for committing disorders in the forest, and not for preventing them.'

The formidable Ruperta Howe decreed otherwise.[1] Withers failed, here and elsewhere, to establish any central bureaucratic control. The allowance of £130 p.a. continued to be paid, until 1790; but the keepers looked upon themselves 'to be only the hired servants of the Lieutenant'. Two of them (in Woolmer) received no wages at all, but were allowed to sell as much peat, turf, heath and stones from the forest as they could dispose of, or, in their own words, 'make what profit they can of the forest'. There were then no deer on Woolmer (nor had there been for thirty years), and although the Lieutenant's father had re-stocked Alice Holt, 'none are supplied for the use of His Majesty, nor any venison warrants now served'.

Thus the interest of the Crown (or of the public) in the forest had been reduced to an interest in the timber growing in the Holt (for no timber grew in Woolmer). The Commissioners here unravelled an extraordinary story. Until 1724, whenever timber was felled all the proceeds were accounted for to the Crown. But when a fall took place in 1729, Ruperta Howe asserted (without precedent) a claim to the 'lop and top' and bark of all trees felled by warrant. The claim was allowed, and one seventh part of the proceeds of the sale of timber was paid to her. So matters continued for several decades, the Lieutenant taking the lop, top and bark in kind, or payment in lieu of this, until 1770, when the then Lieutenant (the Countess of Hillsborough) upped her claim from one seventh to one fifth, in money value, of all timber felled. She not only succeeded in getting this accepted, but also got it backdated over the previous decade; and, in addition, was saved all trouble of paring, cutting and carrying the lops, tops and bark herself. By virtue of an office whose only duties (the preser-

---

1. See Ruperta Howe's 'Objections' to Withers taking authority 'over her head', and paying the keepers directly instead of through her: T1.247 (23 March 1724). Withers appears to have won the point in form, but Ruperta Howe in fact.

vation of the timber) were performed by servants paid by the Crown, she was exacting a payment of one fifth part of the produce of the forest.

In 1777, for the first time in the eighteenth century, a fall of timber was ordered for the direct use of the navy. Naval timber, from Crown property, was accounted for at around half of its market price, and this the Lieutenant, Lady Hillsborough, highly resented. In a memorial to the Treasury she pointed out that her one fifth share of the timber, if valued by auction on the open market, would have been about £500, whereas under the Crown's terms to the navy she was allowed only £178. She therefore prayed that a further impending fall for the navy 'might be revoked, and that for the future all the timber might be sold by public auction as usual'.

In this she overreached herself, and overlooked a changing mood in Parliament and in public office. The claim drew upon it an investigation of the terms of the Lieutenant's grant, and raised the suggestion that she had no right to the lops, tops and bark at all, but only to boughs casually cut off (as when dead trees were felled) or thrown down by wind. The matter went into some circumlocution office for a decade, and meanwhile Lady Hillsborough's successor, Lord Stawell, continued to receive in kind the lops and tops of each fall, and continued to demand a money payment in lieu of this calculated at one fifth market value. It was 'a very singular demand', the Land Revenue Commissioners noted, 'that in this forest, maintained by the public at very considerable expence, as a nursery of timber for the navy, no more timber should be cut for the public service, but that all should be sold by auction, in order that the Grantee might receive a greater advantage . . .' They were irritated enough by the claim to draw up a balance-sheet of the forest revenue for the century, from 1700 to 1786, by which it appeared that the total produce from wood sales and naval timber was £15,414 19s. 3d., and the expense of salaries, allowances and other charges £24,089 10s. 10d., 'so that instead of producing any clear revenue, during the present century, this forest has occasioned a loss to the public of £8,674.11.7d.'. As for venison, 'the grant has been completely reversed in practice; the Lieutenant retains the whole in his own disposal'. The original grant (they noted) 'is not a grant of the forest, but of an office to which duties are annexed, as well as emoluments, and those duties have been neglected, while the emoluments have been increased'. For this the laxity of Government was no doubt to blame: 'One of the worst effects of this relaxation . . . is that the Grantees of Offices, being left so long in the undisturbed possession of the profits of what has been entrusted to their care, are gradually led to look upon the property itself as their own.'[1]

1. 6th Report of the Land Revenue Commissioners, *Commons Journals*, 1790, pp. 120–78, *passim*.

These then were the roof-timbers of the foresters' world, the juridical and administrative conditions within which they scratched for their own livelihood. These were the great themes of the Commissioners' Report, played on the soaring strings of money and the sounding brass of 'interest'. There were subsidiary themes of substantial corruption as well: for example, a big timber contractor (perhaps played on a bassoon?) who was knocking down trees at the naval half price and knocking them off at the full market price on his own account. But every now and then a small subsidiary theme, like a flurry of piccolos, comes into the Report. Whenever a fall of timber took place, the people of the forest villages – Frensham, Binstead, Bentley and Kingsley – avowed that they also had a right, to the 'offal' or stack wood – the faggots and small broken boughs left by the fall. It is not recorded that any Ranger or Surveyor was inattentive enough to allow such an outrageous claim. The poor took the wood nevertheless. In Ruperta Howe's time (when the poor inhabitants of Farnham also were involved) they came 'in a tumultuous and riotous manner' and carried their portion away.[1] In 1741 the 'pretended right' of the poor was tried at Winchester Assizes, and they lost their case.[2] But they asserted it again and again, notably in 1777, 1783, 1784 and 1788. In 1784 Lord Stawell commenced more than forty actions against 'the poor people of the adjoining parishes . . . They all entered appearances, but suffered judgement to go by default.' Nevertheless, in 1788 at the next fall: 'The offal wood, after having been made into faggots, and a day appointed for the sale of it, was openly carried off by the people of Frensham, to the number of 6,365 faggots in one day and night.'[3]

The value of these perquisites, pretended or allowed, was unequal. In 1777 the stack wood taken by all the poor villagers was valued at £80, whereas the Ranger claimed for himself £250 (or one fifth of the fall). But the decisive inequality lay in a class society, wherein non-monetary use-rights were being reified into capitalist property rights, by the mediation of the courts of law. When the people of Frensham claimed their 'rights', openly and with a solidarity so complete that in 1788 no tithingman could be found to execute a warrant, they were subject to prosecution. When the Land Revenue Commissioners found that Lord Stawell and his predecessors had grossly exceeded their perquisites and neglected their duties, the question which most troubled them was, if the Crown were to resume its own, what compensation should be awarded to the Ranger, what 'Recompence for the Loss of Advantages which, though

---

1. Ruperta Howe, memorial to Treasury, n.d., C(H) 62.60.
2. 6th Report of the Land Revenue Commissioners, pp. 126, 160–61.
3. ibid., pp. 126 and 161; see also White, op. cit., Letter IX.

at first improperly taken, have received a Kind of Sanction from the Inattention or Forbearance of Government'.[1]

It is astonishing the wealth that can be extracted from territories of the poor, during the phase of capital accumulation, provided that the predatory élite are limited in number, and provided that the state and the law smooth the way of exploitation. One thinks of the maharajahs of petty Indian states in the nineteenth century, or of the great servants of the East India Company fifty years before. The fortunes of the great speculators, politicians, generals and courtiers of the early eighteenth century in England have the same baseless, insubstantial air: they exist, but, in a country where wages, salaries, rent and tithes are counted in tens of pounds, it is not clear what these fortunes of thousands per annum rest upon. In many cases – Cadogan, Cobham, Chandos, Walpole – the fortune rested in origin upon access to public money, lands, perquisites of office, sinecures, percentages on public transactions.

So the game of the great predators went on. No doubt the people of the forests and chases could see well enough how it was being played. They can have felt little allegiance, no manorial deference, to Rangers who speculated upon their land, bought and sold their grants over their heads, and lived in luxury in the lodges. The forest conflict was, in origin, a conflict between users and exploiters. And so the matter was seen and expressed by 'King John', when he reviewed his followers on Waltham Chase: 'they were determined not to leave a deer on the Chase, being well assured that it was originally designed to feed cattle, and not fatten deer for the clergy.'

iii. The Exercise of Law

As for the law, the Black Act was to remain a part of it for a century; and the virtual repeal of the Act, in 1823, took place after prolonged resistance.[2] In the present state of knowledge, no firm estimate can be made as to the frequency of its employment.[3] But the number of cases which come to hand, with little research, and the amount of case-law bred by the Act show that it did not fall into desuetude.

An informed guess might be this: in the first two decades after enactment, it was employed regularly (although infrequently) against deer-

1. 6th Report of the Land Revenue Commissioners, pp. 133–4.

2. See Radzinowicz, *A History of English Criminal Law and its Administration from 1750*, 1948, I, pp. 580–81.

3. Only the examination of indictments in the Assize Records of more than one circuit over a period of one hundred years would provide evidence for such an estimate. This has not been attempted.

stealers and poachers.[1] Thereafter it was rarely used against such offenders, unless some aggravation such as 'malicious shooting' was involved. And by a decision in 1783 it was held that the clause in the Act relating to the killing of deer should be deemed repealed by subsequent legislation which imposed more lenient penalties.[2] But the other clauses in the Act remained active. These included those against arming and disguising, threatening letters demanding venison, money or 'other valuable thing', several classes of incendiarism, malicious shooting, maiming of cattle, cutting of young trees, etc.

By the nature of the offences, recourse to the Act was most likely in a context of agrarian disturbance, especially when this was combined with class insubordination – as, for example, when resistance to enclosure took the form of firing into windows, threatening letters or the houghing (or malicious wounding) of cattle. Among cases which have come to hand, without extensive inquiry, we have those of Lewis Gunner, firing his pistol *in terrorem*; that of Henry Aburrow, breaking the head of Foxcroft's fish-pond; the case of Paul Lewis, in 1763, who fired a pistol in order to terrify a farmer whom he was attempting to rob;[3] the case of young Thomas Chester in Northamptonshire ('a quiet honest and industrious inoffensive and sober person') who cut down some young trees of a Mr Blinco of Marston St Lawrence;[4] and the case of Nathaniel Rand, in

1. The use of the Act against deer offenders in Hampshire, Surrey, Middlesex, Hertfordshire, etc. in the 1720s has been illustrated sufficiently above. It was used in the 1730s against offenders in the Forest of Dean: see MSS and printed Calendars, Gloucester Assizes, 1736 – five cases for appearing in disguise with guns, iron hedge-bills etc., in 1735: MS Rawl. C452, Bodleian Library; also C. H. Hart, *The Commoners of Dean Forest*, Gloucester, 1951, p. 78. But the Dean affair involved substantial riot; I suspect that after 1731 it was unusual to prosecute unaggravated deer-stealing under the Black Act. It may be significant that a proclamation against deer-stealers of 19 July 1733 did not invoke the Black Act, but increased the reward for convictions under the Act of 5 George I: T53.38, pp. 199–201; *London Gazette*, 23 July 1733. But two men were convicted under the Black Act in Northumberland for poaching eight salmon from a river in 1738: SP36.46, fo. 237.

2. *Rex* v. *Davis* (1783), 1 Leach 271: see Radzinowicz, op. cit., 1, pp. 59–60. But it was still possible to prosecute under other clauses in the Act, against disguising, bearing arms, etc. After a poaching affray in 1805 in which several of Lord Suffield's Keepers were wounded, six men were sentenced to death at Thetford Assizes under the Black Act (commuted to transportation): C. Mackie, *Norfolk Annals*, Norwich, 1901, 1, p. 37.

3. Lewis felt aggrieved because he had been tricked into pleading guilty to the first count of his indictment (attempted robbery) on the understanding that he would be transported, and that the second count (under the Black Act) would be passed over. He suffered for his mistake at Tyburn: *Aris's Birmingham Gazette*, 18 April and 9 May 1763. I owe this reference to Bernice Clifton.

4. Petition of his mother, Susanah Chester, supported by a testimonial as to her son's character signed by four clergy, one baronet, seven gentlemen, and others, in SP36.25,

1788 in Hertfordshire, 'a poor, ignorant, and almost superannuated clown' for setting fire to a cock or stack of unthreshed wheat.[1] As late as 1770 the full rigmarole of proclamation by the Privy Council under the Black Act was employed against James Rylatt, a grazier on Holland Fen, who had been forcibly resisting the fen's enclosure.[2] But in fact a wide variety of offences could be pushed and pulled until they fitted the proper legal forms. The only generalization that may be safely made is that the Act remained available in the armoury of prosecution. Where an offence appeared to be especially aggravated, where the state wished to make an example of terror, or where a private prosecutor was particularly vindictive, then the indictment could be drawn in such a way as to bring the offence within the Act.

It was the last occasion which entered literary tradition; when the oppressive squire, Tyrrel, closed up the old path which gave access to the land of his tenant, Hawkins, young Hawkins went out at night, broke the padlocks and threw down the gates. The young man 'had buttoned the cape of his great coat over his face . . . and he was furnished with a wrenching-iron for the purpose of breaking the padlocks'; and these in turn furnished the Squire's lawyer with the 'arms and disguise' to bring him within an indictment under 9 George 1 c.22.[3]

This is too easily taken for novelist's licence. In fact, within two or three years of its enactment it was evident that neither arms nor disguise need attain any high formality. In a proclamation of 1727 against the raiders of a Hertfordshire deer-park, it was sufficient to cite that 'one of the said persons was disguised with a coloured handkerchief over the lower part of his face'.[4] Two years before this Charles Towers was executed in London, and he has sometimes been regarded as London's first victim of the Black Act. Towers, a butcher of St James's Market, was indicted in that 'he, armed with guns, swords, &c. and face blacked, on the highway called Wapping Wall did, with seven others, rush into the house of John Errington with a large stick, his hair clipt off, without hat, wig or shirt, only with a blue pea-jacket, which flying open showed his breast as well

---

fo. 182. Thomas Chester did not cut down Blinco's trees 'with wicked and mischievous intentions' nor for private advantage, but was drawn on 'by too much zeal for the publick good' since Blinco had lately blocked up and sown with acorns 'what is esteem'd by all people in several adjacent villages to be his Majesties property or highway. . .' Chester was reprieved and transported: *London Journal*, 20 March 1731; *Gloucester Journal*, 23 March 1731.

1. Henry Judd, 'a very opulent and respectable farmer', was charged with hiring and counselling Rand to commit the offence; but poor Rand was convicted, Judd was acquitted: *Aris's Birmingham Gazette*, 17 March 1788.

2. Papers in PC1.15 Box 5.

3. William Godwin, *Caleb Williams*, 1794, I, ch. IX.   4. PC1.4.22.

as his face black and besmeared with soot and grease, and there did rescue John West'.

Errington was a bailiff and Towers was a 'Minter'; that is, he was one of the debtors who had taken refuge in the supposed 'liberty' of the 'New Mint' (or 'Seven Cities of Refuge'). The Minters kept up an extreme loyalty – indeed, a whole ritual of solidarity – in defending each other from the bailiffs. They based their claim to 'sanctuary' upon the supposed privileges of ancient consecrated sites within and around the city. Several such 'sanctuaries' had been closed down at the turn of the century, and in 1720 only that at Southwark and the memory of one at Wapping survived. In the aftermath of the Bubble, their inmates multiplied.

We have in the case of the 'Mint' some kind of metropolitan parallel to the forest matrix of Blacking, with debtors as foresters and bailiffs as keepers. But the debtors were better-organized, the bailiffs more brutal. The bailiffs lived in an immediately symbiotic relationship to London's criminal society; under cover of their function they had the reputation for engaging in armed robbery and blackmail; a 'bum bailiff' had authority to hold debtors for a short time as prisoner in his 'spunging house' – and once held there a man, whether a genuine debtor or not, might be terrorized and bled of whatever money he or his friends had.[1] The debtors organized themselves to resist the bailiffs. Their 'society' was enrolled in a book; oaths of mutual support were made; and from the 'sanctuary' at Southwark they sent their emissaries, who were called 'Spirits', out of the Mint in search of their antagonists. The Spirits were dressed in the fashion which the Ku-Klux-Klan has later made notorious, 'in long black gowns, which go over their heads, with holes made to see out at'. If a bailiff or bailiff's informer was unwise enough to enter the Mint (or was seized and dragged within it) he was subjected to one of a gradation of ritualized punishments: he would be tried by hooded 'judges', and then sentenced to be whipped, or made to utter blasphemies, to eat parchments, drink salt and water, or to be 'pumped'. 'Pumping', with the head held under a street-pump, could be extended to repeated ducking in foul sewers, until at length the filthy victim was forced to kiss a brick covered with human excrement and say:

> I am a Rogue, and a Rogue in Grain,
> And dam me, if ever I come into the Mint again.

The Minters of Southwark – as is testified by their own (anonymous) statements – had a high sense of the legitimacy of their own institutions;

1. Charles Towers maintained that the bailiffs beat and wounded debtors in barbarous ways: a carpenter had had his right arm 'hacked and chopped . . . in such a manner it was obliged to be cut off': *Lives of the Most Remarkable Criminals*, ed. A. L. Hayward, 1927, p. 198.

248

saw themselves as protecting each other against oppression; and even claimed that, so far from supporting criminality, they always apprehended and handed over to the authorities any person seeking refuge with them guilty of theft, murder or other such crime. This seems unlikely, but cannot be discounted. In 1722 Government began to move against Southwark, and a last stand was made by some hundred debtors and their families in the other 'sanctuary' between Ratcliffe Highway and Wapping. At this, the 'New Mint' (the Middlesex Grand Jury presented) there were 'cruel, inhuman and horrid barbarities' practised: the minters 'often run riotously about the streets with desperate weapons, disguising themselves'. And, as with the Blacks, there were suggestions of exactly that mixture of resistance to authority with potential Jacobite disaffection which so much exasperated Walpole. The New Minters were alleged to gather in taverns and sing the most licentious songs:

> We value not the Turnipman or Justice of Peace,
> But we'll duck the Bailiffs, and do as we please,
> Do as we please, boys, with a Huzza . . .
>
> And if that he offer the Mint to put down,
> We soon will dethrone him and pull down his Crown . . .

Although contemporaries supposed that Towers had been convicted under the Black Act, it is probable that he was not. For, in the same parliamentary session which enacted 9 George I c.22, an almost-forgotten Act (9 George I c.28) was passed, with a death-clause for anyone from a pretended place of privilege who joined, in disguise, any riot or who assaulted any officer exercising his duty. Towers, who was selected to make an example of terror, was executed from a special gallows erected on Wapping Wall. He told a sympathetic crowd that 'he was not disguised when he rescued Mr. West, unless the dirty condition he was commonly in could be so termed'. It is a nice comment on eighteenth-century polite sensibility that cropped unpowdered hair and the absence of a wig, and a jacket flying open to reveal his bare breast, should be taken to constitute 'disguise'.[1]

1. For the Mint, *Commons Journals*, xv, 169–70 (23 February 1706), xx, 154–7 (27 February 1723); presentments of Middlesex Grand Jury in KB1.2 (Parts II and IV) – these identify the 'New Mint' as in Green Bank, Anchor and Hope Alley, and Meeting House Alley, adjoining Wapping. See also *Newcastle Weekly Courant*, 12 January 1723; T. J. de Mazzinghi, *Sanctuaries*, 1887; G. Howson, *Thief-taker General: The Rise and Fall of Jonathan Wild*, 1970, pp. 12–13, 23. The Jacobite songs are in SP35.55 (3) (information of William Preston, 4 January 1725). For 9 George I c.28 see Radzinowicz, op. cit., I, p. 623. For Charles Towers, *ON*, 5 January 1725 (Bodleian Library); *Proceedings* (Brit. Mus. press-mark L21 aa2), 4–9 December 1725; Hayward, op. cit., pp. 194–9: this very useful account, published first in 1735, says the indictment was

Thus a stick and a dirty face would do for arms and disguise. And already, in the case of Arnold shooting Lord Onslow, most of the offences in the Act had been severed from the Act's preamble; and for these it was not necessary to prove arming or disguising at all.[1] One of the first to discover this was Bryan Smith, an Irish Londoner, an amateurish operator, who tried to extort money by means of an anonymous threatening letter. He was hanged, in April 1725, from the same tree as John Guy, the deer-stealer, another victim of the Act.[2] Smith was one of the first to try out a new sartorial fashion, that of riding to Tyburn wrapped in his shroud. This was devout in him (he was a Catholic) but also a great blunder, since while his fellows were being prepared by the hangman, he 'made shift to slip his head through the halter, and jump over the cart among the mob, but he was so muffled up in his shroud, and . . . so easily distinguish'd, that he was presently retaken'.[3]

The greatest of all legal fictions is that the law itself evolves, from case to case, by its own impartial logic, true only to its own integrity, un-swayed by expedient considerations. This can scarcely be observed in the evolution of case-law arising from the Black Act. We have noted already (above, p. 210) the critical decision of Lord Hardwicke, C.J., in the case of the Herefordshire turnpike rioters in 1736. The Lord Chief Justice is reported as directing the jury that if 'the prisoners did appear in the high road with their faces blacked, that is sufficient within the act'; thus Blacking was divorced from 'being armed', each being construed as 'a distinct separate crime from the rest' – a direction so much at variance with the wording of the Act that subsequent editors implied that the Lord Chief Justice must have been misreported. This is unlikely. Lord Hardwicke, in presiding over the turnpike rioters' trial, was wearing three hats (or three black caps) at once: in his earlier alias as Philip Yorke he had helped to draft and to secure the passage of the Act; in his role as Lord Chief Justice (and former Attorney-General) he had pressed

actually found on the Black Act (I have not checked this): it also says that at Towers's execution the crowd, 'as is not common on such occasions', lamented him and poured down showers of tears. Southwark Mint was, it seems, closed without such examples of terror, and a Dissenting minister, the Reverend Joseph Fawcett, claimed that this was owing to his 'preachments': 'I have been instrumental to convert many Rebel Insolvents, Papists and Torys, and that without any confused noise of garments rowl'd in blood or halters . . .': Fawcett to Walpole ('Much Esteem'd Great Sir'), soliciting a reward, 17 March 1725, T1.252 (35).

1. For the Onslow case, above, p. 209.   2. For John Guy, above, p. 173.

3. *Select Trials at the Old Bailey*, 1734–5, II, pp. 31–4; *Mist's Weekly Journal*, 1 May 1725; Hayward, op. cit., pp. 221–3. Other blackmailers and authors of 'incendiary' letters were convicted under the Act: thus in London in 1729 Jepthah Bigg, *Select Trials*, II, pp. 292–5, and, in 1731, offenders in Hertfordshire, Lincolnshire and Kent: T53.36, pp. 58, 66: see my study, 'The Crime of Anonymity' in *Albion's Fatal Tree*.

for the most severe measures against such rioters; and he was also sitting in his role as judge. To these hats he was shortly to add a fourth: as Lord Chancellor, he managed to maintain for twenty years his position as the only law lord, so that any appeal against his decisions to the House of Lords, sitting in its judicial capacity, would be, in effect, to himself. In these circumstances, it may be seen as a singular tribute to the luminous perspicuity of his judgements that none of his decisions was ever upset.[1]

Another critical decision was that of Midwinter and Sims at Gloucester Assizes in 1749. This affair arose, once more, out of poaching. The prisoners were being prosecuted for taking a local gentleman's rabbits, and in revenge they killed one of his breeding mares. Sims held the mare around the neck with a girdle, while Midwinter stabbed her in the belly. Both were found guilty; Midwinter was sentenced to death, but the judge (Mr Justice Foster) referred the case of Sims to the consideration of his fellow judges, since that part of the Act 'doth not by any express provision take in aiders and abettors'. He therefore argued that Sims, while guilty, was not excluded from 'benefit of clergy' (i.e. the offence was not, in his case, capital). The judges were consulted over the next two years, in a ragged and informal way, and most appeared to be of an opinion contrary to Foster. Sims also was therefore sentenced to death.[2]

It was a nice point of law, which turned upon whether the statute in question expressly included aiders and abettors (as principals in the second degree) and whether the statute named as capital the offender or the offence. Obviously Midwinter and Sims shared equal guilt in the light of common sense; but in the light of the law this was by no means so obvious, and judges are supposed to adjudicate such nice points in a legal light, since a precedent which appears equitable in one case may appear very much less so when applied to another. An Act 'of so penal a nature' (Foster argued) 'ought to be construed literally and strictly'.

Judges have often in favour of life given way to distinctions, which possibly might never have occurred to persons who have not made the law their principal study. They have done so in favour of life; but they have very seldom done it, and, I think, never ought to do it, against the life of a man.

What is interesting in this case is that Sir Michael Foster saw 'no reason to alter his opinion'; and he was a judge not only humane but also eminent for his learning in criminal law. Some ten years later he prepared

1. John, Lord Campbell, *Lives of the Lord Chancellors*, 1846, v, p. 49; Cas. T. Hard., 291–2, *English Reports*, vol. 95.
2. Both men, however, were reprieved by Foster. For the case, Fost. 415–30, *English Reports*, vol. 168, pp. 90–97.

for the press his *Crown Law*, in the course of which he reported the case of Midwinter and Sims and presented his full reasons for dissenting from the opinion of most of his fellow judges. Prior to publication he sent a copy of the manuscript to the Lord Chief Justice, Lord Mansfield, who wrote back to him with great emphasis: 'I very much wish that you would not enter your protest with posterity against the unanimous opinion of the other judges in the case of Sims.' Mansfield found nothing in Foster's account which was objectionable in point of law. Indeed, the Lord Chief Justice went so far as to agree that the authorities cited by Foster 'prove strongly to the contrary' of the judges' decision; 'but they seem to be founded in subtle nicety, and very literal interpretation'. If the determination of Sims's case 'was contrary to former authorities, there is no hurt in it . . . The construction is agreeable to justice: and therefore, suppose it wrong upon artificial reasonings of law, I think it better to leave the matter where it is.' Lord Mansfield's letter elevates to a surprising authority the judge's sense of 'doing justice to the publick' over his interpretation of the law. As Dodson, Foster's nephew and editor, later pointed out, whatever might be thought to be Sims's deserts, 'no punishment which is not authorised by law ought to be inflicted on any man'.[1]

But Foster's very learned and convincing legal argument came to light only thirty years later, after his death, when his nephew published, in an appendix to the third edition of *Crown Law* (1792), his full report and argument. In the first edition (1762) Foster was obliged to suppress this, in deference to the Lord Chief Justice's request, which carried the force of a command. No doubt Mansfield was pleased that the matter was 'left where it was', since in 1767 the case of *Rex* v. *Royce* came up to him for decision. Royce was accused, on several counts, of taking part in a riot in Norwich in which some hundred rioters had pulled down a dwelling-house. The jury acquitted Royce on all counts of taking part in the riot, but on one count they returned a special verdict finding Royce guilty of 'aiding' the rioters by standing by and shouting encouragements. (No doubt the jurors hoped that they had got their fellow citizen off, while still throwing a sop to the law.)

Now for Sims, who had held the mare's head, to be found equally guilty with Midwinter, who had stabbed her, might seem to conform with natural justice. But Foster's 'artificial reasonings of law' turned out not to be so artificial after all, since Royce, who cheered on a crowd committing a felony, was scarcely on a par with those who pulled a building

---

1. ibid., p. 92; Michael Dodson, *The Life of Sir Michael Foster*, 1811, pp. 30–34; Radzinowicz, op. cit., I, pp. 52–5; M. Foster, *A Report of Some Proceedings on the Commission, &c.*, 3rd edn, 1792, Preface, p.v.

252

down. Lord Mansfield, however, had no hesitation in finding against Royce in the strongest terms. 'Tenderness,' said His Lordship,

ought always to prevail in criminal cases; so far, at least, as to take care that a man may not suffer otherwise than by due course of law; nor have any hardship done him, or severity exercised upon him, where the construction may admit of a reasonable doubt or difficulty. But tenderness does not require such a construction of words . . . as would tend to render the law nugatory and ineffectual, and destroy or evade the very end and intention of it: nor does it require of us that we should give in to such nice and strained critical objections as are contrary to the true meaning and spirit of it.

In coming to this decision Mansfield was fortunate in being able to recall a very telling precedent on his side of the question. 'In the course of the argument,' the law reporter noted,

a case of one *Simms*, at Gloucester Assizes in 1749 upon the Black Act . . . was mentioned by Lord Mansfield, and remembered by Mr Justice Aston. . . The case was very deliberately considered by the twelve Judges . . . and eleven Judges thought the man that held the mare to be a felon . . .

Humming and hawking through his learned memories, Mansfield did allow that Mr Justice Foster was 'of a different opinion, and continued to be so'. But he did not enlarge upon the arguments in which Foster had shown 'a reasonable doubt or difficulty', and, in citing certain precedents on his side, he neglected to mention the longer and more persuasive list of precedents on the other side which Foster had drawn up.

This is a curious episode of justice, since, first, Foster was now dead, and, second, Mansfield had himself ensured the suppression of Foster's report of the case and no other printed report was available. So that posterity, for this important precedent, could rely only on Lord Mansfield's memory. And his memory was very selective. (So far from the twelve judges considering the case 'very deliberately', in Foster's account there had been a brief meeting of six judges, in which the case was not argued by counsel, and in which the judges had divided three on each side; two of these had subsequently changed their view (finding against Sims); and there had subsequently been a further meeting of 'such of the judges as were then in town' – Foster and another being absent – which had decided the question.) In any case, the precedent was upheld and Royce was sentenced to death.[1]

Royce's case was under the Riot Act and not the Black Act, but the

1. 4 Burr. 2,073, *English Reports*, vol. 98, pp. 81–8; Radzinowicz, op. cit., I, p. 85. Royce was neither executed nor pardoned, but died while still in King's Bench prison in February 1771.

precedent held good for both,[1] and it was further enforced by the decision
the next year in the Coal Heavers' Case (1768). This arose from a tumult
in Shadwell, and a night-long – and very violent – attack by coal-heavers
on the house of a Mr Green, by whose agency their status was being
threatened and their wages reduced. Shots were exchanged for some
hours, and Green was lucky to escape with life and limb, as several of his
attackers did not. In ensuing trials, seven coal-heavers were condemned
to death under the clause in the Black Act relating to the firing of offensive
weapons, even though three of them clearly had not been in possession of
firearms and had simply joined (unarmed) in the attack. As Dodson
noted, if Foster's opinion in the case of Midwinter and Sims had been
correct, then 'it follows necessarily that three of those men suffered a
more severe punishment than the law authoriseth'. Lord Mansfield, C.J.,
still keeping to himself the reasons for Foster's opinion, presided over this
hearing also, and again cited the case of Sims as a precedent for dis-
allowing the appeal.[2]

In this way the Act evolved and enlarged itself, nurtured by the sense
of natural justice of such men as Hardwicke and Mansfield. From time to
time voices were heard suggesting that it be even further enlarged. Thus a
reverend pamphleteer argued, in 1783, that it be extended to all night
poachers: 'as to being *disguised*, any one may be said generally to be so
in the night . . .'[3] But by this time there were contrary voices as well.
Blackstone in his *Commentaries* singled out the capital penalty for cutting
down the mound of a fish-pond as 'outrageous, being seldom or never
inflicted' and 'hardly known to be law by the public'.[4] Men whose
sensibility had been nourished by *Joseph Andrews* or by Goldsmith
found the Black Act less easy to stomach. William Eden, influenced by
Montesquieu and Beccaria, brought many provisions of the Black Act
under criticism in his *Principles of Penal Law* (1771). Prosecutors became
more reluctant to put the Act into effect: in a Leicester case of destroying

1. Although, as Dodson pointed out, since the Riot Act mentioned 'offenders' whereas
the Black Act designated only the offences, Royce's conviction may have been within
the statute: Foster, op. cit., Preface, pp. vi–vii.

2. Dodson's preface to Foster, op. cit.; 1 Leach 64–7; and Radzinowicz, op. cit.,
1, p. 56, who points out that Blackstone (4 *Comm.* 373) shared Foster's opinion. For
the coal-heavers' dispute see M. D. George, 'The London Coalheavers', *Economic
History, Supplement to Economic Journal*, 1, no. 4 (1926–9), pp. 229–48; G. Rudé, *Wilkes
and Liberty*, Oxford, 1962, pp. 91–104; W. J. Shelton, *English Hunger and Industrial
Disorders*, 1973, Part II; Peter Linebaugh, 'Eighteenth Century Disorders', *Bulletin of
the Society for the Study of Labour History*, no. 28, spring 1974, pp. 57–61.

3. H. Zouch, *An Account of the Present Daring Practices of Night-Hunters and Poachers*,
1783, p. 10.

4. Blackstone (12th edn, ed. E. Christian, 1795), 1 *Comm.* 4.

trees, in 1793, the prosecutors 'from motives of humanity declined giving evidence, the Judge having stated the offence to be *capital* under the *Black Act*'. The judge instructed the accused to 'enter into his Majesty's service'; the indictment would still 'hang over their heads, as a security for their future good behaviour'.[1] But a gathering reluctance to use the Act was by no means the same thing as obsolescence. Cases continued to come up in the first two decades of the nineteenth century, up to the edge of repeal. Thus in 1814 an Essex labourer, William Potter, was executed for cutting down the orchard of a neighbouring miller. The sentence of death, the committing magistrate said later, 'rather struck us all with surprise', and a petition was presented against it, signed by the magistrate and the prosecutor among others. Potter also was struck with surprise, and the magistrate added (in extenuation of his offence) that 'very few of the lower orders of the people are acquainted with the terms of the Black Act'.[2] Undoubtedly many even among the governors of England were coming to feel that the Act's clauses – apart from those on malicious shooting and incendiarism – were too severe. There were exceptions – among the judges, in the House of Lords and in the *Quarterly Review*[3].

We may leave this subject, which has occupied us long enough and which is not such as to incline one to close with a romantic peroration either on man's nature or on British traditions. We will close with two brief cases and two vignettes, which illustrate the resources and complexities of the Act's heritage. In the first case, John Haywood was sentenced to death at Coventry in 1801 for driving a nail into the frog of the foot of the prosecutor's horse, thus laming the beast temporarily but doing it no permanent harm. The judges (on appeal) found the conviction good: the word in the statute was 'wound', and the act was done

1. Case of Joseph Bland and John Edgson, Leicester Assizes, July 1793. Very incomplete figures in *PP*, 1819, *Reports*, *VIII* (appendices), suggest that after 1770 the Black Act was rarely employed, and then in cases of cattle-maiming (e.g. Western Circuit, 1770–1818, 7 convictions, of whom 3 executed), of malicious shooting and stabbing (e.g. Norfolk Circuit, 1768–1819, 12 convictions, of whom 4 executed; Lancaster Circuit, 1798–1818, 10 convictions, of whom 2 executed), arson and threatening letters. William Potter appears to have been the only offender executed for cutting trees in England and Wales between 1805 and 1818; there was one conviction in the Western Circuit for cutting hop-binds in 1801 (reprieved).

2. *PP*, 1819, *Reports*, *VIII*, p. 87; Radzinowicz, op. cit., I, pp. 62–3. It was Lord Sidmouth who rejected the petition for a reprieve.

3. Thus the *Quarterly Review*, vol. 24 (1821), p. 199: 'It does not appear that the act was either passed unadvisedly or believed to be unavailing . . .' It should be preserved as a resource against 'the possible recurrence of disorders of an equally formidable nature'.

out of malice.[1] In the second case, there was a contrary decision. Thomas Ross was convicted in 1800 of breaking the mounds of two fish-ponds at Bosworth Park, Leicestershire. But in his case it was proved, from the trampling of the ground, the disturbance of weeds and the presence of a sack, that Ross was motivated not by malice to the owner of the Park (Sir W. Dixie) but by the far more proper economic motive of stealing the fish. He therefore did not fall within the Act. Theft or poaching might, after all, be conformable with a due daylight deference. It was, above all, malice to the gentry which the Act was designed to punish.[2]

Two vignettes. At the Lent Assizes at Thetford in 1802 Elizabeth Salmon was indicted under the Black Act for incendiarism, in setting fire to a stack of hay, fodder and clover. The facts were as follows. Elizabeth Salmon had been living (in her own house) with a man named Frosdike. The stack stood in her own yard, and was made up of some part of fodder from the common, some gleaned in the neighbourhood, and some clover perhaps bought by Frosdike. This man had drifted off, and had returned once more before finally abandoning Elizabeth. On his final visit he had 'sold' a pony and the stack to another man (the prosecutor) for fourteen guineas; the pony (it was alleged) was worth twelve guineas, so that presumably the stack was valued at two. Frosdike was not called as a witness, and no evidence was brought by the prosecution as to the ownership of the stack. One presumes that Elizabeth Salmon had taken some part in the gleaning, and felt that she had some right in it. When the money was paid to Frosdike, she said she would burn the stack to the ground rather than let it be sold. She made no pretence of secrecy, but immediately called some of her neighbours as witnesses, and in front of ten or twelve people took a hod of coals from her fire to the stack. When it failed to burn well, she fetched her bellows. None of the neighbours sought to interfere. For this she was convicted and cast for death. In her defence she said she had been ill-treated by Frosdike. One is left with an impression that she was also ill-treated by the law.[3]

And finally an earlier case, that of Baylis and Reynolds, the turnpike rioters. We have already noted that this case was tried before Lord Hardwicke, and was the occasion for a remarkable decision. At their height, in 1735, the rioters at Ledbury were one hundred strong, armed with guns and swords, some dressed in women's clothes, with high-crowned hats and blackened faces. They called themselves 'turnpike cutters or levellers', and undoubtedly were supported by the local population; a farm labourer swore that 'he looked upon such gentlemen

1. E. H. East, *A Treatise of the Pleas of the Crown*, 1803, II, pp. 1076-7; Radzinowicz, op. cit., I, p. 67.
2. East, op. cit., II, p. 1067.   3. Russ. & Ry. 26-7.

as were for erecting turnpikes about Ledbury [as] the same as persons that robb'd on the highway'.

The legislature had, in fact, had the forethought to provide itself with a new Act (8 George II c.20) only four months previously, making the cutting of turnpikes felony. This included a clause enabling the Law Officers to remove the trial out of the affected county (where juries might be recalcitrant) into an adjacent one. Our old acquaintance, Nicholas Paxton, who was preparing the case, discussed the matter at length:

> Upon inquiry I found that the prisoners had been visited and spirited up, whilst in gaol, by numbers of people and even by some of the persons who were upon the jury, as I am credibly informed, so that . . . prosecutions here would have been ineffectual; and thereupon . . . I removed all the prisoners yesterday by Habeas Corpus to Worcester to be prosecuted at the next Assizes . . .

As to one of the accused, James Baylis, Paxton was under difficulties:

> I am particularly directed by the Order of Council to prosecute him and the other person [i.e. Reynolds] taken with him, upon the Black Act, but Mr. Skipp hath taken an information upon oath from him against several others that were concerned in destroying the turn-pikes, and . . . is therefore desirous that he may be admitted a witness. If it was only intended by the Order of Council that Examples might be made upon the Black Act, there are others in custody that may answer that purpose . . .

In the end it proved to be most convenient to let Baylis and Reynolds 'answer the purpose'. They were tried before the court of King's Bench, at Westminster Hall. Both men were condemned to death, but Baylis was rewarded for his good intentions by a reprieve. Since Thomas Reynolds had proved obdurate, and had refused to buy his life at the expense of his comrades, he was a fit 'example' to be made under the Black Act. He was a collier, aged thirty-four, whom the Ordinary of Newgate described as being a man of 'good character'; 'he had but little learning, but had pritty good natural parts, and own'd he was too apt to drink too deep in his cups'. He was brought within the Black Act for being armed with a pick-axe, and for going disguised with 'a woman's gown and a woman's straw hat'. The old cast was present in force: Paxton worked up the case, Lord Hardwicke directed the jury ('if, upon the evidence, you believe that the prisoners did appear in the high road . . . disguised, you are to find them guilty'), and Sir Francis Page, as the senior judge below the Chief Justice, was awarded the privilege of pronouncing the death sentence.

Reynolds told the Ordinary of Newgate that 'he did not think that crime had been of so heanious a nature as to bring him to that unhappy end'. At the gallows he complained that 'he had never committed any theft nor murder nor done any other crime in his life'. His execution was gruesome. After being suspended the usual time at Tyburn,

> He was cut down by the executioner . . . but as the coffin was fastening, he thrust back the lid, upon which the executioner would have tied him up again, but the mob prevented it, and carried him to a house where he vomited three pints of blood, but on giving him a glass of wine, he died.

This was a curious end to the collier's life, among strangers and far from his native Herefordshire.[1] Professor Plumb has suggested that historians have paid too much attention to revolutions and too little to the creation of political stability. And he sees the decades of the consolidation of Walpole's power as such an historical moment, paying tribute to the 'Great Man' for his realism and his command of the possible.[2] Such a case can, no doubt, be made for Walpole and the hard Hanoverian Whigs. Even if their prime interest was their own private advantage, the very size of the immense private interests at risk made them zealous opponents of a nostalgic and anachronistic Jacobite counter-revolution. Whether other historical alternatives were open, we cannot (from the materials considered in this study) hazard. It is a complex and perhaps unreal question. But at least we must give to plain facts plain names. The Hanoverian Whigs of the 1720s and 1730s were a hard lot of men. And they remind us that stability, no less than revolution, may have its own kind of Terror.

iv. The Rule of Law

We might be wise to end here. But since readers of this study may be provoked to some general reflections upon the law and upon British traditions, perhaps we may allow ourselves the same indulgence.

From a certain traditional middle ground of national historiography the interest of this theme (the Black Act and its evolution) may be evident. But this middle ground is now being eroded, from at least two directions. On one hand the perspective within which British political and social historians have been accustomed to view their own history is, quite properly, coming under challenge. As the last imperial illusions of the twentieth century fade, so preoccupation with the history and culture of a small island off the coast of Europe becomes open to the charge of nar-

1. Paxton's letter of 24 March 1736, SP36.38, fo. 191; Crown briefs in TS11.725.2285 and 11.1122.5824; for case law, Cas. T. Hard. 291–2 and above, p. 210; for Reynolds and his execution, *ON*, 26 July 1736, and (for a slightly different account of his death) P. Linebaugh in *Albion's Fatal Tree*, pp. 103–4.

2. J. H. Plumb, *The Growth of Political Stability in England, 1675–1725*, 1969, *passim* and p. 188.

cissism. The culture of constitutionalism which flowered here, under favoured conditions, is an episode too exceptional to carry any universal significance. If we judge it in terms of its own self-sufficient values we are imprisoned within its own parochialism.

Alternative perspectives must diminish the complacency of national historical preoccupation. If we see Britain within the perspective of the expansion of European capitalism, then the contest over interior rights and laws will be dwarfed when set beside the exterior record of slave-trading, of the East India Company, of commercial and military imperialism. Or, to take up a bright new conservative perspective, the story of a few lost common rights and of a few deer-stealers strung from the gallows is a paltry affair when set beside the accounts of mass repression of almost any day in the day-book of the twentieth century. Did a few foresters get a rough handling from partisan laws? What is that beside the norms of the Third Reich? Did the villagers of Winkfield lose access to the peat within Swinley Rails? What is that beside the liquidation of the *kulaks*? What is remarkable (we are reminded) is not that the laws were bent but the fact that there was, anywhere in the eighteenth century, a rule of law at all. To ask for greater justice than that is to display mere sentimentalism. In any event, we should adjust our sense of proportion; against the handfuls carried off on the cart to Tyburn (and smaller handfuls than have been carried off in Tudor times) we must see whole legions carried off by plague or dearth.

From these perspectives concern with the rights and wrongs at law of a few men in 1723 is concern with trivia. And the same conclusion may be reached through a different adjustment of perspective, which may coexist with some of the same arguments. This flourishes in the form of a sophisticated, but (ultimately) highly schematic Marxism which, to our surprise, seems to spring up in the footsteps of those of us in an older Marxist tradition. From this standpoint the law is, perhaps more clearly than any other cultural or institutional artifact, by definition a part of a 'superstructure' adapting itself to the necessities of an infrastructure of productive forces and productive relations. As such, it is clearly an instrument of the *de facto* ruling class: it both defines and defends these rulers' claims upon resources and labour-power – it says what shall be property and what shall be crime – and it mediates class relations with a set of appropriate rules and sanctions, all of which, ultimately, confirm and consolidate existing class power. Hence the rule of law is only another mask for the rule of a class. The revolutionary can have no interest in law, unless as a phenomenon of ruling-class power and hypocrisy; it should be his aim simply to overthrow it. And so, once again, to express surprise at the Black Act or at partial judges is – unless as confirmation and illustration of theories which might easily be demonstrated without all this labour – simply to expose one's own naivety.

So the old middle ground of historiography is crumbling on both sides. I stand on a very narrow ledge, watching the tides come up. Or, to be more explicit, I sit here in my study, at the age of fifty, the desk and the floor piled high with five years of notes, xeroxes, rejected drafts, the clock once again moving into the small hours, and see myself, in a lucid instant, as an anachronism. Why have I spent these years trying to find out what could, in its essential structures, have been known without any investigation at all? And does it matter a damn who gave Parson Power his instructions; which forms brought 'Vulcan' Gates to the gallows; or how an obscure Richmond publican managed to evade a death sentence already determined upon by the Law Officers, the First Minister and the King?

I am disposed to think that it does matter; I have a vested interest (in five years of labour) to think it may. But to show this must involve evacuating received assumptions – that narrowing ledge of traditional middle ground – and moving out onto an even narrower theoretical ledge. This would accept, as it must, some part of the Marxist–structural critique; indeed, some parts of this study have confirmed the class-bound and mystifying functions of the law. But it would reject its ulterior reductionism and would modify its typology of superior and inferior (but determining) structures.

First, analysis of the eighteenth century (and perhaps of other centuries) calls in question the validity of separating off the law as a whole and placing it in some typological superstructure. The law when considered as institution (the courts, with their class theatre and class procedures) or as personnel (the judges, the lawyers, the Justices of the Peace) may very easily be assimilated to those of the ruling class. But all that is entailed in 'the law' is not subsumed in these institutions. The law may also be seen as ideology, or as particular rules and sanctions which stand in a definite and active relationship (often a field of conflict) to social norms; and, finally, it may be seen simply in terms of its own logic, rules and procedures – that is, simply *as law*. And it is not possible to conceive of any complex society without law.

We must labour this point, since some theorists today are unable to see the law except in terms of 'the fuzz' setting about inoffensive demonstrators or cannabis-smokers. I am no authority on the twentieth century, but in the eighteenth century matters were more complex than that. To be sure I have tried to show, in the evolution of the Black Act, an expression of the ascendancy of a Whig oligarchy, which created new laws and bent old legal forms in order to legitimize its own property and status; this oligarchy employed the law, both instrumentally and ideologically, very much as a modern structural Marxist should expect it to do. But this is not the same thing as to say that the rulers had need of law, in order to oppress the ruled, while those who were ruled had need of none. What was often at issue was not property, supported by law, against no-property; it was alternative definitions of property-rights: for the landowner, enclosure – for the cottager, common rights; for the forest officialdom, 'preserved grounds' for the deer; for the foresters, the right to take turfs. For as long as it remained possible, the ruled – if they could find a purse and a lawyer – would actually fight for their rights by means of law; occasionally the copyholders, resting upon the precedents of sixteenth-century law, could actually win a case. When it ceased to be possible to continue the fight at law, men still felt a sense of legal wrong: the propertied had obtained their power by illegitimate means.

Moreover, if we look closely into such an agrarian context, the distinction between law, on the one hand, conceived of as an element of 'superstructure', and the actualities of productive forces and relations on the other hand, becomes more and more untenable. For law was often a definition of actual agrarian *practice*, as it had been pursued 'time out of mind'. How can we distinguish between the activity of farming or of quarrying and the rights to this strip of land or to that quarry? The farmer or forester in his daily occupation was moving within visible or invisible structures of law: this merestone which marked the division between strips; that ancient oak – visited by processional on each Rogation Day – which marked the limits of the parish grazing; those other invisible (but potent and sometimes legally enforceable) memories as to which parishes had the right to take turfs in this waste and which parishes had not; this written or unwritten customal which decided how many stints on the common land and for whom – for copyholders and freeholders only, or for all inhabitants?

Hence 'law' was deeply imbricated within the very basis of productive relations, which would have been inoperable without this law. And, in the second place, this law, as definition or as rules (imperfectly enforceable through institutional legal forms), was endorsed by norms, tenaciously transmitted through the community. There were alternative norms; that is a matter of course; this was a place, not of consensus, but of conflict. But we cannot, then, simply separate off all law as ideology, and assimilate this also to the state apparatus of a ruling class. On the contrary, the norms of foresters might reveal themselves as passionately supported values, impelling them upon a course of action which would lead them into bitter conflict – with 'the law'.

So we are back, once again, with *that* law: the institutionalized procedures of the ruling class. This, no doubt, is worth no more of our theoretical attention; we can see it as an instrument of class power *tout court*. But we must take even this formulation, and see whether its crystalline clarity will survive immersion in scepticism. To be sure, we can stand no longer on that traditional ground of liberal academicism, which offers the eighteenth century as a society of consensus, ruled within the parameters of paternalism and deference, and governed by a 'rule of law' which attained (however imperfectly) towards impartiality. That is not the society which we have been examining; we have not observed a society of consensus; and we have seen the law being devised and employed, directly and instrumentally, in the imposition of class power. Nor can we accept a sociological refinement of the old view, which stresses the imperfections and partiality of the law, and its subordination to the functional requirements of socio-economic interest groups. For what we have observed is something more than the law as a pliant medium to be twisted this way and that by whichever interests already possess effective power. Eighteenth-century law was more substantial than that. Over and above its pliant, instrumental functions it existed in its own right, as ideology; as an ideology which not only served, in most respects, but which also legitimized class power. The hegemony of the eighteenth-century gentry and aristocracy was expressed, above all, not in military force, not in the mystifications of a priesthood or of the press, not even in economic coercion, but in the rituals of the study of the Justices of the Peace, in the quarter-sessions, in the pomp of Assizes and in the theatre of Tyburn.

Thus the law (we agree) may be seen instrumentally as mediating and reinforcing existent class relations and, ideologically, as offering to these a legitimation. But we must press our definitions a little further. For if we say that existent class relations were mediated by the law, this is not the same thing as saying that the law was no more than those relations translated into other terms, which masked or mystified the reality. This may, quite often, be true but it is not the whole truth. For class relations were expressed, not in any way one likes, but *through the forms of law*; and the law, like other institutions which from time to time can be seen as mediating (and masking) existent class relations (such as the Church or the media of communication), has its own characteristics, its own independent history and logic of evolution.

Moreover, people are not as stupid as some structuralist philosophers suppose them to be. They will not be mystified by the first man who puts on a wig. It is inherent in the especial character of law, as a body of rules and procedures, that it shall apply logical criteria with reference to standards of universality and equity. It is true that certain categories of person may be excluded from this logic (as children or slaves), that other categories may be debarred from access to parts of the logic (as women or, for many forms of eighteenth-century law, those without certain kinds of property), and that the poor may often be excluded, through penury, from the law's costly procedures. All this, and more, is true. But if too much of this is true, then the consequences are plainly counterproductive. Most men have a strong sense of justice, at least with regard to their own interests. If the law is evidently partial and unjust, then it will mask nothing, legitimize nothing, contribute nothing to any class's hegemony. The essential precondition for the effectiveness of law, in its function as ideology, is that it shall display an independence from gross manipulation and shall seem to be just. It cannot seem to be so without upholding its own logic and criteria of equity; indeed, on occasion, by actually *being* just. And furthermore it is not often the case that a ruling ideology can be dismissed as a mere hypocrisy; even rulers find a need to legitimize their power, to moralize their functions, to feel themselves to be useful and just. In the case of an ancient historical formation like the law, a discipline which requires years of exacting study to master, there will always be some men who actively believe in their own procedures and in the logic of justice. The law may be rhetoric, but it need not be empty rhetoric. Blackstone's *Commentaries* represent an intellectual exercise far more rigorous than could have come from an apologist's pen.

I do not know what transcultural validity these reflections may have. But they are certainly applicable to England in the eighteenth century. Douglas Hay, in a significant essay in *Albion's Fatal Tree*, has argued that the law assumed unusual pre-eminence in that century, as the central legitimizing ideology, displacing the religious authority and sanctions of previous centuries. It gave way, in its turn, to economic sanctions and to the ideology of the free market and of political liberalism in the nineteenth. Turn where you will, the rhetoric of eighteenth-century England is saturated with the notion of law. Royal absolutism was placed behind a high hedge of law; landed estates were tied together with entails and marriage settlements made up of elaborate tissues of law; authority and property punctuated their power by regular 'examples' made upon the public gallows. More than this, immense efforts were made (and Hay has explored the forms of these) to project the image of a ruling class which was itself subject to the rule of law, and whose legitimacy rested upon the equity and universality of those legal forms. And the rulers were, in serious senses, whether willingly or unwillingly, the prisoners of their own rhetoric; they played the games of power according to rules which suited them, but they could not break those rules or the whole game would be thrown away. And, finally, so far from the ruled shrugging off this rhetoric as a hypocrisy, some part of it at least was taken over as part of the rhetoric of the plebeian crowd, of the 'free-born Englishman' with his inviolable privacy, his *habeas corpus*, his equality before the law. If this rhetoric was a mask, it was a mask which John Wilkes was to borrow, at the head of ten thousand masked supporters.

So that in this island and in that century above all one must resist any slide into structural reductionism. What this overlooks, among other things, is the immense capital of human struggle over the previous two centuries against royal absolutism, inherited, in the forms and traditions of the law, by the eighteenth-century gentry. For in the sixteenth and seventeenth centuries the law had been less an instrument of class power than a central arena of conflict. In the course of conflict the law itself had been changed; inherited by the eighteenth-century gentry, this changed law was, literally, central to their whole purchase upon power and upon the means of life. Take law away, and the royal prerogative, or the presumption of the aristocracy, might flood back upon their properties and lives; take law away and the string which tied together their lands and marriages would fall apart. But it was inherent in the very nature of the medium which they had selected for their own self-defence that it could not be reserved for the exclusive use only of their own class. The law, in its forms and traditions, entailed principles of equity and universality which, perforce, had to be extended to all sorts and degrees of men. And since this was of necessity so, ideology could turn necessity to advantage. What had been devised by men of property as a defence against arbitrary power could be turned into service as an apologia for property in the face of the propertyless. And the apologia was serviceable up to a point: for these 'propertyless', as we have seen, comprised multitudes of men and women who themselves enjoyed, in fact, petty property rights or agrarian use-rights whose definition was inconceivable without the forms of law. Hence the ideology of the great struck root in a soil, however shallow, of actuality. And the courts gave substance to the ideology by the scrupulous care with which, on occasion, they adjudged petty rights, and, on all occasions, preserved proprieties and forms.

We reach, then, not a simple conclusion (law = class power) but a complex and contradictory one. On the one hand, it is true that the law did mediate existent class relations to the advantage of the rulers; not only is this so, but as the century advanced the law became a superb instrument by which these rulers were able to impose new definitions of property to their even greater advantage, as in the extinction by law of indefinite agrarian use-rights and in the furtherance of enclosure. On the other hand, the law mediated these class relations through legal forms, which imposed, again and again, inhibitions upon the actions of the rulers. For there is a very large difference, which twentieth-century experience ought to have made clear even to the most exalted thinker, between arbitrary extra-legal power and the rule of law. And not only were the rulers (indeed, the ruling class as a whole) inhibited by their own rules of law against the exercise of direct unmediated force (arbitrary imprisonment, the employment of troops against the crowd, torture, and those other conveniences of power with which we are all conversant), but they also believed enough in these rules, and in their accompanying ideological rhetoric, to allow, in certain limited areas, the law itself to be a genuine forum within which certain kinds of class conflict were fought out. There were even occasions (one recalls John Wilkes and several of the trials of the 1790s) when the Government itself retired from the courts defeated. Such occasions served, paradoxically, to consolidate power, to enhance its legitimacy, and to inhibit revolutionary movements. But, to turn the paradox around, these same occasions served to bring power even further within constitutional controls.

The rhetoric and the rules of a society are something a great deal more than sham. In the same moment they may modify, in profound ways, the behaviour of the powerful, and mystify the powerless. They may disguise the true realities of power, but, at the same time, they may curb that power and check its intrusions. And it is often from within that very rhetoric that a radical critique of the practice of the society is developed: the reformers of the 1790s appeared, first of all, clothed in the rhetoric of Locke and of Blackstone.

These reflections lead me on to conclusions which may be different from those which some readers expect. I have shown in this study a political oligarchy inventing callous and oppressive laws to serve its own interests. I have shown judges who, no less than bishops, were subject to political influence, whose sense of justice was humbug, and whose interpretation of the laws served only to enlarge their inherent class bias. Indeed, I think that this study has shown that for many of England's governing élite the rules of law were a nuisance, to be manipulated and bent in what ways they could; and that the allegiance of such men as Walpole, Hardwicke or Paxton to the rhetoric of law was largely humbug. But I do not conclude from this that the rule of law itself was humbug. On the contrary, the inhibitions upon power imposed by law seem to me a legacy as substantial as any handed down from the struggles of the seventeenth century to the eighteenth, and a true and important cultural achievement of the agrarian and mercantile bourgeoisie, and of their supporting yeomen and artisans.

More than this, the notion of the regulation and reconciliation of conflicts through the rule of law – and the elaboration of rules and procedures which, on occasion, made some approximate approach towards the ideal – seems to me a cultural achievement of universal significance. I do not lay any claim as to the abstract, extra-historical impartiality of these rules. In a context of gross class inequalities, the equity of the law must always be in some part sham. Transplanted as it was to even more inequitable contexts, this law could become an instrument of imperialism. For this law has found its way to a good many parts of the globe. But even here the rules and the rhetoric have imposed some inhibitions upon the imperial power. If the rhetoric was a mask, it was a mask which Gandhi and Nehru were to borrow, at the head of a million masked supporters.

I am not starry-eyed about this at all. This has not been a star-struck book. I am insisting only upon the obvious point, which some modern Marxists have overlooked, that there is a difference between arbitrary power and the rule of law. We ought to expose the shams and inequities which may be concealed beneath this law. But the rule of law itself, the imposing of effective inhibitions upon power and the defence of the citizen from power's all-intrusive claims, seems to me to be an unqualified human good. To deny or belittle this good is, in this dangerous century when the resources and pretentions of power continue to enlarge, a desperate error of intellectual abstraction. More than this, it is a self-fulfilling error, which encourages us to give up the struggle against bad laws and class-bound procedures, and to disarm ourselves before power. It is to throw away a whole inheritance of struggle *about* law, and within the forms of law, whose continuity can never be fractured without bringing men and women into immediate danger.

In all of this I may be wrong. I am told that, just beyond the horizon, new forms of working-class power are about to arise which, being founded upon egalitarian productive relations, will require no inhibition and can dispense with the negative restrictions of bourgeois legalism. A historian is unqualified to pronounce on such utopian projections. All that he knows is that he can bring in support of them no historical evidence whatsoever. His advice might be: watch this new power for a century or two before you cut your hedges down.

I therefore crawl out onto my own precarious ledge. It is true that in history the law can be seen to mediate and to legitimize existent class relations. Its forms and procedures may crystallize those relations and mask ulterior injustice. But this mediation, through the forms of law, is something quite distinct from the exercise of unmediated force. The forms and rhetoric of law acquire a distinct identity which may, on occasion, inhibit power and afford some protection to the powerless. Only to the degree that this is seen to be so can law be of service in its other aspect, as ideology. Moreover, the law in both its aspects, as formal rules and procedures and as ideology, cannot usefully be analysed in the metaphorical terms of a superstructure distinct from an infrastructure. While this comprises a large and self-evident part of the truth, the rules and categories of law penetrate every level of society, effect vertical as well as horizontal definitions of men's rights and status, and contribute to men's self-definition or sense of identity. As such law has not only been imposed *upon* men from above: it has also been a medium within which other social conflicts have been fought out. Productive relations themselves are, in part, only meaningful in terms of their definitions at law: the serf, the free labourer; the cottager with common rights, the inhabitant without; the unfree proletarian, the picket conscious of his rights; the landless labourer who may still sue his employer for assault. And if the actuality of the law's operation in class-divided societies has, again and again, fallen short of its own rhetoric of equity, yet the notion of the rule of law is itself an unqualified good.

This cultural achievement – the attainment towards a universal value – found one origin in Roman jurisprudence. The uncodified English common law offered an alternative notation of law, in some ways more flexible and unprincipled – and therefore more pliant to the 'common sense' of the ruling class – in other ways more available as a medium through which social conflict could find expression, especially where the sense of 'natural justice' of the jury could make itself felt. Since this tradition came to its maturity in eighteenth-century England, its claims should command the historian's interest. And since some part of the inheritance from this cultural moment may still be found, within greatly changed contexts, within the United States or India or certain African countries, it is important to re-examine the pretensions of the imperialist donor.

This is to argue the need for a general revaluation of eighteenth-century law, of which this study offers only a fragment. This study has been centred upon a bad law, drawn by bad legislators, and enlarged by the interpretations of bad judges. No defence, in terms of natural justice, can be offered for anything in the history of the Black Act. But even this study does not prove that all law as such is bad. Even this law bound the rulers to act only in the ways which its forms permitted; they had difficulties with these forms; they could not always override the sense of natural justice of the jurors; and we may imagine how Walpole would have acted, against Jacobites or against disturbers of Richmond Park, if he had been subject to no forms of law at all.

If we suppose that law is no more than a mystifying and pompous way in which class power is registered and executed, then we need not waste our labour in studying its history and forms. One Act would be much the same as another, and all, from the standpoint of the ruled, would be Black. It is because law *matters* that we have bothered with this story at all. And this is also an answer to those universal thinkers, impatient of all except the *longue durée*, who cannot be bothered with cartloads of victims at Tyburn when they set these beside the indices of infant mortality. The victims of smallpox testify only to their own poverty and to the infancy of medical science; the victims of the gallows are exemplars of a conscious and elaborated code, justified in the name of a universal human value. Since we hold this value to be a human good, and one whose usefulness the world has not yet outgrown, the operation of this code deserves our most scrupulous attention. It is only when we follow through the intricacies of its operation that we can show what it was worth, how it was bent, how its proclaimed values were falsified in practice. When we note Walpole harrying John Huntridge, Judge Page handing down his death sentences, Lord Hardwicke wrenching the clauses of his Act from their context and Lord Mansfield compounding his manipulations, we feel contempt for men whose practice belied the resounding rhetoric of the age. But we feel contempt not because we are contemptuous of the notion of a just and equitable law but because this notion has been betrayed by its own professors. The modern sensibility which views this only within the perspectives of our own archipeaagos of *gulags* and of *stalags*, for whose architects the very notion of the rule of law would be a criminal heresy, will find my responses over-fussy. The plebs of eighteenth-century England were provided with a rule of law of some sort, and they ought to have considered themselves lucky. What more could they expect?

In fact, some of them had the impertinence, and the imperfect sense of historical perspective, to expect justice. On the gallows men would actually complain, in their 'last dying words', if they felt that in some particular the due forms of law had not been undergone. (We remember Vulcan Gates complaining that since he was illiterate he could not read his own notice of proclamation; and performing his allotted role at Tyburn only when he had seen the Sheriff's dangling chain.) For the trouble about law and justice, as ideal aspirations, is that they must pretend to absolute validity or they do not exist at all. If I judge the Black Act to be atrocious, this is not only from some standpoint in natural justice, and not only from the standpoint of those whom the Act oppressed, but also according to some ideal notion of the standards to which 'the law', as regulator of human conflicts of interest, ought to attain. For 'the law', as a logic of equity, must always seek to transcend the inequalities of class power which, instrumentally, it is harnessed to serve. And 'the law' as ideology, which pretends to reconcile the interests of all degrees of men, must always come into conflict with the ideological partisanship of class.

We face, then, a paradox. The work of sixteenth- and seventeenth-century jurists, supported by the practical struggles of such men as Hampden and Lilburne, was passed down as a legacy to the eighteenth century, where it gave rise to a vision, in the minds of some men, of an ideal aspiration towards universal values of law. One thinks of Swift or of Goldsmith, or, with more qualifications, of Sir William Blackstone or Sir Michael Foster. If we today have ideal notions of what law might be, we derive them in some part from that cultural moment. It is, in part, in terms of that age's own aspiration that we judge the Black Act and find it deficient. But at the same time this same century, governed as it was by the forms of law, provides a text-book illustration of the employment of law, as instrument and as ideology, in serving the interests of the ruling class. The oligarchs and the great gentry were content to be subject to the rule of law only because this law was serviceable and afforded to their hegemony the rhetoric of legitimacy. This paradox has been at the heart of this study. It was also at the heart of eighteenth-century society. But it was also a paradox which that society could not in the end transcend, for the paradox was held in equipoise upon an ulterior equilibrium of class forces. When the struggles of 1790–1832 signalled that this equilibrium had changed, the rulers of England were faced with alarming alternatives. They could either dispense with the rule of law, dismantle their elaborate constitutional structures, countermand their own rhetoric and exercise power by force; or they could submit to their own rules and surrender their hegemony. In the campaign against Paine and the printers, in the Two Acts (1795), the Combination Acts (1799–1800), the repression of Peterloo (1819) and the Six Acts (1820) they took halting steps in the first direction. But in the end, rather than shatter their own self-image and repudiate 150 years of constitutional legality, they surrendered to the law. In this surrender they threw retrospective light back on the history of their class, and retrieved for it something of its honour; despite Walpole, despite Paxton, despite Page and Hardwicke, that rhetoric had not been altogether sham.

Appendix 1
The Black Act

Anno nono GEORGII I. C.22.

An act for the more effectual punishing wicked and evil-disposed persons going armed in disguise, and doing injuries and violences to the persons and properties of his Majest'ys subjects, and for the more speedy bringing the offenders to justice.

I. WHEREAS *several ill-designing and disorderly persons have of late associated themselves under the name of* Blacks, *and entered into confederacies to support and assist one another in stealing and destroying of deer, robbing of warrens and fish-ponds, cutting down plantations of trees, and other illegal practices, and have, in great numbers, armed with swords, fire-arms, and other offensive weapons, several of them with their faces blacked, or in disguised habits, unlawfully hunted in forests belonging to his Majesty, and in the parks of divers of his Majesty's subjects, and destroyed, killed and carried away the deer, robbed warrens, rivers and fish-ponds, and cut down plantations of trees; and have likewise solicited several of his Majesty's subjects, with promises of money, or other rewards, to join with them, and have sent letters in fictitious names, to several persons, demanding venison and money, and threatning some great violence, if such their unlawful demands should be refused, or if they should be interrupted in, or prosecuted for such their wicked practises, and have actually done great damage to several persons, who have either refused to comply with such demands, or have endeavoured to bring them to justice, to the great terror of his Majesty's peaceable subjects:* For the preventing which wicked and unlawful practices, be it enacted by the King's most excellent Majesty, by and with the advice and consent of the lords spiritual and temporal and commons, in parliament assembled, and by the authority of the same. That if any person or persons, from and after the first day of *June* in the year of our Lord one thousand seven hundred and twenty-three, being armed with swords, fire-arms, or other offensive weapons, and having his or their faces blacked, or being otherwise disguised, shall appear in any forest, chase, park, paddock, or grounds inclosed with any wall, pale, or other fence, wherein any deer have been or shall be usually kept, or in any warren or place where hares or conies have been or shall be usually kept, or in any high road, open heath, common or down, or shall unlawfully and wilfully hunt, wound, kill, destroy, or steal any red or fallow deer, or unlawfully rob any warren or place where conies or hares are usually kept, or shall unlawfully steal or take away any fish out of any river or pond; or if any person or persons, from and after the said first day of *June* shall unlawfully and wilfully hunt, wound, kill, destroy or steal any red or fallow deer, fed or kept in any places in any of his Majesty's forests or chases, which are or shall be inclosed with pales, rails, or other fences, or in any park, paddock, or grounds inclosed, where deer have been or shall be usually kept; or shall unlawfully and maliciously break down the head or mound of any fish-pond, whereby the fish shall be lost or destroyed; or shall unlawfully and maliciously kill, maim or wound any cattle, or cut down or otherwise destroy any trees planted in any avenue, or growing in any garden, orchard or plantation, for ornament, shelter or profit; or shall set fire to any house, barn or out-house, or to any hovel, cock, mow, or stack of corn, straw, hay or wood; or shall wilfully and maliciously shoot at any person in any dwelling-house, or other place; or shall knowingly send any letter, without any name, subscribed thereto, or signed with a fictitious name, demanding money, venison, or other valuable thing; or shall forcibly rescue any person being lawfully in custody of any officer or other person, for any of the offences before mentioned; or if any person or persons shall, by gift or promise of money, or other reward, procure any of his Majesty's subjects to join him or them in any such unlawful act; every person so offending, being thereof lawfully convicted, shall be adjudged guilty of felony, and shall suffer death as in cases of felony, without benefit of clergy.

II. *And whereas notwithstanding the laws now in force against the illegal practices above mentioned, and his Majesty's royal proclamation of the second day of* February *which was*

Persons disguised and in arms appearing in forest, &c. and killing deer, &c. deemed felons.

Sending letters without a name, &c. and demanding money, &c. felony.

in the year of our Lord one thousand seven hundred and twenty-two, *notifying the same, many wicked and evil-disposed persons have, in open defiance thereof, been guilty of several of the offences before mentioned, to the great disturbance of the publick peace, and damage of divers of his Majestys' good subjects;* It is hereby enacted by the authority aforesaid, That all and every person and persons, who since the second day of *February* in the year of our Lord one thousand seven hundred and twenty-two, have committed or been guilty of any of the offences aforesaid, who shall not surrender him, her or themselves, before the twenty-fourth day of *July* in the year of our Lord one thousand seven hundred and twenty-three, to any of the justices of his Majesty's court of kings bench, or to any one of his Majesty's justices of the peace, in and for the county where he, she or they did commit such offence or offences, and voluntarily make a full confession thereof to such justice, and a true discovery upon his, her or their oath or oaths, of the persons who were his, her or their accomplices in any of the said offences, by giving a true account of their names, occupations and places of abode, and to the best of his, her or their knowledge or belief, discover where they may be found, in order to be brought to justice, being thereof lawfully convicted, shall be adjudged guilty of felony, and shall suffer death as in cases of felony, without benefit of clergy.

Such persons when to surrender themselves, &c.

III. Provided nevertheless, That all and every person and persons, who have been guilty of any the offences aforesaid, and shall not be in lawful custody for such offence on the said first day of *June* and shall surrender him, her or themselves, on or before the said twenty-fourth day of *July* as aforesaid, and shall make such confession and discovery as aforesaid, shall by virtue of this act be pardoned, acquitted and discharged of and from the offences so by him, her or them, confessed as aforesaid; any thing herein contained to the contrary in any wise notwithstanding.

Who intitled to a pardon.

IV. And for the more easy and speedy bringing the offenders against this act to justice, be it further enacted by the authority aforesaid, That if any person or persons shall be charged with being guilty of any of the offences aforesaid, before any two or more of his Majesty's justices of the peace of the county where such offence or offences were or shall be committed, by information of one or more credible person or persons upon oath by him or them to be subscribed, such justices before whom such information shall be made as aforesaid, shall forthwith certify under their hands and seals, and return such information to one of the principal secretaries of state of his Majesty, his heirs or successors, who is hereby required to lay the same, as soon as conveniently may be, before his Majesty, his heirs or successors, in his or their privy council; whereupon it shall and may be lawful for his Majesty, his heirs or successors, to make his or their order in his or their said privy council, thereby requiring and commanding such offender or offenders to surrender him or themselves, within the space of forty days, to any of his Majesty's justices of the court of king's bench, or to any one of his Majesty's justices of the peace, to the end that he or they may be forth coming, to answer the offence or offences wherewith he or they shall so stand charged, according to the due course of law; which order shall be printed and published in the next *London Gazette*, and shall be forthwith transmitted to the sheriff of the county where the offence shall be committed, and shall, within six days after the receipt thereof be proclaimed by him, or his officers, between the hours of ten in the morning, and two in the afternoon, in the market-places upon the respective market-days, of two market-towns in the same county, near the place where such offence shall have been committed; and a true copy of such order shall be affixed upon some publick place in such market-towns; and in case such offender or offenders shall not surrender him or themselves, pursuant to such order of his Majesty, his heirs or successors, to be made in council as aforesaid, he or they so neglecting or refusing to surrender him or themselves as aforesaid, shall from the day appointed for his or their surrender as aforesaid, be adjudged, deemed and taken to be convicted and attainted of felony, and shall suffer the pains of death as in case of a person convicted and attainted by verdict and judgment of felony, without benefit of clergy; and that it shall be lawful to and for the court of king's bench, or the justices of *oyer* and *terminer*, or general gaol-delivery for the county, where the offence is sworn in such information to have been committed, upon producing to them such order in council, under the seal of the said council, to award execution against such offender and offenders, in such manner, as if he or they had been convicted and attainted in the said court of king's bench, or before such justices of *oyer* and *terminer*, or general gaol-delivery respectively.

V. And be it enacted by the authority aforesaid, That all and every person and persons, who shall, after the time appointed as aforesaid, for the surrender of any person or persons, so charged upon oath with any the offences aforesaid, be expired, conceal, aid, abet or succour, such person

Marginal notes:

Justices to return informations to a secretary of state,

who is to lay the same before the King and council, who may make an order for their surrender.

Persons not surrendring themselves pursuant to such order, deemed to be convicted, &c.

Persons abetting them, &c. deemed felons.

or persons, knowing him or them to have been so charged as aforesaid, and to have been required to surrender him or themselves, by such order or orders as aforesaid, being lawfully convicted thereof, shall be guilty of felony, and shall suffer death as in cases of felony, without benefit of clergy.

VI. Provided nevertheless, and it is hereby declared and enacted, That nothing herein contained shall be construed to prevent or hinder any judge, justice of the peace, magistrate, officer or minister of justice whatsoever, from taking, apprehending and securing, such offender or offenders, against whom such information shall be given, and for requiring whose surrender such order in council shall be made as aforesaid, by the ordinary course of law; and in case such offender or offenders, against whom such information, and for requiring whose surrender such order in council shall be made as aforesaid, shall be taken and secured in order to be brought to justice, before the time shall be expired, within which he or they shall be required to surrender him or themselves, by such order in council as aforesaid, that then in such case no further proceeding shall be had upon such order made in council against him or them so taken and secured as aforesaid, but he or they shall be brought to trial by due course of law; any thing herein before contained to the contrary in any wise notwithstanding.

*Offenders appre-
hended within the
time limited by
order of council,
shall be tried
according to law.*

VII. And be it enacted by the authority aforesaid, That from and after the first day of *June* one thousand seven hundred and twenty-three, the inhabitants of every hundred, within that part of the kingdom of *Great Britain* called *England*, shall make full satisfaction and amends to all and every the person and persons, their executors and administrators, for the damages they shall have sustained or suffered by the killing or maiming of any cattle, cutting down or destroying any trees, or setting fire to any house, barn or out-house, hovel, cock, mow or stack of corn, straw, hay or wood, which shall be committed or done by any offender or offenders against this act; and that every person and persons, who shall sustain damages by any of the offences last mentioned, shall be and are hereby enabled to sue for and recover such his or their damages, the sum to be recovered not exceeding the sum of two hundred pounds, against the inhabitants of the said hundred, who by this act shall be made liable to answer all or any part thereof; and that if such person or persons shall recover in such action, and sue execution against any of such inhabitants, all other the inhabitants of the hundred, who by this act shall be made liable to all or any part of the said damage, shall be rateably and propor-

*Hundred charge-
able for damage
sustained in
maiming cattle,
&c.*

tionably taxed, for and towards an equal contribution for the relief of such inhabitant, against whom such execution shall be had and levied; which tax shall be made, levied and raised, by such ways and means, and in such manner and form, as is prescribed and mentioned for the levying and raising damages recovered against inhabitants of hundreds in cases of robberies, in and by an act, intituled. *An act for the following hue and cry*, made in the twenty-seventh year in the reign of Queen *Elizabeth*.

27 Eliz. c.13.

VIII. Provided nevertheless, That no person or persons shall be enabled to recover any damages by virtue of this act, unless he or they by themselves, or by their servants, within two days after such damage or injury done him or them by any such offender or offenders as aforesaid, shall give notice of such offence done and committed unto some of the inhabitants of some town, village, or hamlet, near unto the place where any such fact shall be committed, and shall within four days after such notice, give in his, her or their examination upon oath, or the examination upon oath of his, her or their servant or servants, that had the care of his or their houses, out-houses, corn, hay, straw or wood, before any justice of the peace of the county, liberty or division, where such fact shall be committed, inhabiting within the said hundred where the said fact shall happen to be committed, or near unto the same, whether he or they do know the person or persons that committed such fact, or any of them; and if upon such examination it be confessed, that he or they do know the person or persons that committed the said fact, or any of them, that then he or they so confessing, shall be bound by recognizance to prosecute such offender or offenders by indictment, or otherwise, according to the laws of this realm.

Persons injured to give notice within two days after the offence committed,

and to be examined within four days after notice, touching their knowledge of the offenders.

IX. Provided also, and be it further enacted, by the authority aforesaid, That where any offence shall be committed against this act, and any one of the said offenders shall be apprehended, and lawfully convicted of such offence, within the space of six months after such offence committed, no hundred, or any inhabitants thereof, shall in any wise be subject or liable to make any satisfaction to the party injured, for the damages he shall have sustained; any thing in this act to the contrary notwithstanding.

Hundred not liable, if the offender is convicted within six months, &c.

X. Provided also, That no person, who shall sustain any damage by reason of any offence to be committed by any offender contrary to this act, shall be thereby enabled to sue, or bring any action against any inhabitants of any hundred, where such offence shall be committed, except the party or

Action to be commenced within a year after the offence.

parties sustaining such damage, shall commence his or their action or suit within one year after such offence shall be committed.

XI. And for the better and more effectual discovery of the offenders above-mentioned, and bringing them to justice, be it enacted by the authority aforesaid, That it shall and may be lawful to and for any justice of the peace, to issue his warrant to any constable, headborough, or other peace officer, thereby authorizing such constable, headborough, or other peace-officer, to enter into any house, in order to search for venison stolen or unlawfully taken, contrary to the several statutes against deer-stealers, in such manner, as by the laws of this realm such justice of the peace may issue his warrant to search for stolen goods.

Justices may issue warrants to search for stolen venison.

XII. And be it further enacted by the authority aforesaid, That if any person or persons shall apprehend, or cause to be convicted any of the offenders above-mentioned, and shall be killed, or wounded so as to lose an eye or the use of any limb, in apprehending or securing, or endeavouring to apprehend or secure any of the offenders above-mentioned, upon proof thereof made at the general quarter-sessions of the peace for the county, liberty, division or place, where the offence was or shall be committed, or the party killed, or receive such wound, by the person or persons so apprehending, and causing the said offender to be convicted, or the person or persons so wounded, or the executors or administrators of the party killed, the justices of the said sessions shall give a certificate thereof to such person or persons so wounded or to the executors or administrators of the person or persons so killed, by which he or they shall be entitled to receive of the sheriff of the said county the sum of fifty pounds, to be allowed the said sheriff in passing his accounts in the exchequer; which sum of fifty pounds the said sheriff is hereby required to pay within thirty days from the day on which the said certificate shall be produced and shewn to him, under the penalty of forfeiting the sum of ten pounds to the said person or persons to whom such certificate is given, for which said sum of ten pounds, as well as the said sum of fifty pounds, such person may and is hereby authorized to bring an action upon the case against such sheriff, as for money had and received to his or their use.

Persons killed or wounded in apprehending offenders, to be rewarded.

XIII. *And whereas the shortness of the time within which prosecutions for offences against the statute made in the third and fourth years of the reign of their late majesties King William and Queen Mary, intituled,* An act for the more effectual discovery and punishment of deer-stealers, *ar*

3 & 4 W. & M. c.10.

limited to be commenced, has been a great encouragement to offenders; be it therefore enacted by the authority aforesaid, That any prosecution for any offence against the said statute, shall or may be commenced within three years from the time of the offence committed, but not after.

Prosecutions may be commenced within three years after offence committed.

XIV. And for the better and more impartial trial of any indictment or information, which shall be found commenced or prosecuted for any of the offences committed against this act, be it enacted by the authority aforesaid, That every offence that shall be done or committed contrary to this act, shall and may be enquired of, examined, tried and determined in any county within that part of the kingdom of *Great Britain* called *England*, in such manner and form, as if the fact had been therein committed; provided, That no attainder for any of the offences made felony by virtue of this act, shall make or work any corruption of blood, loss of dower, or forfeiture of lands or tenements, goods or chattels.

Such offences may be tried in any county.

Attainder not to work corruption of blood, &c.

XV. And be it further enacted by the authority aforesaid, That this act shall be openly read at every quarter-sessions, and at every leet or law-day.

This act, where to be read.

XVI. And be it further enacted by the authority aforesaid, That this act shall continue in force from the first day of *June* one thousand seven hundred and twenty-three, for the space of three years, and from thence to the end of the then next session of parliament, and no longer.

Farther continued by 24 Geo. 2. c.57.

XVII. And be it further enacted by the authority aforesaid, That if any venison, or skin of any deer, shall be found in the custody of any person or persons, and it shall appear that such person or persons bought such venison or skin of any one, who might be justly suspected to have unlawfully come by the same, and does not produce the party of whom he bought it, or prove upon oath the name and place of abode of such party, that then the person or persons who bought the same, shall be convicted of such offence, by any one or more justice or justices of the peace, and shall be subject to the penalties inflicted for killing a deer, in and by the statute made in the third and fourth year of the reign of their late majesties King *William* and Queen *Mary*, intituled, *An act for the more effectual discovery and punishment of deer-stealers.*

3 & 4 W. & M. c.10.

Appendix 2
Alexander Pope and the Blacks

i.

In *The Times Literary Supplement* of August and September 1973 Professor Pat Rogers and I outlined our independent discoveries of the fact that Charles Rackett, the poet's brother-in-law, was accused of being a Berkshire Black.[1] Although we interpreted the evidence in different ways, there is little dispute between us as to the rather slender set of facts which make this evidence up. It may be useful to rehearse these facts again.

First, there is an abstract of the deposition of Thomas Sawyer, under-keeper of Swinley Walk in Windsor Forest, dated 27 October 1722 which is headed 'Account of Michael Racket's killing and dressing deer'.[2] This referred to three occasions (25 June, 30 June and 1 July 1722) on which the keeper had seen three men hunting deer; on the third occasion Sawyer watched them kill a calf, followed them back to Hall Grove near Bagshot (the Rackett home), and found there Michael Rackett and two servants, James Goddard (or Gosden) and Daniel Legg, dressing the calf. Sawyer asked to speak to Michael's father, Charles, who 'begged deponent not to take notice of it, offering him a guinea'. Below this abstract there is a list of eleven Berkshire Blacks all of whom got into very serious trouble in May 1723. The list is in another hand, and was probably set down at a later date, when informations were coming to hand. The list includes Rackett senior, Michael Rackett and the two servants. Beside Michael's name is written 'absent'.

---

1. Pat Rogers, 'A Pope family scandal', *The Times Literary Supplement*, 31 August 1973, p. 1005; E. P. Thompson, 'Alexander Pope and the Windsor Blacks', *The Times Literary Supplement*, 7 September 1973, pp. 1031–2.
2. SP35.33, fo. 102.

This abstract is the only detailed evidence as to the affair which survives in the state papers. There is also a subsequent summary of it, among other notes on deer-stealers, which enlarges the accusation to 'Mr. Rackett, his Son and his Servants Horses & Dogs frequently were seen hunting and maliciously destroying the Deer in Windsor Forest . . .'[1] The witnesses to this were Sawyer and (for a subsequent occasion) William Clements, an accused Black who turned King's evidence.

There are one or two other passing mentions of Racketts. The most interesting is in 'A List of the Blacks Taken by Capt. Brereton', dated 15 May 1723. Overleaf are some hastily jotted notes, probably by Delafaye, of further accused and of evidences.[2] This series of notes is difficult to interpret; in my reading the word 'Jacobites' is scribbled, not at the head of the list, but beside the first name – 'Mr Ragget of Hall Grove near Bagshot, worth £20,000 & his son Michael, his 2 Servants and Horses and Dogs'. The next man on the list, James Barlow, the innkeeper, is also accused of being a Jacobite, and against two others in the list of nine names there is jotted 'suspicion of High Treason'. Clements, who turned evidence, is one of the nine.

The warrant for the arrest of Rackett, Michael, his son, and their two servants is dated 18 May.[3] Charles Rackett and the two servants were taken up by Baptist Nunn (acting with the help of soldiers) on 19–20 May.[4] Goddard and Legg, the servants, were committed on 21 May, and Charles Rackett was not, it seems, committed but was bound over to appear at the Court of King's Bench on 25 May.[5] He was bailed in £500, with sureties of £250 each provided by Richard Pottenger and Colonel James Butler.[6]

We know little more than this. The hardest evidence in the case appears to be against Michael, the son, and not against Charles. While the father was a suspected Jacobite, and was believed to have hunted the forest, Sawyer could only prove that he had offered to buy him off with a guinea

1. SP35.47, fo. 72.   2. SP35.43, fo. 23.

3. SP44.81, fo. 261. The warrant was for night-hunting with arms and in disguise – the offence made capital by the old act of Henry VII, recently revived by Proclamation; see above, p. 58.

4. T1.244, (63).   5. SP44.8, fos. 251, 258.

6. Richard Pottenger was married to a cousin of Pope's, and hence was related to the Racketts: see George Sherburn, *The Early Career of Alexander Pope*, New York, 1963, p. 29. Pottenger was Recorder of Reading and became M.P. for Reading in 1727. James Butler was (Professor Rogers thinks) one of the Butler clan of the Jacobite Duke of Ormonde and of his brother, Charles Butler, Earl of Arran, of Bagshot Park (see above, p. 110). When Pope had visited Hall Grove in 1717 he also paid a call on Lady Arran and Colonel Butler at Bagshot Park: see *The Correspondence of Alexander Pope*, ed. George Sherburn, Oxford, 1956, I, pp. 427–8.

(a familiar forest procedure). The other witness, Clements, himself lay in danger of indictment, and would have carried less weight. But Michael was in serious trouble. I think it a safe assumption, from the 'absent' beside his name in one list, and from the fact that although the Secretary of State's warrant was issued for his arrest he appears in none of the lists of arrested men, that he had – like many other accused – become a fugitive.

We are now on the grounds of inference. Most of the other prisoners bailed at about the same time remained under active prosecution. Barlow, the Jacobite innkeeper, bailed on the same day as Rackett and in the same high recognisances (£500 and two sureties of £250), still had the charges hanging over his head as late as 1729.[1] Thus on 25 May there was an intention to bring Charles Rackett to trial – or perhaps to threaten to do so in the absence of his son.

It seems that no trial ensued. The evidence is largely negative. Cracherode, the Treasury Solicitor, prepared in each law term statements of the causes under official prosecution. Such a statement, dated 14 June 1723,[2] lists a number of accused Blacks – some of them fugitives – but omits any mention of either Rackett. Successive statements over the next two or three years do not include them. It might therefore seem that Charles Rackett faced a serious threat of prosecution on 25 May; but by 14 June he had somehow got 'off the hook'.

We could also suppose that he escaped prosecution through the urgent representations of his brother-in-law. Even through a muffled press, one can detect that the gossip about Rackett and Pope was going around. Thus the *London Journal* (25 May) evidently confused the father and son: noting that some of the accused Blacks had evaded arrest, it added, 'among them one Mr. R— a gentleman of good estate; they tell us he is brother-in-law to the famous Mr. P—'. The same confusion of Charles and Michael may possibly lie beneath a report in *Applebee's Original Weekly Journal* (also 25 May): among those seized as Blacks are some 'of considerable substance; and ... one now in Newgate is, beyond contradiction, of a very reputable family in Berkshire, and heir at law to a valuable fortune; and great application is making to men in power in his favour'.[3]

If Pope was making this 'great application' it would be of interest to know which channel of influence he chose. For legal help he is likely to

1. See above, pp. 90–91.   2. T1.243 (1).

3. Professor Rogers has pointed out to me that this report first appeared in the *Daily Journal*, 22 May 1723, and there mentioned 'three' as being of 'considerable substance'. The *Whitehall Evening Post*, 15 June (copied in *Newcastle Weekly Courant*, 22 June) reports that two messengers had been dispatched 'in quest of two gentlemen of considerable Fortunes that are charged with belonging to the Blacks'.

have turned to his friend William Fortescue. But some greater interest was needed. *Habeas corpus* was then in suspension and actions against the Blacks were being carried forward directly on the authority of the Secretaries of State – Townshend, until he went with the King to Hanover at the end of May, and thereafter, and with great vigour, by Walpole. Pope was not yet on terms to dine with Walpole (as he was to be in several years). But he could have enlisted the aid of Viscount Harcourt, with whom he was at that time on cordial terms, and who was one of the Lords Justices of the Regency Council in the King's absence. On 21 June he wrote to Harcourt: 'You have done me many & great favours, and I have a vast deal to thank you for.'[1]

At any rate, it appears that Charles Rackett was back at Hall Grove in July 1723. Pope wrote to him (July 13): 'Dear Brother, – Every day past, we had a designe to see yourself & my Sister, at Hallgrove.' Mrs Pope, aged eighty-one, wished to make the journey as well, but her poor health and the 'excessive dry weather' was delaying the journey. 'If any of you can come this way, we hope to see you, & very much desire it . . . Pray be assured of our hearty Loves & Services.'[2]

But this evidence is not conclusive. And the other possibilities should be stated. First, Rackett could have been proceeded against, not by the Treasury Solicitor, but – as were other offenders – by forest officials at the Assizes. In this event the case could well have been held over (as were others) until the spring or summer of 1724, and it is possible that the records have (with other Black records) been lost.[3] Second, Rackett could have skipped his bail, or he could have been advised (by Pope?) to leave the country. This could explain a reference in a letter from Pope to Michael Rackett some years later to 'the Sums of money and Bonds' which his father 'took away with him before he Dyed'.[4] I think this possibility unlikely, although the reference still remains to be explained. Third, the threat of prosecution could have been kept hanging, for a year or two, or indefinitely, above his head.

It is this third possibility which seems most likely. Although both Racketts disappear from the records, the name of at least one of his servants, Daniel Legg, does not. Baptist Nunn's expenses account records

1. Sherburn, *The Correspondence of Alexander Pope*, II, p. 175. But the letter goes on to thank Harcourt for an even greater favour – his intercession on behalf of Bolingbroke.

2. ibid., II, p. 181. This letter is undated as to year, and has been placed by the editor in 1723 on only slender evidence.

3. If two other undated letters of Pope were to be placed in 1724 these could suggest that one of the Racketts could have been tried at Oxfordshire Assizes in that year. See ibid., II, pp. 80, 172. But it seems most unlikely that no other evidence would have survived.

4. ibid., IV, pp. 160–61.

for 11 June 1723: 'Before Mr. Hayes wth Mr. Racketts man for conviction ab^{t} killing deer in forest expences 0.4.6.'[1] This suggests that one of the two servants (perhaps James Goddard or Gosden) was summarily convicted before a Berkshire magistrate. (His penalty was perhaps not severe, since Justice Hayes was no enthusiast for forest law, and in October Walpole wrote directly to him, reproving him for his 'faint prosecution' of the Blacks.)[2] But the case against Rackett's other servant did not end here. Assize papers for 1724 include the recognisances for five offenders who were bound over to appear as evidences against other Blacks who (one must presume) were regarded as even greater offenders. Thomas Hambledon and James Stedman were bound over to appear as evidences against the fugitive William Shorter 'and others', William Terry to appear against John Plumbridge (another Black fugitive), James Barnet to appear against Charles Simmonds (another fugitive, possibly of genteel status),[3] and (the first of these recognisances) William Clements of 'Winsum' (or Windlesham) Surrey, *agricola*, was bound over to give evidence against 'Daniel Legg and others concerning certain misdemeanours by them committed'. This recognisance was drawn by the undersecretary, Charles Delafaye, on 16 August 1723; bail was in £200, with two securities at £50 each, one of whom was the trusty Baptist Nunn.[4] These recognisances were (it seems) taken out once again in February 1724, when the evidences were bound over to appear at the next Assizes for Berkshire.[5] But the recognisances were kept securely in the hands of central government: of Delafaye or of the Treasury Solicitor, whose clerk did not dispatch them into the keeping of the Berkshire Clerk of Assize until mid-July 1724.[6]

Thus Rackett's man was being accorded similar treatment to that afforded to William Shorter, the 'King' of the Berkshire Blacks: for at least fifteen months a very serious charge was kept hanging above his head. In the formula 'Daniel Legg and others' it is difficult not to read in the names of Charles and Michael Rackett; and this procedure was being supervised by Walpole, with his customary attention to detail, through the agency of Delafaye, Baptist Nunn and the Treasury Solicitor. If Daniel Legg was never brought to trial it may have been because Walpole found it to be more serviceable to keep him on ice.

But, where, in all this, is the case against young Michael? The other Black fugitives end up, after a year or two in Cracherode's lists, with the

1. T1.244 (63). 2. See above, p. 79. 3. See above, p. 88 n.2.
4. Assi. 5.44 (ii). 5. SP44.8, fo. 334.
6. The Clerk of Assize has left a note with these recognisances: 'received these five recognisances of Mr. Delafaye's the 13th of July 1725 from Mr. Cratchrode's clerke & not before'.

note that proceedings of outlawry will be taken against them. The puzzle is that Michael's name is not among them. He appears to have lived abroad for the next sixteen and more years, and he has afforded to Pope scholars and to the learned editor of Pope's correspondence some puzzles. It has generally been assumed that he lived abroad to escape his debts.

We can construct something of his situation from two letters from his uncle: the first to an unidentified duke, 2 September 1731, the second a detailed business letter, 22 January 1739.[1] The first concerns a proposed lease for the Hall Grove house. Charles Rackett had died in 1728. But it seems probable that the Racketts had given up their Hall Grove house two or three years before this date.[2] From the first letter it is evident that Pope was trying to help his half-sister (Mrs Rackett) to lease the house to the duke and the land to a farmer. Difficulties had arisen because the Rackett estate was in fact vested upon Michael, her son, and was perhaps also entailed upon his two younger brothers. Pope explains that drawing up a proper lease will take a little time, since his nephew, Michael, is abroad, and has left his mother to 'transact all his affairs' for 'many years', acting for him by power of attorney. Michael is in his mother's debt 'for her jointure & a farther sum of money', but Pope hastens to add that for this reason his nephew acts 'in all things with utmost complyance & tenderness to her . . .' It is clear that Michael's prolonged absence, and the attendant legal complications, are frightening off prospective tenants from both house and land.

Pope's letter to his nephew, over seven years later, continues the story of Hall Grove. The Rackett estates have been terribly impaired by 'Mortgages, Law Suits, and by your Father's Neglect, as well as by the Sums of money and Bonds he took away with him before he Dyed'. Although Michael had sought to execute a deed transferring Hall Grove to his mother, 'the Laws here against Papists render it Ineffectual'. 'Compares Executors' have 'taken out an *Outlawry* against you'; by which means, 'the Moment my Sister Dyes, they will inevitably Enter upon the Estate and Receive the Rents in your Stead, till all the Debt is pay'd'. This debt is 'now near £800 principal and Interest'. Pope advises his nephew to sell the reversion to the estate to a protestant, 'which sale will be good notwithstanding the Laws against papists; and notwithstanding your OutLawry'. From the money received, Michael may obtain the necessary

---

1. Sherburn, *The Correspondence of Alexander Pope*, III, pp. 223–4 and IV, pp. 160–61.

2. In 1731 Pope said that Hall Grove had been leased to a Mr Butler: ibid., III, p. 223. The Verderers' Books (LR3.3) show that the Forty Days Court on 2 May 1726 granted a licence to George Butler of Hall Grove to shoot in Windsor Forest. I have not found out the degree of relationship, if any, of George Butler to James Butler, who was Rackett's security.

£150 'for your present purpose of purchasing in the Army', and a surplus to be put to use in England 'or otherwise in ffrance'.

There are difficulties in interpreting these documents, which involve simultaneously legal points of entail, debt, outlawry and the 'Laws here against Papists'. Process of outlawry against a fugitive might lie for trespass with force of arms (Michael's supposed offence in 1723), and outlawry for a misdemeanour could bring with it forfeiture of goods and chattels. (No such forfeiture could take place while the estate remained settled upon Mrs Rackett, in jointure.) On the other hand, Michael appears to have a debt of some £800 (which would probably have descended upon him from the impoverished estate), and the process of outlawry could arise from this. In theory, no such process was good if the debtor was out of the country; it could (if taken) be upset by a writ of error, with the plaintiff carrying costs.[1] I can find no explanation which exactly fits the letter. Pope's references to outlawry could carry two different meanings: (a) Michael was already an outlaw, as a fugitive from justice, and (b) his creditors had taken out a process of outlawry against him for debt. The purchase of a commission in 'the Army' (one might note) did not necessarily indicate the British army. Michael could possibly have been enlisting (as did other Jacobite émigrés) in the French.

Certain facts about the Rackett case do, however, seem clear. First, the family finances suffered some catastrophe, which can probably be dated from 1723. Charles Rackett, already beset by the additional punitive tax which Walpole levied upon Catholics in that year, took measures to secure his wife's future by settling an annuity upon her, secured by a loan (or investment) of £1,100 to Lady Carrington at 5 per cent.[2] Payment of this interest (£55 p.a.) commenced in October 1723. Within ten years the family's reputed £20,000 had tumbled to this annuity, an unleasable Hall Grove, and a heap of debts and claims. Second, Michael Rackett kept very clear of England; he could not even pay a brief visit to the country at a time when his presence could have sorted out awkward legal tangles, and he left all such matters in his mother's hands, under the advice of Pope.

We should, at this point, ask more carefully: who exactly were the Racketts, in what degree of relationship did they stand to the poet, and

1. William Holdsworth, *History of English Law*, 1966 edn, III, p. 70; IX, p. 255.

2. Details of this are in an unsigned note in the *Athenaeum*, 30 May 1857, pp. 693-5, based on accounts of Lady Carrington in the author's possession. Lady Carrington, a fellow Catholic and a relation of Pope's friend, John Caryll, was at that time living in Paris: Brit. Mus. Add. MSS 28,238. Many English Catholics avoided punitive taxation by investing funds in France, and Lady Carrington appears to have arranged such matters. Thus we need not suppose that Charles Rackett had taken himself to Paris, although there remains that unexplained reference to the sums of money and bonds which he 'took away with him before he Dyed'.

what claims may they have had upon him? Little is known on the first point. The poet's father was twice married, and Magdalen (who married Charles Rackett) was a child of the first mother, Alexander of the second. Pope's half-sister must have been nine years older than he was, perhaps a little more. It is easy for the twentieth-century mind, which regards kinship obligations lightly, to assume that the relationship was a distant and casual one. This is an error. Eighteenth-century kinship reciprocities and obligations were normally more imperative than our own. And to this certain important familial, cultural and economic facts must be added. Pope's mother had fostered Magdalen as a child, and it is clear from surviving scraps of correspondence that she kept a close interest in the Rackett family and visited (or contemplated visiting) Hall Grove into her eighties; Magdalen's children were the only grandchildren that Mrs Pope had or was likely to have. Pope and his half-sister had shared a few years of childhood in their Berkshire home (at Binfield) and there were not, on either side, any other surviving siblings. The Racketts were Pope's only close kin, and the quality of the relationship is expressed in a letter of as late as January 1740, when Pope, who was attempting to recoup his health in Bath, prepared to hurry back to London under 'the necessity of serving my next Relation immediately'. Michael still needed the £150 to purchase a commission – 'a great opportunity of making his fortune much easier' – and the money was needed within a fortnight. Pope proposed to borrow the money from Fortescue. He wished he could stay at Bath – 'But I cannot be wanting to my Sister's Son on this occasion'.[1]

The Racketts, then, were Pope's 'next relations' and acknowledged as such. And the family reciprocities may well have been stronger than that. Little is known of Pope's father, but it seems possible that he had been 'put to a merchant in Flanders', made 'a moderate fortune' perhaps dealing in 'Hollands wholesale', retiring to Windsor Forest at some time after the Revolution of 1688.[2] The house where the Pope family settled, Whitehill House in Binfield, had been bought at first (in 1695) by Charles Rackett of Hammersmith, who sold it to Pope's father (at the same price) in 1698.[3] This was, perhaps, the time at which Rackett moved to Hall Grove[4] and

1. Sherburn, *The Correspondence of Alexander Pope*, IV, p. 215. Pope seems to have obtained the loan of £150 in the end from Ralph Allen of Bath.

2. Sherburn, *The Early Career of Alexander Pope*, p. 31; Joseph Spence, *Observations, Anecdotes &c*, ed. J. M. Osborn, Oxford, 1966, I, p. 7.

3. Sherburn, *The Early Career of Alexander Pope*, p. 36.

4. As late as 1689 Hall Grove was perhaps in the possession of Thomas Bullock, who was presented at the Forty Days Court on 25 July (LR3.2) for felling its coppice. This reference is of interest since it shows that although Hall Grove was in Surrey, the forest courts still claimed that it lay within the Forest of Windsor. If such claims continued to be exercised in Charles Rackett's time it might help to explain his involvement with Blacking.

the two men were obviously already acquainted. Moreover, both men were Catholics, and they appear to have shared the services of at least one Catholic priest.[1] This would have greatly strengthened normal familial bonds. Finally, it seems quite possible that Rackett and Pope senior were linked by their commercial activities. Protracted Chancery cases suggest that young Michael Rackett was apprenticed in 1715 to a merchant connected with the Dutch West India Company, perhaps based on Antwerp.[2] This could suggest that the foundation of both Rackett and Pope fortunes lay in some part of the Flanders trade, and that the two men could even have been business partners. Magdalen's marriage to her father's partner, of the same proscribed faith, would be a natural way of cementing the alliance. And Michael, if he was 'put to a merchant in Flanders', would have been following in the steps of his father-in-law.

Thus the Rackett–Pope relationship was a close one, and one which the poet fully respected. Critics have been a little impatient with the Rackett family who are seen (through surviving correspondence) as only a drag upon the poet's genius; for Pope was concerned, over many years, with the financial problems and legal entanglements which Magdalen inherited from her husband, and he was also at pains to try and help Michael's two younger brothers in their careers – careers made the more insecure by anti-Catholic legislation. Professor Pat Rogers, who is the most severe of contemporary critics, dismisses Charles Rackett as 'a somewhat inadequate man', refers to Charles's 'three troublesome sons', and concludes that 'for years the Racketts were a millstone round the poet's neck'.[3] Against this we must set Pope's letters and his actions. The letter which outlines the appalling state of the Rackett finances, of January 1739, concludes: 'Believe me, dear Nephew, Glad of any occasion to serve you, and at all times very Sincerely and Affectionatly Your Faithfull and real Servant.'[4] The poet's accurate and economical pen would not have run on so far unless impelled by genuine feeling. Similarly Pope was at pains to assure the unidentified duke in 1731 that his nephew 'is a very honest and tractable man'. There is at no point in these letters the least hint of disapproval or rebuke (except as to Charles Rackett's 'neglect'), as there

1. One priest, who helped to educate young Pope, was named John Banister, but I know of no evidence which relates him to the Finchampstead Bannisters, for whom see above pp. 112–13: Spence, op. cit., i, pp. 7–10.

2. Chancery proceedings, C11.2224.33 and C11.2618.16 suggest that Michael Rackett was apprenticed with one Magbrucci, a merchant of London, from June 1715 to December 1720, when Magbrucci found no work for him 'and began to be unkind to him'.

3. See *The Times Literary Supplement*, 31 August 1973 and Pat Rogers, 'The Waltham Blacks and the Black Act', *Historical Journal*, XVII, 3 (1974), p. 483.

4. Sherburn, *The Correspondence of Alexander Pope*, IV, p. 161.

must surely have been if we accept the view that the indebtedness of the family estates was due to Michael's extravagance.

I really do not know what underlies this story. But I will propose one possible solution. Power in this matter undoubtedly lay, in the summer of 1723, with Walpole. It is absolutely clear from the state papers that he was overseeing, and in detail, the campaign against the Blacks. And Walpole was a hard man to bargain with. He was by no means likely to have allowed a Catholic gentleman and a reputed Jacobite, against whom, and against whose son, he had a good case of association with Blacking, to go free without obtaining something in return. The father might be left unprosecuted; but some large sum of money might have been exacted for that, as well as an undertaking that the son remain an outlaw. Meanwhile the prosecutions might remain dormant. Michael, if in France,[1] might well have burned his fingers further in the Jacobite cause. Pope would not have regarded him the worse for that; he remained, throughout, the friend of Atterbury and of Bolingbroke. He would see his nephew as the actor in a rash, youthful escapade, and thereafter as the victim of 'the Laws against Papists' and of Hanoverian rancour.

But if any such deal were made, Walpole would stand to gain one other asset. He had two hostages to hold against Alexander Pope. Pope had seemed, in the early months of that deeply disaffected year, 1723, to be moving towards open criticism of the Walpole regime. He had given testimony on behalf of his friend, Francis Atterbury, the Jacobite Bishop of Rochester, when on trial in May before the House of Lords; and his correspondence with the Bishop, when imprisoned in the Tower, was well known. This can have pleased Walpole very little. But from June onwards – and until Charles Rackett's death in 1728 – Pope had to tread very warily. It is my impression that, for several years, he did.

ii.

So much for the Rackett affair. No doubt, in due course, more may come to light about the family's fortunes.[2] The immediate bearing of the affair, as it influenced Pope's relations with Walpole, must remain a matter of speculation. But we have also to consider the possible implications of these events as they bore upon the poet's imaginative life. Through much of his childhood and 'teens Pope was with his family at Binfield in the western part of the forest. This experience (which he never ceased to value) underlay much of his pastoral poetry. One of his earliest

1. There is as yet no clear evidence as to where Michael was.
2. More evidence may lie in Chancery records, whose complexity is such that I abandoned my own search.

major poems, published in 1713 when he was twenty-four, was 'Windsor Forest'.[1]

The first ninety-odd lines of the poem celebrate the harmony of the forest economy:

> Not *Chaos*-like together crush'd and bruis'd,
> But as the World, harmoniously confus'd:
> Where Order in Variety we see,
> And where, tho' all things differ, all agree.

This harmony is expressed not only in the variegated forms of natural beauty but in the adjustment of interests between hunters and farmers. Pope's point was given explicit political expression:

> Rich Industry sits smiling on the Plains,
> And Peace and Plenty tell, a STUART reigns.

The equilibrium established under Queen Anne is contrasted with the discord of earlier times:

> Not thus the Land appear'd in Ages past,
> A dreary Desart and a gloomy Waste,
> To Savage Beasts and Savage Laws a Prey,
> And Kings more furious and severe than they:
> Who claim'd the Skies, dispeopled Air and Floods,
> The lonely Lords of empty Wilds and Woods . . .

> In vain kind Seasons swell'd the teeming Grain,
> Soft Show'rs distill'd, and Suns grew warm in vain;
> The Swain with Tears his frustrate Labour yields,
> And famish'd dies amidst his ripen'd Fields.
> What wonder then, a Beast or Subject slain
> Were equal Crimes in a Despotick Reign;
> Both doom'd alike for sportive Tyrants bled,
> But while the Subject starv'd, the Beast was fed.

The explicit reference here to 'sportive Tyrants' is to William I and to the legend of his depopulation of the New Forest. But Pope was very probably encouraging readers to associate the names of William I and III, and was contrasting the harsh enforcement of the forest laws under William III with a sense of relief in the forest at the milder regimen of Anne.[2]

If an obtuse social historian may read the poem in a literal sense, this regimen was indeed mild. There are peaceful cottages, gathering flocks on the hills, yellow harvests amidst the sandy wilds. The 'vigorous Swains'

1. The first passages of the poem may have been written as early as 1707.
2. See J. R. Moore, 'Windsor Forest and William III', *Modern Language Notes*, LXVI, 1951, pp. 451-4.

are apparently pursuing lesser game (partridge, pheasant, hare, woodcock and fish) without restraint from the keepers. The forest youth join eagerly in the chase when the Queen turns out to hunt deer. Meanwhile, to give this harmony a more universal dimension, the 'earthly Gods' attend the Court at Windsor, while within the forest retired statesmen and scholars, like Pope's patron and friend Sir William Trumbull, could find retreat. The oaks of the forest themselves become symbols of Britain's imperial destiny, the timber for peaceful commerce which will knit the world into the same harmony. Meanwhile on 'Thames's shore' –

> . . . each unmolested Swain
> Shall tend the Flocks, or reap the bearded Grain:
> The shady Empire shall retain no Trace
> Of War or Blood, but in the Sylvan Chace,
> The Trumpets sleep, while chearful Horns are blown,
> And Arms employ'd on Birds and Beasts alone.

What occasions surprise is not that the poem embellishes reality but that it holds a remarkably close correspondence to it. As we have seen, the Court Books of the Verderers give an explicit quantitative index as to the mild enforcement of forest law in Anne's reign.[1] And the poet's observation may be more exact than that. For when he was about sixteen – and perhaps had already started work on the first part of the poem – he won the friendship of Sir William Trumbull of Easthampstead, who was for many years an elected Verderer. At one time Pope and his patron rode in the forest three or four days in each week – and one must suppose that Trumbull kept a paternal eye on forest regulations. Thus the image of an easily regulated harmony of interests may have been idealized, but it was nourished in genuine experience.

Pope was only an occasional visitor to the forest in the years after 1716 when the Hanoverian forest bureaucracy attempted to reimpose the full rigour of forest law. He is likely therefore to have been unprepared for the violence which erupted between 1721 and 1723. But he cannot have been surprised to observe the old conflict between foresters and officials reviving, nor to have noted the exacerbation of feelings between old Catholic or Tory families and Whig courtiers.[2] He would have had ample sources of information as to forest affairs, not only through the

1. See above, p. 46.
2. Howard Erskine-Hill has pointed out (*The Times Literary Supplement*, 14 September 1973, p. 1,056) that Pope could have learned from his friend John Caryll of his brush with Richard Norton in the Forest of Bere in 1716, in another case where disputes over game rights were exacerbated by anti-Catholic feelings. See also above, p. 138. On this occasion Norton went out of his way to advise Caryll's friend (and Pope's acquaintance) Robert Dormer that the papists should be quiet and keep to themselves:

Racketts, but through a network of old friends and associates.[1] His patron Sir William Trumbull had died, but Pope was probably still in touch with the Trumbull family which his friend (and collaborator in the *Odyssey*) Elijah Fenton joined, as tutor, in 1724. His Catholic friends, the Englefields of Whiteknights near Reading, were cousins to Sir Charles Englefield, the Catholic baronet who got into trouble for encouraging deer-stealers;[2] and the cousinship extended to Pope's lifelong friend, Martha Blount, the granddaughter of Anthony Englefield, from another forest village, Mapledurham. Undoubtedly he would have known – as his friend Swift did, at a far greater distance – the whole story of Thomas Power and of his provocations. And he would have known, better than we can know, what grievances against forest law his brother-in-law and nephews may have had.

It is in this context that we must guess at his reactions to the affair. Professor Pat Rogers has suggested that Charles Rackett's involvement in this criminal and Jacobite-tainted episode 'must have been a deeply shaming event for Pope'. Thereafter he had to suffer 'this skeleton in the family cupboard – Rackett, the Berkshire Black'. It was a 'lasting disgrace': 'But the dishonour was more than personal; it threatened Pope's entire artistic stance. He had forged from the sylvan haunts of his boyhood a symbol of rustic purity . . .' The forest was expressive 'of a kind of blessed retirement', and 'he had used the rapacious hunter-kings as an emblem of cruel despotism'. When Rackett the 'plunderer' was taken up, Pope's 'symbolism collapsed around him'. 'His brother-in-law had polluted one of the most cherished spots in his imaginative world.' One is left only to admire the 'striking testimony to his domestic loyalty' which Pope continued to show towards his sister's troublesome sons.

We are on the grounds of inference again. But I think that this is to get the matter upside-down. It is true that the episode polluted one of the most cherished spots in Pope's imaginative world. But it was not Charles Rackett, nor even the Blacks, but people like Thomas Power, Baptist Nunn, Judge Page and the Hanoverian Black-hunters generally who were the agents. And, beyond this again, the forest as an image of harmony and of reconciled interests was utterly polluted by the discord and bloodshed of the new regime.

'there must be no thoughts of medling and spreading and getting folks together . . . the tyde will turne, and the closer you keep together the better': Brit. Mus. Add. MSS 28,237.

1. See L. Fitzgerald, 'Alexander Pope's Catholic Neighbours', *Month*, CXLV (1925), pp. 328–33. But on the Catholic culture and its general context, see especially Howard Erskine-Hill's study of the Caryll family in *The Social Milieu of Alexander Pope*, New Haven, 1975.

2. See above, pp. 102–3.

One need not propose that the poet had any active sympathy with Blacking. But one does note that several men who were Black targets or actors in the prosecution of the Blacks turn up as subsequent targets for Pope's satire; these include Cadogan, Governor Thomas Pitt, Sir Francis Page and Paxton.[1] Pope kept on friendly terms with one only of the prosecuting cast, Lord Cobham; but Cobham was replaced as Governor of Windsor Castle in June 1723, and throughout the earlier months of the year Colonel Negus, his deputy, appears to have performed his duties.

All this is only indirect, inconclusive evidence. It confirms only that the general run of Pope's values would have been against the courtiers, the fashionable and moneyed settlers in the forest, the judges and prosecutors. But if we look again at the symbolism of 'Windsor Forest' we may infer with more precision what Pope's feelings might have been. The world of his adolescent poem symbolizes, as we have seen, a coincidence of variety in harmony, an equilibrium both in the natural and human worlds. This world of harmonized interests – farmers and hunters, scholars and courtiers – is specifically contrasted with that of William I (and perhaps William III) in which 'savage' forest laws were exercised in the interests of royal sport, frustrating the labour of the farmers, feeding beasts while subjects starved –

> What wonder then, a Beast or Subject slain
> Were equal Crimes in a Despotick Reign . . .

By contrast the reign of 'a STUART' has brought peace and plenty, rich industry, and forest laws so lax that all enjoy the lesser game. The hunting horn can now seem 'chearful', and arms are 'employ'd on Birds and Beasts alone'.

Thus for 1713, when the poem was first published. But in 1723, turn where you would in Windsor Forest (the real forest), you could not but encounter that 'barbarous Discord' against which the whole of the poem had been an invocation. Those evil personifications whose everlasting exile had been invoked at the conclusion to the poem – 'pale Terror', 'gloomy Care', 'purple Vengeance', 'Persecution', 'Faction' and 'gasping Furies' thirsting for blood – found actual expression, centring upon the parish of Winkfield so well known to him from his rides with the Verderer, Trumbull, on the margins of which lay his old home, Binfield, East-hampstead Park and Hall Grove. The forests were once again a prey to 'savage laws', and the Black Act had indeed made 'a Beast or Subject slain' into 'equal crimes'. (In the next few years several men were indeed hanged for the offence of hunting deer in royal parks – and for doing it close to Pope's new homeland, at Richmond.) Moreover it was

1. See above, pp. 211, 213 n.3.

at Trumbull's old seat that Thomas Power had woven those provocations which had helped to bring men to the gallows. It might seem that a 'Despotick Reign' had returned once more.

It is not easy to conceive of a more terrible pollution of the image of harmony established in the poem. I doubt whether Pope would have felt, in 1723, shame or dishonour at this 'skeleton in the family cupboard'. He is more likely to have shared the feelings of Thomas Hearne, of Will Waterson, and of those juries which refused to convict. As for the poem itself, it was too late to rewrite that. Pope did, perhaps, allow one indication of his feeling to be glimpsed. In an early version of the poem lines 85-94 had read:

> Succeeding Monarchs heard the Subjects Cries,
> Nor saw displeas'd the peaceful Cottage rise.
> Then gathering Flocks on unknown Mountains fed,
> O'er sandy Wilds were yellow Harvests spread,
> The Forests wonder'd at th'unusual Grain,
> And secret Transport touch'd the conscious Swain.
> *Oh may no more a foreign master's rage*
> *With wrongs yet legal, curse a future age!*
> *Still spread, fair Liberty! thy heav'nly wings,*
> *Breath plenty on the fields, and fragrance on the springs.*

The four italicized lines had been discarded when the poem was first published, in favour of the more gummy and discreet couplet:

> Fair *Liberty*, *Britannia's* Goddess, rears
> Her chearful Head, and leads the golden Years.

But when Pope's *Works* were published (1736) he was at pains to put the lines back in a footnote. It was a prayer which had not been answered.

There is altogether too little to go on. But undoubtedly Pope was moved by unusually sombre feelings in 1723. Professor Sherburn found the years 1718-23 to be 'one of the most tranquil periods in Pope's life'. He dates the end of this tranquillity to the seizure of Pope's edition of the Duke of Buckingham's *Works*, on a suspicion of Jacobite passages.[1] This was in January 1723. The next months were preoccupied with the matter of Atterbury, Bishop of Rochester, and Pope's flaunted loyalty to him. And immediately upon Atterbury's sentence of banishment there came the blow of the Rackett crisis. May 1723 also saw the imposition of a punitive tax upon Catholics. On 2 June, Pope wrote to Judith Cowper: 'I have not wanted other Occasions of great melancholy (of which the

1. See Sherburn, *The Early Career of Alexander Pope*, p. 201; Pat Rogers, 'Pope and the Social Scene', *Alexander Pope*, ed. P. Dixon, 1972, p. 129.

least is the Loss of part of my Fortune by a late Act of Parliament).'[1]
The greatest of these (he told her) was the taking leave of his friend,
Atterbury. His mood remains sombre; on 14 July to Broome: 'Every
valuable, every pleasant thing is sunk in an ocean of avarice and corruption.
The son of a first minister is a proper match for a daughter of a late South
Sea director, – so money upon money increases, copulates, and multiplies,
and guineas beget guineas in *saecula saeculorum*.' The letter concludes:
'My body is sick, my soul is troubled, my pockets are empty, my time is
lost, my trees are withered, my grass is burned!'[2] And to Swift, in
August: 'The merry vein you knew me in, is sunk into a Turn of
Reflexion . . .' And, earlier in the same letter, 'Tis sure my particular ill
fate, that all those I have most lov'd & with whom I have most liv'd, must
be banish'd.'[3] The reference is evidently to Atterbury and to Bolingbroke,
and to his fears for Lord Peterborough. But those 'with whom I have
most liv'd' might carry a reference to the Racketts. At a deeper level the
episode could have turned Pope away, finally and decisively, from any
thought of the pastoral mode, and directed him more urgently towards
satire. And yet, although evidently working inside him, the satire was
delayed expression for several more years. It is customary to attribute this
to his preoccupation with the work on his Homer. But if we recall the
earlier suggestion that – at least until Charles Rackett's death – Pope
remained in some way a hostage to Walpole's favour, one may see his
predicament in a different way.

These questions should be pursued by better Pope scholars than myself.
But a social historian may be allowed to offer one suggestion to literary
scholars. Some critics appear to suppose, when they discuss the bitter
satires of the early Hanoverian decades, most of which come from a Tory
or near-Jacobite position which is both traditionalist and radical in its
humanist implications, that they are dealing with a literary form which
may only be understood by bringing in some notion of hyperbole. That is,

1. Sherburn, *The Correspondence of Alexander Pope*, II, p. 174. For a helpful summary
of the influence upon the poet of successive anti-Catholic measures, see Pat Rogers,
'Pope and the Social Scene', pp. 102–4.

2. Sherburn, *The Correspondence of Alexander Pope*, II, pp. 182–3.

3. ibid., II, pp. 184–5. We know the text of this letter only through a doubtful transcription. It is not impossible that Pope's reference in his original letter to Swift had
been more explicit than this. The transcriptions are unreliable, since they were often
amended or embellished by the poet for subsequent publication: an explicit reference to
the Rackett affair will certainly have been dropped. But we also have a (more reliable)
transcription of Swift's reply, which responds paragraph by paragraph to Pope's
original. His reply at this point is: 'I have often made the same remark with you of my
Infelicity in being so strongly attached to Traytors (as they call them) and Exiles, and
State Criminalls . . .': Sherburn, *The Correspondence of Alexander Pope*, II, p. 198.

the satirist no doubt had grievances (some of them petty and personal), but we are dealing with certain conventions and a certain style in which satire is pushed, for the sake of literary effect, to an extreme which bears little correspondence to the vices portrayed.

There is something in this, no doubt. But to work on only this one episode of the Blacks has turned up evidence enough as to the actualities of a spy-system, of blood-money, direct corruption and the callous manipulation of men and the purchase of principles. It becomes apparent that there was, for the political and economic losers, and for those Catholics or suspect Jacobites like the Rackett family, oppressed by –

> . . . certain laws, by sufferers thought unjust,
> Denied all posts of profit or of trust . . .

an alternative way of viewing the whole political process, in particular during the years of Walpole's ascendancy. In this view, the ascendant Hanoverian Whigs appeared as no more than a sort of state banditry. And the fact that such an alternative view was possible may mean that critics should review the assumption of hyperbole. Swift's comment on Power[1] was not, after all, made in consequence of his having been passed over for a favour, or of poor digestion, or even of anal fixation; it was an accurate and morally poised comment on an event which actually occurred. We should read some satires not as extravaganzas but in a more literal way – expertly flighted and with a shaft of solid information.

1. See above, p. 221.

Note on Sources

The character and possible limitations of this study can only be understood in the light of the sources employed, and the curious absences in these sources.

Public Record Office. In the main series of state papers (SP) a limited amount of correspondence survives, a few fragments of depositions, the Secretary of State's Warrant Books, the minutes of the Lords Justices of the Regency Council (and correspondence between Delafaye or Walpole in London and Townshend in Hanover, which occasionally refers to the Blacks). In reconstructing the government of the forests, this can be supplemented by materials in other classes; memoranda from all forests which touched upon financial matters survive in the Treasury papers, especially the in-letters (T1). There are a few relevant cases in the Court of Exchequer (E), very useful papers on Enfield Chase in the papers of the Duchy of Lancaster (DL), a few scraps survive on marginal cases in the records of the Court of King's Bench (KB), and bits here and there among the papers of the Crown Estate Commissioners (Crest.), the Forestry Commission (F), the Office of Land Revenue Records and Enrolments (LRRO), and of course in the Privy Council register (PC). Most important of all are the Verderers' Books for Windsor Forest, in the Exchequer papers, Office of the Auditors of the Land Revenue (LR); these include a record of presentments which arose regularly before the Forty Days Court or Court of Attachment, together with what seems to be a rough draft of the proceedings of the Swanimote Courts (when held). The final copy of these records was presumably sent under seal to the Chief Justice in Eyre, whose records I have not found.

While this is much, again and again the sources collapse just at the point where we should expect them to reveal most about the Blacks.

Assize papers (Assi.) are especially disappointing: little more survives than formal minutes (often with erroneous attributions of occupation etc.), one or two indictments in marginal cases, and a few recognisances. But cases against the Blacks were state prosecutions, mounted by the Treasury Solicitor, and one might have expected records to have survived in this office. They do not appear to have done so, although it should be said that TS records have had a curious history, even in this century. The other place where these records might be expected to lie is in the Court of King's Bench, which as a court of record covering all offences *vi et armis* against the King or his officers, sometimes preserved treason, sedition, riot materials etc. in its *baga de secretis* (KB 8). But the Black records, including the records of the Special Commission at Reading, are not here either.

What is missing? Essentially – and in addition to the Crown briefs, indictments, depositions, etc. – all the central materials as to Black infiltration and surveillance. If it were not for the survival of Baptist Nunn's extraordinary expenses claim (among Treasury in-letters) we would not know of his activity in placing spies among the Blacks at all, nor of his regular contacts with Colonel Negus and with Walpole. None of Parson Power's informations survive; nothing much as to Colonel Negus's dossiers; none of the depositions as to Barlow's or Fellows's possible Jacobite activities. That a great deal of such material existed is confirmed by an entry in the Secretary of State's Warrant Book (SP44.81, fo. 236) which lists a hefty bundle of papers forwarded to the Attorney-General; these include informations of soldiers and others as to Richard Fellows enlisting men for the Blacks, records of the examinations of Blacks before the Secretary of State, the affadavits and 'relations' of Blacks who turned King's evidence, three 'transactions with Power' (17 and 23 July and 1 August 1723), supplementary affidavits and correspondence relating to Power, and, finally, a 'Memorandum of the Crimes charged against the Blacks'.

Can we assume that all these materials have been lost or destroyed? Very probably: I have inspected the extensive Hardwicke papers in the British Museum – Lord Hardwicke was, as Philip Yorke, Solicitor-General at this time, and shortly to become Attorney-General (when he would have inherited his predecessor's active papers). I can find nothing, and, while it is possible that I missed the relevant volume, this is unlikely, since the papers are in general in chronological order. It almost appears as if all Black materials have been weeded from his records. But the same is true, and in the most infuriating way, about the extensive Walpole papers in the Cholmondeley (Houghton) (C(H)) collection in the Cambridge University Library. Once again we come repeatedly to the edge of Black matters – a few papers on Enfield, Richmond, etc.– but there is silence on Blacking, on Charles Rackett, on Huntridge. Some weeding is suggested here also; and it is my tentative conclusion that all central records on the Blacks were held by the Treasury Solicitor (Cracherode, followed by Paxton) and eventually destroyed or lost. But a possibility still remains that they might surface at some time, either from some private collection, or else from among some uninspected legal papers from a subsequent decade; for the cases against some Blacks were held in suspension until the 1730s and Walpole was not a man to allow the destruction of incriminating evidence which might, at some future time, serve his uses.

Other Collections. The *Cholmondeley* (*Houghton*) and *Hardwicke* collections have already been mentioned: they proved to be disappointing. Nor have I been able to find any series of private papers, of magnates or of gentry in the disturbed districts, which offered central documentation. Once again, it is possible that, subsequent to this study, such sources may surface. The *Trumbull Correspondence* in the Berkshire Record Office revealed a little: but in 1723 Sir William Trumbull had died, and his son was a minor. The Berkshire Record Office, in its other collections, provided fragmentary insights into certain forest parishes. Of greater importance for the government of Windsor are the *Constable's Warrant Books*, preserved in the Queen's Library: while these include only business which is strictly official and formal, they contain memoranda from Colonel Negus, details of the appointment of all forest officers, etc., which, when put together with the Verderers' Books, allow a reconstruction to be made. But, for Windsor Forest, there are once again serious gaps in the records – gaps which drew critical comments as early as 1809, when the Parliamentary Commissioners inquired into the forest. In the case of the Hampshire forests no papers of Swanimote or other courts have come to light, although there is evidence that forest courts were still being held. Affairs there have been reconstructed largely from Treasury in-letters, supplemented by some materials in the Hampshire Record Office, including a few papers of the Norton family. Evidence as to ecclesiastical lands in Hampshire is more substantial: the accounts and papers of the *Bishopric of Winchester* (transferred to the Hampshire Record Office from the Ecclesiastical Commissioner's records at Millbank) can be supplemented by some *stewardship papers* of Bishop Trelawny's time (also transferred in recent years to the Hampshire Record Office from Farnham Castle) and by papers of the extensive holdings of the *Dean and Chapter of Winchester*, still housed in Winchester Cathedral. The facilities available for consulting the latter were limited, since extensive research would inconvenience the Dean and his staff. But the materials on Church lands in both places are excellent, and invite the attention of any scholar who wishes to reconstruct the finances and administration of the eighteenth-century Church. The correspondence of Archbishop Wake, in Christ Church, Oxford, threw a little more light on Sir Jonathan Trelawny. *Quarter-Sessional* records have been uninformative about Blacking in the major counties, but those which touch upon Farnham and Richmond, in the Surrey Record Office, are the fullest and most useful.

A number of other collections have been used, and their whereabouts should be clear from the acknowledgements and footnotes: while useful at this or that point, none offer central documentation on the Blacks. Only three other sources require a particular comment: among the family papers of the Right Honourable the Earl St Aldwyn, at Williamstrip Park, near Cirencester, there are some copied extracts from two reports of *Charles Withers*, the Surveyor-General of Woods and Forests, which appear to have survived in no other form. Charles Withers was one of the few officials of this parasitic period who appears to have taken his duties seriously: his tours of the forests were extensive, and his comments were observant. But unfortunately the copyist was more interested in extracting passages on other forests (Forest of Dean and New Forest), and unless the originals of these reports turn up, the observations on Berkshire and Hampshire forests do not survive.

Second, we have the one printed contemporary source of substantial value. This is the thirty-two page pamphlet, by an anonymous author, *The History of the Blacks of Waltham in Hampshire; and those under the like Denomination in Berkshire*, which was published by A. Moore in December 1723. Professor Pat Rogers (*Historical Journal*, XVII, 3 (1974), p. 466) feels able to attribute the authorship to Daniel Defoe, on inferential evidence. This is possible. The pamphlet, in any case, is not important as an independent source. The history is culled from the newspapers, especially, in the case of the Hampshire Blacks, from the correspondent of the *London Journal*. And the details of the seven condemned Hampshire men is not as full as that given in the Ordinary of Newgate's *Account*. But the author of the pamphlet did visit the condemned in Newgate, and he reports a little which is new.

Finally, some description is required of the *Waterson Books* which, while not providing information as to Blacking, do tell us something of the parish of Winkfield, and get us as close as we may ever get to the thoughts of one forest farmer. I was led to these by finding a curious manuscript book (referred to here as Waterson (Reading)) in the Reading Reference Library, in eighteenth-century script. The book (Reading Ref. BOR/D) had been savagely torn and defaced, with some 100 pages ripped out. From this I was led to the Ranelagh School at Bracknell, which holds other books and papers of the Reverend Will Waterson, its first headmaster. Here are kept two complete and undefaced memorandum books, which bear some kind of relationship to the defaced volume in the Reading Library. At first it looked as if the latter might be a copy of the former, made by some hand, and then the original defaced by some accident; or that Will Waterson, at the end of his life, made a fair copy of his own notes into the two Ranelagh Books and himself – as he proceeded – tore out the finished pages in the Reading Book.

Stricter examination revealed a different sequence, and these are my conclusions. The Reading Book is in fact Waterson's own memorandum book, commenced in 1727 or before and continued intermittently until he prepared, in his old age, the Ranelagh Books I and II, probably in 1755–6. Although the latter books represented a codification of materials in the former book, there is no evidence that Waterson tore out the sheets in the former while transcribing materials into the latter. In fact the original Reading memorandum book was passed on, when Waterson died in 1759, to his successor, the Reverend Timothy Wylde, who probably entered details of a perambulation of Winkfield in 1767.

In fact, both books contained much sensitive matter. As mentioned in Chapter 1 (pp. 49–50), Will Waterson, as parish priest and schoolmaster, felt it his duty to act as 'memory' to his parishioners, and to record all evidence which appertained to their institutions and rights. Materials in both books relate to the church, the parochial charities, the school, titles to parks and manors, forest laws and common rights. Waterson, at the end of his life, drew together all that he had gathered about parish institutions, drawing upon his earlier (Reading) memorandum book, and completing the two which are now at Ranelagh School. He had some notion of publishing the latter, and he certainly hoped that his information would continue to be used by the parishioners. But, equally, he suspected that his records might prove to be unwelcome to certain powerful persons, and in his will he left them to successive headmasters of the school, ordering that they be kept in a carefully locked chest, which was to be opened only in the presence of the Master. The living of Winkfield was in the gift of the Dean and Chapter of Salisbury, and hence Waterson was free from dependence upon local aristocratic or gentry interests. But he seems to have had good reasons for his anxiety. I suggest that after his death the Reading Book passed into the hands of some interested person and was deliberately and systematically defaced: among sections ripped out are those on Winkfield's common rights (the word 'turfs' survives on one torn margin), on the nobility and gentry's title to certain claimed privileges, on the parks, on the manor, and on tithe disputes with local gentry.

This much can be deduced from the context of surviving pages, and from words in torn margins. We must be grateful that the Ranelagh Books did not fall into the same hand, although these – compiled when Waterson was in his seventies and when the episode of Blacking was thirty years in the past – are probably of a more softened character than had been the original memoranda. But it is clear enough that *someone* had an interest in erasing Waterson's records. For there had been a little vandalization of the Winkfield parish register also. This register (Berks Rec. Off. D/P/51/1/4) contains in most years a place where Waterson entered a brief note of interesting events ('Not. Paroch.'). But the notes for the years 1723 and 1724 have been altogether erased, perhaps with a knife, and attempts to recover them with an ultra-violet reader have been unsuccessful. Since 1723 had been the year in which Waterson had had the sad duty of entering in the register the burial of John Gilbert, Leonard Thorne and Thomas Hatch, '*infurcati*', it is probable that the erased notes concerned the Blacks.

I have prepared a more detailed discussion of all these points, copies of which are held in the Berkshire Record Office and by the Headmaster of Ranelagh School, who will no doubt make them available to any researcher. Altogether Will Waterson's careful collection and preservation of the records of his parishioners' rights does credit to him in his dual profession as priest and as schoolmaster, and is in pleasing contrast to the indifference or subservience to the gentry of many eighteenth-century vicars. He was a man of honour.

I should perhaps add a final note of bewilderment, not as to a source but as to an absence. Harriet Martineau published in 1845 a book of *Forest and Game-Law Tales*. In the second volume there is a long story entitled 'The Bishop's Flock and the Bishop's Herd', which is very clearly based upon the story of Bishop's Waltham Chase. The author claimed for her stories a 'substantial basis of truth'; and in this story – which is bad and moralistically sentimental – there is a presentation of conflict between farmers and the Bishop which conforms to the evidence, as well as certain touches, such as the suggestion that some Waltham hunters were Londoners with a Hampshire background who came down for a few days at a time, which cannot be confirmed but which are not implausible. But where could Harriet Martineau have got these stories from? She appears to have had no connections with the district, and I know of no published account in the intervening 120 years. This suggests, once again, that I may have overlooked some source – and perhaps an obvious one. But at a certain point one must cut through the lines of possible further investigation, or no history book could ever go to the press.

Index of Persons and Places

Subject Index

Index